£6

THAT WAS
SATIRE
THAT WAS

By the same author

W.H. Auden: a biography
Benjamin Britten: a biography
The Brideshead Generation
The Envy of the World: fifty years of the BBC Third Programme and Radio 3
The Inklings
Jesus (Past Masters series)
The Oxford Companion to Children's Literature (with Mari Prichard)
Dennis Potter: a biography
A Serious Character: the Life of Ezra Pound
Robert Runcie: The Reluctant Archbishop
Secret Gardens: the Golden Age of Children's Literature
J.R.R. Tolkien: a biography

EDITED

The Letters of J.R.R. Tolkien
The Puffin Book of Classic Children's Stories

FOR CHILDREN

The Mr Majeika series
Shakespeare without the Boring Bits
The Joshers
The Captain Hook Affair

THAT WAS
SATIRE
THAT WAS

....

Beyond the Fringe,
The Establishment Club,
Private Eye
and
That Was The Week That Was

Humphrey Carpenter

VICTOR GOLLANCZ
LONDON

First published in Great Britain in 2000 by Victor Gollancz
An imprint of Orion Books Ltd
Orion House, 5 Upper St Martin's Lane, London WC2H 9EA

ISBN 0575 06588 5

Printed and bound in Great Britain by
Butler & Tanner Ltd, Frome and London

Contents

···············

Preface

....

Forty years ago, on 22 August 1960, four young men stepped on to a stage in Edinburgh and changed the face of comedy. Whether *Beyond the Fringe* was or was not satire is an argument that has raged ever since. But its arrival in London the following year created a fashion for the satirical, or would-be satirical, that was one of the first manifestations of what would soon be called 'The Swinging Sixties'.

The satire virus spread. Parental, authoritarian *mores* began to come under fire from performers at an establishment called The Establishment, billed as 'London's first satirical night-club'. Meanwhile, quite coincidentally (since its perpetrators had been developing the idea for years) but with perfect timing in view of the sudden public appetite for lampooning, a scruffy yellow pamphlet calling itself *Private Eye* began to be obtainable in certain London coffee bars. Eventually even the BBC woke up to the fact that comedy was changing, and inaugurated the satirical Saturday night television programme *That Was The Week That Was*. Pubs experienced a drastic downturn in sales as millions came home before closing time to watch it. For a few months, everyone wanted to be a satirist.

Then, just as suddenly, it was all over. *Beyond the Fringe*, though still running, was being performed by a substitute cast, and had become just another West End tourist attraction like *The Mousetrap*. (The real *Beyond the Fringe* had gone to New York where the Americans could enjoy its quaint Britishness while themselves remaining comfortably unsatirized by it.) The Establishment Club fell into the hands of gangsters who beat up the audience, which was more than even the most daring satirist had attempted. Just as suddenly as the BBC had found its nerve for satire, it lost it, and abruptly pulled the plug on the Saturday show – though (typically for the BBC), having killed off this type of show, it then spent several years fruitlessly trying to revive it again. Meanwhile the 1960s moved on, into such later phases as Carnaby Street Fashions, Beatlemania and Flower Power.

Satire – apart from in the pages of *Private Eye*, which somehow survived – dwindled to a distant, rather embarrassing memory.

Had it achieved anything? It is true that shortly after the end of the satire boom an ageing and worn-out Conservative administration had finally given way (albeit by only a few votes) to a government that claimed to be socialist. The satirists had done a little to help expose the Profumo scandal, a débâcle that seems almost innocuous by the standard of today's goings-on in public life, but which contributed to the departure of the Tories. Maybe more significantly, the rules about what could and couldn't be said in public, and the younger generation's attitude to authority, had changed quite radically during the brief heyday of satire.

This book is meant equally for those who (like myself) were young and idealistic when the curtain first rose on *Beyond the Fringe*, and for later generations who have heard the legend that there were satirical giants in those days, and who wonder what really happened. A certain amount has already been written about the satire boom, but nobody has tried to explain what it was all about. Or, as Jonathan Miller, who was one of those four young men who walked on to that Edinburgh stage in 1960, puts it: 'It's an interesting story, and I think that it's never been really got quite right, largely because it hasn't been set enough in its broad social context – either diachronically, to use that awful technical term, in the sense of what came before, or synchronically, with what was going on at the same time. And there were all sorts of currents that were moving.'

So this, if you like, is the diachronically synchronous story of the Satirical Sixties.

Prologue

·····································

Permission to speak

'Satire,' wrote the American playwright George S. Kaufman, commenting satirically on the lack of commercial success the genre usually enjoyed, 'is what closes on Saturday night.' *Beyond the Fringe* proved him wrong, packing in the audiences on Broadway as well as in the West End; and for just over a year, during the run of *That Was The Week That Was* on BBC Television, satire was what gripped the British nation on Saturday nights.

It was all largely due to the Tory Prime Minister of the day, Harold Macmillan, who inspired more satirical attacks during the early 1960s than any other public figure. Yet he himself seemed confused about the meaning of 'satire'. Visiting the BBC Television Centre in Shepherds Bush, home of *TW3*, as the TV satire show was widely known, he murmured to the Director-General, Hugh Carleton Greene, 'I hear that you have some sort of saturnalia out here on Saturdays.'

To understand the climate in which 1960s satire was born, we need to understand the political and cultural climate of the 1950s, which really started in 1945 with the end of the Second World War. In a party political broadcast a month after the German surrender, Winston Churchill warned the British people of the perils of electing a Labour government. They would be wishing on themselves a 'Continental conception of human society called Socialism, or in its more violent form Communism'. It would mean the introduction of 'political police' much like the Gestapo, who would suppress 'expressions of public discontent'. He ended: 'On with the forward march! Leave these Socialist dreamers to their Utopias or nightmares.'

The electorate had other ideas. Jonathan Miller recalls his father crowing over the results of the General Election on 26 July, as he sat in a railway carriage: 'He was triumphantly going, "So-and-so's *out!*" as yet another Conservative lost his seat. And there was a bowler-hatted figure sitting opposite, who was giggling nervously at all this, realizing that he had some frightful Jewish radical sitting in front of him.'

Labour had won with 393 seats, a huge majority over the Conservatives. 'Things are going to be different after the war' had become a catchphrase of Other Ranks in the armed forces during hostilities. Now, undistracted by the victory celebrations, those who voted for Labour were remembering the hunger marches of the 1930s and hoping to continue to enjoy in peacetime the comparatively classless society the war had brought to Britain.

Clement Attlee's Labour government duly pushed through a massive programme of nationalization and welfare provision; but the country had been virtually bankrupted by the cost of the war, and the late 1940s proved to be an era of austerity, with stricter rationing of food and other commodities than had proved necessary during the war itself. By 1950 the country's economic position had improved enormously, and better times could be prophesied with confidence; but the electorate had been given no proof of this, and in February 1950 Labour's huge majority in the Commons was reduced to a mere half-dozen. The outbreak of the Korean War a few months later necessitated further cuts and economies. In the autumn of 1951 there was another General Election, and the Conservatives came back to power.

Family holidays, 1958-style.
(a page from the *Radio Times*)

From our perspective of early twenty-first-century Britain, with fashionable restaurants and designer clothes shops jostling for attention on every shopping street, the austere drabness of the immediately post-war years seems almost beyond belief. Doris Lessing, who had arrived in London from Southern Rhodesia in 1949, aged thirty, with a small child and the manuscript of her first novel, vividly recalls this period of British life:

> That London of the late 1940s, the early 1950s, has vanished, and now it is hard to believe it existed...No cafés. No good restaurants. Clothes were still 'austerity' from the war, dismal and ugly. Everyone was indoors by ten, and the streets were empty...Rationing was still on...The [municipal] Dining Rooms, subsidized during the war, were often the only places to eat in a whole area of streets. They served good meat, terrible vegetables, nursery puddings. Lyons restaurants were the high point of eating for ordinary people – I remember fish and chips and poached eggs on toast...You could not get a decent cup of coffee anywhere in the British Isles.

After a brief taste of socialism, British society had reverted to its pre-war hierarchical norm. Doris Lessing notes that respect for the monarchy was ubiquitous: 'In cinemas and theatres, we stood up for the national anthem.' Indeed the social scene had largely reverted to that of the 1930s. The novelist Emma Tennant, who grew up in an aristocratic family in London during the early 1950s, describes this period as an 'attempt to echo the decade before the German bombs flattened so much of the city', an era that harked back to '*Brideshead* snobberies with a vengeance'. Tennant's parents held a coming-out ball in her honour at their house in Regent's Park, and as a débutante she was presented at court, curtseying to the Queen: 'We had queued in a stuffy ballroom and, one by one, stood a split second in front of the Royal Family on the dais, before dropping down to perform what looked, from the rear, very like the laying of an egg.'

Newspapers reported royal doings with unquestioning politeness: 'Prince Charles, six next month, may have boxing lessons when the Royal Family returns from Balmoral in a week – the Duke of Edinburgh wants him to, and the Queen has not made up her mind.' As late as 1957, Malcolm Muggeridge was sacked from the editorship of *Punch* – the nearest to a satirical magazine that 1950s Britain could manage – for trying to print a mildly facetious poem about the Queen's choice of Cheam preparatory school for Prince Charles. 'Shortly afterwards,' Muggeridge writes, 'other verses expressing a proper love of the monarchy appeared in the magazine.'

Royalty and others in authority did not have to endure 'investigative' reporting or paparazzi with intrusive cameras. Photo-journalism was confined to such magazines as the lively but innocuous *Picture Post* and the deeply conservative *Illustrated London News*. Television – still in its

infancy in the early 1950s, and found in only a small minority of households
– offered only very limited and respectful 'newsreel' coverage of public
events. (There were also cinema 'newsreels', invariably several days out of
date and again utterly conservative in content, with commentaries spoken
by deep-toned 'Empire' voices.) The overall style of the media was set by the
formality of *The Times*, which carried few photographs and relegated news
to its inside pages; the front was taken up with classified advertisements:
Births, Marriages, Deaths, Club Announcements – 'Roehampton Club –
children's party, conjuror, 3.30 p.m., six shillings' – and the famous personal
column: 'The Society of Old Seafordians Annual Dinner in London on
March 18th…Salmon fishing wanted, Scotland, for two rods…Education
for girls in the country; games and sea bathing, ponies to ride.'

There were few stirrings of feminism. When in May 1949 Norman
Mailer's novel *The Naked and the Dead* reached London, *The Sunday
Times* condemned it in an editorial that gives some indication of the male
attitude to women at this period: 'Mr Mailer is a writer of exceptional gifts
and much of the book has real value, but large parts of it are so grossly
obscene that it is quite unfit for general circulation. No decent man could
leave it lying about the house, or know without shame that his womenfolk
were reading it.' Even in 1960 the prosecuting counsel in the *Lady
Chatterley's Lover* obscenity trial took a similar line when he asked the
jury, 'Is it a book you would even wish your wife or your servants to read?'

Females in the 1950s did not dress badly, but in his cultural history of the
emergence of pop from the austerity of post-war England, George Melly
observes that for most of the decade 'fashion' had the sole meaning of French
styles for rich women: 'English upper-class girls were expected to dress like
their mothers, and only tarts or homosexuals wore clothes which reflected
what they *were*.' An exception was the Teddy Boy style of the mid-1950s,
but this was solely for working-class males. As to middle-class adolescent
boys, 'You bought what your parents thought you ought to wear,' says
Jonathan Miller. 'As you got older, you wore slightly smaller versions of
your father's clothes. People remained large schoolboys until they were
eighteen, and then went to university and became Varsity Men.'

As this suggests, there was no self-conscious 'youth culture'. Teenagers
were scarcely identified as a social group with its own tastes and needs, and
young adults found themselves precipitated into a prematurely middle-
aged lifestyle. There were few complaints, a rare exception being an article
in the *Daily Herald* in 1954, written by a twenty-three-year-old with the
appropriate name of Phoebe Young:

> The Young – Who are the Young? My mind conjures up a gang of rather irre-
> sponsible – but in the most wholesome way – Bright Young Things, who are out

for a good time, full of zest for life, and with an endearing tendency towards practical jokes.

But the Young of the 1950s are not like that at all. They are usually married, responsible, sober citizens.

The Young are no longer young: they are prematurely middle-aged.

The Young are now The Young Marrieds, worried and harassed by children, bills, hire purchase and mortgages.

We won't look back at the 1950s and say wistfully, as our elders do of the 1920s and 30s: 'What fun we had.' The 1950s aren't fun in that sense at all …

The Young of the 1950s have sold their souls for Security … We like possessions: we keep buying washing-machines and television sets. Like the Victorians we are anxious to put our best false fronts to the world …

What nonsense it is for us to waste our youth by ignoring it and sinking into middle age!

This abrupt transition from childhood to adulthood was largely the consequence, at least where boys were concerned, of National Service, which kept them fully occupied – and usually out of the country – for two years when they might otherwise have been finding their own voices as a pressure group. Yet, paradoxically, National Service was one of the factors that began to unsettle the structure of 1950s society in Britain.

Wartime conscription had continued when peace came, so that at the age of eighteen every male in the country was required by law to register with the military authorities. Call-up for the two years of compulsory military service could be deferred until after an apprenticeship or university course, but most boys chose to get it over without delay. Apart from supplying NATO with troops to eyeball the Red Army along the Iron Curtain, National Service provided manpower for military action in Malaya (1948–60), Korea (1950–3), Kenya (1952–5), Cyprus (1955–9) and Aden (1957–60).

Broadly speaking, all these campaigns were to defend British interests – remnants of Empire – either from communism or local independence movements. Yet, although they generally achieved the intended political result in the places concerned, they tended not to reinforce but to undermine the imperial value system in the minds of the young Britons who fought there.

'I felt increasingly distressed by what I was being asked to defend [in Malaya],' recalls one of them. 'It seemed to be a system based on political injustice.' Another says of the Arabs in Aden, 'Living with them, working with them and sometimes fighting with them, I found them to be good people, and it's no good us putting Western values on them.' A third, who took part in the Korean campaign, admits that he 'never really understood' why the British were fighting there.

A 1950s solution to marital stress: drink Horlicks.

National Service – like wartime military service – also created a social mix which unsettled class assumptions. 'I spent life in a complete cross-section of the population,' recalls another conscript, 'and got to know boys from Newcastle or Glasgow or whatever who'd had pretty hard upbringings.' The painter and performance artist Jeff Nuttall writes, 'The Army changed me immensely. I got to know the urban working class intimately by being forced to live with them. They shattered my middle-class fastidiousness and the intolerance that goes with it.' To many, it all seemed a black farce. The writer Karl Miller recalls his National Service as 'burlesque…interlarded with scenes of horror and desolation', and Nuttall says much the same: 'Most of all, best of all, I learned that life is a desperate, terrible, magnificent joke. You can distinguish ex-National Servicemen by this sense.'

Dennis Potter, who did part of his National Service as a clerk in Whitehall, recalls having to bawl 'Permission to speak – SAH!' every time he wanted to ask one of his superiors something. 'That little phrase seemed to me to sum up the whole of English life at that time.' Nicholas Luard, who from 1961 to 1963 ran The Establishment Club with Peter Cook, says of the early 1950s, 'Authority was everything: you disobeyed any form of it, from a schoolmaster to a doctor, at your peril. You didn't even think about it.'

*

The Suez crisis of 1956 played a big part in changing such attitudes. National Service might have continued indefinitely if it had not been for this political débâcle. In late July 1956, President Nasser of Egypt announced the 'nationalization' of the Suez Canal. Britain was the majority shareholder in this crucial trade route (for oil) and means of naval access to the Far East. The British Prime Minister and Leader of the Conservatives, Sir Anthony Eden, determined to take 'a firm stand', supported by his predecessor Churchill, who declared, 'We can't have this malicious swine sitting across our communications.' The British press felt the same; even the pro-Labour *Daily Herald* carried the front page headline 'NO MORE ADOLF HITLERS!' Harold Macmillan, then Chancellor of the Exchequer, said, 'This is Munich all over again,' adding that if England did not accept 'Egypt's challenge' she 'would become another Netherlands'.

The British military plan, supported openly by France and secretly by Israel, but opposed by the United States, was to knock out Egypt's airforce with bombs and land troops at Port Said, with the aim of occupying the Canal Zone, though some politicians might have expected an occupation of Egypt itself. Meanwhile Nasser blocked the canal by sinking concrete-filled ships, and the British press and public began to come rather belatedly to its senses. 'THIS IS FOLLY,' declared the *Daily Herald*, and there were big protest rallies in Trafalgar Square and the Royal Albert Hall, with students chanting, 'Eden must go.' Even the *Daily Telegraph* admitted to 'deep anxiety', while *The Times* observed that there were 'very great risks'. Some ex-National Servicemen who received recall papers from the Suez campaign sent them back with 'bollocks' scrawled across them.

The landing of allied troops at Port Said nevertheless began, but the USSR sent a threatening note to Eden reminding him that Soviet nuclear rockets were far superior in power to the British forces being deployed in Egypt. The United Nations voted in support of an American resolution for a ceasefire, and on 7 November the *Daily Herald* headline was 'EDEN CALLS IT OFF'. The paper's leader-writer commented, 'A squalid episode ends in a pitiable climb-down … Our moral authority in the world has been destroyed.' One immediate result was the reintroduction of petrol rationing in Britain.

At Oxford before the ceasefire, the undergraduate magazine *Isis* had attacked 'the folly of the government's crime', and a Union debate voted decisively to condemn the sending in of the troops. Michael Frayn, who was at Cambridge in 1956, says he recalls demonstrations there 'of colossal ferocity – terrible fights breaking out between the pro and con factions'. Dennis Potter, who became an Oxford undergraduate in the autumn of 1956, wrote in the *New Statesman* two years later, 'Suez … was a shock … For the first time many undergraduates realized that politics was much too important a thing to be left to the government.'

If Suez created genuine anger and increasing political awareness among the young, the episode of the 'Angry Young Men', a literary movement dating from around the time of Suez, was (as we would put it now) largely a hype, the invention of the press. Nevertheless the writers labelled as belonging to it did demonstrate, in their different ways, a growing insurgence in the younger generation of British intellectuals.

John Osborne's *Look Back in Anger* opened at the Royal Court in London in May 1956. The first and for a while the only critic to recognize its importance was Kenneth Tynan, who would be a key figure in the development of 1960s satire. He immediately perceived that the ranting of Osborne's young hero was an accurate representation of the feelings of many young people in Britain. Some of Jimmy Porter's ranting is against his father-in-law, who has served the British Empire in India: 'He's … still casting well-fed glances back to the Edwardian twilight from his comfortable, disenfranchised wilderness.' But most of Jimmy's anger is directed at his own disillusionment and that of his generation: 'Nobody thinks, nobody cares. No beliefs, no convictions and no enthusiasm.' And again:

> I suppose people of our generation aren't able to die for good causes any longer. We had all that done for us, in the thirties and forties, when we were still kids … There aren't any good, brave causes left. If the big bang does come, and we all get killed off, it won't be in aid of the old-fashioned, grand design. It'll be

just for the Brave New-nothing-very-much-thank-you. About as pointless and inglorious as stepping in front of a bus.

Jimmy Porter had had a comic predecessor in Kingsley Amis's Jim Dixon, pulling faces at the older generation in *Lucky Jim* (1954), and soon after Porter came Joe Lampton in John Braine's *Room at the Top* (1957) raging against the 'zombies' in authority: 'To Charles and me it [their home town] was always Dead Dufton and the councillors and chief officials and anyone we didn't approve of were called zombies.' Alan Sillitoe's young hero Arthur Seaton in *Saturday Night and Sunday Morning* (1958) declares himself beyond morality: 'That's what all these looney laws are for, yer know: to be broken by blokes like me.'

The label 'Angry Young Men' was invented accidentally by the Royal Court's press officer, George Fearon. When a journalist asked about Osborne, Fearon replied that he supposed the new playwright was 'a very angry young man'. Seizing on the phrase, the media also applied it to twenty-four-year-old Colin Wilson, who had just become famous when Victor Gollancz published his first book, *The Outsider*, a study of alienation – or, as Christopher Booker puts it, 'a rambling survey of some of the more conspicuously neurotic and self-destructive misfits of the past three hundred years, such as Van Gogh, Nijinsky and T.E. Lawrence'. Wilson writes of being labelled an 'Angry':

London in the 1950s: the age of the bowler hat was not yet over.

Somehow, Osborne and I were supposed to prove that England was full of brilliantly talented young men who couldn't make any headway in the System, and were being forced to go it alone. We were supposed to be the representative voices of this vast army of outsiders and angry young men who were rising up to overthrow the Establishment...[But] the newspaper publicity was on such a moronic level...that it seemed a travesty of what we were trying to do as individuals.

The year of *Look Back in Anger* and Suez also saw the beginning of British pop, or at least its predecessor, rock 'n' roll, with Tommy Steele's first disc 'Rock with the Cavemen'. His second, 'Singing the Blues', reached number one in the charts in January 1957. George Melly describes Steele as 'a new animal, the first realized dream of an entire new class, the model of a new world'.

Television soon began to play a big part in the careers of Steele and his successors, and the fame of *Look Back in Anger* was due largely to its being televised on ITV, live from the Royal Court. Doris Lessing picks on the spread of television during the mid- and late 1950s as one of the most significant social changes:

Before, when the men came back from work, the tea was already on the table, a fire was roaring, the radio emitted words or music softly in a corner, they washed and sat down at their places, with the woman, the child, and whoever else in the house could be inveigled downstairs... They all talked... And then... television had arrived and sat like a toad in the corner of the kitchen. Soon the big kitchen table had been pushed along the wall, chairs were installed in a semi-circle and, on their chair arms, the swivelling supper trays. It was the end of an exuberant verbal culture.

Because of television, the cinema began to decline in popularity, though *Lucky Jim* was signed up for a screen version, and there were press reports that the part of Dixon might go to a brilliant young member of the Cambridge Footlights called Jonathan Miller. But the Angry Young Men were essentially a literary fashion rather than an intellectual revolution. Emma Tennant writes, 'The literary world ha[d] welcomed *Lucky Jim* but appear[ed] to coast along, still satisfied with its smug, pseudo-aristocratic view of itself.'

Jimmy Porter's remark about the 'big bang' refers, of course, to the proliferation during the 1950s of nuclear weapons. The Campaign for Nuclear Disarmament was formally constituted in Britain in January 1958, with Canon John Collins as Chairman, and the first Aldermaston March took place that Easter. 'The bearded boys in blue jeans and no haircuts were along,' writes Herb Greer in his history of CND, 'and so were their long-haired girls, dressed in heavy sweaters, tight slacks and mascaraed tense expressions…[But] the bulk of the marchers were ordinary people from offices, factories, or shops.'

Doris Lessing was in at the beginning of CND: 'The marches united the whole spectrum of the left and far beyond…There were even Tory groups… And many were there not primarily because of the Bomb but because of a general concern for the condition of Britain.' At Oxford, *Isis* devoted an entire issue to the Bomb. 'The next war will destroy most of the people in this country,' stated the opening article – unsigned, like the others. 'But we have all been conditioned…to some sort of acceptance of the inevitability of the arms race.'

Another article in this *Isis* revealed that

> all along the frontier between East and West, from Iraq to the Baltic, perhaps farther, are monitoring stations, manned largely by National Servicemen trained in Morse or Russian, avidly recording the least squeak from Russian transmitters…It is believed, perhaps rightly, that this flagrant breach of the Geneva Convention can provide accurate estimates of the size and type of Russian armaments and troops, and the nature of their tactical methods.

Paul Johnson, then a left-winger and editor of the *New Statesman*, wrote to *Isis* to praise the Bomb issue: 'I believe that there is a real chance of reversing official Labour Party policy on the subject. [Labour was against unilateral disarmament.] Protests such as yours have a bigger effect on Top People than they like to think.' The immediate effect, however, was to bring the Special Branch to Oxford, since it was believed that two of the contributors to the Bomb issue, William Miller and Paul Thompson, had breached the Official Secrets Act by disclosing information they had gained while on National Service, where they had learned Russian and worked as translators. They were arrested and charged, and Dennis Potter, who had just taken over the editorship of *Isis*, opened a fund to contribute to their defence. He received letters of support from (among others) Lindsay Anderson, John Berger, Doris Lessing, Christopher Logue, J.B. Priestley and Kenneth Tynan. Nevertheless when Miller and Thompson appeared at the Old Bailey, the Lord Chief Justice, Lord Goddard, sentenced them to three months' imprisonment.

Despite Paul Johnson's hope, the Labour Party and its leader Hugh Gaitskill continued to withhold official endorsement of CND, though some of the Shadow Cabinet were unilateralists. In his 1960 book *The Glittering Coffin* – published by Victor Gollancz, who was clearly hoping for another 'Angry' bestseller like *The Outsider* – Dennis Potter complained that Labour had become almost indistinguishable from the Tories. Still in power, the Conservatives were now led by the urbane, aristocratic, sixty-six-year-old Harold Macmillan, destined to be the first and chief target of the

1960s satirists. He had succeeded Eden when the latter resigned on grounds
of ill-health soon after Suez. 'Gaitskell and Macmillan', wrote Potter,

> came close [in the 1959 General Election campaign] to resembling two funfair
> barkers, with false noses and six inches of greasepaint. The shouting and the
> drumming get louder and louder as the big tents become tattier and tattier.
> Labour, however, put up a pretty good performance, and almost beat the Tories
> at their own game – their appeal to our stupidity and general selfishness was
> almost as effective.

Potter's book expresses an unease, typical of educated members of the
younger generation in the late 1950s and early 1960s, at the fast-growing
consumerism in Britain – television, washing-machines, cars. As Emma
Tennant puts it, 'The struggle of the 1950s to return to the 1930s ha[d] on the
whole been lost and there ha[d] come the two-car family and an abundance
of machines.' The country was at last enjoying economic prosperity, and
naturally the Conservatives were claiming the credit for this. In a speech at
Bedford on 20 July 1957, Macmillan told his supporters, 'Let's be frank about
it; most of our people have never had it so good. Go around the country, go
to the industrial towns, go to the farms, and you will see a state of prosperity
such as we have never had in my lifetime – nor indeed in the history of this
country.' The left-wing cartoonist Vicky responded, in the *Evening
Standard*, by caricaturing Macmillan as an elderly Superman – 'Supermac'.

Clothes in the mid-1950s 'were still
"austerity" from the war,' writes Doris
Lessing, 'dismal and ugly'.

But far from inciting mockery, this actually improved the Prime Minister's public image. Meanwhile Dennis Potter ranted against the times:

> Maybe the big emotional orgies have disappeared, as Jimmy Porter raves, but a great greyness has blanketed all the rest – Admass [the fashionable term of disapproval for advertising-led consumerism], a diluted Welfare State, a sense of shame and disillusion, contempt for authority, a widespread desire to emigrate or cheat … a feeling of the flatness and bleakness of everyday England … Doesn't it all make you sick? Or does it make you certain of the need to be awake and articulate, pompous perhaps, but *alive*?

Potter's call would soon be answered, but not by Jimmy Porter lookalikes. A new, more characteristically English style of subversion was about to be born, and a crucial part would be played in it by someone who had arrived at Oxford before Potter – someone who was less like Osborne's angry hero than Kenneth Grahame's mild-mannered Mole.

I've got a viper in this box

1

·······························

Doing silly turns

Three years before Macmillan's 'never had it so good' speech, in October 1954, a tall, fair-haired, bespectacled twenty-year-old Yorkshireman arrived at Oxford to read Modern History. 'The lodge of my college,' he recalls,

> was piled high with trunks: trunks pasted with ancient labels, trunks that had holidayed in Grand Hotels, travelled first-class on liners, trunks painted with four, nay even *five*, initials ... They were the trunks of fathers that were now the trunks of sons, trunks of generations. These trunks spoke memory. I had two shameful Antler suitcases that I had gone to buy with my mother at Schofields in Leeds – an agonizing process, since it had involved her explaining to the shop assistant, a class my mother always assumed were persons of some refinement, that the cases were for going to Oxford with on a scholarship and were these the kind of thing? They weren't. One foot across the threshold of my college lodge and I saw it, and hurried to hide them beneath my cold bed. By the end of the first term I hadn't acquired much education but I had got myself a decent second-hand trunk.

Alan Bennett was the first of his family to go to university. Two years later, in 1956, Dennis Potter came up to Oxford from the Forest of Dean determined to flaunt, even exaggerate, his working-class origins as a way of achieving fame among his fellow undergraduates. Bennett, however, saw nothing in his background to shout about: 'I was born and brought up in Leeds, in what I suppose must have been a working-class family. When I say "I suppose", I do not mean that I did not actually notice, but imply that it all seemed perfectly satisfactory to me at the time. I had, after all, nothing to compare it with.'

He claims that his childhood in the 1930s and 1940s was dull rather than deprived – 'the Utility version, childhood according to the Authorized Economy Standard' – and he had no great expectations of university. Yet his personal manner was misleading: 'People ... think I'm sad ... I think it's because I've got an unfortunate face. But I always feel much more cheerful than they imagine that I am.' And his upbringing had in fact been mildly unusual: 'I already knew at the age of five that I belonged to a family that without being in the least bit remarkable or eccentric yet managed never to be quite like other families.'

He was the younger son of Walter Bennett, a butcher working for the Co-Op in the Armley district of Leeds. Mr Bennett was an amateur violinist who had also once taken up the double-bass to play in a dance band – usually an indication of at least mild eccentricity. He was also something of a writer and regularly entered competitions in such magazines as *Tit-Bits*, and was even sometimes paid for sending in short humorous paragraphs. He was expert (recalls Alan) at coming up with 'a telling phrase on a given topic', something 'witty, ironic or ambiguous – in effect a verbal cartoon'; a good mimic, too, who could take off his sisters-in-law, Alan's aunts. One of them had played the piano in the silent cinema, and the other was the manageress of a shoe shop; Alan alleges that for every birthday she gave him the same present, a pair of shoe-trees.

Alan's mother Lilian was less ebullient than her husband, obsessed with household cleanliness and prone to depression. Yet she too had literary inclinations, at least as a reader, being addicted to stories of escape from humdrum life into something more exciting. Alan says she hoped that when he grew up he would become a gentleman farmer. (When he began to portray North Country women of her generation in his television plays in the 1970s, she joked that she was supplying him with most of his dialogue.)

Bennett loved and admired his parents, and was distressed, though also amused, by their obvious feeling of insecurity in the class hierarchy of Britain in the 1940s and 1950s. Oxford confused them. Visiting him at Exeter College, 'they took my scout for a don', and it was worse if all three Bennetts went out for a meal:

> When we were at home we always had our dinner at lunchtime. For my parents, anything that came after that was never more than a snack. But when I was at university and they came to see me, we'd go into the hotel dining room at night and the waiter would present the menu, and my Mam would say the dread words, 'Do you do a poached egg on toast?' and we'd slink from the dining room, the only family in England not to have its dinner at night ... 'Would you like the wine list?' the waiter would ask. 'Not really,' Dad would say, and one had to be quick in order to stop Mam explaining about his duodenal ulcer. Mind you, what wine was there that would go with spaghetti on toast? 'Which is really all we want at this time in the evening. Mr Bennett has to watch his tummy.'

Alan gradually realized that literature seemed to his parents to offer an escape from the rigidity of class: 'They imagined that books would make them less shy and (always an ambition) able to "mix". Quiet and never particularly gregarious, they cherished a lifelong longing to "branch out", with books somehow the key to it.' Their son was eventually to do the 'branching out' for them; yet in childhood it never seemed to him 'that great hopes were set upon me'.

He and his brother Gordon[1] were sent to local grammar schools. Alan found his school dull: 'It wasn't old. It wasn't new. There was not even a kindly schoolmaster who put books into my hands. I think one may have tried to, but it was not until I was sixteen, and a bit late in the day.'

In childhood, many of the children's books he encountered had been an uncomfortable reminder of his parents' social uncertainty:

> The families I read about…had dogs and gardens and lived in country towns equipped with thatched cottages and mill-streams…[and] comfortable pipe-smoking fathers and gentle aproned mothers, who were invariably referred to as Mummy and Daddy. In an effort to bring this fabulous world closer to my own …I tried as a first step substituting 'Mummy' and 'Daddy' for my usual 'Mam' and 'Dad', but was pretty sharply discouraged. My father was hot on anything smacking of social pretension.

There were no such social nuances in Hugh Lofting's wistfully comic Doctor Dolittle books about talking animals, and these became 'my favourite'.

Another refuge was music. With school friends, he attended Saturday concerts by the Yorkshire Symphony Orchestra, feeling that 'music showed you how to live your life'. Brahms's Second Piano Concerto made him believe his future would be lofty: 'I saw myself modestly ascending shallow staircases to unspecified triumphs.' But reality soon broke in. A character in his 1971 play *Getting On* says, 'I thought life was going to be like Brahms… Instead it's, well, it's been like Eric Coates.'

Another spell was less easily broken. In his mid-teens he was 'a fervent Anglican'. Having gained his initial religious upbringing in a Congregational Sunday school, he had become attracted by Anglo-Catholicism, and at fifteen was confirmed by H.H. Vully de Candole, the Bishop of Knaresborough, in St Michael's, Headingley. He recalls 'Easter at St Michael's…the great lilies on the altar, the copes and the candles and the holy ladies plummeting to their knees at any mention of the Virgin's name'. Here, he became

> devoutly religious, a regular communicant who knew the service off by heart. It might be thought this would rejoice a vicar's heart and maybe it did, but

---

[1] Bennett once said, 'I always feel guilty that I never write about my brother. I always write as if I were an only child, which is rather peculiar…He never mentions this, but I always feel this is a rather significant fact.' Gordon Bennett eventually became an estate agent.

actually I think the parish clergy found my fervour faintly embarrassing. A fervent Anglican is a bit of a contradiction in terms anyway, but I was conscious that my constant presence at the Eucharist, often midweek as well as Sundays, was thought to be rather unhealthy... Shy, bespectacled and innocent of the world I knew I was a disappointment to the clergy. What they wanted were brands to pluck from the burning and that was not me by a long chalk; I'd never even been near the fire.

He emphasizes that in his teens he was 'an awful Tory... Oh, awful. It was dreadful, the list of right-wing convictions that I had.' To some extent this never changed. In the 1970s he described himself as politically left-wing but socially right-wing. When attending church as a teenager, he was devoted to the language of the 1662 Book of Common Prayer; years later it was still 'the only work of literature of which I know large sections off by heart'. As to a choice of career, 'I... thought I would be a clergyman.'

That he did not become the Revd Alan Bennett, a right-wing traditional-ist High Churchman, was largely the consequence of National Service. Most of his schoolfellows assumed this would be a bore, but for him it was worse, partly because he was physically a late developer: 'It was touch and go which I got to first – puberty or the call-up.' Yet when National Service began, it proved to be 'the happiest time of my life'.

Like other recruits, he had to begin with basic infantry training – 'I actually didn't even mind the drill' – and he was soon selected for the Joint Services Russian Language course. The Cold War was then at its height, and the aim was to train a body of young men in the language of the enemy. First, they studied Russian at A level, and some were then sent to work in the War Office as translators of Russian documents (Dennis Potter was among these), while others were posted to NATO monitoring stations along the Iron Curtain. An elite, Bennett among them, were picked out to spend the rest of their National Service improving their Russian still further at Cambridge; in theory they could then be recalled in time of emergency to use their linguistic skill.

Bennett therefore found himself in the Cambridge School of Slavonic Studies. He says that, compared to most National Service postings, it was 'a cushy number'. He remembers writing much about 'the Russian soul... it was always a useful theme to pad out one's weekly essay'. Outside the classroom, 'the discipline was lax', and he was able to experience a life very much like that of a Cambridge undergraduate: 'What most people get at university I had in the army in a much more intensified form.'

He soon found himself part of 'a congenial group which included Michael Frayn'. Bennett and Frayn both wrote material for mess-room cabarets. 'He wrote a few items,' explains Frayn, 'and so did I – I don't think we actually

Alan Bennett and Michael Frayn on the National Service Russian language course at Cambridge, 1953.

collaborated together on a script. But one of the things Alan used to do in those cabarets was a prototype of the clergyman he had in *Beyond the Fringe*.'

Considering the importance of this impersonation in his future life, Bennett himself retains surprisingly little memory of its birth. 'I did something with Frayn,' he says, 'and I can't remember what it was.' Fortunately Frayn recalls it in some detail:

> He did it as a minor canon at a provincial cathedral, taking morning muster parade – setting off the army against the church. Every morning in an army unit, everyone has to go on parade in order to be counted, like a school, and there's a set drill. Alan just imagined that they would do the same at cathedral – would

check all the deans and minor canons. He did it with that preposterous ecclesiastical accent he later used in the sermon in *Beyond the Fringe*.

Asked if he was impersonating any particular clergyman, Bennett says, 'If it was based on anybody – and I don't recall that it was – the sermons I heard most often were from the Vicar of St Michael's, Headingley, who was Canon R.J. Wood, a Canon of Ripon. He had a very round, grand style, and if it came from anywhere it was him.' The real target of his mockery seems to have been not the Church but his own previously pious persona. He explains that his view of himself changed considerably during these years:

> I think that until I went into the army I thought that being a clergyman was what I was going to do, and then it faded away, for all sorts of reasons. Before I did my National Service, I was worried as to whether I ought to be a conscientious objector, but I chickened out of that. However, having done National Service, I began in my first year at Oxford to feel much more strongly about it. Ex-National Servicemen had to do Reserve Training in the long vacation, and I certainly felt I ought to object to that. CND hadn't really started yet, but there was already much more of a pacifist feeling around. But if you did refuse to do Reserve Training on moral grounds, there was no tribunal you could go in front of – it was regarded as a military offence, and you were sent to one of the military prisons. And I certainly failed that test, did the Reserve Training, and became reconciled to the fact that I didn't have much moral fibre!

This process of readjustment included the fading of what he had regarded as religious faith. 'It would be easy to say I no longer believed,' he told an interviewer years later, 'but I don't think I ever believed in the first place.' He also fell in love.

Before beginning National Service he had managed to win an under-graduate place at Cambridge, but during the Russian course he decided to try for Oxford. It was partly that he had already experienced Cambridge, but chiefly because 'I had a hopeless crush on one of my fellow officer cadets, who was bound for Oxford.'

Years later he said that, until his mid-forties, he assumed that he was exclusively homosexual: 'I'd always been in love with guys, you see, but always unhappily. They were always straight, and it was always totally unfulfilled.' Yet he was not celibate: 'I was interested in sex, and whichever way any sex came along, you just had to take it – that's how it seemed to me. And it very, very seldom went with being in love, which I tend to regard as totally separate, separate from sex.' Even loveless sex was hard to come by. In the 1980s the actor Ian McKellen, crusading for gay rights, asked Bennett about his sexual orientation. He replied, 'That's a bit like asking a man crawling across the Sahara whether he would prefer Perrier or Malvern water.' However, in 1993 Bennett revealed to a *New Yorker* interviewer that for some years he had been having a relationship with Anne Davies, described by the interviewer as a 'darkly attractive woman who had been doing his house-cleaning'. Ms Davies, whom Bennett had installed as the proprietor of a café in the Yorkshire village where he had his country home, told the *Daily Mail*: 'I suppose you could describe me as his common-law wife.'

He got a scholarship to Oxford, not to the athletically minded Brasenose College, where the object of his affections had gone, but to Exeter, which proved to be 'inward-looking'. This suited him: 'I was happy to settle down in the cosy, undemanding atmosphere of the Exeter Junior Common Room.' Yet initially Oxford was a disappointment after National Service; he was socially uneasy there, and lonely. 'I became a member of no clubs; no cards decorated my mantelpiece; no societies met in my room. It was all very dull and, apart from the fact that I had to share a set [of rooms] with someone who had been in the same barrack room for much of my National Service and whom I loathed and who loathed me, I was quite happy.'

Michael Frayn had stayed on at Cambridge, as an undergraduate, and had immediately joined the Footlights, the university revue club. Bennett found that there was no such organization at Oxford. 'I'm sure if there had been I would have failed to join that too.' Indeed, he avoided all university theatre groups: 'I had no theatrical ambitions. I might have acted a bit, but I was overawed by the people who did. I lived a college rather than a university life, and steered clear of the Oxford University Dramatic Society and the Experimental Theatre Club.'

Yet fairly soon he found an outlet for his humour – the unlikely one of the Exeter College Junior Common Room (JCR) Suggestions Book. 'As a respository of actual suggestions,' Bennett writes,

> the Suggestions Book was useless, but it served besides as a college newspaper, a diary, a forum for discussion, and a space in which those who were so inclined could attempt to amuse and even paddle in the direction of literature. The result was a volume (in time a succession of volumes) that was parochial, silly and obscene, but to me, and possibly to others, of a particular value. A family atmosphere, a captive audience and a set of shared references are good conditions in which to learn to write, and I think it was through my contributions to the JCR Suggestions Book that I first realized I could make people laugh and liked doing it.

The Suggestions Books for Bennett's years at Exeter have been preserved in the college library, and his handwriting appears frequently in them. At first his entries were short and pithy:

Thir,
>Pleathe can we have a-full length mirror (looking-glath I mean) in the J.C.R.
>Yths. etc.
>A. Bennett

Another letter included a bloodstain:

Sir,
>A *serious* suggestion. There is no first-aid box in college – not even in the lodge.
>This is *my blood* and there's lots more where that came from – but one day there mightn't be, unless we get a first-aid box, if only for the sake of us haemophiliacs.
>Yrs etc & bleeding steadily
>Alan Bennett

Besides his own contributions, there are jokes about him by other undergraduates, and caricatures emphasizing his owl-like gaze and spindly legs. He had quickly become a college 'character'. One undergraduate even cut off a lock of his fair hair and glued it into the book, with the comment: 'Someone has Raped a Lock of A. Bennett's hair. But the fringe is still immaculate.' (A curious anticipation of the significance of the word 'fringe' in his life.) In a later volume, there is a verse by Bennett himself:

>Marcel Proust had a very poor figure,
>He hadn't the chest for sexual rigour.
>He lay with Albertine tout nu;
>Ce n'est seulement le temps qu'il a perdu.

Bennett explains that this was from a cabaret act he was doing at Oxford: 'There were some other verses to it, I think.'

*

Universities are natural breeding grounds for satire. Clever young people, coming inevitably into conflict with an older generation of academics, turn to wit and mockery. Topical comedies satirizing such conflict were performed at Oxford and Cambridge as early as the sixteenth century, but it was not until the 1880s that the Cambridge Footlights Dramatic Club was formed to put on an annual May Week light entertainment. The club's historian, Robert Hewison, notes that its first original production, a one-act comic operetta called *Uncle Joe at Oxbridge* (1885), included a little of 'what in a later age might have passed for satire' – for example, one character proposing to blow up the University Senate House, and another advising him that dynamite could be easily bought in Ireland.

By the turn of the century, Footlights scripts were sparkling with topical

(*left to right*) Bennett, Frayn and two fellow National Servicemen.

references. For example, their 1909 revue gibed at a Joint Select Parliamentary Committee which was reporting on the censorship of plays. The Lord Chamberlain had been the licenser and censor of public theatrical performances in Britain since 1737, but until now had worked without guidelines.[2] The Committee recommended that His Lordship should censor anything indecent, blasphemous, or inciteful to crime; also the 'invidious' representation on stage of 'a living person, or a person recently dead', and anything 'calculated to impair friendly relations with any Foreign Power'.

'Oh it's going just a bit too far,' sang the Footlights as a comment on this,

> When our Censor's lack of humour is a bar
> To our drama being potted
> And what's rotten being rotted.

[2] Robert Hewison writes, in his history of the Cambridge Footlights: 'An Act of 1737 had formally placed the censorship of plays in the hands of an official of the Royal Household, the Lord Chamberlain. In London he also controlled the use of theatre buildings, though elsewhere the licensing of theatres was carried out by local magistrates ... The Act of 1843 consolidated these powers, but created a fundamental division between the "legitimate" and the "musical" theatre, by excluding from censorship performances that consisted mainly of music, singing, dancing and short sketches, the sort of entertainments put on in public-houses. In the 1850s these entertainments began to develop into music-hall, which remained outside the Lord Chamberlain's jurisdiction until 1911, when all theatre shows came under his control. Theatre censorship remained in force until 1968.'

The new censorship guidelines had immediate consequences for them. Their next May Week revue, in 1910, was called *The Socialist* and described itself as a 'musical satire'. It set out to mock George Bernard Shaw, H.G. Wells and the Fabian Society; but to get past the Lord Chamberlain the script had to be very mild, and a reviewer from the Cambridge *Gownsman* complained that the satirical content of the show had not been 'trenchant enough to rouse any political excitement'.

However, not all the Footlights shows were public and therefore liable to censorship. They and the Oxford University Dramatic Society (OUDS) regularly gave private smoking concerts or 'smokers' in their clubrooms, with an audience of members and their guests – strictly men only. 'The admission of smoking implied the exclusion of women,' writes Hewison, 'so "smokers" were understood to be relaxed, somewhat drunken and usually coarse-minded affairs.'

Being private, smokers were rarely written up in the press. The *Cambridge Review* described one in 1897 which sounds innocent; one performer did 'imitations of various musical instruments' and a cod scientific lecture; another had 'a large fund of dry humour'. On the other hand the actor and playwright Emlyn Williams, recalling his undergraduate days at Oxford, fully confirms Hewison's description when he writes of an OUDS smoker: 'Sketches of the crudest ribaldry were directed at an audience of cackling undergraduates and daringly tipsy dons.' Williams himself, in drag, sang a torch song in the role of a French prostitute: 'Je m'appelle Yvette,/Yvette des trottoirs ...' At this period, cross-dressing played a big part in smokers, and indeed in the public revues, since both the Footlights and the OUDS excluded women from their membership.

Colleges as well as drama clubs held their own smokers, among them Exeter, and Alan Bennett was soon attending. He recalls these JCR entertainments as 'just a dramatized version of the Suggestions Book: vulgar, private, silly ... uproarious drunken affairs, confined to members of the college'. The atmosphere was 'friendly'; nevertheless, 'I didn't pluck up courage to take part ... until my third year.' That he finally did so was the result of his friendship with one of the few other North Country working-class undergraduates in his college, a greengrocer's son from Lancashire, the future television and radio personality Russell Harty. 'If one had to point to the quality that distinguished Russell throughout his life, it would be cheek,' Bennett recalled after Harty's death in 1988. 'He had learned then, by the age of twenty, a lesson it took me half a lifetime to learn, namely that there was nothing that could not be said and no one to whom one could not say it.' Bennett was also impressed by Harty's unashamed homosexuality, at a time when it was still illegal. 'He didn't look on it as an affliction,' Bennett writes, 'but he was never one for a crusade either. He just got on with it ...

His funniest stories were always of the absurdities of sex and the ludicrous situations it had led him into.'

Harty was taking part in an Exeter smoker, and persuaded Bennett to join in. He performed a new version of the Cathedral Muster Parade monologue, this time abandoning the military setting and presenting it as a cod Anglican sermon, full of oily platitudes. A few people were under the impression that he was mocking the college chaplain, Eric Kemp, later Bishop of Chichester, but Bennett denies this: 'It's not based on him at all, because he had a very non-rhetorical preaching style.'

It ran through many versions. 'Once I had hit on the form,' he says, 'I used to be able to run up sermons for all sorts of occasions, choosing texts at random from any book that came to hand.' His other notable performance in the Exeter smokers was as the Queen, giving her Christmas broadcast. In his autobiographical compendium *Writing Home* he refers to this rather gingerly as if it were someone else's work – a 'regular feature' of the smokers, and 'very tame it would seem now, but in those pre-satirical days, when HMQ's annual pronouncement was treated with hushed reverence, the very idea of it seemed sacrilegiously funny'. However, when questioned, he admits that it was another of his own monologues, which was regularly updated with topical references, and he reduces himself to giggles as he recalls it: 'They were so obscene. There was one about – oh, a terrible, obscene thing –' (He puts on the Queen's voice.) '"This year I opened up this passage, this wonderful passage" – I think she'd had a baby that year! And the "passage" turned out to be the St Lawrence Seaway – she'd done the royal opening of it.'

Michael Frayn says he received a stream of hilarious letters from Bennett at Oxford: 'They were incredibly, magically funny, illustrated, often written on bits of wallpaper, eccentric shapes. And I just cried with laughter.' Yet Bennett recalls himself in Oxford days as essentially introspective. Reading his diary for 1956–9 forty years on, he found it to be dominated by 'my slightly sickening obsession with, coupled with lack of insight into, my own character. It's full of embarrassing resolutions about future conduct and exhortations to myself to do better. Love is treated very obliquely, passing fancies thought of as echoes of some Grand Passion.' Even the spoof sermon seemed, in retrospect, part of his undergraduate attempts at self-discovery – the search for his essential self: 'Art ... begins with imitation, often in the form of parody, and it's in the process of imitating the voices of others that one comes to learn the sound of one's own.' Also, by making his first public appearances behind the mask of mimicry, he was protecting, rather than exposing, his deep shyness. 'It *is* contradictory,' he once remarked in an interview. 'You show off and yet you say you're shy. I don't think it's hypocrisy. A lot of actors are personally quite shy ... And that's because

Frayn, Michael Collings and Bennett in cabaret during National Service days. Frayn recalls
that Bennett 'used to do a prototype of the clergyman in *Beyond the Fringe*'.

there's a mask when you're acting; you're actually not revealing yourself.
It's a controlled situation.'

*

By the time that Bennett began to perform the sermon in college smokers,
the Suez crisis had pushed Oxford politically to the left. Alan Coren, who
came up to Wadham College in 1957, recalls that even ex-public schoolboys
were claiming to be left-wing: 'My room-mate was from Eton and genuinely
embarrassed about the fact.' One of Bennett's friends at Exeter, Alan
Shallcross, who had been at a Cheshire grammar school, says the same:
'When I was an undergraduate, there was no deference paid to men from
Eton or Harrow or the public schools.' This, says Shallcross, liberated the ex-
grammar-school men like himself and Bennett – the first generation to
benefit from the 1944 Butler Education Act, which had raised the school
leaving age from fourteen to fifteen, and greatly increased the provision of
free places for high-quality secondary education, making it possible for a
much larger proportion of children from poorly off homes to get a
sufficiently good education to qualify them for university places. Shallcross
says that he and other beneficiaries of the Act had a sense of being the

instruments of social change: 'We were the first to feel that nothing was sacred – we could think the unthinkable and do the un-do-able, which of course largely centred round making fun of the Royal Family, which we thought was frightfully daring. The atmosphere was very much cocking a snook.'

Shallcross met Bennett's parents when they came to Oxford, and emphasizes that they were not 'characters' like Russell Harty's father and mother: 'They both had the kind of private qualities that Alan possesses still. And that has often made me wonder what was the impetus for the performer in him, as opposed to the writer.'

Sitting his Final Examinations in the summer of 1957, Bennett got a First. Later he described this as a 'fluke result', and guessed that, without it, 'I would never have picked myself up to do much except possibly teach – and teach badly.' However, Russell Harty, with whom Bennett went on holiday to Venice soon after Finals, described the First as well deserved, and said that Bennett was 'doing his shy best' to hide the achievement. (Harty himself had got only a Third in English.)

Deserved or not, the First gave Bennett what he calls a 'breathing space' to stay on at Oxford and 'go on doing silly turns'. He enrolled for postgraduate studies and, during his fourth year at Oxford (1957–8), began tentatively to perform outside his own college. A third-year Trinity College undergraduate, Andrew Hichens, saw him give the cod sermon at an OUDS smoker. 'Nobody knew anything about him,' Hichens recalls, 'and he looked as though he'd just come out of the woodwork – as if he was a freshman reading theology. But in a few moments he had everybody falling about.' John Wells, three years Bennett's junior at Oxford and reading Modern Languages at St Edmund Hall, saw him at about the same time, when he had enlarged his repertoire of monologues, and recalled that one of them took off the posh mother of a débutante: 'And there was a very very funny one which I've never seen him do since, which was about an atomic scientist.' Bennett recalls that this sketch required an elaborate prop: 'I had a sort of molecular diagram, made up of bits of curtain wire, little wooden balls and a hatstand. When I was doing it in cabaret at Oxford, you'd see me walking through the streets carrying this hatstand.'

Wells himself performed comic turns at smokers, but he realized that Bennett's pieces were much more carefully crafted: 'I thought it was infinitely better, much better worked, much more intelligent that anything I was doing. We all ad-libbed, but Alan used to take tremendous trouble writing, and every single line was perfect. And very well performed. And the notable thing was that when Alan came to do a smoker, the whole room went quiet.'

2

This suet and this sangfroid will get you nowhere

John Wells had begun to perform cabaret sketches in the army, during National Service. The son of a Sussex vicar, he had gone on from public school (Eastbourne College) to a commission as a second lieutenant in the Royal Sussex Regiment, and had sailed for Korea in 1956:

> From Southampton, we went down through the Bay of Biscay, and stopped at Gibraltar, with the Union Jack flying. We then went across the Mediterranean without stopping, and through the Suez Canal, just before the Suez crisis, and the next stop was Aden, with the Union Jack flying. Then we went to Colombo, with the Union Jack flying; then we went to Singapore, with the Union Jack flying; Hong Kong, the same; and we just didn't stop where there wasn't a British presence. And it just seemed perfectly natural. There was no sense of colonial shame.

Wells adds that at Eastbourne College 'the level of political sophistication was absolute zero. The Sixth Form had a talk from a Labour MP, and we looked at him as if he was a kind of green man from Mars. Everybody was Conservative, and there was really an absolute acceptance that those in charge knew how to run everything.'

When the ship reached Korea, Wells found that his regiment was conducting itself in full imperial style:

> There had been a ceasefire, and all we had to do was patrol, and we had taken all the regimental silver, and the band, and even in temperatures well below freezing the band played during dinner, and we all wore full Number One Mess Kit, and we entertained the Americans and Swedes and French, and afterwards there was tremendous pride in showing these other United Nations forces how British officers whiled away the evenings.

To Wells's astonishment, the after-dinner entertainment consisted of nursery games:

We played High Cockalorum, which was simply getting on each other's shoulders and knocking each other off. And the most absurd game was called Torpedoes – it wasn't only absurd, it was extremely dangerous. They cleared a big table, and propped one end of it up, and as a junior officer you were put on the table, face down, and then you were given a box of matches in one hand, and a match in the other, and then they'd say, 'Grease the tube!' And all these dirty old buggers then rubbed you up and down the table, and then when they shouted 'Fire!' they threw you off. And you had to light the match before you hit the floor. Well, if you lit the match you landed very heavily on your balls and it was extremely painful. If you protected yourself, you didn't light the match, so you had to do it again.

I thought this was ridiculous, so a friend of mine called Simon Wood and I suggested that they might like us to do a cabaret instead. And I used to do impersonations of drunken American generals, or Swedes, for the amusement of other nationalities, when the Americans or Swedes weren't there. It did go down very well. And I suppose in retrospect they would be recognized as satirical sketches.

In 1957 Wells went up to St Edmund Hall, Oxford, on a scholarship to read Modern Languages, 'and I had the most shatteringly boring first year – it was mostly people going, "Bang, bang, you're dead." Teddy Hall was a very philistine college.' He spent his second year in Germany, 'teaching at a very nice boarding school outside Munich, and going to satirical night-clubs'. Returning to Oxford in the autumn of 1959, 'I saw a poster for an Experimental Theatre Club cabaret evening, and I turned up, and there was no competition. All I really did was people I'd met the army – just impersonating people.'

Wells's appearance was almost gauchely schoolboyish, with tousled hair and an oddly protruding upper lip, but he could make himself look astonishingly like John Betjeman or Field Marshal Montgomery (two of his favourite impersonations). That evening, he found himself performing to people he had never seen before,

a very, very smart set, with sort of Christ Church girls, long legs and very pretty. And to my amazement it went very well. And the next morning a Balliol undergraduate called Peter Usborne turned up at my room over the sweet shop in St Giles, and said, 'I hear you're the funniest man in Oxford. Will you come round to Balliol?' And I went round to Balliol, and in Usborne's room I met Paul Foot and Richard Ingrams, and very shortly after that Willie Rushton came up for the weekend. And I really, absolutely fell for them. First of all, Richard was incredibly charismatic, a schoolboy hero, very funny, and we just got on immediately. And we started doing tape-recorded improvisations and things, writing articles for *Mesopotamia*. So that was how I got caught up in it.

Wells was a late addition to a set of friends and fellow humorists that had been gradually coming together over the previous nine years, since the autumn of 1950.

*

That term, a thirteen-year-old listed as 'Ingrams, R.R.' had arrived as a new boy in Churchill boarding house at Shrewsbury School in Shropshire. Although his father had been at the school, and he had an elder brother already there, Richard Reid Ingrams was, at first, isolated and lonely. An early report from his housemaster describes him as 'silent…sober…still a child in many ways'. However, he soon found companionship.

Another new boy turned out to have a birthday just a day before him, and to live near him in London, which gave them something in common. Moreover this boy, a plump-faced broadly built child called William George Rushton, could whistle the tunes from all the latest musicals, and had immersed himself in P.G.Wodehouse and the comic *Daily Express* column by 'Beachcomber'. Rushton was soon entertaining Ingrams with the Beachcomber characters, among them Mr Justice Cocklecarrot, perpetually plagued by a troupe of red-bearded dwarfs; the cad and cheat Captain Foulenough; Dr Smart-Alick, unprincipled headmaster of Narkover School; the tireless inventor Dr Strabismus (Whom God Preserve) of Utrecht; and the archetypal seaside landlady Mrs McGurgle. 'Willie knew quite a lot of it by heart,' says Ingrams.

Beachcomber, whose real name was J.B. Morton, gradually became a role model for Ingrams, both as a humorist and as an individual. Born in 1893, he wrote the 'By the Way' humour column in the *Daily Express* from 1924 until 1975. In his *Dictionary of National Biography* article on Morton, Ingrams (who has edited *The Bumper Beachcomber* and played Mr Justice Cocklecarrot in a radio version of Beachcomber) writes:

> His humour was based on a strong dislike of the twentieth century… Nevertheless his funniest work was pure nonsense which had little or no reference to the real world…Morton was a stocky thickset man who wore his hair in a crew-cut like his mentor Hilaire Belloc. In his early days as a journalist he was a familiar figure in the pubs of Fleet Street with his loud laugh, muddy boots, and blackthorn walking stick…He became a Roman Catholic in 1922.

'The other person beside Beachcomber that Willie and I were influenced by was Tom Lehrer,' adds Ingrams. Lehrer's 'sick' humour, displayed in such songs as 'Poisoning Pigeons in the Park' and 'The Masochism Tango', began to circulate in Britain from 1953, following the issue in America of his first LP, *Songs by Tom Lehrer*. 'He was a real breath of fresh air,' Ingrams says. 'We could sing all his songs – they were very outrageous. Lehrer was very satirical, well ahead of his time.'

CORONATION BLANCO

There were four boys from Blanco's
    Hall
Who went to the coronation ;
They caught the half-past two express
From Rodentbury station.

And when they reached fair London
    Town
" The flour of cities all,"
They pitched the I.T.C's best tent
In the middle of the Mall.

They took a coach to Westminster
And entered by the door
They said : " We are four Johns
    who've come
To scrub the vestry floor."

They took the Coronation Stone
And carved their names upon it,
With a heart and Zsa Zsa Gabor
And a rather doubtful sonnet.

They called the Bishops naughty
    names,
They called the dean a gorgon ;
They played French cricket in the nave
And chopsticks on the organ.

The bishops shuddered at the strains
Of that triumphant song ;
The verger to the sexton said
" I think there's something wrong."

Now when our friends from Blanco's
    sensed
Episcopal alarm,
They changed their tune at once and
    sang
A reverential psalm.

But 'twas too late, the Yard had
    come,
Policemen by the score :
A fire brigade, the Coldstream guards
And ambulances four.

And so at last, they gave it up
And were put into gaol ;
(The re-endowment fund was used
To get them out on bail).

OTIS.

121

A poem by Richard Ingrams, illustrated by Willie Rushton, printed in their school magazine, the *Salopian*, to mark the Coronation in 1953.

The young Rushton could draw excellent cartoons. 'From the earliest days that I remember,' Ingrams says,

> he seemed to be a fully-fledged cartoonist. I don't know where he got it from; he had no ancestral cartoonists. All the time he doodled, on any piece of paper. His style was his own and owed little or nothing to other cartoonists. Not many artists would wish to be reminded of their early efforts, but Willie's stand up very well.

Christopher MacLehose, who arrived at Shrewsbury a little after Ingrams and Rushton (and is now the head of the publishers Harvill Press), agrees that Rushton's cartoon style was already fully developed – as was the cartoonist:

> He'd dash his drawings off at the back of the class, and they'd be passed along the line with ripples of merriment. Nobody minded them – I think people were encouraged at Shrewsbury to be pretty insolent. The school certainly wasn't regimented. Rushton himself was already quite circular in appearance, and seemed to have no ambition at all. While I was gradually going up academically, he was going down. We met in the Lower Sixth, where he'd sit with his cronies at the back of the class. In appearance and voice he was already a fully developed man in a child's clothes – a grown-up, but a lazy one.

There was a subtle difference in the backgrounds of Ingrams and Rushton. Ingrams's Old Salopian father was a tall, inscrutable banker with mysterious interests abroad. Ingrams had inherited his father's height, taciturnity, and fundamental melancholy; while his mother, the daughter of Queen Victoria's surgeon, had bequeathed to him and her three other sons a patrician, almost aristocratic conviction of their secure social position. Rushton was not so high in the English class system. His father was a quiet, reserved man who worked for the London publishing firm of Chapman & Hall, while his mother was a vivacious Welsh redhead. Ingrams notes that Rushton modelled his own mock-blimpish comic persona largely on his paternal grandfather, 'Herbert "Bertie" Rushton… a ruddy-faced Wodehousian clubman with a twinkling eye and a fondness for horse-racing'.

Ingrams played the cello and treated school chapel services seriously (his mother was a Roman Catholic). Rushton was neither musical nor religious – 'Good heavens, no I was spared that' – but Ingrams detected a serious streak in him:

> I never thought Willie changed throughout his life. He always seemed to be exactly the same person, as far as I was concerned, though he grew a beard later on. He seemed to be very grown up, even at that stage. Though never in the least

bit religious, he seemed to have found the answers to life, in some strange way, that I hadn't. At any rate, he remained untroubled by ambition. Perhaps because he was an only child, Willie always seemed very mature, self-sufficient and sensible compared with myself and most of our contemporaries. He only wanted to do what he enjoyed doing, and I don't think he wanted to do anything else or be anything else, and I think that was partly why he was loved.

Ambition at Shrewsbury in the early 1950s meant keenness to shine in sport and classics. As in all British preparatory and public schools at that time, Latin and Greek predominated in the curriculum, at least up to O level, and the school magazine, a dull affair called the *Salopian*, tended to quote untranslated Homer in its editorials, while the bulk of its pages were filled with reports of sporting fixtures. Like John Wells's Eastbourne College, the school was unquestioningly Conservative. At the beginning of Ingrams's and Rushton's third year, Queen Elizabeth II, as yet uncrowned, visited the school to mark its 400th anniversary. Afterwards one of the senior boys wrote in the *Salopian*: 'I understand now, as I never understood before, what the word "homage" ought to mean.'

Considering that this was the accepted attitude, it is rather surprising that, a few months later, just before the Coronation, the *Salopian* printed a comic ode about four Salopians going to London for that event and causing mayhem in Westminster Abbey. 'They called the Bishops naughty names,' ran one stanza,

> They called the Dean a gorgon;
> They played French cricket in the nave
> And chopsticks on the organ.

The poem's author was named as 'Otis', and it was accompanied by an illustration signed 'R'. This was the first public collaboration between Ingrams and Rushton. Ingrams had taken his pseudonym from one of his favourite screen performers, Groucho Marx, who was 'Otis B. Driftwood' in *A Night at the Opera*.

The *Salopian* was edited by senior boys, and the intrusion of young Ingrams and Rushton into its stuffy pages would probably not have happened without the encouragement of the master in charge of the magazine, a young Shrewsbury history teacher with mildly left-wing views called Lawrence LeQuesne. 'He was the reason I pursued comedy,' said Rushton many years later. 'LeQuesne laughed at every joke [in the *Salopian*], with the loudest laugh you'd ever heard.'

Looking back to those days, LeQuesne emphasizes that Ingrams was not openly subversive as a schoolboy. 'He kept the rules, and in some of the externals did conform to the established model of the successful Salopian.'

Yet his 'basic inspiration was a deep-rooted hostility to taking things seriously'. In later years, neither Ingrams himself nor his friends could identify the roots of this sense of the absurd – nor, indeed, could the friends explain any of the fundamentals of his personality. 'The more I saw of Ingrams, the less I seemed to know of him, the less there was to grasp,' writes (somewhat despairingly) his biographer, radio and TV comedy producer Harry Thompson. 'As I saw more of his friends and colleagues, I realized that I was not alone in this perception… "You'll never get to the bottom of Ingrams," said [Alan] Coren, taking me to one side. "There isn't a bottom to get to," smiled Ingrams.'

If explanations are to be attempted, Ingrams's parents seem, unsurprisingly, to provide some of the answers. He describes his father as 'an ultra-traditionalist' who nevertheless had a sardonic sense of humour; while his mother's Catholicism meant that he grew up with a sense of man having fallen from grace. He has the melancholy wit of someone who sees human history as a perpetual falling away from the ideal, and knows that nothing can be done about it except to laugh.

Certainly his comic style at Shrewsbury sometimes involved posing – or perhaps it was not posing – as an ultra-Conservative. Making his maiden speech in the school debating society at the age of fifteen, during a debate on crime, he argued that 'the stocks were the answer to everything'; he reported this in a letter to his mother, who he evidently knew would approve. More often he opted for a freewheeling, almost surrealist type of humour. Elected secretary of the debating society during his next school year, he proposed a motion deploring 'the inactivity of the School Ghost' – and reported on his own performance somewhat ironically in the *Salopian*: 'The secretary said that if there was a school ghost its inactivity should most certainly be deplored. He said no less, he certainly said no more: but he said it very well and some, but only some, people found it funny.' For another meeting he devised the motion 'That this House prefers to sit in its bath facing the plug'.

This brand of humour was partly derived from Rushton. The two had now developed a talent at acting. 'R.R. Ingrams was very effective as the leader of the mob when, with high-pitched, harsh, and strained voice he shouted for the death of Christ,' wrote the *Salopian* reviewer of the school Passion Play; but the Ingrams–Rushton forte was comedy. 'Rushton… specializes in the impersonation of pomposity,' noted the critic when the two of them appeared in J.M. Barrie's *The Admirable Crichton*, Rushton taking the part of Lord Loam. Indeed,

> the play [was] chosen to fit Rushton's talents… Of the others, Ingrams as the Hon. Ernest Woolley was measurably the best. The part suited his peculiar talents admirably… [Ernest's] sublime egotism and flow of fatuous epigrams

were handled as to the manner born, in a most witty and delightful performance.

Their chief field of comic activity was, however, the *Salopian*. Its correspondence column often printed unctuous letters from boys thanking masters for giving up their spare time to referee and umpire sporting fixtures. Ingrams contributed a spoof letter in this vein, thanking one of the school clocks: 'It has now been working since the beginning of this term, and may it ever continue to work for the generations to come.' This was mockery of Shrewsbury's narrow-mindedness. As Rushton puts it, 'Shrewsbury was isolated from the outside world ... [in P.G. Wodehouse's] Blandings country ... The sort of place you go to die, not to be educated.' And when Ingrams was chosen by LeQuesne to be editor of the *Salopian* at the start of his fifth year, assisted by Rushton and several other boys, he began to attack Shrewsbury's limitations more openly.

'They say that these are the happiest days of life,' he wrote in one of his first editorials;

> all one can say is Life can't be up to much. The enemy is Stodge. The new boys do not know this; for the first few days of the happiest of their life they hop happily along singing sweet songs; but then the Stodge, with a green spotlight lighting up its yellow face, rears its ugly foot and brings it down with a squelch on the innocent victims. Down they sink into the mud and begin to become the leaders of the future ... You see, it's no good. This suet and this sangfroid will get you nowhere.

Suet and sangfroid were not solely found at Shrewsbury. Ingrams was attacking the average middle-class Englishman of the 1950s. It was the sort of sneer that two other Catholic traditionalists, Hilaire Belloc and G.K. Chesterton, had made at their suburban-minded compatriots earlier in the twentieth century.

The same issue of the *Salopian* (Christmas 1954) included a mock-sixteenth-century number of the magazine – a spoof on the school's recent quatercentenary celebrations. Again, there was an editorial attacking the character of the English – 'ye stiffe upper lippe is a forry bane and fufficeth not' – and this time various sub-groups were singled out: 'Hearken unto me ye weedes alle, ye that are y-bloated ... ye yobbes and ye hackes ... ye pfeuds ...' Ingrams believes that this last term of abuse, 'pseud', was his own invention. He first aired it in a poem printed in the *Salopian* the previous term. 'There is a tribe that in the world exists,' he wrote alongside a Rushton drawing of a Shrewsbury-style aesthete, with a gramophone record floating above his head like a halo,

Who might be called the pseudo-culturalists.
Who think they can to heavenly realms aspire
By warbling Handel in the concert choir;
He who acclaims as masterpieces all
The tawdry paintings of the mad Chagall.
Who quotes from Blake or from Professor Freud,
This man I label with the title 'Pseud'.

Ingrams was criticizing the Shrewsbury system not merely as an insider, but from a position of considerable success. During his sixth and final year at school he was chosen to be head boy of his house, a school prefect, and the house platoon commander in the army cadet corps; he was also elected to senior positions in several school clubs – an indication that boys as well as masters approved of him. Indeed, one boy a year younger than Ingrams who now joined the editorial team of the *Salopian* looked up to him with '*total hero-worship*'.

This was Paul Foot, a member of a leading English family of left-wing intellectuals – most of them Liberals, like Paul's diplomat father Hugh Foot, but one of them, his uncle Michael Foot, a Labour MP. Paul was as tall as Ingrams, with the same slow smile; but he had inherited his family's total commitment to liberalism, and he soon realized that Ingrams suspected him of 'taking things too seriously' in that department of life.

This was borne out in a school debate on the motion 'That this House deplores the decline of the landed gentry'. Foot made a serious speech attacking the old privileged upper class, but Ingrams, who half belonged to that class, responded mockingly. 'He delivered the most ferocious attack on me,' recalls Foot, 'saying that the world was full of weeds and wets, and that I was one of them, and the only thing that *mattered* was the landed gentry.' Foot was bemused by this, and he remained essentially out of tune with Ingrams's sardonic mock-conservatism. Yet the two shared a dissatisfaction with the *status quo*, a discontent with the world as they found it; and for a while this provided them with an excellent basis for partnership and collaboration.

Reporting this debate, the *Salopian* noted that Rushton had got to his feet and provided 'a light interlude', while the proposer had been 'Mr C.J.P. Booker'. Christopher Booker, the same age as Ingrams and Rushton, soon joined the *Salopian* editorial team. 'He had spectacles and golden curls,' recalls Ingrams mockingly, 'and he was very keen on butterflies and fossils. He used to go out on his bicycle and look for fossils on Sunday afternoons.' Ingrams soon nicknamed Booker 'Fotherington-Thomas', after the goody-goody in Geoffrey Willans's books about the comic schoolboy Molesworth. Booker responds:

It's true that I was keen on geology, and used to spend my Sunday afternoons pedalling out to look for fossils – but not in a Fotherington-Thomas way. After all, Darwin [an Old Salopian] had done it when he was at the school. But then Ingrams has his own rather limited view of the world. He's not a very serious or deep character.

Booker's parents ran a girls' prep school in Dorset. 'My dad was a keen Liberal – he stood for the Salisbury constituency a couple of times in the 1950s. And I'd been very keen on politics from an early age.' Again, Ingrams sneers – 'Booker is the only man I know who can instantly tell you things like who the prime minister was in 1931' – and Booker answers back:

Richard's invention of the concept of the Pseud says a lot about him – people are either Pseuds or Bores, unless he happens to like them, and in that case they can do no wrong. 'Good man, good man,' he will growl, even though they may be utterly fraudulent. He comes to his judgements entirely viscerally. And in a way I find him incredibly dark. Even to those of us who know Richard reasonably well, and have worked with him for decades, he's secretive and un-transparent. You get the feeling that, not far below the surface, there's a great dark area.

The Pseud – later a target for the scorn of *Private Eye* – makes his début in the *Salopian*, created by Ingrams and Rushton.

" PSEUD "

THE PSEUD

There is a tribe that in the world exists
Who might be called the pseudo-culturists.
Who think they can to heavenly realms aspire
By warbling Handel in the concert choir ;
He who acclaims as masterpieces all
The tawdry paintings of the mad Chagall
Who quotes from Blake or from Professor Freud,
This man I label with the title " Pseud. "

OTIS.

But it would be wrong to present Booker and Ingrams as essentially hostile to each other. Booker had arrived at Shrewsbury (from the Dragon School in Oxford) a year after Ingrams and Rushton, and he was amused and impressed by their already thoroughly formed personalities: 'Willie, and to a certain extent Richard, really stood out as characters. They were particularly good in the debating society, especially Willie, who was a spontaneous wit.'

The Ingrams–Rushton double-act was seen to advantage during an evening of spontaneous debates in the spring term of 1956:

> It was then the turn of Mr Rushton and Mr Ingrams to respectively move and oppose the third motion: 'This House considers the annexation of Rockall an act of unprovoked aggression.' Mr Rushton was concerned lest the birds on Rockall might be disturbed. 'How would you like to be a pregnant gannet pestered by battleships and platoon organizations?' he asked his audience. Mr Ingrams was in favour of extending the Empire, and he produced a book from which he proceeded to read a long extract. At the end of his recital he remarked that the passage was indeed interesting but, of course, totally irrelevant. He then quoted, 'Lest we forget, lest we forget'; and this was greeted from across the way by Mr Rushton adding – 'the pregnant gannet' … Frivolity at its best.

During this term Ingrams handed the chief editorship of the *Salopian* to Rushton, so that he could work for A levels. Christopher Booker was now part of the editorial team. 'I wrote an editorial on why the Army Cadet Corps should be abolished,' he recalls,

> which would have been unthinkable at Shrewsbury four years earlier. We'd arrived at a school that was still very traditional in its outward forms, with very strict hierarchies: junior boys couldn't speak to anyone from the year above them unless they were spoken to, whereas seniors could wear their jacket open and walk on certain bits of grass – all the traditional privileges and punishments of public-school life. But society in the 1950s was beginning to open out and become more relaxed, and that was particularly noticeable in the official response to my article.
>
> After it had been printed, I was called in by the master in charge of the Corps, Major Fowler. In the past, he would have been terrifically angry, but now his attitude was 'I do understand what you're saying' – the old order at school was trying to be sympathetic to the young people who were keen on chucking it all aside. And in that sense Shrewsbury was a very good school.

*

Booker was turned down for National Service on account of poor eyesight – he spent a 'gap' year in London and then went to Cambridge – but the rest of the Ingrams gang joined the army. Paul Foot emphasizes that public school-boys almost always got commissions: 'All you had to do was say you'd been to public school and you were automatically marked out for being an officer.' Foot himself not only became a second lieutenant but, thanks to family influence, secured a safe and comfortable posting to the West Indies. However, Ingrams and Rushton experienced a very different kind of army life.

'We neither of us made it into the officer ranks and class,' says Ingrams.

> I never understood quite how Willie failed to get a commission. He failed to get to university, first of all. He tried to take O level Maths, I think six times, and failed. Then they said, 'Why don't you do Biology?' So he did Biology, and he went into the exam, and there was something in a test tube, and they said, 'What is this?', and Willie put down 'Disgusting.' And he walked out. And he did something like that in the army too.

Rushton was sent as a trooper to the British Army of the Rhine. Ingrams, meanwhile, had similarly been judged by the interviewing panel not to be officer material. Paul Foot guesses that he answered their questions 'with that satirical and contemptuous attitude ... and would have been demoted for that reason'. Ingrams says that his failure to get a commission was a 'deep shock' to his mother. His father had died of a heart attack three years earlier, while Rushton's father succumbed fatally to diabetes while he was doing National Service. For Ingrams, the loss may have deepened his identification with his father's traditionalism and sardonic melancholy.

He became a sergeant in the Education Corps, and was posted to Korea and Malaya to teach literacy to ill-educated soldiers and help run the camp library. John Wells glimpsed him in Korea, not knowing who he was, and not exchanging a word with him: 'I saw him playing the harmonium at mattins in the garrison chapel, looking like a baboon, and I thought "What an odd man."' National Service deepened Ingrams' already ingrained scepticism about society, as it dawned on him that 'the officers weren't really fit to be in charge and that it was the NCOs who knew how to run things. That discovery made me more of a bolshevik.' Rushton had similarly eye-opening experiences:

> It was the first time I had met my fellow man ... London Teddy Boys, Glaswegians, Liverpudlians ... Everyone had something to offer. I was staggered, really ... I suddenly realized what a waste of brain there was [in] these guys who had left school at fifteen, sixteen. I think it was when I started moving left.

*

In 1959, after his two years' National Service, not knowing what else to do, Rushton joined a London solicitor's office as an articled clerk. In his spare time he continued to draw cartoons, occasionally submitting one to *Punch*. It always rejected them.

Founded in 1841, *Punch* had announced in its first issue that it would include 'original, humorous and satirical articles', and for a while it did display a radical outlook, analysed here by the modern literary critic John Sutherland:

> Its position can best be defined by a comprehensive negativity; it was anti-royalist, anti-aristocrat, anti-Cockney, anti-Semitic, anti-Irish, anti-Whig, anti-Tory. Personalities were guyed ruthlessly, and all game was in season ... It was quite typical, for example, that *Punch* in 1846 should make jokes about starving Irishmen.

This is remarkably like *Private Eye* in the 1960s; and like the *Eye*, *Punch* retained its writers on a salaried basis, as Sutherland explains:

> An original factor was Mark Lemon's system of paying his men on *Punch* salaries, rather than by-the-line rates. Long-term engagement encouraged contributions more substantial than the usual 'guffawgraphy' of cuts, squibs, puns and comic verse. There emerged from *Punch* a string of quite ambitious comic surveys of English society and institutions.

A prime example of these surveys is Thackeray's 1846–7 *Punch* serial 'The Snobs of England' (later published as *The Book of Snobs*) which exposed 'toadyism' at every level of society. The early *Punch* could also be passionately serious about contemporary issues. It printed Thomas Hood's *The Song of the Shirt*, a monologue by a seamstress protesting against overwork and starvation wages:

> O! men with sisters dear,
> O! men with mothers and wives!
> It is not linen you're wearing out,
> But human creatures' lives.

However, from the beginning, much of *Punch* was on the Christmas-cracker level, like this joke from an early number: 'Why is a loud laugh in the House of Commons like Napoleon Buonaparte? – Because it's *an M.P. roar* (an Emperor).' The radicalism soon disappeared, and *Punch* became the uncritical, harmless jester of the Victorian Establishment. Thackeray obviously regretted this. In 1854 he wrote of the decline of satire under Victoria:

> We have washed, combed, clothed, and taught the rogue good manners ... but he has put aside his mad pranks and tipsy habits; and ... has become gentle and harmless, smitten into shame by the pure presence of our women and the sweet confiding smiles of our children.

Yet satire is more likely to flourish when empires are in decline, rather than while they are being built; certainly at times when value systems have collapsed, or are being reassessed and challenged – a process to which it contributes – rather than maintained uncritically. In a 1961 article, Jonathan Miller associated the fading away of British satire in Victorian times with 'the development of the nineteenth-century English public school with its emphasis on loyal and unquestioning service: with the rise of a new [middle] class anxious to establish itself with unshakeable values and a reputation for reliability and sound judgement'. He continued:

> Good manners have suffocated English satire more effectively than any secret police. The smug courtesy of the public-school sixth-former, neatly adjusted to the demands of loyal service in a growing Empire, takes all the life-blood out of satire...It is the same spirit that makes it a breach of good taste...to discuss politics or religion in the intimacy of a club.

During the 1950s *Punch*, proverbially to be found in dentists' waiting rooms, purveyed the same cosy, unchallenging humour that it had done for the previous century. Malcolm Muggeridge, editor from 1953 to 1957, recalls that the political content was feeble: 'Our deliberations on the week's cartoon were lengthy and confused. Usually someone would suggest showing President Eisenhower as Humpty Dumpty, or General de Gaulle as Alice. Usually we did.'

3

Joined at the hip

Despite having done no more work at school than Rushton, Ingrams won an award to University College, Oxford. Arriving there in the autumn of 1958, he was surprised and delighted to find that Paul Foot, though a year junior to him at Shrewsbury, had chosen the same college and was among the freshmen. Foot says, 'I heard this voice saying "Foot" and I looked up and there was Richard ... We immediately clung together from the nervousness of being in a new place ... and very, very quickly became close friends – much closer than we'd been at school.'

Ingrams was especially pleased to have Foot's companionship, since (like John Wells in his first year) he was disappointed by Oxford. Hoping to encounter 'eccentrics and aesthetes and witty people', he found instead 'just a lot of men in duffel coats wandering up and down the High Street'. More specifically, he had expected to meet 'funny people ... wanting to do the kind of things that I wanted to do'; but again there was a dearth.

However, the previous term a Christ Church undergraduate, Adrian Berry, had started a pamphlet-sized humorous magazine. The son of Lord Hartwell, owner of the *Daily Telegraph*, Berry had come up to Oxford from Eton with an itch to contribute gossip to the undergraduate journals *Cherwell* and *Isis* (named after Oxford's principal rivers). 'But they were too nervous to publish it,' he recalls, 'so I started *Parson's Pleasure*.' He named the magazine after the bathing place on the river Cherwell where male members of the university swam naked – a spot, inevitably, with mildly scandalous associations. 'It cost me about £25 an issue,' says Berry. 'The Proctors [the pair of dons in charge of university discipline] occasionally objected to things in it, and W.H. Smith wouldn't sell it because it was too scandalous, so we had to sell it in cafés, and people kept pinching the money.'

The first issue of *Parson's Pleasure* claimed, in an editorial signed by Berry and headed 'The Power of the Pen', that the new magazine would be satirical:

> The aim and purpose of this magazine is to bring a new and healthy breeze into Oxford life … We have no intention of publishing any libel, but do not imagine that we shall flinch from lashing out brutally at all signs of pomposity and vainglory … I give my solemn word of honour that any undergraduate who outspokenly condemns this magazine will be savagely lampooned … Our general policy can be summed up in four words: 'Justice tempered by prejudice.'

In fact the bulk of the first issue, which was written by Berry himself and a small group of helpers, consisted not of satire but undergraduate gossip, chiefly about Berry's upper-class friends at Christ Church – characters such as '"Jinks" Grafftey-Smith' and 'balding ex-teenager Ron Angel', described as a pair of 'sexual aristocrats', who were said to have 'caused many a deb to reach for her chastity belt'. A whole article was devoted to the exclusive Gridiron dining and drinking club – the university's most aristocratic haunt, far beyond the pockets of most undergraduates – and there was an entirely serious column reporting on games of bridge.

The gossip column in the second issue of *Parson's Pleasure* mentioned a Magdalen undergraduate who was a leading Oxford Conservative:

> Kenneth Baker ('tall, dark and handsome' – *Daily Express*) is gradually discarding his veneer of genial bonhomie, to reveal the gleaming metal of his ruthless political ambition. 'Tell me, Lord Attlee,' he asked at dinner, 'is it comfortable at No. 10?'

The third issue printed an 'exposé' of its rival *Isis*, currently being edited by the left-wing Dennis Potter: 'His frequent displays of histrionics are not the product of a domineering megalomaniac, but of a slightly hysterical, soft-centred, anxiety-complex-ridden Make-Gooder with a winning way with his underlings' (an extraordinarily shrewd summary of Potter which remained accurate for the rest of his life). By this time, Berry's hope of being satirical seemed to have faded: he was now commissioning serious articles by dons (Nevill Coghill on an OUDS production of *All For Love*, Roy Harrod on Marx), and he printed three bad poems by the celebrated Oxford aesthete of the 1920s, Harold Acton. The bridge report occupied a lot of space in each issue, and there was news of another upper-class pastime – 'the opening meet of the Christ Church and New College Beagles'; also 'A Day with the Drag Hounds'.

By the spring of 1959, Berry was approaching his Finals, and he was keen that others should take over the editorship of *Parson's Pleasure*. He knew Paul Foot through a National Service acquaintance, and Foot, now in his second term, saw the opportunity for himself and Ingrams to resume something like their version of the *Salopian*. Ingrams did not know or care twopence about the Christ Church 'bloodies' who featured in the *Parson's*

Pleasure gossip columns, yet he had enjoyed reading their supposed exploits. 'I remember Adrian Berry being a very loud and engaging figure,' he says, 'and his *Parson's Pleasure* was very wild and libellous and funny.' He shrewdly perceived from this that there was a readership for scandal about total strangers. 'It brought home to me that you don't have to know who people are to enjoy reading about them,' he recalls. 'In fact, people *like* reading about people they don't know anything about.'

The issue of *Parson's Pleasure* for 9 May 1959 announced: 'Editor – Paul Foot'. Referring to Berry as a 'great reformer in Oxford journalism', Foot declared, 'Now the torch has been passed on and it is our duty to uphold the tradition of which he has laid the foundations. We will do so fearlessly, with integrity and purpose. Between the turgid waters of Isis and Cherwell we will steer our jolly little barque.'

There was an immediate change in the *Parson's Pleasure* style. The correspondence column began to carry letters from imaginary characters. 'Hubert Drivel' protested against 'the exclusive maleness in the May Day Morris Dancers', and 'Sir Reginald Ball' complained, 'There are too many foreigners in the country…wops, wogs, dagos, what?' The magazine's gossip column ('Parson's Table Talk') now began to report, even more incomprehensibly than under Berry's editorship, on the doings of quite a different set: 'Who is the Provok'd Wife in *That Was No Lady*? It is not Mary All-my-friends-have-been-sent-down-except-Herbie I-knows-everyone-in-Oxford-except-Mary-Borg Butterfield-Borg. She plays the part of the maid, seduced by Razor (Richard "Pater Impotens" Ingrams).'

From an article in the same issue, signed 'Hugo Prayermat', it was possible to deduce that this referred to an undergraduate production of a musical based on Vanbrugh's *The Provok'd Wife*:

> The ubiquitous Ken Loach is playing the male lead and the female side of the cast is studded with stars…Glancing down my OUDS card, I see that Master John Spurling has written a new 'play'…perhaps the new effort has some characters in it; it had better! Otherwise Prayermat and his cronies will be in the gallery booing heartily…Hugo Prayermat will shortly be appearing in *A Woman Killed with Kindness*, a production by Univ. Players and LMH Dramatic Society…Prayermat is taking the part of kindness.

If 'Hugo Prayermat' had any real existence, he was Ingrams, who was now immersing himself in Oxford theatricals. *That Was No Lady* was reviewed by 'Charlie Chucklehead' in a later issue of *Parson's Pleasure*: 'Razor, played by Richard Ingrams, is absolutely brilliant(?).'

Ingrams recalls that the name 'Hugo Prayermat' was invented by Willie Rushton, who had begun to come down from his clerk's job in London to spend weekends in Oxford, helping Foot and himself with *Parson's*

Pleasure. They decided to retain the 'Bridge' column for one more issue, but with a difference; this time it reviewed Oxford bridges, including Magdalen Bridge and Folly Bridge – 'unhappily neither of these are of great interest to the serious connoisseur'.

Having made his début, Foot remained as sole editor for the next issue of the 1959 summer term, which announced on the front cover in an enormous typeface: 'VICE IN OXFORD'. This was explained on the last page: 'We would like to welcome to Oxford Mr Donald Vice who speaks tomorrow to St Peter's Hall numismatic society on "Coins – their various uses".' There was also a letter from 'Cuthbert Dither' which began in the style of CND protests:

> Dear Sir,
>
> Though many of my contemporaries seem to be apathetic and indifferent towards the issue I nevertheless feel that it is one on which every thinking man must be committed. Over all our lives there hovers a threat, a menace of disaster, something which is there whether we like it or not. It is our duty to get together and rid ourselves of the concomitant despair.
>
> To what do I refer? The Radcliffe Camera [a prominent university building]. For too long it has drably dominated our lives, for too long we have crouched in its dismal shadow. Let it be removed before it is too late.

In the autumn of 1959, the *Parson's Pleasure* front cover announced: 'Editors – Paul Foot & Richard Ingrams'. Foot was only too glad to share the job – indeed, to hand it over. 'I've always been a rotten editor,' he says. 'He [Ingrams] is the one who assessed the stuff, put it in, and ruthlessly spiked things. He was plainly an editor from the beginning.' Indeed Ingrams was already marking himself out as less a humorist than someone who caused others to be humorists, providing them with an audience, a context, and an assurance that he would laugh at them if they were funny. 'In conversation,' writes his biographer Harry Thompson, 'he likes to sit back and soak up the jokes and anecdotes of others…his eyes quickly glaze over if the performance begins to falter…[friends'] main function is to entertain him.'

The front-cover headline of this first jointly edited issue was 'GIRAFFE FOUND IN PUB'. Inside, a Rushton cartoon depicted a giraffe standing at a bar and saying: 'No, no, I insist – the highballs are on me' – a joke that aroused the disapproval of the Proctors. The spoof letters continued. 'Chadmore Chastlebed' protested about an editorial that had mocked 'Grey Men' – undergraduates who wore ties and wrote their essays on time – and in a later issue 'Mable Crutchworthy (Mrs)' complained that she could not find the free plastic gnome promised on the front cover. The editors explained: 'When we tried to enclose the gnomes in the magazine, we found that they invariably fell out.'

Other contributions came from 'Slycrutch', 'E. Bladder, 'Muriel Prawnwinkle' and 'A.J. Hotayr', who complained in tortuous philosophical terminology about a review of his latest work of philosophy (a gibe at Oxford's most distinguished philosopher, A.J. Ayer). There was also a rather feeble parody of James Bond by 'Ian Phlegm', notable only for the villain's name: 'The story so far: Ball, deserted by Ethel, has inadvertently prevented Vuckoff's escape from the Bodleian ...' Meanwhile an editorial complained – like the *Salopian* – about dullness:

> Everywhere we see the dreariness of Man. We see the squat-bottomed pipe-smokers ensconced in pubs discussing the day's rugger.
>
> We hear the bloodies staggering home to bed regaling one another with silly military songs.
>
> What is more, we can envisage them in 40 years' time. And what will they be doing?
>
> You can bet your bottom and your dollar that they will be squatting in suburban pubs talking about the day's rugger.

Parson's Pleasure was now running out of money. Adrian Berry was no longer financing it, and though Paul Foot's uncle Michael had supported it for a few issues by buying (out of his own pocket) a whole-page advertisement for the Labour journal *Tribune*, this situation could not continue indefinitely. After the autumn term of 1959 *Parson's Pleasure* stopped abruptly.

Or so it seems. Oxford's Bodleian Library does not have a complete run of the magazine, and Adrian Berry says that the only person claiming to possess all the issues is 'someone who lives in Africa'. At some point, Auberon Waugh, then a Christ Church undergraduate, made an unsuccessful attempt to acquire it from Ingrams and Foot: 'I made a sort of takeover bid – I went to Foot's rooms in Univ, and Ingrams was there, and I was treated with some scorn, shown the door.' Certainly it was revived for at least two more issues in 1961, edited by another undergraduate, Noel Picarda. One of these carried a photo-story called 'Manhunt', in which John Wells played a hapless student caught by the Proctors buying nylon stockings from a slot machine, and submitted to 'nameless tortures ... DEEP in the dungeons of the Clarendon Buildings'. Berry recalls that the Proctors were offended by this, and called a final halt to *Parson's Pleasure*.

Berry himself went on to become science correspondent of the *Daily Telegraph*. 'Eventually I realized that *Parson's Pleasure* had been the start of *Private Eye* – who have never been unkind to me. They've sometimes printed articles supposedly by "Adrian Batty, our Telescope correspondent", but nothing worse than that.'

*

By the time they finished with *Parson's Pleasure*, Ingrams and his friends had found a bigger and more sophisticated outlet for their bizarre collection of talents. This was provided by Peter Usborne, the Balliol undergraduate who introduced Ingrams and Foot to John Wells. Usborne was a former scholar of Eton who had determined to found a humorous magazine at Oxford. 'At school,' he explains,

> I'd always thought that running a magazine was romantic. My uncle, Richard Usborne, the great expert on P.G. Wodehouse, had bought up what we'd now call a London listings magazine – though it quickly ran out of money – and his hero was Harold Ross of the *New Yorker*. And I became aware of *Le canard enchaîné*, the French satirical magazine, and *Simplicissimus* in Germany; I knew nothing about them, but I was aware that something called satire existed on the Continent.

Usborne explained in the first issue (May 1959) that *Mesopotamia* – named after a stretch of land between two streams of the Cherwell, near Parson's Pleasure – was meant to be 'a progressive, meaningful, distinctive, semi-demi-surrealist, neo-dadaist ANTI-MAGAZINE; as you will see, it is not.' He had instead opted for a smartly produced glossy with many pages of advertisements, twice the size of *Parson's Pleasure*. Its opening list of contributors included Rushton, but not Ingrams or Foot.

Rushton had now given up his legal career. 'He was nearly run over by a London bus,' recalls Ingrams, 'and he decided then that he was never going to do anything that he didn't enjoy, in his future life. And he immediately gave up being a solicitor, and took to freelance cartooning. And all he could get was a job on the *Liberal News*.' Rushton himself gives a slightly more detailed account of this period of his life:

> Briefly I served under Michael Foot on *Tribune* but he was looking for another Vicky...I also became political cartoonist of the *Liberal News* where I ran a strip cartoon called 'Brimstone Belcher' who was a Fleet Street journalist in the Chapman Pincher/Sefton Delmer mould. It was finally withdrawn due to public incomprehension.

A member of the *Mesopotamia* team was struck by Rushton's curiously middle-aged appearance:

> I remember him always wearing a neat little trilby hat, tweed overcoat, jacket and tie – he made no concessions whatever to undergraduate fashion. He was a sprightly chap, light-hearted, witty, rotund, unassuming, yet quietly sure of himself. English and proud of it, he was fond of cricket and beer. Compared to us students, Willie was a grown-up person...At the time we underrated him, when in fact he was miles ahead of us.

The description is by Andrew Osmond. Ingrams had briefly met this handsome, dark-haired ex-public schoolboy during National Service, and had thought him 'arrogant', chiefly because he was a smartly turned-out junior officer in the Gurkhas. Coming up to Brasenose College, Osmond had conformed to this image, opting for a socialite life at Oxford; Ingrams and Foot referred to him in the *Parson's Pleasure* gossip column as 'Outrageously handsome ex-Gurkha Andrew Osmond', and Osmond himself admits that 'I was what was called a "deb's delight". I just went to parties in London with pals from the army.'

Nevertheless Ingrams began to find Osmond amusing, and co-opted him into his gang – which in turn Usborne soon co-opted into *Mesopotamia*. Their names all appeared under fanciful titles in the third issue. Osmond was listed as 'Pencil Sharpener', Ingrams as 'Caterer', Rushton as 'Special Effects', and Foot as 'Type Writer'. A notice in this issue, inviting contributions, emphasized: 'Political satire, cartoons and captions for cartoons are particularly suitable.'

A Rushton cartoon in this issue did attempt political humour, portraying the four major international leaders of the day, Macmillan, Eisenhower, Khrushchev, and de Gaulle, afloat in a rowing boat, on which a sign is hanging: 'Peace at last'. But it is not clear what (if anything) Rushton meant by this. Indeed *Mesopotamia* had an uncertain touch with any kind of humour. *Parson's Pleasure* had been a joke about its own genre, a non-magazine that made almost no sense to anyone; whereas, beneath its self-consciously humorous veneer, *Mesopotamia* was a seriously ambitious project, an attempt (by Usborne) to attract attention in the world beyond Oxford, not satirizing itself and therefore failing whenever individual jokes failed.

Even Ingrams managed to be unfunny in its pages, contributing to the third issue a spoof obituary of a public school master which started well – 'All generations of Corrodians will be grieved to hear of the death at 89 of Mr L.P. ("Porker") Stringhurst' – but then petered out. Foot wrote an equally disappointing spoof report of a Union committee meeting, and then abandoned *Mesopotamia* for the Union itself, with the intention of making his mark as a serious undergraduate politician. The next issue named Ingrams and Osmond as joint assistant editors under Usborne's editorship, and included a parody of the easily mockable columnist and author Godfrey Winn – 'I am tall and dark and (although I say it myself) rather lovely with flowing hips and willowy hair.' There was a renewed attempt at political satire with a board game called 'Arms Race', featuring world leaders and a nuclear explosion at the finish, and, more successfully, a spoof advertisement mocking a new social group far removed from Oxbridge:

DO YOUR FRIENDS SMELL?
NO? Then it's time you applied to:-
THE LONDON SCHOOL OF BEATS
The Basement, 420 King's Road, London SW3

Naïve? Gullible? Stable? Frustrated? Untalented? Send NOW for 6-week
correspondence course ...

Unsolicited Testimonial

Look, man, I must sing to you of the new holy life, swinging with the starry
cosmos and warm in the soft belly of the earth mother ... I am found, man,
bathing is unclean ...

A pair of accompanying photographs showed a young bowler-hatted City
gent metamorphosing into a Beatnik. This was John Wells.

Though Usborne had eagerly recruited Wells for *Mesopotamia* on the
strength of his skills as a cabaret performer, Wells was not immediately
welcomed by the Ingrams–Rushton–Foot trio of Old Salopians. 'Coming
from Eastbourne College was a major handicap,' says Wells, 'because the
Salopian snobbery made them regard Shrewsbury as a secret kind of crypto-
Eton. They were a very snobbish school.' On the other hand (he continues),

> Ingrams was incredibly funny, and he was this very irresistible gang leader, in
> that he always seemed to know exactly what he wanted. When he was actually
> writing – he has this big round handwriting – he never crossed a word out; that
> was what used to impress me very much. I'd do eight or nine drafts on the
> typewriter, and throw it away. He never never did that. He just seemed to have
> an absolute confidence.

Elsewhere, Wells has described Ingrams as having 'an instinctive feel for the
bogus and the genuine'.

Did Wells feel, from the outset, that the two of them had the same sense
of humour? 'Well, I'd been brought up on Wodehouse, and certainly I knew
Beachcomber. But I think what Richard and I had in common from the
beginning was funny voices. We'd both been through the same experiences
in the army. And a great deal of the jokes were army – sergeant-majors and
droopy officers, and comic working people.' This sounds like the same
humour as the outstanding radio comedy series of the 1950s, *The Goon
Show*, and Wells, when asked about this, partly agreed about the affinity:
'Certainly *The Goon Show* was what we all knew by heart.'

Until the Goons appeared in 1951, radio comedy had been derived from
music-hall, and rarely ventured into the subversive. Then along came Spike
Milligan, the son of an Irish regimental sergeant-major and himself a gunner

in the Second World War. Milligan's Goon scripts brought anarchic army humour to the nation's loudspeakers:

> 'You there – that guard over there!'
> 'Da – yeah?'
> 'Why is your uniform so dirty?'
> (*Proudly*) 'I'm a mud guard.'

As *Beyond the Fringe* would dare to do later, *The Goon Show* mocked the portrayal of the war in 1950s films and radio documentaries: 'The English Channel, 1941. Across the silent strip of grey-green water, coastal towns were deserted, except for people.' Minnie Bannister (played by Milligan) tells Henry Crun (Peter Sellers): 'Come, Henry, we'd better be getting home – I don't want to be caught on the beaches if there's an invasion.' Henry answers, 'Neither do I – I'm wearing a dirty shirt.'

Milligan's scripts sometimes have touches of Shakespeare. This scene could feature Falstaff:

> SEAGOON: Major Bloodnok, I must ask you to parade your men.
> BLOODNOK: Why?
> SEAGOON: I'm looking for a criminal.
> BLOODNOK: You find your own – it took me years to get this lot.

Another influence is the strictly logical nonsense of Lewis Carroll:

> MORIARTY: My socks keep coming down.
> GRYTPYPE-THYNNE: Oh? Say 'Ahh'.
> MORIARTY: Ahhhhhh.
> GRYTPYPE-THYNNE: Gad, you've got hoar-frost on the ankle.
> MORIARTY: Is that dangerous?
> GRYTPYPE-THYNNE: If it kills you, yes.

The Goons were so funny that it is easy to miss the mockery. Jonathan Miller, however, sees them as crucially subversive, an influence on *Beyond the Fringe*:

> The Goons did an enormous amount to subvert the social order. After all, half of the *Goon Show* is a send-up of British imperialism – endless jokes about Henty-like characters, the British defending absurd salients on the North West Frontier, and idiotic figures like Major Bloodnok, endlessly shitting himself in lavatories – 'Ohhhh, Ali, get me a clean shirt, I'll never eat Bombay duck again!' That was very much our sort of stuff.

There was indubitably a Goonish touch to the opening paragraphs in a *Mesopotamia* of the summer of 1960, a supposed greeting from 'Colonel Sir Ethelred Cabbage…Military Attaché to the British Consulate in

Mesopotamia' (Rushton portrayed him in full dress uniform and a 'Miss Bognor' sash). The message began: 'We live in a world of change. I know. My wife's a man now.' Besides their radio show, the Goons had made comic gramophone records, such as 'The Ying-Tong Song' and 'I'm Walking Backwards for Christmas'. This – and the presence in Oxford's Broad Street of the Isis Recording Studios, which could be hired to manufacture gramophone records of amateur performances – seems to have given the *Mesopotamia* gang the idea of recording their own disc of funny voices. The 1960 summer number announced itself as 'Mesopotamia Rock', and had a detachable plastic record fixed to its front cover – 'Cut out record and play at 33⅓ r.p.m. … The record was directed by John Wells.'

Copies of the disc have long since vanished, but Peter Usborne recalls that the issue to which it was attached 'sold like the clappers – I remember, just after it came out, walking across the quad in Balliol, and hearing John Wells's voice coming out of every other window'. Ingrams recalls that the disc included Wells impersonating an army sergeant-major growling at a recruit: 'What's your name?' and receiving the answer 'Lady Violet Bonham-Carter'.

Indeed, Wells was the star of this entire issue of *Mesopotamia*. One page

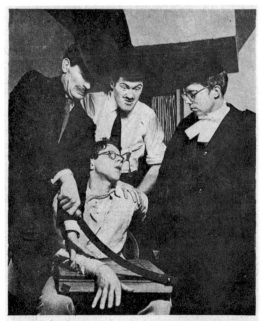

Parson's Pleasure depicts John Wells suffering at the hands of the university authorities – the standing figures are (*left to right*) Andrew Osmond, Richard Ingrams and unknown.

DEEP in the dungeons of the Clarendon Buildings, Oxford's equivalent of Flossenburg, nameless tortures are practised upon innocent youth by these vile sadists attempting to wring confessions from their swollen lips. Should they weaken and confess, they can be dragged before a secret tribunal and trial without defending counsel or right of Appeal.

PARSON'S PLEASURE CRIES SHAME TO THIS BLOT ON HUMANITY

featured snapshots from the photo album of a fictitious freshman at Keble (considered a dim college), with Wells playing the part of this archetypal Grey Man. There was a snap of him proudly showing off 'my new glasses!', while another of Keble itself had a hand-drawn arrow pointing to 'my room'. Wells also contributed a parody of Second World War reminiscences: '...those grim days in 1939 when I stood for three and a half hours in the rain waiting to be drafted – a fitting prelude to those five terrible years of fears and privations in the Home Guard Blanket and Webbing Equipment Sub-Depot at East Hoathly'.

He starred again in the next *Mesopotamia* (November 1960), which described itself as 'Once upon a Mesopotamia'. The 'O' of 'Once' was created by the shield of the crusader-in-armour from the masthead of the *Daily Express* – except that Rushton had drawn him with bent sword, and modelled him on Wells playing the dim freshman. This would eventually reappear on the masthead of *Private Eye*.

Half of this issue was taken up with a Rushton strip cartoon (co-written by him and Ingrams, Osmond and Wells) featuring the further adventures of the dim freshman, now called Little Gnittie, and still recognizably Wells. Caroline Seebohm, who was one of the most glamorous and popular girl undergraduates of this era at Oxford, recalls that, compared to the rest of the Ingrams gang, Wells did seem rather grey and dim. She gives this portrait of them:

> They were all brilliant and funny and also joined at the hip in some way, each one playing a slightly different role. Ingrams himself was really quiet and low-key, but his chokey, snorting laugh – I can still see the shoulders of his tweed jacket heaving up and down – somehow added to the others' funniness. He played the same role as Andy Warhol did later, I think, in *his* circle (though minus the drugs) – always observing and egging people on. And his mysterious aloofness added to his magnetism.
>
> Paul Foot was always outraged at something, full of energy, pacing up and down, declaiming, being shot down, arguing in his high-pitched voice. Andrew Osmond seemed incongruous in the group, being so smooth and debs'-delighty, always wearing upper-class Savile Row clothes, such as those wide-striped shirts that seemed more appropriate on trendy bankers. But it's interesting how, so often, incongruously connected people make a brilliant whole.

The Little Gnittie strip cartoon began: 'There was a little boy called Gnittie, who went to Oxford to find his Self.' In his progress through the university, Gnittie travels to Bloodyland' (populated by the rugger-playing hearties of Christ Church), learns to write a Tutorial-Postponement Letter, attempts to grow a beard, tries religion (both High and Low Church), and is introduced to 'the Birds' (Oxford women) by a Casanova-like 'Expert'. Rushton's drawing of this character is recognizably Ingrams, who was reputedly having considerable amorous success with Oxford under-graduettes. Gnittie also goes to the Union – which is full of literally faceless men – and eventually finds his Self in the form of a bowler-hatted statue, which he recognizes as his future. At the end, he falls 'into a Sea of Bowler Hats, NEVER TO BE SEEN AGAIN'; a conclusion that may reflect the *Mesopotamia* contributors' faint anxiety about their own future.

Rushton, however, was optimistic about the gang's prospects, believing that they could all continue doing exactly the same thing after Oxford. 'Willie was marking time,' recalls Ingrams,

> waiting for the rest of us to leave Oxford when he was convinced that our day would finally dawn. Memories of those times are blurred (partly because so many of the vital decisions were made in pubs), but the surviving members of the Oxford gang all agree that Willie was the person who first mooted the idea of a magazine, at a boozy picnic near Aynho [a village north of Oxford]. '*Mesopotamia* could continue,' he boomed, before falling asleep.

Andrew Osmond recalls this too:

> We were lying there in the sunshine and Willie said, 'What are you all going to do when you leave this place?' We all had our different plans, and he said, 'You're all mad. We should do a magazine. The public would buy this stuff.' And we all said, 'Yes, Willie have another drink.'

*

Paul Foot, meanwhile, was taking on the faceless men of the Union, and winning. In his third and final year he achieved the double feat of being elected to its presidency and being chosen to edit *Isis*, thereby implicitly turning his back on the antics of the Ingrams gang and opting for conventional success. Yet he invited Ingrams to contribute to *Isis* (Ingrams wrote a sentimental piece on the disappearance of the traditional English pub); and during his term's editorship Foot managed to do what *Parson's Pleasure* and *Mesopotamia* had never dared to attempt, organize an act of subversion that divided the university.

Under the deceptively mild heading 'Dons', Foot began (in the *Isis* issue for 18 January 1961) to print candid comments on Oxford lectures. An introductory article observed: 'The first thing that is seriously wrong with lectures is that it is easy for them to be so bad…a boring and infuriating exhibition of opinionated egotism.' The writer observed that, in medieval Oxford, scholars had argued with each other in public disputations, but nowadays the dons simply held forth to their audience uninterrupted for an hour, without even taking questions.

The article, signed 'Spartacus', was the work of John Davis, an undergraduate at University College. With Foot's approval, he organized a team of reviewers to report on individual lectures in the next issue's 'Spartacus' column. The reviewers did not pull punches:

> Professor Kneale's treatment of the distinction between the necessary and the contingent was disappointing…To spend five minutes on Plato's realms of Being and Becoming is too cursory for Greats and seemingly irrelevant to most PPE men …
>
> Mr Charles Taylor on 'Explaining Behaviour' was excellent…But…it is hoped that [he] will speak a little more slowly.

A Nuffield College don, J.P. Plamenatz, who lectured on Rousseau, Hegel and Marx, was described as 'academic in the worst sense of the word', guilty of 'a watery and abstract liberalism'. But the most scathing comments – the work of John Davis himself – were reserved for Mrs Evelyn Roaf of Somerville, lecturing on Dante's *Divine Comedy*.

Reporting that the audience in her first lecture had been a mere seven people (most of whom were said to be her own pupils), and that the numbers had shrunk to three the second week, Davis accused Mrs Roaf of 'cosy-prosy evasions' in her remarks on Dante. Calling her lectures 'dull and void', he went on: 'There is no atmosphere of intellectual excitement: Mrs Roaf's own enthusiasm does not communicate itself, and the *Comedy* is made to appear domestic and comfortable rather than divine and epic.'

John Wells, who had written one of the other reviews, recalls that, when this issue of *Isis* came out, Mrs Roaf 'had a nervous breakdown'. A few dons – including (remarkably) the much-attacked Plamenatz – felt that the experiment had been justified, and they supported the right of undergraduates to express their opinions on teaching in the university; but many were outraged, and the Proctors immediately summoned Foot and forbade him to continue with the reviews.

In the next issue of *Isis*, the series title 'Dons' appeared once again, but this time the page was blank, except for the words 'Censored by the Proctors'. Foot was, however, able in his editorial to give an account of the fracas:

> The ban was total, unconditional. On NO ACCOUNT were we to publish any more reviews of individual lectures…First, the lectures were private, and therefore – no public comment … Then I was told that the academic quality of the lectures would suffer from such criticism. The force of this argument was summed up by the Senior Proctor's unforgettable remark: 'D'you realize what this would mean? It would mean dons would take more trouble with their lectures, and give fewer of them.' The sheer horror of this situation was almost too much to bear.
>
> Thirdly, the case of extreme personal distress [Mrs Roaf]. I am of course very

sorry that there should have been personal distress. And I apologize for that. But it does not in any way affect the issue. The reviews may have been harsh. That is not a reason for banning them altogether.

The national press seized on the row, and *The Times* rumbled pompously that the reviews had caused 'a sense of outrage among graver minds'. In a letter to the *Sunday Telegraph*, Professor Max Beloff of All Souls asserted that the *Isis* 'agitation' was the work of scruffy left-wingers – 'a particularly active minority' committed to 'the cause of nuclear disarmament', who displayed 'a studied and unpleasant slovenliness of dress and deportment, a neglect of the elementary precepts of good manners'. Beloff declared that undergraduates, far from having a right to criticize their teachers, were privileged to be granted 'junior membership of a society of learned men' (no mention of women), and concluded, 'So far from being bold pioneers, the rude young men of *Isis* will seem to future historians of our universities no more than flotsam on the surface.' In which he was wrong, for John Davis, the chief perpetrator of the outrage, eventually became Warden of All Souls.

4

A little bit of something for everyone

Following his Finals at Oxford, Alan Bennett looked for a research subject, and a supervisor. 'I paid a disastrous visit to Beryl Smalley at St Hilda's, thinking I might do something on the Franciscans. There had been a torrential thunderstorm and forgetting to wipe my feet I trailed wet footsteps all across her white carpet, thus putting paid to any hope of research into the friars, barefoot or otherwise. I then went to see K.B. McFarlane.'

A Fellow of Magdalen, known for his deflating comments, McFarlane had written only a few books and articles, but was nevertheless, in Bennett's opinion, 'the leading medieval historian of his time'. Bennett recalls of their first meeting: 'I marched awkwardly into the room, stood on the hearthrug and said, "I'm Bennett," at which he laughed.'

Bennett's special subject in Finals had been the reign of Richard II, and McFarlane agreed that Richard's retinue should now be his topic of research. 'Thereafter,' writes Bennett,

> I used to go down and see him pretty regularly, though not in my recollection talking much about work; these visits, very often around teatime, gradually became less tutorial and more social … McFarlane was a great teacher, and yet he scarcely seemed to teach at all. An hour with him and, though he barely touched on the topic of my research, I would come away thinking that to study medieval history was the only thing in the world worth doing. McFarlane himself had no such illusions, once referring to medieval studies as 'just a branch of the entertainment business'.

McFarlane soon began to hand over some of his undergraduate pupils to Bennett for teaching. Bennett was uncomfortable in this role: 'I could never find sufficient comments to fill the necessary hour, and nor could my pupils. If I ventured on argument I was soon floored, and the tutorials ended in awkward silence. Eventually I took to putting the clock on [i.e. forward] before my pupils arrived, so there was less time to fill.' One of the pupils was Adam Roberts, now Professor of International Relations at Oxford. 'I knew Alan already,' says Roberts,

> because he was in a group of friends of which my sister (an undergraduate at Somerville) was also a member, and I'd met him quite a few times before he ever had the misfortune to tutor me. So that added an element of artificiality and absurdity to what was already a pretty absurd situation. Here was this character trying to teach me about – as far as I can remember – thirteenth- and fourteenth-century kings of England, and queens if there were any; a subject in which I had absolutely zero interest. And if he had an interest in this topic, it didn't come over as being electric.
>
> His own description of his tutorials is very accurate – his practice of setting his clock fast to shorten the whole thing. On several occasions I recall Alan saying, when I had finished reading my essay and all possible conversation about it had been exhausted, 'Let's wander over to the King's Arms and have a drink.' He was quite friendly – it was just the awful feeling on both sides that we had to go through this charade.
>
> I think it's true that he was shy, in a way, and he always rather acted that part. But he did in fact have lots of good friends. And after I left Oxford, for some time I was living in a house in London where several of his friends were living too, and Alan quite frequently visited us. He would often produce his tiny notebook in which he kept jokes, or bits of vivid conversation he'd overheard on the bus. One didn't get the feeling that he was an isolated figure, though he didn't seem to have a close partner of either sex, and sometimes one wondered about this.

For a while, Bennett remained a member of Exeter College Junior Common Room. Someone commented in one of the 1957 Suggestions Books on his 'long practice of imitating sermons', and his cabaret performances seem to have increased his popularity in college, since he was elected President of the Junior Common Room for 1958–9. 'I was never sure whether that was a distinction or a betrayal,' he says, laughing. 'Because you normally have to be quite hearty to be President of the JCR. But Exeter was a very peculiar college, and it was only because I could make people laugh.' His election gave him the privilege of writing presidential replies on the left-hand page of the Suggestions Book. 'This side of the book absolutely paralyses me,' he wrote at the beginning of term. 'I feel so alone out in the middle of this Great White Page.' And in reply to a complaint from an under-graduate: 'I promise you a New Deal.'

McFarlane eventually persuaded Magdalen to appoint Bennett to a junior lecturer post, with membership of its Senior Common Room and the right to dine at its high table. After the cosiness of Exeter JCR he felt adrift. His neighbours at dinner often included C.S. Lewis, Gilbert Ryle, and

A.J.P. Taylor, all of whom he found 'daunting', and his 'vivid and painful' memories of these meals included the occasion on which 'I found that, in sitting down, the sleeves of my gown had caught under the legs of my chair, effectively reducing my range of movement to a few inches. I was too shy to stand up and loosen it. So I sat there, refusing dish after delicious dish, simply because I couldn't reach the plate.'

Nor did he feel comfortable lecturing. On the one occasion that he gave a paper to a historical society, there was 'total silence' when the chairman asked for questions. 'Not a single one, until an undergraduate at the front leaned forward and whispered, "Could I ask you where you bought your shoes?"'

He realized that he was in the wrong profession. 'The only thing that fitted me for a don's life was my appearance. I *look* like a don. That isn't enough. I wasn't suited to academic life by temperament or capabilities.' Nevertheless during 1959 he applied for a lectureship in medieval history at the University of Hull. 'The professor kicked off the interview by empha-sizing that train services were now so good that Hull was scarcely four hours from King's Cross. It wasn't that he'd sensed in me someone who'd feel cut off from the vivifying currents of capital chic; rather that my field of study was the medieval exchequer, the records of which were then at Chancery Lane.' If he had gone to Hull, he would have come to know the university's librarian, Philip Larkin, later to become an inspiration and to some extent a role model for Bennett. In the event, they never met.

Bennett had a feeling that 'making people laugh was not a proper activity for a postgraduate and that I ought somehow to be acquiring more dignity; except that by now I was being asked to perform in other colleges and do cabaret for dances and Commem Balls, and was sometimes even paid.'

In the summer of 1959 he made his first appearance at Edinburgh.

*

Since it began in 1947, the Edinburgh Festival had included, alongside its official programme of events, a number of 'Additional Entertainments', financed and staged by a variety of amateur and professional groups. During the 1950s these became known as the 'Festival Fringe', and a society was eventually formed to co-ordinate them. The first Fringe revue was in 1951, a late-night professional production called *After the Show* which had transferred from the West End.

The word 'revue' is of course French, and was first used to describe a type of performance in the 1830s, when topical 'revues' of the year's events would be put on in Paris theatres. The first person to introduce revue successfully to England was André Charlot, a Parisian theatre manager who took over London's Alhambra in 1912 and staged bright, swiftly moving spectaculars featuring glamorous chorus girls in lavish dresses, sandwiching comic turns of various kinds. One of Charlot's stars immediately after the First World War, Jack Hulbert, recently down from Cambridge, soon began to stage his own 'little revues' in the Little Theatre just off the Strand. Comedy played more part in these, but it was mostly as tame as *Punch*. In the 1940s came the *Sweet and Low* revues, starring the waspish Hermione Gingold, and after the war an actor, playwright and director called Laurier Lister mounted another series of what were now known as 'intimate revues', beginning with *Tuppence Coloured* (1947). Among Lister's performers was Joyce Grenfell; his writers included Michael Flanders and Donald Swann,[1] and the young Sandy Wilson, fresh from Oxford and soon to create *The Boy Friend*. 'What was Intimate Revue?' Wilson asks in his autobiography, and answers: 'a pot-pourri…a little bit of something for everyone…Thus a satirical sketch may be followed by a romantic ballad, a dance interlude by a "point" number. The "running order"…may be changed a hundred times: And nothing – *nothing* – must go on too long.' John Wells gives a more sarcastic description of the genre:

> Directors literally insisted on the cast cleaning their teeth in the wings before they went on, and the glittering smiles were accompanied by a good deal of dancing about in frilly things and waving one's hands around. There were also lots of songs about things like the Income Tax. In fact, within the conventions of punchlines and neat blackouts, it was not unlike an animated copy of *Punch*.

The 1951 Edinburgh revue *After the Show* was intimate revue at its worst, depending chiefly on mildly blue jokes. 'Half-past ten and curtain time,' began the opening chorus,

> And once again we're here
> To give you a dose of libel
> And jokes with a kingly leer.

There was in fact no 'libel' in the show, but plenty of leering of the feeblest sort:

> After the show
> Where can you go?
> It must be cheap but smart

---

[1] The Flanders and Swann shows *At the Drop of a Hat* (1956) and *At the Drop of Another Hat* (1963) were not quite intimate revue and not quite satire. They verged on the whimsical, with jolly songs about animals, but there was an underlying elegiac quality about the material, perhaps springing from Flanders' disability (he was confined to a wheelchair by polio). In the second show, Flanders alluded wryly to the great change that had come over revue since the first *Hat* performances: 'Satire squats hoof in mouth under every bush. The purpose of satire, it has been rightly said, is to strip off the veneer of comforting illusion and cosy half-truth. And our job, as I see it, is to put it back again.'

> Why not make your way
> To Paddington buffet
> And try and get your teeth into a British Railways tart.

Other numbers included 'Two Old Queens', with the performers dressed as the Cunard transatlantic liners *Queen Elizabeth* and *Queen Mary*:

> To and fro
> To and fro
> Across the romantic Atlantic we go
> We long for something we didn't oughta
> A change from just passing Southampton Water.
>
> I once met a cruiser
> A regular bruiser
> But all the brute did was decamp.
> Ignoring my gender
> In spite of my splendour
> He made this lady feel just like a tramp …

They break off for dialogue: 'The brute rammed me amidships.' 'Did it damage your propeller shaft?' 'Damage it? Ever since I've been the only ship in the line with a soprano hoot!' The last sentence, implying castration, has been marked with a blue pencil by the official theatrical censor – one of the play examiners working on behalf of the Lord Chamberlain, in whose playscript archive (now in the British Library) this and other pre-1968 revues have been preserved.

The next professional revue at Edinburgh, in 1953, was *See You Later*, written by Sandy Wilson and starring Fenella Fielding. Since Wilson was primarily a songwriter, most of the numbers were musical, and one of them dipped its toe a little uncertainly into politics, albeit American rather than British. Inspired by the McCarthy witch-hunt, then in full cry, it was sung by Fenella Fielding in the character of an American typist; she pleads to 'Dear Mr McCarthy' to spare her boss because 'He's just wonderful in bed,/So he really can't be, can't be, can't be Red!'

The same year saw the arrival at Edinburgh of the Oxford Theatre Group (OTG), a company of student performers drawn both from the OUDS and the Experimental Theatre Club. They brought two straight plays and a revue, *Cakes and Ale*. Most of the latter was in verse (presumably sung), and the humour was sharper and more experimental than the 'intimate revues'. In the opening number, 'Going Away', a group of guests at a wedding comment acidly on the failings of the ceremony, the bride and the groom. Then comes a calypso – a genre much in fashion in 1953 – on biblical themes, called 'Revelations':

> Oh you've all read in the Old Testament
> How the wife of Lot became condiment.
> It was her curiosity started the rot
> She only peeped a little but she had lost her Lot.

This pioneer Oxford revue also directed its attention to the fashionable target of Admass, parodying current advertising and market research. One song featured the 'Mr and Mrs Average' of consumer surveys:

> *He*
> I work eight hours a day for fifty weeks of the year,
> Smoke 4.7 cigarettes and drink a pint of beer,
> Go weekly to the pictures, fill in the pools,
> Complain of the weather, think the government are fools,
> On Sunday afternoon I take a nine-minute nap;
> In fact I'm an extraordinarily ordinary chap.

> *She*
> I'm a typical housewife, my cooking's just fair,
> My complexion is average, I've nondescript hair,
> I'm seven times more interested in fashion than news,
> Eight per cent of my time I spend standing in queues.
> I lead a monotonous and uneventful life,
> I'm really an extraordinarily ordinary wife.

Oxbridge and the public schools came in for some gentle mockery. In 'Old Boys' Day', three middle-aged men revisit their old school, and one bellows his own words to the school song to show how much he hates the place. Another number featured a pair of gormless upper-class Oxford graduates looking for jobs:

> Two public-school officer-class potentials,
> Hardly intellectuals, but quick to grasp essentials ...
> Both joined the army, both got commissions,
> Impressed the CO so much we were nearly requisitioned ...
> Then we went to Oxford for a smattering of learning,
> Smartened up our wits, became artistically discerning ...

Cakes and Ale – submitted to the Lord Chamberlain without indication of authorship – was not revolutionary, but it showed how university humour was diverging from professional revues, and was beginning to stick a tentative pin into certain aspects of contemporary society.

The Oxford revues continued at Edinburgh, and by 1959 were a well-established feature of the Fringe. The show that year was to be written and directed by an American postgraduate, Stanley Daniels (later a television producer in the USA). Alan Bennett auditioned for it. He was now twenty-five and says he felt 'immensely old'. Fortunately Daniels looked 'at least forty', and had 'no dignity at all'. Bennett was accepted into the cast. The revue, called *Better Never*, was performed at the OTG's regular Edinburgh home, a gloomy hall in Cranston Street hired to them by the city's Parks and Burials Department.[2]

The script of *Better Never* included a sketch about nuclear war called 'Atom and Eve', in which a radioactive couple sing a romantic song:

> In our cottage by the sea,
> Where it's relatively free
> From deadlier contaminations,
> We just sit and hear the sweet
> Patter-patter of little feet
> Of our dear little mutations.

GIRL: (*Calling offstage*) Are you there, Junior?
VOICE: Yes, Mummy.
GIRL: Then let's hear you count your fingers.
VOICE: One, two, three, four, five, six, seven, eight, nine, ten.
GIRL: Isn't he a dear? Now the other hand.
VOICE: One, two, three, four, five, six, seven, eight, nine, ten.
GIRL: And now the other hand.

Most of the sketches were written by Stanley Daniels, but Alan Bennett was allowed to contribute the monologue that John Wells had seen him perform at Oxford (with the aid of his hatstand), 'At Home with the Atom' – again, the subtext is the nuclear threat:

Good evening. I'm a scientist. I'm one of those chaps – boffins they used to call us in the war – boffins. I'm a back-room boy. I work at a big nuclear research station... You know, it's very, very difficult for us scientists to talk to you laymen. Only this morning someone said to me, 'Oh, that's as plain as a pikestaff.' Well, (*he points to an excessively complicated molecular model*) this is a pikestaff, atomically speaking... Here is an ordinary simple piece of molecular structure. (*He shows the audience a set of contemporary-type clothes pegs.*) Now, fifty years ago, we used to imagine this as something quite different. We thought it looked like this. (*Indicates old-fashioned curly-type hatstand.*) And we're continually making discoveries. All the time...

Now there are all sorts of questions I know you want to ask. How big is an

---

[2] I remember it well; I was in the band there for the OTG revue six years later, when the cast included Michael Palin.

Harold Macmillan takes a ride on the Miniature Railway at the Conservative Party Summer Fête in Bromley.

atom? What does an atom feel like? What does it look like? Are they available for general consumption? Well, I obviously can't answer all your questions here, but there is just one I would like to deal with which a lot of viewers have sent in. What is a geiger counter? It's really very simple. A geiger counter is like a clock. Except that where a clock goes tick tock tick tock a geiger counter goes tick – tick – tick – tick. You see? If you have any questions like this – just write them on a postcard and send them to the Ministry of Defence. I'm sure they'd be only too pleased to answer them. But postcards, please.

Bennett's sermon sketch was not included, but on the last night he arranged with the stage manager to let him slip it in without asking Daniels. 'It was an unforgivable thing to do,' he says, 'and there was a tremendous row about it, but it was a great success.'

Even without the sermon, Bennett was picked out by reviewers. In the *Observer*, Alan Pryce-Jones wrote that the show had been

done on a shoestring by a cast of young people who deserve the packed audiences they got. Stan Daniels, as scriptwriter, established himself overnight; and Alan Bennett, a sad comic, was as successful as Patty Thorne, a gay one. The almost impossible task of making yet another joke out of *Hamlet* was achieved [*Better Never* included *Hamlet* performed as a Rodgers and Hammerstein musical]; and a special word of praise must be given to the music and the welcome acidity of the lyrics.

Similarly the theatre critic of the *Daily Herald*, David Nathan, admired 'the sharp, acid wit of the revue's writer, Stanley Daniels', and 'the solemn-faced comedy of a tow-thatched student called Alan Bennett'.

Bennett himself writes that the revue was 'a great success, to the extent that the official Festival took note'. Alan Pryce-Jones had been complaining, in his *Observer* column, that Edinburgh had become 'a testing ground for subsequent London productions, or a shop window for Scottish repertory companies'. He felt there was more 'creative energy' on the Fringe, and went on, 'The Oxford Theatre Group … is just the kind of fringe organization which ought to be encouraged more actively by any city preparing a festival.' It was probably as a consequence of this that, as Bennett notes, the Festival decided that in 1960 it would 'put on a revue of its own'.

5

Danny Kaye of Cambridge

The Festival Director at this time was Robert Ponsonby, an Old Etonian and former Oxford organ scholar, who later became the BBC's Controller of Music. After a couple of years in the job, he had begun to feel that the Festival was 'a bit pompous, and that late-night entertainment, which was of course flourishing on the Fringe, was something the Festival proper ought to be doing'. For 1958 he booked the musical comedienne Anna Russell, who did take-offs of operas in funny hats, and for 1959 Flanders and Swann. For 1960, he decided to have a different late-night show during each of the Festival's three weeks. The first was to be given by Louis Armstrong, the second by a group called Les Frères Jacques, and the final one by Beatrice Lillie. 'And it was all going fine,' Ponsonby recalls,

> but eventually Armstrong's agent said, 'Look, I can't find any other British dates for him, and it's not worth him coming across just for that.' So at a rather late stage we were stuck. And because I'd been pretty irked by the constant theft of our thunder by clever undergraduates from Oxford and Cambridge, on the Fringe, I said to Johnny Bassett, 'Let's put on our own revue, let's beat them at their own game.'

John Bassett, recently graduated from Wadham College, Oxford, had become Ponsonby's assistant the previous year. Although his first love in the arts was jazz – he played the trumpet and had run a band at Oxford – he felt he had theatre in his blood: 'My grandmother was a Gaiety Girl, and I've always considered myself to be a sort of substandard Serge Diaghilev.' The first person he recruited for the revue was the pianist in his band, Dudley Moore, who was making a reputation as a cabaret performer.

Dudley Stuart John Moore had been born in Charing Cross Hospital in 1935 with a club-foot and a slightly deformed, shorter left leg. His father was an electrician, and his mother had been a shorthand typist. He was brought

Dudley Moore (centre) with the Bassett Hounds – John Bassett is immediately to the left of
Moore, holding a trumpet.

up on a council estate in Dagenham, to the east of London, near the Ford car
plant. 'We didn't seem poor,' he says, 'but we didn't seem rich, either.'

The club-foot was inherited from his maternal grandmother. During
Dudley's childhood, it required a series of surgical operations so that he
could walk normally, and when obliged to stay in hospital he often felt that
he had been abandoned by his parents. Also, his mother had an ambiguous
attitude towards his disability:

> My mother didn't want me to feel there was anything wrong – and yet she did.
> On the one hand, she was very anxious about my foot, and on the other, she
> pretended that it didn't exist, which made me very confused. She either over-
> inflated or under-inflated me. It was either: 'You're perfect; there's nothing
> wrong with you' or 'You're a complete cripple.' So with that came the idea that
> I was either a genius or a piece of crap.

There was a piano in the house and, encouraged by his mother, he soon
showed precocious musical talent. At thirteen, he won a scholarship to
attend Saturday junior sessions at London's Guildhall School of Music,
studying violin as well as piano. He also learned the organ, though this
required a reinforced heel on his bad leg, so that it could reach the pedals. He
had stopped growing after reaching five feet two and a half inches.

As a pupil at Dagenham County High School, he found that he could deflect the bullies by making them laugh. 'I was a very pompous little boy who was *driven* to humour. I got funny so I wouldn't get beaten up any more.' Yet despite his physical problems, he proved very popular with girls at school – again largely because he amused them. He alleges that for his first kiss, 'I had to stand on a pile of bricks to reach her.' Not wishing to expose his bad leg and foot, 'I was quite attuned to the possibility that I would have to make love in my duffle-coat and snow boots, with just the offending member emerging and splurging.' In fact his dark, puckish good looks easily compensated for his hidden deformity, and he had a prodigious sexual appetite. 'I went right from the midwife to the mid-life crisis... What else is there to live for? Chinese food and women – there *is* nothing else.'

Blending his two talents, music and humour, he became known for comic turns at the piano, singing in a falsetto voice. He may have got some of his ideas from the Danish-born musical entertainer Victor Borge, whose Broadway shows became available on LP records in Britain during the mid-1950s – Borge's sketches included a ten-minute Mozart opera, sung in falsetto, and Dudley Moore would similarly launch into a mock-Schubert *Lied* called 'Die Flabbergast'. He was also converted to jazz, when he heard a recording of the pianist Erroll Garner playing 'The Way You Look Tonight'. Moore's own jazz left-hand piano style was modelled closely on Garner's pulsing four-to-the-bar chords.

His deformed leg ruled out National Service, and he won an organ scholarship to Magdalen College, Oxford, going up in 1954. 'There was I,' he says, 'this club-footed wanker sitting on the organ seat, playing this beautiful organ in this stunning chapel. I felt I really didn't deserve to be there.' However, the college organist, Dr Bernard Rose, thought him highly talented, and raised no objection when Moore began to embroider his organ voluntaries with quotations from the day's pop songs.

Magdalen was very aristocratic. 'The toughest part that first year,' Moore recalls,

> was not knowing how to open my mouth without having it sound like an old saw, because, coming from Dagenham, I spoke in a very lazy accent – not Cockney but sort of suburban. I went through a terrible stage of trying to imitate other people's voices, so I ended up with a peculiar voice, very untidy, with vowels lurching in every direction. I still talk that way today.

He soon became known at Oxford as Cuddly Dudley. The stage director Patrick Garland, then an undergraduate actor with the OUDS, says he was called this with good reason: 'He had an unforced, unpretentious wit which was very appealing, and people genuinely admired and liked him very much.'

As well as being much in demand as a musician at Oxford, Moore soon turned to acting, joining the Experimental Theatre Club and playing Enobarbus in *Antony and Cleopatra*, for which he also wrote the music. He could also be found on Saturday nights in the Union cellars, playing with John Bassett's traditional jazz band, the Bassett Hounds, who soon began to be hired for débutante balls in London. 'Then in my third year,' Moore recalls, 'I started doing cabaret, and it was like being the school clown all over again. I found a niche and became rather well known around campus as a cabaret performer, a guy who improvised and generally made a fool of himself.' He was sometimes on the same bill as Alan Bennett, though Bennett says they made no particular impression on each other.

After taking his degree in 1957, Moore stayed on at Oxford to read for a postgraduate degree. Bernard Rose suggested that he apply for the post of Organist and Tutor in Music at Queen's College, but Moore did not see himself as a don. Indeed he soon abandoned his studies, rented a bedsitter in London, and began to freelance as a jazz pianist and cabaret entertainer. He formed a trio with a bass player and drummer, made his début at Ronnie Scott's club, gigged with the Bassett Hounds at the Dorchester and the Savoy, and was hired to write incidental music for the Royal Court Theatre. He worked in the Vic Lewis Band, which took him briefly to New York, and with bandleader Johnny Dankworth, though Dankworth says that his piano style (with its insistent Erroll Garner left hand) tended to swamp other people's solos: 'Dudley was a soloist from the start. He wasn't meant to be a rhythm-section pianist.'

He soon became so well known in jazz and cabaret circles that the BBC Television arts programme *Monitor* chose him as one of two young musicians whose work and lifestyles were contrasted in a documentary; the other was composer Peter Maxwell Davies. During 1959 Moore cut his first disc, with George Martin producing – a jazz single he had written called 'Strictly for the Birds'.

To his friend John Bassett, the multi-talented Moore was an obvious choice for the proposed Edinburgh revue. (He had already appeared on the Fringe in the 1958 Oxford revue, which had the future film director Ken Loach in the cast – he remembers Moore as 'hilarious'.) Bassett asked Moore for other names, 'and I recommended another person...I suggested Alan Bennett.' Taking up the suggestion, Bassett 'saw Alan doing cabaret, and I booked him'. Meanwhile Bassett himself had thought of a young Cambridge graduate who had been a star of Footlights shows a few years earlier, and was now a medical student in London.

*

Jonathan Wolfe Miller was born in 1934 into a highly successful London Jewish family. His father, Dr Emanuel Miller, was an eminent psychiatrist, and his mother Betty wrote novels and biographies.

The Miller great-grandparents had come to Britain from Lithuania in the 1860s, and Jonathan's grandfather Abram had been in the fur trade, doing well enough to send Emanuel to Cambridge, where, studying philosophy, he was taught moral science by Bertrand Russell. But Emanuel was a restless polymath – like his son – and he soon turned to medicine, working first as a neurologist, researching the effects of shell-shock during the First World War. Later he moved into child psychiatry and criminology, established London's first child guidance clinic in the East End, founded an Institute for the Scientific Treatment of Juvenile Delinquency, and wrote prolifically – his books included *Types of Mind and Body* (1926), *Modern Psychotherapy* (1930), *Insomnia* (1935) and *The Growing Child and its Problems* (1937). Peter Cook has observed that Jonathan Miller 'had a very early established feeling planted in him by his family that medicine was what was worthwhile', and felt guilty whenever he turned aside from it.

Miller's mother Betty, née Spiro, had been educated at St Paul's School for Girls and University College, London. She published her first novel when she was nineteen, and went on to write many more, as well as a biography of Browning. She was the niece of the French philosopher Henri Bergson, who developed the concept of the *élan vital* and wrote a famous essay called *Laughter*, subtitled 'On the Meaning of the Comic'. In his own 1987 paper on 'Jokes and Joking', Jonathan Miller sums up, and criticizes, his great-uncle's theory on the subject:

> Bergson claimed that we laugh at people in situations where they revert to a more automatic type of behaviour. When the herd observes a reduction in the versatility and flexibility of one of its members, it goes through loud respiratory convulsions which as it were ask the offending individual to 'pull its socks up'... It would be wrong to laugh this theory out of court; but as it stands, it deals with so little of the topic. This is a common feature of theories about humour ...

Though Emanuel Miller had been brought up to practise Judaism, and felt some guilt at abandoning it, he reared Jonathan as an unbeliever. 'I am Jewish in the residual sense of only half belonging,' Miller has said. 'I deeply distrust Israel and Zionism and I have a loathing of all monotheistic religions.'

The Millers lived at a series of addresses in the Harley Street area of London, and were well enough off to employ a nanny for Jonathan and his sister. Home life became unsettled during the Second World War, with the family following Emanuel around as he moved from one military hospital to another. 'There were strange, long-delayed train journeys in the middle of wartime England,' Miller remembers. 'We would be pushed into hot summer sidings while troop trains rattled by three platforms away. I don't think I was a very happy child, but I look back on childhood with tremendous longing for those endless summer days.'

After the war he was sent to St Paul's School in London, where he devoted much effort to getting out of organized sports, bringing notes to school claiming that he suffered from flat feet. But one sport, boxing, could not be evaded at St Paul's, 'a giant, Darwinian struggle, in which every single person in the school was forced to contest'. He remembers that 'as soon as you were hit on the nose, there was this very strange smell of aluminium. When the aluminium smell came, I would try to lie down and avoid the rest of the contest.'

He grew to be six foot three, and became almost as self-conscious about his giraffe-like height as Dudley Moore was about his shortness. He talked unceasingly and precociously, almost like a parody of an intellectual, but had developed a stammer which could strike at unexpected moments:

> It always got troublesome when I was on trains or buses, having to ask for my fare; and then there were all these stammerers' circumlocutions that I had to go through.
>
> The awful thing about stammering is that you never know which consonants are going to be the fatal ones. You think that you've got it all taped – avoid 't's and 'd's today and it'll be all right. Then, suddenly, you'd find that you'd be tripping up over an 'n'. I remember once having a very bad time with initial 'm's, which made the noise which tube trains make when they're waiting – a sort of Westinghouse stammer – and, very foolishly under the circumstances, travelling to Marble Arch. I could see the conductor coming down the corridor towards me and I knew that I would have to say 'M–M–M', and finally, as often happens with stammerers, a fantastic act of creation took place. I said, 'One to the arch that is made of marble, please.'

Despite the stammer, he began to appear on stage at St Paul's. He had fallen in love with the theatre when taken to pantomimes in early childhood – 'a world of such wonderful, artificial, fantastic brilliance that it seemed to me the acme of desirability' – but he did not go in for 'straight' acting at school. 'I just did revue sketches.'

The annual revues at St Paul's were a rare chance for the boys to indulge in licensed mockery. Miller recalls them as 'those enchanted occasions once a year when I did school revues, when somehow all the school rules were alleviated'. He had an unlikely role model as a performer: 'For some reason, as a fourteen-year-old boy I became completely intoxicated with the image of Danny Kaye. I just wanted to be as much like him as I could possibly be.'

Asked to explain this obsession, he says:

> When I was thirteen, at a time of austerity and restriction, [Kaye] represented a

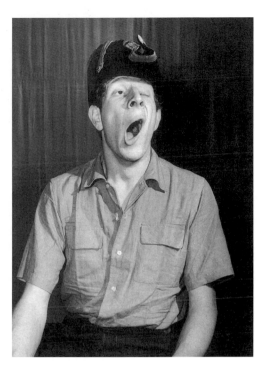

Jonathan Miller in the Cambridge Footlights – 'a mimic the like of whom has never before been seen,' wrote Harold Hobson.

curious, glowing image of happiness and success. [He] was cheerful, blond, graceful, handsome, wealthy, much applauded, and possessing unspeakable qualities of elocution. He was for me the highest aspiration.

In fact the young Miller bore a considerable physical resemblance to the American-Jewish Kaye (real name Kominski), whose manic energy as a performer seems to have suggested to him how he might unleash on stage the torrent of words that rushed through his own mind. A friend from his early years suggests that he stammered because he had too much to say – that 'words jostled, and sometimes jammed, in the only exit available to them'.

His Kaye-style acts had a surrealist edge, and were laced with chicken noises and other vocal sound effects; but he could also do more conventional impersonations, and during his last year at St Paul's (1953) he was selected to appear in a BBC radio programme featuring young performers, *Under Twenty Parade*, where, billed as 'John Miller', he took off announcers and other familiar radio voices.

Arriving at Cambridge in the autumn of 1953, to read medicine at St John's College, he made an immediate impression, largely because of his appearance. One contemporary describes him as 'built like an Anglepoise lamp', and Michael Frayn remembers seeing him 'walking barefoot in the street' (though Miller denies this), while in rapt conversation with a friend. The philosopher Ludwig Wittgenstein, long resident at Cambridge, had died two years earlier, and Miller says he had left behind an 'atmosphere of intense pursuit into the nature and meaning of words'. Miller himself felt caught up in this 'enormous explosion of ideas', and another undergraduate, the future writer Frederic Raphael, noticed how, as Miller talked, his 'eloquent hands made distinct Wittgensteinian boxes'.

Opting for intense conversation, Miller at first eschewed comedy, preferring to spend his spare time in such clubs as the History of Science Society. He was also elected to the Apostles, the celebrated semi-secret club which, since the last century, had met weekly to read essays and talk. 'It was a very important part of my life when I was at Cambridge,' Miller has said of the Apostles. 'We discussed things and formed friendships there. It wasn't like the Freemasons. There were no rituals. There was no commitment to some metaphysic. All we did was discuss ideas.' Meetings were often held in the King's College rooms of E.M. Forster – 'I used to like going every Saturday night to Morgan Forster's rooms and reading papers,' says Miller. Previous generations of Apostles had had a reputation for homosexuality, but Miller claims that by the mid-1950s being a member 'helped the seduction of girls. One would say, "I'm an Apostle, get your knickers off!"'

In his second or third term he did agree to take part in a revue, but merely a college one – a show put on in the unlikely venue of the St John's bicycle shed. However, the then President of the Footlights, the future writer of musicals Leslie Bricusse, was in the audience, and persuaded Miller to take part in the 1954 Footlights May Week revue, *Out of the Blue*.

Miller recalls that this show included 'an awful lot of stuff with people walking around in blazers and flannels and boaters, and singing songs about Proctors and punts, and things of that sort', and the script (in the Lord Chamberlain's collection) confirms this. But there were sharper items: a spoof of the evangelist Billy Graham (written by Bricusse and Frederic Raphael); a mock-interview with a starlet; a monologue by a company director addressing his shareholders; a sketch about a black man being refused a room in a West End hotel; a song called 'Follow My *Lieder*', which suggested that post-war Germany might turn Nazi again; and a duologue in verse, by Raphael, for two people impersonating the Catholic-pessimistic novelists Evelyn Waugh and Graham Greene ('It's gloom, gloom, gloom, that puts our names in lights'). The Lord Chamberlain was informed that a 'Stop-Press Calypso' would include 'a topical stop-press item each day'. The script included some sample calypso verses, one of which commented on the failure of Labour to keep its left-wingers under control:

> Pandemonium reigns supreme in the Labour Party,
> So there'll be a meeting called by Mr Attlee,
> Mr Morrison will use hand grenades and dynamite,
> To rid the Labour Party of the Bevanite.

Jonathan Miller appeared in several sketches written by others, but his main contribution to *Out of the Blue* was two monologues. One of them, 'Down Under', a parody of a travelogue about Australia, is missing from the script submitted to the Lord Chamberlain, though a photograph exists of Miller performing it, with a large aeroplane propeller on his head. The other monologue, 'Radio Page', is in the script, but chiefly in the form of a synopsis – evidently Miller performed most of it ad lib.

It begins with him impersonating the BBC's 'pips' – the Greenwich Time Signal – followed by the weather forecast: 'The South of England will move in a westerly direction late tonight.' Then: 'Police message … police anxious to interview man with long blue hair. They've never met a man with long blue hair.' After a news bulletin, with racing news and a report from Washington, comes a natural history programme, including the sound of the 'lesser spotted pillow-wort'; then *The Critics*, who review an 'exhibition of Persian digestive biscuits', and make 'animal noises' during their discussion. Next, a parody of a radio drama with a John Buchan-esque storyline:

> Curtain UP! We present James McKechnie [a popular radio actor of the day] in an unending series of radio plays. He provisions himself at Totnes and cuts across country, cuts himself a stout stick of hickory. Kurt and the boys in the car suddenly appear. No one but a blind chauffeur could have missed him. It was a blind chauffeur. Runs into a church and makes himself a rude bed, stays the night. Wakes and cuts himself a stout stick of liquorice. Meets girl with terrible affliction. They kiss. That was *The Blue Mountain* with James McKechnie. Here is Inspector Morris from Scotland Yard to say a few words. 'Use the 999 system and you won't get into any scrapes.'

Miller then turned his attention to the highbrow Third Programme: 'Timid announcer announces chamber-music concert. After one folk song Bertrand Russell is introduced who talks about Prof. Moore and the apples.' Ten years later, Miller reused this material in the Broadway production of *Beyond the Fringe*:

> [ANNOUNCER:] In the third of our series, *Portraits from Memory*, Bertrand
>   Russell reminisces about his early days at Cambridge.
> [RUSSELL:] One of the advantages of living in Great Court Trinity, I seem to
>   recall, was the fact that one could always pop across at any time of the day or
>   night and trap the then young, and somewhat beautiful, G.E. Moore into a

logical falsehood by means of a cunning semantic subterfuge. I recall one occasion with particular vividness. I had popped across and knocked on his door. 'Come in,' he said. I decided to wait awhile in order to test the ethical consistency of his proposition. 'Come in,' he said once again. 'Very well,' I replied, 'if that is in fact truly what you desire.' I opened the door accordingly and went in. Moore was seated by the fire with a basket upon his knee. 'Moore,' I said, 'have you any apples in that basket?' 'No,' he replied, and smiled seraphically as was his wont. I decided to try a different tack. 'Moore,' I said, 'have you *some* apples in that basket?' 'No,' he replied again, leaving me in a logical cleft stick from which I had but one way out. 'Moore,' I said, 'have you then *apples* in that basket?' 'Yes,' he replied, and from that day forth we remained the closest of friends.

In the 1954 Footlights version, the sketch ends with Russell being 'asked to request a tune and, for the Moral Sciences faculty and Professor Gilbert Ryle, chooses Berkeley's theme tune: "I hear voices and there's no one there." [The eighteenth-century philosopher Bishop Berkeley argued that objects exist only in the mind of the beholder.] Announcer says good-night.'

Like the once-religious Bennett with his parody sermon, Miller was mocking the intellectual world that was dear to him.

*

Out of the Blue transferred to the West End for three weeks at the Phoenix Theatre in July 1954. The *Sunday Times* drama critic Harold Hobson was hugely impressed by Miller, calling him

> a mimic the like of whom has never before been seen in the Charing Cross Road. Nothing in nature is alien to him. One moment he is an explorer…Then, astoundingly, he becomes Australia itself. He is the Thinker and the Thought …He makes his subjects and unwitting collaborators flow together in a vast incredible harmony of nature in his superbly funny philosophic fantasy.

In consequence of this and other glowing reviews, Miller received offers from several theatrical managements, but turned them all down, and announced that he would not appear in any more revues.

However, he was back the following year. The 1955 Footlights show, *Between the Lines*, had among its cast the future professional actor Peter Woodthorpe, and also Rory McEwen, who became a successful folk singer; but once again it was Miller who got almost all the praise from reviewers. The *Daily Telegraph* sent a critic to Cambridge, and the result was a headline that dogged Miller ever after:

DANNY KAYE OF CAMBRIDGE

> The Footlights revue, *Between the Lines*, is primarily a vehicle for Jonathan Miller, who made his name a year ago. He has developed his fantastic talent to

such a pitch in the last twelve months that he is infinitely more like Danny Kaye than Danny Kaye himself.

His range of expression equals the variety of his imagination: his timing has acquired a polish that makes a critic regret that he is dedicated to the noble profession of medicine. If laughter be therapeutic he should be certain of success.

Once again, the script gives only a sketchy notion of what Miller said and did in the two monologues he contributed to the show. The first was entitled 'Culture'. The synopsis for this begins:

Enter: Talk in a homely voice about books:
1. The nineteenth-century novel: imitate trees, wind, rain, thunder and lightning: the mad governess: hostess asks her in, saying she will enjoy *Wuthering Heights*: a howl is heard. 'What's that?' 'Only Father.'
2. Tennyson: *The Idylls of the King*: Arthur finds the sword Excalibur and is not amazed: the lady of the lake making the sword. Arthur rows out to get sword. 'Nice sword you've got there.' Rows back: Sir Lancelot singing Tirrah Lirrah by the river: imitations of a weedy knight.

When *Between the Lines* transferred to London for three weeks at the Scala Theatre, this part of the monologue was singled out by another reviewer from the *Daily Telegraph*: 'His portrayal of the sword Excalibur being forged under water by a breathless lady of the lake seemed to me the most pointed criticism of Tennyson ever made, certainly the most amusing.'

The 'Culture' monologue continued with a 'History of Western Philosophy', with 'imitations of Isaiah Berlin and woman talking on Wittgenstein', and there was a section on music: 'Music has charms to soothe a savage breast: sing into shirt.' Miller's second monologue, 'Island Heritage', was largely devoted to the death of Nelson. This, too, was eventually performed on Broadway:

But what *were* his dying words? There is some historical doubt about this. Some people say that Nelson said, 'Kiss me, Hardy,' in which case a young cabin-boy would have been dispatched up on deck to fetch Captain Hardy – 'Admiral's compliments, sir, Captain Hardy, sir, says you're to come below and kiss him.'

In London in 1955, the *Daily Telegraph* reviewer thought this 'even funnier' than the Tennyson take-off, and concluded:

Mr Miller's method is surrealistic, his approach uninhibited...I advise all connoisseurs of the comic not to let the opportunity pass of seeing an amateur in action who can compare with the best of the profession. With curly hair looking just like a wig and a cunning, almost maniacal, expression about the eyes, Mr Miller reminded me of Harpo Marx. His antics live up to that illustrious name.

Again, he was offered professional engagements, and this time he accepted a few, appearing in a radio programme written by others, called *The Man from Paranoia*, about a Cambridge don who owns a singing goldfish, and with Rory McEwen in cabaret in an upstairs room at the Royal Court Theatre in Sloane Square. He even rose to the height of delivering the Bertrand Russell monologue in *Sunday Night at the London Palladium*, one of the top television variety shows, transmitted live on ITV. Then, having taken his degree at Cambridge in the summer of 1956, he went to continue his medical studies (which exempted him from National Service) at University College Hospital in London.

His life remained schizophrenic. He intended to specialize in neuro-psychology – 'I was interested in higher disorders of brain function' – and he married a Cambridge graduate who had taken up medicine. 'Jonathan has a very good double act with Rachel,' John Wells once observed, 'in that Rachel manages him and is probably the only person who gets away with teasing him.' At the hospital he founded a Thomas Browne Society to hold discussions which ranged beyond medicine. Yet he also appeared in a couple of hospital revues, and continued to broadcast as a comedian, contributing to more radio programmes and performing his 'Death of Lord Nelson' sketch on BBC TV's *Tonight*, where he was watched somewhat anxiously by the BBC's future Director-General Alasdair Milne: 'A hilarious turn ... where he impersonated Nelson fumbling for the fatal bullet inside his waistcoat, [but] it was no help that Jonathan, at the time uncontrollable in terms of studio discipline ... lurched past the cameras in his enthusiasm and so disappeared from view altogether for a while.'

John Bassett, looking for his Edinburgh performers, had been at school at Bedales with Miller's future wife Rachel. He called on Miller at the hospital, and found him keen to join the Edinburgh show as a release from the strain of his work. 'This man Bassett came and asked if I wanted to take part in this revue,' is how Miller himself recalls it.

> I did it because it was going to be a holiday ... The young junior hospital doctors complain, quite rightly, about the hours they work now, but those are nothing compared to the hours we worked – and there was nobody that spoke up for us in those days ... Also, I was married by that time and I knew how many people crucify their families on the unremitting demands of junior medicine. So I was therefore very vulnerable and susceptible to the appeals of the theatre as an alternative.

As well as signing Miller up for the projected revue, Bassett asked him to suggest a fourth member of the cast. Miller had no difficulty in thinking of a name: 'I said Peter

6

At right-angles to all the comedy we'd heard

Eleven days after Alan Pryce-Jones in the *Observer* had praised Alan Bennett's performance in the 1959 Oxford Fringe show *Better Never*, a first-night audience at the Apollo Theatre in Shaftesbury Avenue assembled to watch Kenneth Williams and Fenella Fielding in a new revue. Williams had become popular through his whining, nasal performance on Tony Hancock's radio show, and Fielding had made her name under the auspices of song- and revue-writer Sandy Wilson. He had provided some of the songs to this new show, which had the sort of meaningless title that was typical of intimate revue, *Pieces of Eight*. But the audience that evening, 24 September 1959, found themselves watching something entirely different.

The show's writers included the twenty-nine-year-old Harold Pinter, whose play *The Birthday Party* had been put on briefly and disastrously in the West End the previous year. Pinter's sketches tended to be just that: impressionistic studies of how people really speak and behave, rather than comic items with punchlines. In one, an old newspaper-seller and a barman talk with aimless monotony about which evening paper is usually the last to be sold. Nevertheless Pinter was capable of writing jokes; in another sketch, an applicant for a job is asked, 'Are you *virgo intacta*?' and when he reluctantly answers, 'Yes,' is then asked, 'Have you *always* been *virgo intacta*?'

The greater part of the script of *Pieces of Eight* was experimental in quite a different way, the work of a writer seven years younger than Pinter. Some of his material was obviously influenced by *The Goon Show*, such as a strange song about a man called Onu Beeby Friski. However, other sketches by this writer betrayed no influences at all (except possibly that of Lewis Carroll). The most notable of these featured a weird individual called Grole.

Seated in a train with a cardboard box on his knees, Grole buttonholes the man opposite: 'I've got a viper in this box, you know.' He emphasizes that it's a viper, not an asp: 'Cleopatra had an asp, but I haven't...I don't want one either; I'd rather have the viper myself … Not that they're cheaper to run, if anything the viper is more voracious than the asp; my viper eats like a horse.' The sketch is partly built around puns and verbal misunder-standings; when the other man echoes the words 'like a horse', Grole responds, 'Oh yes, I'd like a horse; I've nothing against horses, I could do with a horse; mind you, you'd never get it into this box.' But mostly it is just the unstoppable Grole freely vouchsafing crazy information: 'Serpents hear through their jaws, you know, it's the bone structure that does it. Oh yes, good gracious, yes, there's no doubt that it's the bone structure.'

Kenneth Williams did his best as Grole; but those who knew its author found the Williams version – with lots of eye-rolling, leering and whining – far less funny than the performance that Grole's creator had been giving for years to his friends at school and at Cambridge, where he was still an undergraduate when *Pieces of Eight* opened. His name was Peter Cook.

Jonathan Miller first set eyes on Cook while *Pieces of Eight* was running in London. Miller had gone back to Cambridge, and was inveigled into watching a college revue with Cook in the cast. 'There was this astonishing, strange, glazed, handsome creature,' Miller recalls,

> producing weird stuff the like of which I'd never heard before. I remember his first line when I was shot up in my seat by him. He was playing some person in a suburban kitchen concealed behind a newspaper. He didn't say a word. But all eyes were drawn to him. Then he rustled the newspaper and simply said, 'Hello, hello. I see the *Titanic*'s sunk again.' One knew one was in the presence of comedy at right-angles to all the comedy we'd heard.

After the show, Miller introduced himself to Cook and asked if he had ever worked with schizophrenics, telling him, 'You've perfectly reproduced the schizophrenic speech pattern.' (Grole in *Pieces of Eight* spoke like one too.) Cook, mystified and amused, said he hadn't any experience of schizophrenia – it all came from his imagination.

Yet Cook did have a slightly odd, even dislocated, emotional background, which may account in part for the nature of his humour. Born in 1937 – which made him slightly younger than Alan Bennett, Dudley Moore and Jonathan Miller – he had seen very little of his parents in childhood. His father, a District Officer in Nigeria, had to spend most of his working life separated from his family. 'My father used to receive news by boat,' Peter recalled, 'six months after it was published. He'd open *The Times* and say, "Good God, Worcester are 78 for 6."'

Even before Peter's first birthday, his mother left him to the care of her own mother and went to join her husband in Nigeria. The Second World War meant that he did not see her again until he was six, and he met his father for the first time a year after that. 'He was a total stranger to me,' recalled the adult Cook. Like Dudley Moore, he first developed a talent at humour to defend himself against bullying – in his case at a grim preparatory school in Eastbourne, to which he had been sent at the age of seven. He has said of this, 'I disliked being away from home – that part was horrid. But it started a sort of defence mechanism in me, trying to make people laugh so that they wouldn't hit me. I could make fun of other people and therefore make the person who was about to bully me laugh instead.'

He had been brought up on the usual English upper-middle-class diet of humorous reading: *Punch*, Beachcomber, Wodehouse; but at his public school, Radley, he suddenly developed quite a different brand of comedy, which he alleged was drawn from life. The story is told that the school employed, as a waiter in the dining hall, a strange character called Arthur Boylett, who does indeed sound schizophrenic; he claimed to see stones and twigs move of their own volition, and regarded this as in some way significant. According to Cook, he would buttonhole boys and tell them about his visions, repeating the words, 'I thought I saw it move.' Yet few Radleians of that generation – boys or masters – recollect Boylett as a school character; or, rather, the reality of the man has been totally eclipsed by Cook's reinvention of him. It would be absurd to suggest that the Boylett performance Cook swiftly developed at school, and then carried to Cambridge (where the character was renamed Grole), was a self-portrait; nevertheless the lonely ramblings of Boylett–Grole – as in the viper sketch in *Pieces of Eight* – do seem to reflect in some way the inner monologue of an isolated, parentless child.

Cook made quite a name at Radley as an actor and mimic, and was successful in other departments of school life. Like Richard Ingrams at Shrewsbury, he was no rebel against the system but a conventional achiever – he became head boy of his 'social' (the Radley name for boarding houses) and a school prefect, and was known for his immaculate good manners. Nevertheless when not on stage he seemed quite silent and withdrawn. Old Radleians recall him as 'quite a shy person' behind the comedy, 'a bit of a loner', who was 'surprisingly awkward' in human relationships.

Exempted from National Service because he had suffered from asthma in childhood, he arrived at Cambridge (to read Modern Languages) in 1957 at the age of only nineteen, two years younger than most freshmen, and initially made no attempt to join the Footlights. Like Alan Bennett, his first pieces of undergraduate comedy were created in the college suggestions book – strictly speaking, at Pembroke it was the Food Complaints Book – and, again like Bennett, he then began to perform in college smokers.

Most of his Cambridge sketches featured Boylett–Grole, whose voice could easily be mimicked. This, indeed, was one of the appealing things about Cook's brand of comedy from the beginning. As with the Goons, it was easy for other people to copy the funny voice, if not the brilliant ideas. Consequently the whining, ponderous tones of Grole were soon to be heard around Cambridge. Meanwhile Cook's family, knowing little of this side of him, expected that he would make a career much like his father. Caroline Seebohm, though herself at Oxford (where she was an intimate of the Ingrams gang), went out briefly with Cook while he was at Cambridge, and says, 'He told me quite seriously he was going into the Foreign Service.'

Cook's huge success in Pembroke College smokers emboldened him to start performing in Footlights smokers. There he was seen by a postgraduate called John Bird, who was about to direct N.F. Simpson's theatre-of-the-absurd play *A Resounding Tinkle*. 'It was the first time it had been done complete,' recalls Bird. 'The Royal Court had just done a truncated version.' Like Jonathan Miller, Bird was astonished by Cook's brand of comedy:

> Peter exemplified the idea that language writes you. I often felt that he was at the mercy of the connections his mind made. As far as writing and performing comedy goes, I've always felt I could (as it were) go home and give it a rest, but Peter never could. He was wired up to be funny. Sometimes you had the feeling that he wanted to stop it and couldn't. I always feel my talent, such as it is, is constructed, whereas his seemed to be completely natural.

A Resounding Tinkle was a success – the cast also included Eleanor Bron, then reading Modern Languages at Cambridge – and on the strength of it Bird was invited to direct the 1959 May Week Footlights revue. 'I said I'd only do it if I had absolute control over the material,' he recalls. 'I wanted to do something political. We were living in a nuclear age, and it was time to break from the camp tradition of the Footlights. It felt absolutely imperative that this creaky, old, outmoded political structure, with a self-serving ruling class, should be attacked.'

Bird had come to Cambridge from a grammar school in Nottingham, where his father managed a chemist's shop. John Fortune, who later collaborated with him (and was at Cambridge at this time, but junior to Bird and not in his productions), says that Bird 'has always been very political, quite far to the left, and of all of those in our group [of satirists] he's the nearest to having a kind of moral disgust'. Bird denies this:

> At Cambridge I was much more interested in the theatre than politics – I reckoned I'd end up running the National Theatre! But I do seem to have the reputation of being the Robespierre of our group, and I suppose it developed out of wanting to be something that I'm not – very rigorous and definite. Because I've always had an admiration for people who are. I think it was a search for a clarity, though clarity wasn't really part of my own make-up.

Bird's Footlights revue was called *Last Laugh*. He wrote most of it himself, but Peter Cook contributed the Grole viper sketch, in which he himself played Grole, and several others. In the first-night audience was the then secretary of the university Amateur Dramatic Club, the future publisher Tom Rosenthal, who was doing some talent-scouting for a London theatrical agent, Donald Langdon. After the show Rosenthal telephoned Langdon and reported that the revue cast included 'the funniest man I'd ever seen'. Langdon came down to Cambridge to see this Peter Cook, and persuaded two impresarios to do the same. One was the West End producer Michael Codron, who was looking for material for his new revue *Pieces of Eight*. The other, William Donaldson, describes himself as 'probably the worst producer ever'. He later played a crucial role in the success of *Beyond the Fringe*.

Donaldson had himself only recently graduated from Cambridge. While he was still a student, his father had died, leaving him a very large interest in the family shipping line, Elders & Fyffes. 'It was something like half a million,' Donaldson recalls, 'split between me and my sister – that doesn't sound much now, but of course then it was huge wealth.' He immediately spent some of it on starting a Cambridge literary magazine, *Gemini*, which he co-edited with the young Julian Mitchell; among the student poets who contributed were Ted Hughes and Sylvia Plath. After Cambridge, Donaldson began to squander his funds in the theatre, purchasing a run-down theatrical management company and looking around for shows to put on. 'I'd always been fascinated by the glamour of the theatre, and I thought I'd be auditioning actresses. But I was a complete prat at it. I didn't have the faintest idea about anything.'

He had scarcely begun in the business when Langdon approached him about Peter Cook:

> He rang up and said, 'The Footlights revue is very good this year, there's a brilliant bloke called Peter Cook in it.' So I went up to Cambridge in my impresario's overcoat – aged twenty-three, and knowing fuck-all about it – and watched *Last Laugh*. And I didn't rate Cook at all. But I thought John Bird was a genius. So I bought everything in the show except Cook's material.

Pressed as to whether he was really so silly as to reject all Cook's sketches, Donaldson – a master of the subtly embroidered anecdote, who later became famous for his book of hoax letters to the famous written as 'Henry Root' – admits to doubts: 'It may be that Michael Codron had already bought Cook's stuff. It's one of my stories, which I've probably exaggerated.' Codron had indeed immediately signed up Cook to write for *Pieces of Eight*.

Under Donaldson's wildly inexperienced management, *Last Laugh* was reborn in the summer of 1960 without Cook or his material, and with a professional cast including Cleo Laine, Lance Percival, Sheila Hancock and

Robin Ray. The show was now called *Here is the News*, and Bird – who was again directing – had replaced Cook's sketches with some rather galumphing attempts at political satire; for example, this version of 'The House that Jack Built':

> This is a member of the Engineering Sharpeners and Screwers Organization, the only Trade Union allowed to use the screwdriver that fits the handle on the door in the house that Jack built…This is a member of the Society of Heavy Engineers and Light Labourers, who for eight months have been in dispute with the Engineering Sharpeners and Screwers Organization about the right to use the screwdriver which turns the screw which fits the handle on the door in the house that Jack built …

Lance Percival says that this sort of material went down very badly with the audience: 'We opened in midsummer in Coventry, which was not a good start for a satirical revue – they were expecting end-of-the-pier stuff.' Sheila Hancock claims that posters around Coventry had accidentally billed the show as *Here is the Nose*, suggesting red-nose stuff, whereas 'the jolly opening sketch' included 'a huge nuclear explosion'. Willie Donaldson says that Bird's determination to give the show a totally political slant made it

> terrible gloomy stuff – the punchline of every sketch was people dying – and we made it worse because we didn't have any lighting. Bird thought that Sean Kenny, who was designing the show, was looking after the lighting, and Sean Kenny thought that Bird was. And I was so inexperienced I didn't know there was such a thing as a lighting designer; I thought someone just turned on a switch.

Bird himself agrees that *Here is the News* was a nightmare. It limped to Oxford, where it expired.[1]

Though its attempt to wed politics and comedy had failed, the Cambridge version (*Last Laugh*) may have influenced Peter Cook. Adrian Slade, President of the Footlights at this time, thinks that working with Bird on it encouraged Cook to experiment with political material himself. Certainly it was after the October 1959 Tory election victory that he began, in college and Footlights smokers, to impersonate the new prime minister, Harold Macmillan.

Meanwhile *Pieces of Eight* was an immediate West End hit, running for 429 performances, so that Cook's income soon rose spectacularly above that

---

[1] Ned Sherrin recalls another touring show mounted by Donaldson around this time which came to an equally ignominious end – 'a revue that Moira Lister and David Kernan were in, which folded in Liverpool, and Willie went off on a train to London saying, "I'm going to get some more money," and he never returned. They were left high and dry in Liverpool.' Taxed with this anecdote, Donaldson gives a groan and changes the subject.

of most undergraduates. He bought a sports car and began to dress nattily. However, on leaving Cambridge in the summer of 1960 (with a Lower Second) he took a temporary job with a London advertising agency, in case this theatrical success was merely a flash in the pan. In the longer term, his family still expected him to join the Foreign Service. There was, of course, the Edinburgh Festival revue for which he had been enrolled by Jonathan Miller, to be performed in August; but this was merely a brief summer diversion with no further performances planned after its one week at the Festival. Certainly he had no notion that he was about to become famous as a satirist.

PART TWO

Boom

1

Funnier than anything we had ever seen

In his preface to *The Oxford Book of Satirical Verse*, Geoffrey Grigson writes that it is 'famously difficult' to define satire. Nevertheless he tries:

> One can say gravely that satire postulates an ideal condition of man or decency, and then despairs of it; and enjoys the despair, masochistically. But the joke must not be lost – the joke of statement, of sound, rhythm, form, vocabulary, rhyme, and surprise. Without the joke everything goes, and we may be left only with complaint, invective, or denunciation.

Nearly three centuries earlier, Jonathan Swift, author of one of the classics of the genre, gave a snappier definition which is itself satirical: 'Satire is a sort of glass, wherein beholders do generally discover everybody's face but their own.'

The first-century rhetorician Quintilian claimed that the Romans had invented satire: 'Satura quidem tota nostra est', which means 'Satire is wholly our own'. Actually they had only formulated the word.[1] Although the Greeks had no term for satire, they practised it widely, in prose and poetry ranging from Aesop's fables in the sixth century BC to Aristophanes' comedies a little later. Aristophanes frequently mocked Cleon, the Athenian political leader of his day; a couple of lines in his play *The Wasps* describe Cleon as 'the greatest monster in the land... With camel's rump and monstrous unwashed balls'. Another public figure, Alcibiades, was guyed by Aristophanes for his lisp. Aristophanes sometimes got into trouble for this sort of outspokenness, but generally the Athenian city state allowed comic poets to write what they wanted.

---

[1] The word 'satire' comes, rather oddly, from the Latin *lanx satura*, originally meaning 'a dish full of fruit' and hence 'a medley of food' or simply 'hotchpotch'. The Satyrs, the boozy, randy half-goats, half-men of Greek mythology, seem to have influenced the change of spelling to *satira*, the word applied to Latin poems ridiculing folly.

The Roman Empire gave no such licence, and Horace, in the first century BC, wrote wistfully of the days when Aristophanes and his contemporaries could expose individuals for their malpractices:

> Whenever a person deserved to be publicly exposed for being
> a crook and a thief, a lecher or a cut-throat, or for being notorious
> in any other way, they would speak right out and brand him.

Horace himself wrote urbane light verse on human follies without much naming of names. A century later, Juvenal lashed out scornfully at the decadence of imperial Rome. He too had to stick to general terms, but in this typical passage, translated by Peter Green, he emphasizes that his satires are inspired by the daily sight of corruption:

> Don't you want to cram whole notebooks with scribbled invective
> When you stand at the corner and see some forger carried past
> On the necks of six porters, lounging back like Maecenas
> In his open litter? A counterfeit seal, a will, a mere scrap
> Of paper – these were enough to convert him to wealth and honour …
> Who can sleep easy today? If your greedy daughter-in-law
> Is not being seduced for cash, it'll be your bride: mere schoolboys
> Are adulterers now. Though talent be wanting, yet
> Indignation will drive me to verse …

Ian Hislop, the present editor of *Private Eye*, says he is 'very keen on Juvenal – he has an amazing contemporary feel'.

Horace and Juvenal define, roughly speaking, the two types of satire that a writer or performer may opt for: an urbane attack on stupidity, or an indignant outburst against malpractice and injustice – though of course the two are not mutually exclusive. Samuel Johnson seems to be making this distinction in his dictionary definition of a satire as 'a poem in which wickedness or folly is censured'. The great age of English literary satire was about half a century before Johnson, when John Dryden and the Restoration playwrights had directed their scorn at the corruption, bawdiness and cynicism of a 'permissive society' that was lustily celebrating its release from the grip of the Puritans. Dryden's satirical device of the mock-heroic couplet was then perfected by the Pope in *The Rape of the Lock* – 'The hungry Judges soon the Sentence sign,/And Wretches hang that Jury-men may Dine' – and by Swift, in the adventures of Lemuel Gulliver, using what we would now call 'fantasy' to highlight the follies of religious bigotry and foolish government. Two years after that, John Gay's *The Beggar's Opera* (1728) suggested that Hanoverian government and high society were no better than a gang of thieves.

As we have seen, Victorian England flinched at looking at itself in the satirical mirror. Even Thackeray, who started out as a satirist in *Punch*, declared himself disgusted with the writings of Swift, calling them 'horrible, shameful, unmanly, blasphemous'. Thackeray's contemporary Dickens was moved to anger by social abuses, and his novels include an element of satire; but it is only one ingredient in the rich Dickensian soup. In another age, the Victorian light-versifier and librettist W.S. Gilbert would probably have become a true satirist; but his *Bab Ballads* (1869) and his librettos for Arthur Sullivan poke only the mildest of fun at typical Victorians ('Oh, I am the very model of a modern Major-General'). Rare exceptions to the absence of satire in Victorian times are to be found in George and Weedon Grossmith's *The Diary of a Nobody* (1892), and the *Cautionary Tales* of Hilaire Belloc, ostensibly written for children – such as the one about the wimpish Lord Lundy, a disappointment to his family on account of his very un-stiff-upper-lip proneness to weeping:

> We had intended you to be
> The next Prime Minister but three:
> The stocks were sold; the Press was squared;
> The Middle Class was quite prepared.
> But as it is! My language fails!
> Go out and govern New South Wales.

On 12 January 1960, Peter Cook, whose family was still expecting him to go out and govern New South Wales, or at least to follow his father into the Foreign Service, wrote to John Bassett, who was convening *Beyond the Fringe*. Bassett had invited him to lunch in London in order to meet Alan Bennett and Dudley Moore, whom he did not know, and Jonathan Miller, whom he did, so that they could discuss the proposed Edinburgh revue. 'I should very much like to join you all for lunch on the 14th,' Cook replied. 'What time and where?'

Bennett thinks that they met in a restaurant 'on Goodge Street', near University College Hospital where Miller was working in the pathology department. Cook remembered it as 'an Italian restaurant in Swiss Cottage', but Bassett says it was 'near to University College Hospital for Jonathan', and Miller confirms that it was close to the hospital: 'We met ... in a "cayf" in Warren Street ... for an expense-account lunch. I can't remember whose expense, but I think it was our own.'

Bassett says the Festival paid, but his four guests found it a tense occasion. 'We were all jealously guarding our own little province,' recalls Miller. 'I think we were tremendously suspicious of one another and very competitive.' Cook had just turned twenty-two, and was easily the youngest, still in his final year at Cambridge, but Bennett says he nevertheless played the part of the prosperous West End revue-writer:

He dressed out of Sportique, an establishment – gents' outfitters' wouldn't really describe it – at the west end of Old Compton Street. There hadn't really been any men's fashions before 1960 – most of the people I knew dressed in sports coat and flannels, as some of us still do – but when I saw Peter he was wearing a shortie overcoat, a not-quite bum-freezer jacket, narrow trousers, winkle-picker shoes and a silk tie with horizontal bars across it.

Bennett was impressed, indeed dismayed, by the effortless comic verbal fluency that Cook demonstrated over the lunch table. Miller agrees: 'As soon as Peter sat down at lunch, this flow of uncontrollably inventive stuff came out of him. It was impossible to compete with him.' Yet Miller, in his different way, was equally articulate and funny, and Bennett began to feel that 'I was there under false pretences – a feeling that never really left me', while Moore recalls being 'completely mute in front of these intellectual giants ... They were all six foot two, and I was five foot two.' On the other hand Bassett remembers Moore 'doing a Groucho Marx walk behind the waitresses – the one where you take enormously long strides with bent knees – and going into the kitchens through one swing door and coming out again through another. Very physical comedy, and very funny.'

After lunch, Bassett took them to the London offices of the Edinburgh Festival, in St James's, to meet Robert Ponsonby, who recalls that the four 'played the fool, and I could see we were on to something, because they were sparking each other off just in conversation'. Ponsonby signed them up for a flat fee of a hundred pounds each – except that Cook's agent Donald Langdon negotiated a further ten pounds for him, having privately pleaded with Cook not to jeopardize his career by working with amateurs (by which he meant Bennett, Moore and Miller). Ponsonby says he told the four, 'You have *carte blanche* to do a revue, and I don't mind how much you send up the Festival.'

Ponsonby had already decided on a title for the show. 'Still to this day I have to explain it to people why I thought of *Beyond the Fringe* – it meant that we were doing something which was beyond the talent of the Fringe.' Bennett recalls that none of the cast liked the title,

because it came from Ponsonby. He was a nice man, but we saw him as an embodiment of an upper-class figure. And he seemed to us quite condescending. He suggested the title, and we didn't like it, but I don't think anybody ever put up any serious alternatives – though we thought of calling it *At the Drop of a Brick*, and Peter suggested '*One of the Best Revues for Some Time*' – Bernard Levin.

Levin was then the drama critic of the *Daily Express*.

Eight weeks later *Queen* magazine announced: 'Four very funny men will brighten the Edinburgh Festival this year ... *Beyond the Fringe* ... will run at the Lyceum for the opening week ... The revue will be produced by John

Bassett, Robert Ponsonby's assistant.' The article mentioned that the four performers would also be on stage together some months before the Festival, 'when they join Peter Sellers in an Evening of Divertissement in aid of World Refugee Year, to be held at the R.I.B.A. on April 28th'. But on that occasion they performed solo turns. Nothing had yet been done about writing ensemble pieces for the Edinburgh show.

As Bennett and Miller recall it, no serious efforts were made in this direction until very late. 'We wrote a lot of our own monologues,' says Miller, 'and we knocked stuff around verbally – in my hospital bedroom! And then we put a lot of stuff together up at Edinburgh, in the week before we opened, while we were all staying in a flat – a Mrs Grosset's flat in Edinburgh – and enough came together then.' Bennett says much the same:

> We had various meetings before we went up to Edinburgh, sometimes at the London offices of the Festival, and I think we used to rehearse, but not in any kind of consistent way. And then we went to stay in an Edinburgh flat near the Lyceum, about a week before we opened, and we must have rehearsed then. Of course the individual things didn't get rehearsed, because you knew you could do them. It was the collective things.

Bennett found it impossible to come up with ideas at these writing–rehearsing sessions: 'I couldn't write there. Peter could, but I had to come along with whatever I'd prepared, because I was hopeless at ad libbing, by comparison with Peter.' Everyone agrees that Cook contributed substantially more to the script than the others. 'Peter wrote most of it,' says Dudley Moore with only a little exaggeration. 'I'd say that on a percentage scale, starting with me at zero, Peter probably contributed 67 per cent, and Jonathan and Alan the rest. I didn't contribute a word. I provided music.'

In fact much of the material came from Cook's existing stock of sketches. As for the rest, Bennett emphasizes that 'there was no unified approach at all. We each had our own ideas of what we wanted to be funny about.' Miller made the same point in a 1961 newspaper interview: 'We do not gather our material with any set intention. We chatter away about anything and anybody and see what comes out. If we tried to do it deliberately we would go crazy.' He emphasized this in a radio interview the same year, in which all four took part:

> At the moments in writing the script when we ever felt we were trying to put anything across, the script-writing conferences ground to a standstill. [*Noises of agreement from the others.*]… The best things have been when an idea has sprung into the mind complete, and it's simply a matter of getting this idea scripted and articulated. Then I think that things are funny. But I honestly don't think that we have tried to *do* anything in *Beyond the Fringe* at all. I think we agree about that.

Cook said the same thing more succinctly in 1961 press interviews: 'We don't intend to be specifically didactic... To take an ordinary poke at this and that is so unutterably dreary. They all do that.' He added, 'Our humour is based on Victorian puns.' Certainly many of the jokes in Cook's own Grole sketches could have come from Lewis Carroll. Moreover if there was any satire in Grole, it was satire, by an alumnus of Radley and Cambridge, of the stupidity of the working class. When Grole metamorphosed, in *Beyond the Fringe*, into a coalminer who would like to have been a judge ('but I never had the Latin, never had the Latin for the judging, I just never had sufficient of it to get through the rigorous judging exams'), John Wells identified this as a 'surreptitious right-wing sketch', in which the miner was 'revealed and savagely satirized as a daft old nit'.

To Wells, the originality of *Beyond the Fringe* lay not in its supposed satirical content, but in its oneness with the private jokes of schoolboys and undergraduates: 'They were fooling about on the stage in exactly the same way as they fooled about off it ... getting away with exactly the same kinds of fantasies as we were doing in our rooms in Oxford.' Until then there had been a barrier between the sniggerings of playground and junior common room and what passed for humour on the public stage – a distinction not observed in the time of Shakespeare or the Restoration, but imposed by the Victorians. Cook and his colleagues broke the taboo, drawing on the kind of humour that flourished in college suggestion books but was never seen in public. Alan Bennett emphasizes this: 'It has always seemed to be that what was subsequently labelled "satire" was simply this kind of private humour going public.'

Beyond the Fringe also differed from previous 'intimate revues' in that the latter has usually been written by people whose lives centred on the theatre, and whose intellectual interests scarcely stretched beyond Shaftesbury Avenue. Moreover the writers had then handed over their material to professional actors to perform. Jonathan Miller emphasizes that this was not the case with the *Fringe*: 'We didn't come from the straightforward theatrical tradition, there was a broader range of topics and we naturally strayed into all sorts of things... philosophy and things like this, which haven't featured massively on the English stage.' He adds that London theatre was eager for this change: 'Beckett's ragamuffin metaphysics, Pinter's psychotic menace and the success of Joan Littlewood's saucy productions had all sharpened the climate.'

John Wells was also struck by the visual plainness of *Beyond the Fringe* – no set to speak of, no 'production numbers', and the cast in ordinary clothes (cardigans[2] and grey flannel trousers). Jonathan Miller agrees that this was

[2] The cardigan, which now looks dowdy, was then regarded as casually elegant, possibly because Rex Harrison had recently worn one as Henry Higgins in *My Fair Lady*.

In March 1960, five months before the Edinburgh opening of *Beyond the Fringe*, Bennett, Cook, Miller and Moore pose for *Queen* magazine.

important, remarking that even Peter Cook's sketches in *Pieces of Eight* had been 'softened and blurred by their gay commercial setting … tinselly dance routines, a-fidget with glow-paint and fishnet'. *Beyond the Fringe* (continues Miller) 'tried to rinse away some of this gaudy sediment. We abandoned décor, dancing and all the other irrelevant dum-de-da of conventional revue, hoping to give the material a chance to speak for itself'. Cook, however, said he would have been 'delighted' to have 'a hundred chorus girls' in the show, and Ned Sherrin believes that 'they wanted to have Julie Christie walking across occasionally, as a sort of running gag – but that was the nearest they got to a girl'. John Bassett says Cook's idea was that Christie would be nude – 'It was just a schoolboy dream.'

This plain style of presentation owed something to a new wave of American comedians. In October 1961, a few months after the London opening of *Beyond the Fringe*, Jonathan Miller wrote in the *Observer*:

American cabaret presents a different aspect [of satire] altogether. Isolated from the baroque traditions of European satirical theatre, the idiom of American satire draws its inspiration from slick-tongued confidence tricksters of the old frontier: the tall-story-teller, the pedlar of patent medicines and the hot-gospeller. The modern American cabaret performer is a distillation of this wise-guy tradition; by Mark Twain out of Elmer Gantry. It is the apotheosis of pure talk.

Today there are many clubs [in the USA] devoted to such acts: where fast-talking hipsters keep up a breathless commentary on the social and political scene in a language which combines urban jargon with the rural, cracker-barrel accents of the West. In San Francisco there is the hungry i where Mort Sahl first made his Custer stand. Chicago has the Second City, New York has the Premise [where] the audience suggest the topics they would like to see dealt with… There are many others.

A few months earlier, Miller had written at length about Sahl in the *New Statesman*:

Mort Sahl is thirty-four, the son of immigrant Jewish parents. He spent his very early childhood in Canada and grew up in California. He spent six or seven years at the University of California…His act grew naturally out of the sharp, sardonic idiom of post-war student life. The time was ripe. Korea, McCarthy, the tawdry values of an anxious and affluent society…In 1953 [the] owner of the hungry i, a small night-spot haunted by students and intellectuals, gave Sahl his first break…He first made headlines with what were then astounding stabs at political figures. His crack about the jacket with the McCarthy flap which zips across the mouth is now an honoured relic in the war museum of his 'battle for truth'…He uses a cartoonist's method…Eisenhower figures…as a golfing dotard.

Miller was also enthusiastic about other American satirists:

Mel Brooks takes a swipe at the sentimental heroism of the New Astronauts ('What do you plan on doing up in space?' 'I guess I'll puke my guts out'). Bob Newhart has a routine which involves Khrushchev being rehearsed for a television appearance ('There's too much glare off his head; we'll have to use a headspray on the night'). Lenny Bruce produces an imaginary conversation between Eisenhower and Nixon in which Eisenhower tries to explain why the Vice-President's Latin-American tour was such a disaster ('It's your wife, Dick. She overdresses!') The American air is a-buzz with these hornets.

Mort Sahl first became known in Britain in 1958, when his LP *The Future Lies Ahead* reached the shops. On this live recording in front of an audience, Sahl delivers his material, which ranges from the political to the Woody Allen 'I'm so vulnerable' style, in a tense, nervy manner, slipping from one topic to another by means of free association:

A lot of people, like myself, have got to yearning after the old days when people were definitive, and they used to make sweeping generalizations...There hasn't been a good sweeping generalization since Senator McCarthy was around, because he used to say what he thought. Now, you might not have *agreed* with it, gang, but at least he said what he thought. He used to say things on television like, 'The State Department is full of nothing but Communists and homosexuals.' And nobody would challenge it, that was the wild part. Though once in a while during the question period, somebody would ask him if it's possible to belong to both groups. (*He gets a big laugh.*) Not yet – I need it later – insecurity in various areas ...

Asked if he had heard Sahl before he and the others wrote *Beyond the Fringe*, Jonathan Miller says:

It's a good question. I think I'd found out about him towards the end of my life as a student, in the late 1950s – I think my friend Joe Melia, who had been at Cambridge, had a record, and I remember sitting at a party in Hampstead listening to this man and being absolutely fascinated by him. But I don't think he influenced us directly, for the very simple reason that we couldn't, any of us, have attempted that sort of free-flowing, commentating monologue. It was very fast Jewish-American stuff which I don't think any of the four of us were remotely capable of. It maybe gave us the feeling that there was something going on in comedy, but I don't think when we started our show we said, 'Sahl gives us the licence to do that,' or 'Let's be as much like Sahl as possible,' because I don't think any of us were remotely like Sahl. Sahl was a direct political commentator. He was writing comic editorials, and I don't think we ever did that at all.

We were parodists, much more.

John Bird says that he too was introduced to Sahl's material at Cambridge by Joe Melia:

The idea of somebody just *talking* like that was extraordinary. Even now [1999], in his seventies, Sahl is extraordinary – he tells you things as if they were true, like that he writes scripts for Robert Redford, or he's been at the Republican Convention, 'And Bob Dole says to me –' And it's only after a bit that you realize it can't *possibly* be true.

Beyond the Fringe, then, was aware of American satire, but not derived from it. It did not need to be. As Miller emphasizes, it was part of Britain's own wide social upheaval:

We were creatures of the post-war generation, and that was the point at which English society was undergoing a great deal of introspection and change. We coincided with the things that happened – perhaps in some ways more significantly – in other ways of theatre, like *Look Back in Anger*. Things were on the move, and we simply expressed the mood of that time – we were creatures of that time.

*

The script for the Edinburgh production of *Beyond the Fringe* was submitted for censorship to the Lord Chamberlain, and consequently survives among his papers at the British Library. In fact the only lines to be censored were in the sketch 'Bollard', where the play examiner has blue-pencilled the two camp actors, hired to advertise a '*man*'s cigarette', addressing each other as 'love' and 'darling'. By 1960, references to sex – particularly homosexuality – were almost the only area in which censorship was still being exercised; and sex played a small part in *Beyond the Fringe*. Theoretically Peter Cook's impersonation of Macmillan could have been banned, as an 'invidious' representation of 'a living person'; but in his history of the Lord Chamberlain's office John Johnston (who worked there) writes that by 1960 politicians seemed 'fair game in sketches and revues'.

The sketches were submitted to the Lord Chamberlain without a running order, but the Edinburgh Lyceum Theatre programme (preserved in London's Theatre Museum, and by John Bassett) gives one – with the caveat: 'Items will be selected from those listed below.' However, there can be no doubt that the show began with the sketch 'Steppes in the Right Direction', in a slightly different version from the one eventually performed in London.

In 1960 most public theatrical performances were still preceded by the playing of the National Anthem, for which the audience rose to its feet. When the Lyceum houselights went down for the opening of *Beyond the Fringe*, Dudley Moore duly came on stage and played 'God Save the Queen' on the piano, whereupon, of course, the audience stood up. Only then was it made clear that this was the beginning of the first sketch:

> PETER: Who is that fellow who keeps playing 'God Save the Queen'? Can't be English. No Englishman would play the National Anthem so often.
> ALAN: Oh, he's not English, certainly.
> JONATHAN: You can tell that by the way he plays the whole piece sitting down.
> PETER: Do you know what I think? I think he's a member of the Leningrad Symphony Orchestra.

Cook claims that the Festival organizers have obliged the *Beyond the Fringe* cast to share 'the smallest bungalow in the world' with the 138 members of this orchestra – a surrealist touch that disappeared after the Edinburgh production, so as not to distract from the way the sketch develops. Cook, Bennett and Miller try to persuade the Russian (Moore) to blow a raspberry at Khrushchev and make approving noises about Macmillan; but he persistently does the reverse – whereupon they all follow suit. *Beyond the*

The Fringe four in Mrs Grosset's flat in Edinburgh, where they lived and rehearsed.

Fringe has thus got briskly down to business in its opening item by mocking both the National Anthem and the Prime Minister, but in such a zany, unpolitical way that it all seems harmless nonsense.

The second sketch in the Edinburgh show's running order was a solo for Jonathan Miller, 'Sunlight from the Sea'. This, in his Footlights 'Radio Page' manner, parodied the style and content of the *Daily Express* and *Daily Mail* (in other words the media were now coming in for a bashing):

THE DAILY MIRACLE. February 9th. Truth and Prosperity. Price 2½d.

St George's Day and a proud day for British mothers as British sportsmen and scientists put the great back into Great Britain. At the White City little Mary Osgood jumps to world class in the Hop, Step and Jump event; in Zurich the bounding pound leaps to parity with the Swiss franc; and on the scientific front it's hats off to Britain's one-man atom team, grammar-school-trained Arthur Peasgood; Sunlight from the Sea, man's age-old dream, now no longer a dream – a remote possibility.

The plan is ludicrously simple. You may have noticed how often the sun shines on the sea, wasting itself while millions starve. Here at Bassingbourne we have succeeded in trapping the natural solar rays and converting them to electricity. We have called this process Sabrina.[3] This stands for Solar Activated Brine – Injection – Solar Activated Brine – er, brine – well, we like the name ...

Next came Alan Bennett's first monologue, 'Let's Face It', a take-off of a typical middle-class reactionary, who supports the South African government and opposes CND: 'Don't let's take any notice of these demonstrators ... This is a democracy. Government isn't run by people like that, it's run by the people.' Bennett says that the four of them 'always referred to this solo as my Boring Old Man sketch', and that he finds it truly boring now. Being topical, it is indeed one of the few items in the show to have dated. Bennett adds, 'I've a dreadful feeling I may have thought I was doing some good.'

The Edinburgh version of a sketch called 'Words ... and things', mocking Oxbridge philosophers in particular, and thus ivory-tower academics in general, was chiefly Bennett's work. 'But Jonathan added things,' Bennett says. 'He knew much more about philosophy than I did.' It is set in the North Oxford household of a don, Bleaney, who is attempting to hold an erudite symposium with his pupils amid domestic chaos:

BLEANEY: Well, I think we might make a start. I've just committed myself to a few thoughts – no principle, of course – just, as it were, to set the cat among the pigeons, and the ball rolling. Now, can you all find yourselves a seat?

CRUTCHLEY: Can I use your floor?

(*They all assume intent listening postures about the room.* BLEANEY *clears his throat, and is about to start when –*)

FEMALE VOICE: (*from upstairs*) Marcus, darling, have you got Teddy?

BLEANEY: Who, darling?

FEMALE VOICE: Teddy, darling. *Adam*'s Teddy.

BLEANEY: Oh, no, dear, Susan's got it. Sorry about that little domestic eruption ...

Dudley Moore claims that he made up his first solo spot in *Beyond the Fringe*, called 'Highly Strung' in the Edinburgh programme, only the night before the show opened: 'I still hadn't got one that I felt was satisfactory. I decided to write a sonata movement using ... "The Colonel Bogey March" ...

[3] A frontally well-endowed actress of the day.

in the style of Beethoven.' Moore was the principal performer in the item that followed it at Edinburgh, 'Royal Box', playing a Grole-like character who attends the same theatrical show night after night in the hope that the Royal Family may turn up: 'That's what they call the Royal Box. But... there's no Royal People in it at the moment ... unless of course they're crouching.' (Moore was proving as adept at Grole-ish voices as Cook himself.) Then came 'Old J.J.', a new version of a sketch conducted almost entirely with initials that Cook had written for *Pieces of Eight* ('Good God, J.G.!' begins the earlier version. 'I haven't seen you since you were M.O. at H.Q. in B.A.O.R.').

These three sketches veered towards more conventional revue material, but they were followed by Cook's devastating impersonation of Harold Macmillan giving a party political broadcast on television. Alan Bennett had gone as far as parodying the Queen, in the privacy of college smokers, with plenty of obscene jokes. Otherwise, says John Fortune, 'it had never occurred to any of us to appear as any contemporary figure'.

Cook shrewdly chose not so much to caricature Macmillan as to impersonate him with devastating accuracy – to the extent that, after *Beyond the Fringe* had established itself, Macmillan began to behave more and more like Cook's take-off of him. The Cook mockery was, instead, directed at Britain's loss of riches and international status in the years since the war:

> Good evening. I have recently been travelling round the world – on your behalf, and at your expense...I went first to Germany, and there I spoke with the German Foreign Minister, Herr – (*he hesitates*) – Herr and there, and we exchanged many frank words in our respective languages; so precious little came of that...I then went on to America, and there I had talks with the young, vigorous President of that great country...We talked of many things, including Great Britain's position in the world as some kind of honest broker. I agreed with him, when he said that no nation could be more honest; and he agreed with me, when I chaffed him and said that no nation could be broker.

John F. Kennedy was elected US President in January 1961, a few months after the Edinburgh *Beyond the Fringe*, and the reference to him was added by Cook for the London production. The choice of such a youthful figure in America only served to highlight the elderliness of Macmillan and the British government.

1960 was World Refugee Year, and another Edinburgh *Beyond the Fringe* sketch took a dig at the British middle-class belief that charity consists of sending old clothes to Oxfam. Two doctors are examining a refugee who has just arrived in Britain:

PESKER: Now, you may realize, Johann, that a lot of people all over Britain – many of them not very well off, old-age pensioners, vicars, schoolmasters and the like, have sent in some of their dearly valued possessions in order to get you kitted out properly. Now, let's see what we've got for you. It's rather like Christmas, isn't it? Or do you have Christmas in – where is it – Bosnia?

BRIGHT: Now, this is a vest which has been kindly sent in by the Vicar of Nastbury. It's a beautiful bit of English worsted aertex, you see, Johann.

PESKER: Completely mothproof. There you are, how do you feel in it? And then there's this splendid shirt. Notice there's no collar, Johann. That will save you having to wear a tie. They don't make shirts like that any more, do they, Bright?

Bennett was cast as Johann, the silent refugee. 'I had to take my clothes off,' he recalls wryly, 'and I hated that.'

Towards the end of the Edinburgh show, Bennett performed his sermon, 'Take a Pew'. Two versions were submitted to the Lord Chamberlain, one including this passage, which exactly catches the pseudo-learned style of many Anglican preachers:

Let us, in the silence together, empty our minds of all useless intellectual jumble, put on one side the so-called lessons of experience, and, clad only in the trappings of our common humanity, let us consider these words. And I use that word, 'consider', you know, advisedly. I'm using it, you see, in its original Greek sense of *con–sider*, of putting ourselves together. *Con*, you see, 'together', in the way of thinking about something. I want us tonight to consider – to put ourselves in the way of thinking about – put ourselves in the way of thinking about – what we *ought* to be putting ourselves in the way of thinking about here together tonight.

Bennett says he could now extemporize the sermon 'on a kind of automatic pilot – I'd done so many by then'.

After the sermon, at Edinburgh, came the *Fringe* team's first attempt at a nuclear war sketch, 'Whose Finger on What Button', which began as follows:

A: Come in.

PERKINS: (*salutes*) You wanted me, sir?

A: Yes, Perkins, I sent for you. I sent for you for two reasons. First of all, we're always delighted to see you in this office. And secondly to ask you about this rather alarming report I have in front of me.

PERKINS: Yes, sir.

A: It appears, if we are to believe this report, that instead of accomplishing your mission of destroying a Russian heavy-water plant in Murmansk you seem to have exploded a hydrogen device in the city of Manchester.

PERKINS: Yes, sir, I am afraid I did … I'm afraid once I got up in the air I couldn't for the life of me remember which it was. I knew it was an M …

The Edinburgh evening concluded with Cook's coalminer–judge monologue, the Shakespeare spoof 'So That's the Way You Like It' (to which all
four had contributed ideas), and Cook's 'The End of the World' (called 'This
is the End' at Edinburgh), in which a loony-fringe religious sect waits for the
apocalypse on a mountain top:

> ALL: (*chanting*) Now is the end – perish the world!
> (*Pause.*)
> PETER: It was GMT, wasn't it?
> JONATHAN: Yes.
> PETER: Well, it's not quite the conflagration I'd been banking on. Never mind,
>   lads, same time tomorrow – we must get a winner one day.

Jonathan Miller says that, when the Edinburgh script was complete, the
four of them felt that they did indeed have a winner: 'I think we did – it
sounds arrogant to say it, but I think we knew that it was funnier than
anything we had ever seen.'

The Edinburgh programme for *Beyond the Fringe* states that the revue has
been 'Produced by John Hammond'. This was John Bassett – Hammond is

'My brother Esau is an hairy man, but I am a
smooth man' – a sermonising Alan Bennett
snapped from the wings on the Edinburgh first
night by John Bassett.

'I have recently been travelling round the world –
on your behalf, and at your expense.' Bassett's
first-night photo of Peter Cook's Harold
Macmillan monologue.

his mother's maiden name – who thought it would be inappropriate that the assistant to the Festival Director should also be staging a revue. 'In any case,' he says, 'they really directed themselves. Jonathan [Miller], I think, had a very dominant role in that area.'

Robert Ponsonby 'saw an early rehearsal, and it was awful. They fluffed, they broke down and corpsed. This was in somebody's sitting room, and I thought, "Oh my God, this is the worst sort of amateurism." But I could see that there was fantastic talent there, and some things were going to be very funny.' Advance bookings were poor, since the performers' names were not well known to the Festival audience. On the first night, at 10.45 p.m. on Monday, 22 August 1960, only a third of the seats were filled, while behind the scenes – according to Jonathan Miller – the Lyceum stage-hands slumbered in the Louis Quinze chairs that had been used earlier in the evening for the Old Vic's production of *The Seagull.*

Seated in the Festival Director's box, Robert Ponsonby nervously watched a sticky start to the show:

> For the first ten minutes, nobody in the audience knew quite what to expect. But already you could see there was phenomenal talent there. And at least two immensely funny men – I mean particularly Peter and Jonathan. In those days Jonathan was very, very funny. Alan, bless him, wasn't obviously funny, but with the famous sermon, of course, we began to get the message, and soon I was watching an audience falling about. Dudley was the least interesting; I can't remember very much of what he did. But altogether I was absolutely delighted.

Yet to Richard Ingrams, who saw *Beyond the Fringe* that week, 'the person who really impressed me was Dudley, because his music was so brilliant. I thought he was the star of the show.'

Among the comparatively few people in the audience on the first night was the future theatre critic Michael Billington, then an Oxford undergraduate. 'It had opened with no fanfares or pre-publicity,' he recalls.

> It was simply shunted on as a late-night show after *The Seagull*. But Alan Bennett and Dudley Moore were well known in Oxford – I had been with Dudley in an Oxford touring production of *Bartholomew Fair* the previous summer – and in the Lyceum gallery on the first night were people from the Oxford Theatre Group, ready to cheer on the home team.
>
> Technically it was a cock-up. They'd obviously had no technical run-through, and the lights went out in the middle of Alan Bennett's sermon. But you knew you were in the presence of something extraordinary. You came out feeling physically slightly ill, because to laugh for that length of time is exhausting. And it was a shock, a slap in the face, to all of us, because we'd seen nothing like this before – we'd never seen names *named* on the stage; we hadn't seen prime ministers actually lampooned, by name.

According to John Bassett, 'The first night at Edinburgh was 32 per cent capacity. And then the word spread, and it took off! The total audience for the whole week was 112 per cent! To make up from the 32 per cent to that, you're talking about cramming in 140 per cent on every other night. Really enormous.' Alan Bennett recalls 'long queues for returns'.

Most national theatre critics responded positively but without great enthusiasm. *The Times* printed a brief, slightly puzzled notice under the headline 'Midnight Gaiety in Edinburgh':

> The pleasingness of this revue is difficult to pin down in words. It keeps the midnight audiences in a continual ripple of easy laughter. The reason may be that each performer is coolly confident of his own power to amuse and also that the comedy is ruled by a nice sense of proportion.

In the *Observer*, Irving Wardle praised the 'economy and ensemble sympathy' of the four performers, which reminded him of Flanders and Swann, but described the script as 'average-level undergraduate revue'. Harold Hobson in *The Sunday Times* gave *Beyond the Fringe* just four words of praise – 'touches of irrational genius' – before devoting the rest of the paragraph to undergraduate Fringe shows. Only the *Daily Mail* spotted a winner, thanks to Peter Lewis, a future scriptwriter for *That Was The Week That Was*. 'I was sent up there as junior second-string *Mail* critic,' he recalls.

> The main offering on the first night was *The Seagull*, but there was a poster in the foyer of the Lyceum saying 'Don't forget – 10.45 – *Beyond the Fringe*'. Nobody knew what this meant, but I thought, 'There's a show on, I must get back for it.' Everyone else went off to their hotels for dinner, but I wrote my notice for the Chekhov in a hurry, and went back, and sat there absolutely entranced by these four young men in identical grey sweaters, larking about in an Oxford and Cambridge manner, but with much more pith than was usual in university revues – wonderful, devastating pieces about Shakespeare ('O saucy Worcester, dost thou lie so still?'), parsons, and dons. I'd been to those Hermione Gingold revues, *Sweet and Low* and all that, which depended mainly on theatrical gossip, fishnet tights, and rather coy references to sex. I'd quite enjoyed them, but suddenly this was about the real world, and one was absolutely astonished.
>
> Well, immediately afterwards I coughed up a few illiterate paragraphs into the telephone – something to the effect that a whole lot of sacred cows had been speared on stage, and left mooing; this is the end of the old-style revue and the beginning of the new one – and of course when it got into the paper, everybody else who hadn't been near the thing was asked by their features editors, 'Why weren't you there?'

Lewis's review was published in the *Daily Mail* on the Wednesday morning, 24 August 1960:

Comedy team   by Coia

Left to right: Dudley Moore, Alan Bennett, Peter Cook and Jonathan Miller, of the "Beyond the Fringe" late
night revue at the Royal Lyceum Theatre, Edinburgh, sketched at the Press Bureau yesterday.

The surprise stars of the 1960 Edinburgh Festival, caricatured in the *Scotsman*.

IT'S THE FUNNIEST REVUE FOR AGES
Beyond the Fringe

Behind this unpromising title lies what I believe can be described as the funniest, most intelligent, and most original revue to be staged in Britain for a very long time.

It is the creation of four, mobile, deadpan young men of Oxford and Cambridge extraction who are in private life a doctor, scriptwriter, historian, and musician.

They take the stage for 90 minutes with grey sweaters, four chairs, and a piano, and proceed to demolish all that is sacred in the British way of life with glorious and expert precision.

Disregarding all the jaded trimmings of conventional sketches, production numbers, dancing, and girls, they get down to the real business of intimate revue, which is satire and parody.

One of their best efforts was a fruity *reductio ad absurdum* of a Shakespearean play, complete with Cousin Westmoreland, incomprehensible clowns, and duel ('Let's to't') and death scene ('Now is this steel 'twixt gut and bladder interpos'd').

There is the occasional lapse into undergraduate humour, but at their best – and that is almost all the 90 minutes – these four high priests of parody make most professional comedians look ham-handed and vulgar.

If the show comes to London I doubt if revue will ever be the same again.

The *Daily Mail* features editor told Lewis to follow the story up, and find out more about the performers. 'So I went to see the four boys. They were all sharing a big flat in Edinburgh, and Jonathan was saying, "Of course, I'm only just doing this as a summer holiday from medicine," and Alan said, "My subject is Richard II, and I'm going back to that."' Michael Billington met them too; he had been asked to write a review for the National Union of Students' newspaper, and on the Wednesday morning he attended a press conference given by them:

> I asked them, 'What are you really attacking, what's your gripe?' And they said, 'Complacency.' It was the complacency of Macmillan's England that they really wanted to get at. And I think it's no accident that *Beyond the Fringe* happened when it did. Because the 1950s (which I was brought up in) had been so complacent, parochial, smug, Little England-ish.

Billington recalls that Jonathan Miller asked for criticisms of the show, and he responded by suggesting that the 'Johann' sketch about clothing the refugee was rather unfair in its implied attack on charity donors.

> Jonathan seemed to take the point. Anyway, I went back to see the show the next day, and the sketch had (if memory serves) gone. If not, then certainly by the time the show moved to London. Possibly the only time in my life any criticism of mine may have had some effect.

Bennett, who had to take off his clothes in the sketch, says he was 'ever so relieved when it was dropped'.

John Wells, then in his third year at Oxford, was performing in the Oxford Theatre Group's Fringe review, *Never Too Late*. He recalls it as 'earnest and rather evangelical', and the script sent to the Lord Chamberlain confirms this. It includes a calypso satirizing racism, and a song about a girl separated from her lover by the Iron Curtain. Moreover (says Wells) it was staged in the usual revue manner, with costumes and choreography. When he had a night off, Wells went to the Lyceum to see what the fuss was about – the *Edinburgh Evening News* was now reporting that *Beyond the Fringe* was 'the hit of the festival', adding that it 'slays everything it touches'. As soon as the show started, Wells found himself helplessly 'rolling about and roaring'.

Meanwhile in London, Peter Cook's agent Donald Langdon went to make a proposal to a theatrical impresario – none other than Willie Donaldson, fresh from losing money with John Bird's revue *Here is the News*. 'Langdon had advised Peter Cook not to do *Beyond the Fringe*,' recalls Donaldson,

> and when it opened to triumphant reviews everybody rushed to Edinburgh to see it except him. He arrived in my office, showed me the reviews, and said, 'I think I'll get it for you.' And he said, 'You produce it, and I'll have an

investment.' Furthermore I lent him the money to invest in it. It was all slightly
dodgy.

He then went off to Edinburgh. Bennett, Miller and Moore all hated him,
because he'd tried to persuade Cook not to do it, but within twenty-four hours
he had persuaded them to let him represent all of them. By this time, every
qualified impresario was up there with their cheque books, people like Michael
Codron, offering them everything under the sun. But Langdon wouldn't let
them talk to anyone, and he persuaded them to do it with me, on the grounds
that I wouldn't fuck it up by adding dancing girls. But my qualifications were
really absolutely nil. I can't imagine why they didn't suspect something funny
was going on.

Rather oddly, Ponsonby and the Edinburgh Festival had not considered the
possibility of future productions of *Beyond the Fringe*, nor made any con-
tractual agreement by which they would benefit from them. 'My lasting
regret,' says Ponsonby, 'is that I didn't have 5 per cent of everything they did
subsequently!'

As soon as they had finished their week in Edinburgh, the four performers
were introduced (in London) to Donaldson, and they agreed that he could
back *Beyond the Fringe*, although Miller and Bennett were dubious about
reviving the show. 'Only Dudley and I seemed to want to do it,' recalled
Cook. 'The other two were perpetually struggling with their consciences.'
Miller returned to his hospital and Bennett went back to Oxford for the start
of the 1960 autumn term. Cook, who was writing sketches for a successor to
Pieces of Eight, chose to pass the time in Cambridge. Donaldson now had to
fend off Michael Codron, who was still keen to invest in *Beyond the Fringe*.
'Codron tried to persuade me to let him in on it,' says Donaldson, 'but I told
him I needed someone who owned a theatre. So I went to Donald Albery and
he came in on it. Actually I'm surprised I didn't let Codron in too – I could
have let everyone in, like in that Mel Brooks film, *The Producers*, and got a
200 per cent investment!'[4]

By the following spring, Donaldson had booked *Beyond the Fringe* into
the Arts Theatre at Cambridge, to be followed by a week at Brighton. It was
hoped that a London run would follow, but when Donaldson had the cast
perform a run-through in front of Donald Albery in the bar of one of his West
End theatres, the Prince of Wales, Albery's response was frosty. He was
particularly scathing about Alan Bennett, telling Donaldson, 'The fair-
haired one will have to go.' Fortunately Donaldson talked him out of this.

---

[4] In *The Producers*, a crooked impresario and his accountant persuade a number of little old ladies to
invest in a musical, to a much higher level than its actual costs. They plan that it will be an immediate
flop, closing after the first night, so that they can pocket all the money without the investors discovering
the fraud. The plan is frustrated by the unexpected success of the show, and they land up in gaol.

Albery proposed financial terms for the four writer–performers: £75 a week, with no box-office royalties. This seemed lavish to Jonathan Miller. 'It's ten times what I'd be receiving as a junior doctor,' he told Alan Bennett, who comments, 'It was fifteen times what I'd be receiving as a medieval historian but something told me even then that this was not really the point.' Willie Donaldson freely admits that the terms were 'pretty mean, considering what Albery and I were going to make'. John Bassett, who had brought the team together, was to receive £30 a week. In the London programme, he is credited (under his own name this time) as having 'originally conceived and produced' the show, and is also listed as its press representative.

The Cambridge version of *Beyond the Fringe*, which opened at the Arts Theatre on 21 April 1961, was more than twice as long as the Edinburgh production. 'They threw everything in, and it was riotous,' says Bassett. Miller recalls that the new material had been devised under the eye of a professional director, Eleanor Fazan. The Albery management had hired her because she had made a great success of a 1957 revue called *Share My Lettuce*. This had been written by Bamber Gascoigne, then a Cambridge undergraduate, for performance in his college, and was then brought to London with a professional cast. 'We sat round a table in Eleanor Fazan's flat,' says Miller, 'just joking out loud, and someone wrote down what we said.'

The new version experimented with 'quickies', short sketches like this:

Two men sitting on couch.
A: These nuclear disarmers go on and on and on and on and on –
B: I quite agree. They go on and on and on –
A and B: (*in endless duet*) On and on and on and on –
(*Slow fade out.*)

Another quickie referred to the excuses frequently offered for the 'colour bar':

Enter JONATHAN *and* ALAN, A. *dressed as landlady.*
J: Excuse me, I am from the London School of Economics and I am looking for lodgings for students.
A: I am sorry, I don't take coloured people, but don't think it's because of what the neighbours say, it's me, I am prejudiced.
(*Pause for* J*'s reaction, then blackout.*)

This was dropped before the show reached London, but later became one of the regular sketches at The Establishment Club.

Peter Cook had a solo quickie in which he endlessly sang the words 'I'm dancing about in the nude' – to which someone else remarked, 'What absolute rubbish. You are fully clothed and you're standing stock still.' Cook answered, 'I am essentially a radio performer.' But the best quickie of all, which survived into the London version of the show, was 'Real Class', in which Cook pointed out to the audience that 'Jonathan Miller and myself come from good families and have had the benefits of a public-school education', whereas the other two 'have worked their way up from working-class origins'. To which Bennett replied, 'I wonder how many of these people have realized that Jonathan Miller's a Jew ... I'd rather be working class than be a Jew.' Miller responded, 'I'm not really a *Jew*. Just Jew-*ish*. Not the whole hog, you know.' John Fortune was shocked by this, 'because when I went up to Cambridge I thought Jews were only in the Bible – though there was a don at my college, King's, who was Jewish, and I heard he'd been refused membership of a golf club because of it'.

Cambridge saw the first appearance of many of the show's most accomplished sketches. These included Moore's Schubert *Lieder* parody (his lethal impersonation of a wobbly Peter Pears singing a Benjamin Britten folk song came later, in London); the rock-'n'-roll vicar ('Don't call me Vicar – call me Dick,' says Miller, to which Moore responds, 'Well, Dicker ...'); a black African politician who has had his skin pigmented white to avoid the colour bar; and a lecture by Civil Defence volunteers – a far sharper way of handling the nuclear-war issue than the absent-minded bomber pilot in the Edinburgh sketch:

> PETER: Now, we shall receive four minutes' warning of any impending nuclear attack. Some people have said, 'Oh my goodness me – four minutes? – that is not a very long time!' Well, I would remind those doubters that some people in this great country of ours can run a mile in four minutes.

John Bird describes this as 'a joke which brilliantly clamped its teeth on that era's self-delusion and hopeless nostalgia for power and glory'.

Not all the new material written for Cambridge was of this quality, and the revue was now enormously long. Yet John Cleese, then aged twenty-one and at Downing College, recalls it as 'quite simply the funniest show that I'd ever seen in my life', and goes on:

> The great delight of it was that there were four people on stage who were all somewhere near the genius level. It never occurred to us, though, that it was satirical ... To us it just seemed the natural content of comedy, the sort of things that you would make jokes about.

A Cambridge magazine, *Broadsheet*, carried a review by Tom Bussmann, which began:

> Only when confronted with the excellent does the inadequacy of the good become painfully manifest. After what seems and probably is years of revues

varying in quality from highly competent with one or two good numbers, down to the stinking, *Beyond the Fringe* is just too good to be true.

Bussmann detected a transatlantic influence – 'Though it would be wrong to draw too close a parallel with the *Beyond the Fringe* quartet and the new American school of humour, it is perhaps worth noting that both developed and thrived initially in a university before undergraduate audiences' – and concluded that Bennett, Cook, Miller and Moore had created a show that rose 'to the level of *satire*, inevitably disquieting but essentially positive and constructive'. This was the second review of *Beyond the Fringe* to use the word 'satire' (the first being Peter Lewis's at Edinburgh).

In Brighton, where *Beyond the Fringe* opened at the Theatre Royal on 1 May 1961, it produced the opposite effect on its audience. Alan Bennett recalls that 'the seats were going up like pistol shots throughout the performance so that, come the curtain, there were scarcely more people in the audience than there were on the stage'. He adds, 'I am convinced that one of the chief pleasures of going to the theatre in Brighton is leaving it. The sleek Sussex matrons sit poised in the stalls like greyhounds in the slips. The first "fuck" and they're a mile down the front, streaking for Hove.'

There was no swearing in *Beyond the Fringe*, but many Brightonians were outraged by the sketch that was arguably the show's finest, 'The Aftermyth of War', which had been added to the script in Cambridge. This mocked such 1950s Second World War films as *The Dambusters* and *Reach for the Sky* (the film biography of Douglas Bader) and, in doing so, laughed at all the clichés about the war itself:

> ALAN: I had a pretty quiet war, really. I was one of the Few. We were stationed down at Biggin Hill. One Sunday we got word that Jerry was coming in – over Hastings, I think it was. We got up there as quickly as we could, and everything was very calm and peaceful. England lay like a green carpet below me, and the war seemed worlds away. I could see Tunbridge Wells, and the sun glinting on the river, and I remembered that last weekend I'd spent there with Celia that summer of '39, and her playing the piano in the cool of the evening. Suddenly, Jerry was coming at me out of a bank of cloud. I let him have it, and I think I must have got him in the wing, because he spiralled past me out of control. As he did so – I will always remember this – I got a glimpse of his face, and, you know – he smiled. Funny thing, war.

Bennett recalls that Cook was nervous about performing this sketch, and Bennett himself made it even more daring by impersonating Douglas Bader, 'coming downstairs with a pipe in my mouth and exaggeratedly stiff legs (though I never quite dared to make them as stiff as they should have been). One night I was hissed and was very pleased with myself.' He also performed

8

Beyond the Fringe hits Brighton. The four's mood in Lewis Morley's photo under the pier probably reflects the lukewarm audiences they were getting.

it on BBC Television's topical magazine programme *Tonight* – and was acutely embarrassed to realize that Kenneth Allsop, the interviewer, had lost a leg in the war.

The critic of the *Brighton & Hove Herald* declared that *Beyond the Fringe* had 'nearly sent me to sleep', and said he thought it 'vaguely indecent for twenty-year-olds [*sic*] to be making fun of Battle of Britain pilots'. Peter Cook was now in favour of dropping 'The Aftermyth of War' when they reached London. Indeed, Bennett recalls that the cast's theatrical friends were advising against a West End run: '"We loved it, darlings," they told us … "but don't, whatever you do, take it in."' Donald Albery, still sceptical, was unwilling to provide one of his own theatres. But the Brighton audience had included a theatrical lawyer named David Jacobs. His clients included Bernard Cribbins, then appearing in a revue called *And Another Thing* at the tiny 440-seat Fortune Theatre, off Drury Lane. 'The Fortune was a funny little theatre,' says Barry Humphries. 'It had done revues all through the

Lewis Morley catches them again, this time at the London Zoo before the opening at the Fortune Theatre.

1930s, and it stood next to the great, majestic Theatre Royal, Drury Lane, like a David alongside Goliath.' The Cribbins show was about to close for a few weeks, for a revamp with new material, and meanwhile the management needed to put a show briefly into the Fortune to cover the gap. Though not over-impressed by *Beyond the Fringe*, Jacobs thought it might do the job.

Bennett recalls that the four of them felt extremely anxious about the prospect of even this limited run. They spent a few hours posing for publicity photos, arranged by John Bassett. Some of these were taken on a derelict industrial site in North Acton. To Bennett this seemed 'appropriately stark and gritty for the enterprise on which we were to embark'.

2

....

It really is a Rolls

Beyond the Fringe opened at the Fortune Theatre in London on the night of Wednesday, 10 May 1961. The next morning's *Daily Express* carried a review by Bernard Levin:

> The theatre came of age last night. Four young men ... gave it the key of the door, and showed how the lock works.
>
> On the tiny stage of the tiny Fortune Theatre erupted a revue so brilliant, adult, hard-boiled, accurate, merciless, witty, unexpected, alive, exhilarating, cleansing, right, true, and good that my first conscious thought as I stumbled, weak and sick with laughter, up the stairs at the end was one of gratitude.
>
> Gratitude that there should be four men living among us today who could come together to provide, for as long as memory holds, an eighth colour to the rainbow.
>
> Satirical revue in this country has been, until now, basically cowardly. First, it has picked on the easy targets. Second, however hard it hit the targets (and it rarely hit them at all, let alone in the middle), it left its audience alone, to leave the theatre as fat and complacent as it came in.
>
> This sorry tale went on for so long that some of us began to despair of the form itself. We believed that satirical revue was impossible in this country.
>
> And now we know we were wrong: blessed were they who did not see, but being blind, believed.
>
> These four immortals take on such targets as the Prime Minister, Dr Verwoerd, Mr Mboya,[1] the H-bomb, Mr Cousins' opposition to the H-bomb,[2] capital punishment, patriotism, Shakespeare, the clergy, the linguistic

---

[1] The Kenyan African nationalist leader Tom Mboya, whom Levin assumes to be the original of 'Mr Akiboto Nobitsu' in the sketch about the black politician who has his skin whitened.

[2] Frank Cousins, General Secretary of the Transport and General Workers' Union, mocked in the sketch 'Frank Speaking': 'We sent round a referendum to all our local branches phrased in this form – "Would you like to see your wife and kids go up in smoke?" Ninety-four per cent of the replies said, "No." If that is not a mandate for unilateral nuclear disarmament I do not know what is.'

philosophers, the Sunday-night religious television programmes, history, lunacy, and anti-Semitism…And this is not all: not by any manner of means. For they not only take on these targets, they roll them gasping and howling in the mire…

The satire…is real, barbed, deeply planted and aimed at things and people that need it. But this is still not all. For the final target, the real victim, the ultimate object of the whole proceedings, is the audience. It is they who feel the final punch, the last twist of the knife, who are taken up and dropped from a great height and thoroughly, healingly, beneficially, beautifully, and properly shaken up in the process…

Mr Peter Cook's parody of the Prime Minister's inability on television to time his gestures right is one of the most diabolically clever pieces of political comment ever created…

Like Levin, Pearson Phillips in the *Daily Mail* treated the show as primarily satirical:

If you have ever been tickled with a sharp scythe you will know what it is like to be entertained by the four young men who have taken over at the Fortune Theatre…I predict it will cause a sensation…Between them they carve up a clutch of sacred British institutions – the National Anthem, the 'Few', Civil Defence, Mr Macmillan and the Church of England. And then suddenly they stifle our laughter, stuffing it down our throats with some vicious sweep of wit which has the audience gasping.

The other daily newspaper critics made no mention of satire. Felix Barker in the *Evening News* called it 'the perfect revue for which we have all waited through so many a groaning and fatuous night'; Milton Shulman in the *Evening Standard* described it as 'unashamed, adult, provocative and uncompromising'; W.A. Darlington in the *Daily Telegraph* reported that the 'cascades of delighted laughter' which had greeted it in Edinburgh were to be heard again at the Fortune; T.C. Worsley wrote in the *Financial Times* that it was 'the kind of thing people will go to again and again for the pleasure of introducing it to their friends and hearing them laugh'; and the anonymous reviewer in *The Times* described the sketches as superior to 'the clichés of Shaftesbury Avenue'.

Despite the fact that only Levin and Phillips used the word 'satire', Michael Frayn, who was in the audience on the second night, describes the arrival of *Beyond the Fringe* in the West End as 'the official opening of the Satirical Sixties'. Frayn, who had joined the *Guardian* after Cambridge, was himself currently writing a mildly satirical column in that paper; for example, two days after the opening of *Beyond the Fringe*, he was mocking Moral Re-Armament as 'Moral Re-Gurgitation'. The *Guardian* critic who reviewed *Beyond the Fringe*, John Rosselli, wrote, 'To readers of this newspaper one may say that it is a lot like Michael Frayn's best "Miscellany" columns animated. In other words, it is very funny.' Frayn says of the comparison, 'I suppose there were satirical elements in my column. I don't think it had very much in common with the rest of the satire movement, but maybe there were the beginnings of that slightly disrespectful tone. And I think that partly came out of National Service, when there was a widespread feeling of disgruntlement – not that those of us on the Russian course had much right to feel it; we had a very pleasant time.'

Bernard Levin was writing a mildly satirical column too, the weekly parliamentary sketch in the *Spectator*, signed 'Taper', in which he frequently gave politicians deriding nicknames; for instance the Attorney-General, Sir Reginald Manningham-Buller, became 'Bullying Manner'. Peter Lewis (who had helped to 'discover' *Beyond the Fringe* in Edinburgh) came to know Levin well when they were both on the *Daily Mail*, and describes his background:

> Bernard's father was a Camden Town tailor who left the marital home and went off to Canada. Bernard was very silent on this subject; he never talked about his family. He went to Christ's Hospital and then to the London School of Economics. He's not at all Oxbridge; that's been one of his strengths. He was never assimilated by the Establishment, so he was able to pick up his lance and go for them. And he modelled himself on George Bernard Shaw – a Shavian polemicist.

Though Frayn regards the London opening of *Beyond the Fringe* as the beginning of the satire boom, he emphasizes that much of the show – perhaps the greater part of it – was not satirical at all. 'Several of the items,' he writes in his 1963 introduction to the published script, 'Jonathan Miller's monologue on the trousers, for instance, ["The Heat-Death of the Universe", in which Miller wove flights of hilarious fancy around how 400 pairs of brand-new corduroy trousers came to be in the Lost Property office of London Transport] are clearly in the old whimsical–fantastical school of Paul Jennings.' Frayn stresses that the show was nevertheless novel in three respects: first, the performers had written all the material themselves; second, there were no interruptions for non-comic items (opening choruses, torch songs and the like); and third – as John Wells remarked – the sketches were about 'things that human beings talked about outside the theatre'. On the other hand Frayn did allow that, running throughout the show, there was an undercurrent of mockery that was entirely new to the London revue stage: 'The show made the audience laugh at the unthinking attitudes of respect which up to then they themselves had shared.'

The reviewers in the two significant Sunday newspapers were in no doubt that it was satirical. Harold Hobson of *The Sunday Times*, whose response to the Edinburgh production had been less than euphoric, was clearly made uncomfortable by the satire, describing the cast as

> four young men, till recently undergraduates in Oxford [*sic*] and, armed only with their own wit, [who] give an entertainment securely founded in their conviction of their natural superiority to all that they discuss, attack, or caricature. Their cleverness is such that not once does it occur to us to ask if this feeling of superiority is justified.

Hobson was puzzled that the target of these attacks and caricatures

> takes on various guises in the course of the evening. Sometimes [it] looks like Mr Macmillan, and then again like Mr Cousins. Sometimes like Negro-baiters, and sometimes like Negroes. Sometimes like the H-bomb, and sometimes like the anti-H-bomb. Sometimes like a parson, and sometimes like a Jew … *Beyond the Fringe* gives no indication about their ultimate attitude …

The remainder of Hobson's review was devoted to praise of Jonathan Miller. 'The star that danced when he was born trod a strange measure; its disturbing poetry is the one absolutely irreplaceable thing in this extraordinarily diverting entertainment.'

Hobson, who was in his late fifties, had failed to see that *Beyond the Fringe*, in the form in which it arrived in London, was not mocking from a specific moral and political standpoint, but was scoffing at (in Frayn's words) 'the unthinking attitudes of respect' which still predominated in Britain in 1960. The picture that gradually emerges from the show is of a bankrupt, defenceless little country run by a ridiculously elderly prime minister. (Cook's Macmillan reads out a letter from an elderly Mrs McFarlane of Fife, and replies to her 'as one Scottish old-age pensioner to another'.) Britain is also a class-ridden, racist society where the only defence against nuclear attack will be to run a mile in four minutes, or climb into a paper bag. 'That's the rule,' says a Civil Defence leader (Cook). 'The bomb drops, the dust settles, hold your breath, jump into your brown paper bag.' Nuclear war seems inevitable, as another of the Civil Defence team (Bennett) makes clear:

> What if one of our American friends … sends up one of their missiles by mistake? It could not happen. You see, before they press that button they've got to get on the telephone to Number 10 Downing Street … And Mr Macmillan will say 'yes' – or 'no' – as the mood takes him … What if Mr Macmillan is out? Perfectly simple! Common sense, really – we'd ask Lady Dorothy.

Britain's loss of greatness is equally discernible in the national church, represented by Bennett's parson, whose sermon is bland to the point of absolute meaninglessness, and by Miller's vicar who has leaned so far to

A moment from the West End production – the sketch 'Bread Alone', caricaturing behaviour in restaurants.

accommodate the young that he has reduced God to a trendy caricature: 'God is as old as he feels and that's the message I'm trying to get across to you youngsters.' As for the monarchy, it has become a mere public image, available for the price of a ticket: 'They're not worth the fifteen shillings,' observes Moore in the 'Royal Box' sketch. British intellectual life has declined into the near-meaningless babble of linguistic philosophers: 'Are you using "yes" in its affirmative sense here?' asks Miller, in the London version of 'Words … and things', now a dialogue between two dons (himself and Bennett), and receives the answer, 'No, no.' The nation's past glories are sentimentally mythologized ('The Aftermyth of War');[3] attitudes to sex are hypocritical (the 'Bollard' sketch, in which homosexuals pretend to be straight, and a Miller monologue about visiting a porn shop); and the law is

---

[3] Though this sketch caused less outrage in London than in Brighton, the cartoonist Nicholas Garland recalls that 'the actor Sebastian Shaw, who was a good friend of mine, was simply beside himself with rage about it'.

a barbarous ass (in one sketch capital punishment is justified as being a mere 'six of the best' for a naughty schoolboy). Culture has become absurdly precious and elitist, as evidenced by Moore's Britten and Schubert *Lieder* parodies, the mock-German of the latter emphasizing that most concert audiences have no idea what the words mean. British theatre is obsessed with the perpetual staging of Shakespeare plays which have long since become meaningless – this sketch (a nonsensical high-speed mock-Shakespeare play) has the deeply ironic title 'So That's The Way You Like It'. Though *Beyond the Fringe* had not set out to be satirical, it had gradually developed into a devastating survey of the state of Britain in 1960.

Its effect on at least some of its audience was powerful. The humorist Tony Hendra recalls:

> When I went up to Cambridge University in the early 1960s it was to complete my studies as a Benedictine monk ... But then I bought a ticket for *Beyond the Fringe*. I went into the show a monk, and I emerged having completely lost my vocation. I didn't know things could be so funny. I didn't realize that authority was so absurd. The next day I went round to the Footlights Club and asked if I could join.

Hendra performed in cabaret for a while, then moved to the USA, where he edited a string of humorous magazines. Much later he returned to Britain and worked on *Spitting Image*.

Harold Hobson's opposite number on the *Observer* was a quarter of a century his junior, and had no difficulty in understanding the 'ultimate attitude' of *Beyond the Fringe*. Kenneth Tynan, born in 1927, the illegitimate son of a businessman, had been easily the most prominent and flamboyant undergraduate at Oxford in the years immediately after the war. Becoming the *Observer* drama critic in 1954, he did much to change British theatre by championing *Look Back in Anger* in 1956 as 'the best young play of its decade'. By 1961 he had, for some while, been bemoaning the lack of political cabaret in Britain. A few months before *Beyond the Fringe* came to London, Tynan had suggested in the *Observer* that 'the theatre as a whole has been infected, and injured, by our weakness in the tiny, ancillary department of satirical cabaret' which could 'pierce to the quick of the ulcer'. He pointed to such American satirical performers as Mort Sahl, Lenny Bruce, Mike Nichols and Elaine May, and asked, what was there in England?

His *Observer* review of *Beyond the Fringe* was headlined 'English Satire Advances into the Sixties', but curiously Tynan did not use the word 'satire' in the review itself. He began it by describing the oddly sepulchral set which the Donaldson–Albery management had thought fit to provide for the Fortune Theatre stage:

The curtain rises on what might be a crypt, or perhaps a denuded wine-cellar. It is anyway the kind of place into which the late Ted Slaughter used to lure his leading ladies, preparatory to hurling them down a disused sump. On the right-hand side of the stage a flight of stone steps leads up to a sort of platform. To the left of centre, and partly hidden beneath the platform, is a grand piano. Somewhere to the rear a flying buttress is distinctly visible.

Tynan then gave an account of the opening sketch ('Steppes in the Right Direction', with Moore as the Russian who plays 'God Save the Queen'), and continued:

The entire scene lasts only a few minutes; I have described it at such length and in such detail because it is the exordium of *Beyond the Fringe*, which I take to be the funniest revue that London has seen since the Allies dropped the bomb on Hiroshima. Future historians may well thank me for providing them with a full account of the moment when English comedy took its first decisive step into the second half of the twentieth century.

The show began as a late-night experiment at last year's Edinburgh Festival, since when it has been shrewdly revised and much expanded... Among other marvels, Mr Miller gives us a hearty, broad-minded vicar, exhorting his lads to 'get the violence off the street and into the churches where it belongs'; a squirming teacher of linguistic philosophy, frenetically distinguishing between 'why-questions' and 'how-questions'; and... a condemned man, persistently asking the question we would all ask in that extremity: 'Will it hurt?'

Mr Moore satirizes folk-singers, fashionable composers, and the collaboration of Peter Pears and Benjamin Britten; during the interval, he crops up in the orchestra pit, tinkling away like a local incarnation of Erroll Garner. Mr Cook, meanwhile, qualifies thrice for the revue anthologies: once as a Beaverbrook journalist, nervously protesting that he has not ditched his liberal principles, and proudly declaring that he still dares, when drunk, to snigger at his employer;[4] again as the Prime Minister, casually tearing up a letter from an old-age pensioner and again as a Pinteresque outcast who would have liked to be a judge ...

Mr Bennett, in manner the mildest of the quartet, is perhaps the most pungent in effect. One will not readily forget the oleaginous blandness with which [he] delivers a sermon on the text: 'My brother Esau is an hairy man, but I am a smooth man.'

I have omitted the collective numbers, among them a devastating attack on Civil Defence, and the only successful parody of Shakespeare that I have ever heard. Certainly *Beyond the Fringe* lacks a great deal. It has no slick coffee-bar

---

[4] This sketch, 'The Sadder and Wiser Beaver', is still bitingly relevant today if 'Murdoch' is substituted for 'Beaverbrook'.

scenery, no glib one-line blackouts, no twirling dancers in tight trousers, no sad ballets for fisherwomen clad in fishnet stockings, no saleable kitsch. For these virtues of omission we must all be grateful; but it can justly be urged against the show that it is too parochial, too much obsessed with BBC voices and BBC attitudes, too exclusively concerned with taunting the accents and values of John Betjeman's suburbia. *Beyond the Fringe* is anti-reactionary without being progressive. It goes less far than one could have hoped, but immeasurably farther than one had any right to expect.

*

Jonathan Miller afterwards claimed, rather irritably, that Tynan had 'shoved this banner [satire] into our hands'. Alan Bennett writes, 'Whether *Beyond the Fringe* was satire was much debated ... It scarcely mattered, as there was no debate about how funny it was.'

Three days after it had opened, a *Daily Herald* reporter, Alan Dick, took Miller, Cook and Bennett to lunch at the Caprice, 'London's show-busiest restaurant' (Moore was absent, 'rehearsing with a band in Southampton'). Miller gave Dick a donnish analysis of *Beyond the Fringe*: 'Our humour is really a social commentary. But it is a highly personal thing, too ...' Dick wrote that they were 'overgrown schoolboys ... They had been told a Rolls-Royce was waiting for them, but did not believe it. I left Dr Miller rushing across the street yelling: "Gosh! It really *is* a Rolls." '

The Rolls made another appearance in the press. In the show's second week, the *Daily Mail* reported that Bennett 'performs at the Fortune Theatre in the evening – returning to Oxford in a Rolls-Royce lent by impresario Donald Albery to lecture at the university during the day. "Fortunately, I've had an easy term with only three lectures a week," he said. "So I can fit in both jobs with ease." ' In this case it really wasn't a Rolls. 'It was just a hired car,' says Bennett, 'and it wasn't every night, it was about three or four nights a week.' He claims that he 'wasn't getting any better' at his Oxford teaching, 'though the celebrity of the revue to some degree compensated my pupils for the shortcomings of the tuition'.

Needing a London *pied-à-terre*, he rented a basement bedsitter from Jonathan Miller, who had bought a house in Camden, and was leading a similarly double life. 'Every night after the curtain falls on *Beyond the Fringe*,' wrote another reporter, 'Dr Miller chugs on his Lambretta up the darkened Camden High Street ... Every morning he chugs down again on his way to the London Hospital, where he does post-mortems by day.' (Barry Humphries says he remembers John Betjeman talking about *Beyond the Fringe*, 'and he hadn't really cared for it. "But I liked Jonathan Miller," he said, "because he's a doctor, so he must be a kind man." ') Dudley Moore recalls that 'when *Beyond the Fringe* took off ... I was living in a small room that cost me ten shillings a week and I stayed there. I drove a silly little car, a 1935 Austin box car, which I finally had to abandon on the side of the road. I bought another car for £40.' Peter Cook rented a flat in Battersea with his girlfriend.

Only a week after the show had opened, Parlophone Records set up their equipment in the Fortune Theatre for two performances, with George Martin producing, and extracts from *Beyond the Fringe* were soon issued as an LP. Michael Billington says that the disc, which made it possible to learn the show by heart, had an enormous influence on his generation of twenty-somethings: 'At parties, we would recap the sketches with a trainspotter's line-by-line accuracy, in much the way that we had replayed *Goon Show* sketches at school. The show quickly acquired a mythical power for the people of my age.' The journalist Christopher Hitchens, then still a schoolboy, has similar recollections:

> At my boarding school, the authorities didn't quite know what to do when the show became a bestselling record. The players were Oxbridge types, after all, and the Edinburgh Festival was 'culture'. But somehow the boys who found it funny and could do all the scenes from memory were just those boys who always set a bad example.

Meanwhile, despite the show's immediate and phenomenal success, the relationship between the four *Fringe* cast members remained as edgy as it had been at that first lunch, a year and a half earlier. Bennett still felt that his own performing and writing skills were inferior to Cook's vast powers of comic invention, especially when Cook was performing his coalminer–judge monologue, 'Sitting on the Bench':

> Peter could tap a flow of mad verbal inventiveness that nothing could stem…
> He would sit there in his old raincoat and brown trilby, rocking slightly as he wove his ever more exuberant fantasies…I had the spot in the show immediately following Peter's monologue, which was scheduled to last five minutes or so but would often last for fifteen, when I would be handed an audience so weak from laughter I could do nothing with them.

Bennett was also resentful at what he saw as a paucity of writing credits: 'I did have a hand in some of the best stuff in the "Aftermyth of War" and the "Civil Defence" sketches…I didn't get much credit for this at the time and that rankled. Peter was so fertile and Jonathan so articulate that it was generally assumed they were responsible for the bulk of the writing.' In fact there were credits in the London programme; as well as being named for having written his own monologues, Bennett is identified as the author of 'Words…and Things' (the philosophy sketch); but it is true that 'Aftermyth of War' and 'Civil Defence' are simply credited to 'The Company'.

As in Footlights days, Miller attracted a disproportionate amount of attention in the press; even Tynan's review was adorned with a portrait photo and brief biography of him (an honour not awarded to the others); whereas in Bennett's view, Miller was not very skilful at handling the audience: 'He gets bored very easily and would often throw the whole performance away because the audience had failed to respond to some remark. As often as not they hadn't heard it, as he talked too fast. His boredom would annoy Dudley, who is a very conscientious performer, plugging away right till the end even on a bad matinée.'

For his part, Miller hugely admired Bennett's performing skills: 'He had a sort of pin-sharp accuracy ... of portraiture ... He was a miniaturist ... perfect ... ' Yet the two of them got on badly offstage. 'I felt,' says Miller, 'that I was regarded by [Alan] as a sort of frivolous, non-contributing dilettante, whose capering around on stage got more attention than he, the diligent writer, got.' Bennett agrees that they 'were always getting on one another's nerves ... Once when Jonathan was being more than usually grandiloquent, and I was being particularly sour, he, with characteristic extravagance, threw a tea service at me. Though, again characteristically, it missed.' Even Moore, who by nature wanted to get on well with everybody, and at first often dined with Bennett before the show, eventually experienced his disapproval. 'There was one sketch,' Moore recalls,

> where an interviewer was supposed to be asking Alan something ... Jonathan had tried, Peter had tried, and then, last but least, I tried it. And it never used to go down well until I started doing my usual performing bit, which was trying to get in with the audience, and twinkling at them, and stuff – which was something Alan did not approve of. And I remember coming offstage having done that, and I said, 'I thought that was the most wonderful performance of that particular sketch – terrific, wasn't it?' And he said, 'No, I thought it was the worst performance ever.' And from then on he never spoke to me. It was as though he'd never met me. We never went out for a meal again – nothing.

Yet despite these tensions, Bennett says that during the years of *Beyond the Fringe*, 'I laughed more than I can ever remember since.' Peter Cook has written, 'Alan was delightfully shockable. It gave me enormous pleasure to come up with some piece of smut and watch him writhe and moan in agony or amusement, stuffing his handkerchief into his mouth.'

Bennett recalls that one evening Harold Macmillan himself came to see *Beyond the Fringe*, and that 'Peter therefore went several steps further [in his Macmillan impersonation], remarking on the Prime Minister's presence in the audience.' According to his biographer Harry Thompson, Cook added this sentence to the monologue: 'When I've a spare evening, there's nothing I like better than to wander over to a theatre and sit there listening to a group of sappy, urgent, vibrant young satirists, with a stupid great grin spread all over my silly old face.' Bennett continues, 'Macmillan buried his face in the programme, and the audience, out of embarrassment, gradually froze. This didn't stop Peter. On he plunged.'

Eventually, after *Beyond the Fringe* had been running at the Fortune Theatre for almost a year, Lord Scarborough, who was then the Lord Chamberlain, brought the Queen to see the show.[5] Bennett was warned that she was coming, and was asked to omit the word 'erection' from one of his lines. 'I priggishly refused,' he says. 'I must be one of the few people who have said "erection" in front of the Queen…I don't suppose either of us profited from the experience.'

It was not until some months had passed, with the show still packed out every night, that the four performers entirely woke up to the fact that they were being grossly underpaid by the management. As Willie Donaldson puts it, they were each receiving a mere £75 a week, while 'Albery and myself were pocketing £2000 every Friday'. Donaldson persuaded them that it was not in his hands, so they wrote to Albery requesting a meeting, and – according to Donaldson – he invited them to tea:

> Over seed cake and Earl Grey he patiently explained the economics of the theatre. 'Difficult times – rising costs – laundry – bricks and mortar – the successes have to pay for the flops – review the situation when I return from Juan les Pins in late September – have another cup of tea'…Miller and Co. retired in confusion and [Albery] and I…struggled along on £2000 a week, but only for the moment. When the show moved to New York we did a great deal better.

Since the beginning of the London run, there had been talk of transferring *Beyond the Fringe* to Broadway. Miller – who had been approached about playing Fagin in the film of Lionel Bart's musical *Oliver!* – was enthusiastic. 'If we go to New York,' he told a *Daily Express* reporter, 'I hope to get a job at the Columbia University – it's a good thing to have worked in the States. And pathology is particularly easy because all your patients are dead anyway.' Bennett (who 'buried himself under a pile of cushions' during this interview) claimed that he would rather remain an academic: 'I don't want to do this revue thing permanently…If I was offered a decent job [at Oxford] I'd rather stay.' Miller protested, 'But, Alan, if we go to the States it'll make us rich for a long time. It'll give us such academic freedom we can even take an unpaid job for a year.' Bennett remained unimpressed, but Moore said he wanted to participate in American jazz, adding, 'I've suddenly got the feel for

---

[5] John Johnston records this in his book *The Lord Chamberlain's Blue Pencil* (1990), and it is confirmed in the *Daily Mail* (2 March 1962), which states that the Queen saw the show 'last Wednesday night'. Harry Thompson records that she was sitting between the Lord Chamberlain and the Earl of Home (later Sir Alec Douglas-Home).

money.' Cook said he would go to America only 'if I get a post in the Kennedy Administration'. In any case, he had a scheme which required his presence in London – and that of the other three – for some time to come. 'Peter Cook,' noted a reporter two months after *Beyond the Fringe* had opened in London, 'has sunk his savings into a new venture that will involve them all – the establishment of The Establishment.'

Peter Cook – with cigar – gives the *Evening Standard* award a quizzical look; Miller, Bennett and Moore seem a little more enthusiastic.

3

....

Satire was in

John Wells writes that 'the great myth of the satire boom' had caught on by the summer of 1961. 'According to the myth... The Establishment... grew naturally and directly out of *Beyond the Fringe*. In fact it had been thought of by Peter Cook in Cambridge a year before *Beyond the Fringe* began.'

Before going up to Cambridge in 1957, Cook had spent some time in Germany, and in Berlin he had visited one of the current satirical cabaret clubs, the Porcupine. 'The show was terribly bad... the humour was very juvenile... but I thought... "Why isn't there the equivalent of this in London?" For a long time my major fear was that somebody would do the obvious and start it before me.'

The Porcupine was an inheritor of a long-standing European tradition of satirical clubs that went back to 1881. In that year, a young painter called Rodolphe Salis opened a club called the Chat Noir in Montmartre. Its star performer, singing blackly comic songs about low life, was Aristide Bruant, who appears in paintings by Toulouse-Lautrec in his characteristic broad-brimmed black hat, with a scarlet scarf around his neck and a flowing black cape. At the turn of the century the cabaret movement spread to Barcelona, where some of the publicity material for Els Quatre Gats (The Four Cats) was designed by the teenage Picasso, and to Munich, where Die Elf Scharfrichter (The Eleven Executioners) featured the radical German playwright Frank Wedekind, who accompanied himself on the guitar as he sang *Moritaten*, blackly comic songs about crime, chiefly murder. Bertolt Brecht saw Wedekind performing some years later, and described him singing 'in a brittle voice, slightly monotonous, and quite untrained. No singer ever gave me such a shock, such a thrill... ugly, brutal, dangerous.' The song that opens Brecht's *Threepenny Opera* (1928) shows the influence of Wedekind: it is a *Moritat* cataloguing the crimes of Mack the Knife.

Wedekind was a contributor to the weekly German satirical magazine *Simplicissimus*. An issue two years after its foundation, in 1898, which jeered at the Kaiser's foreign policy, landed Wedekind and an illustrator in gaol for six months. Nevertheless the magazine continued its lampooning. As Jonathan Miller puts it, 'European satire thrived best under the old-fashioned, indolently repressive regimes in which offensive comment was punished by short terms of imprisonment rather than by execution.'

Berlin is widely thought of as the home of the best satirical clubs; yet its first political cabaret, the Buntes Theater, opened in 1901, was tame and inoffensive. More radical and innovative material was staged by a group convened by the Jewish actor–director Max Reinhardt. Calling themselves Schall und Rauch ('Sound and Smoke'), they featured a character called Serenissimus, a spoof of the Kaiser himself, who sat in the 'royal box' and interrupted the performance with ridiculous comments.[1]

The First World War hardly interrupted Berlin night-life, and during the 1920s its cabarets went in for lavish production styles, with syncopated bands on stage and sophisticated costumes – re-created with a fair degree of accuracy in the 1966 musical *Cabaret*. As the Nazis began to seize power, Werner Finck, front man of a cabaret called The Catacombs, would raise his arm as if giving the Hitler salute, and then say, '*That's* how deep we're in the shit.' If there were uniformed Nazis in the audience, he would ask them politely if it would help if he spoke slowly. 'No, I'm not Jewish,' he would add. 'I only *look* intelligent.'

Surprisingly, Finck's cabaret remained open for a while after the Nazi takeover in 1933, but most performers fled the country, especially if they were Jewish. The Third Reich tried to initiate what it called 'positive cabaret', which would applaud Nazi aims and mock those of their enemies; but of course this was a total failure, and in 1937 Goebbels banned the performance of any political material. Some German exiles established cabarets abroad. Thomas Mann's daughter Erika ran the celebrated Peppermill in Zurich, until the Swiss government was disgracefully persuaded by Germany to object to it, whereupon she moved it to Holland. Erika Mann was able to escape the Nazis when the poet W.H. Auden agreed to marry her so she could have a British passport.

After the war, many cabaret performers and owners went back into business in Germany, among them Werner Finck, who formed a cabaret collective in Munich. The subjects for their satire now included the national folly that had brought about Hitler, and also the policies of Chancellor Adenauer. Jonathan Miller noted in 1961 that, by then, there were a few

---

[1] Berlin and several other German cities also offered a different form of cabaret, known disparagingly as 'Tingeltangel'. This was more like a Soho strip joint of the 1950s or 1960s. Soubrettes would sing sexy songs, sell naughty postcards and wander provocatively among the male audience, encouraging them to buy more drinks and maybe make sexual assignations. Josef von Sternberg's 1929 film *The Blue Angel*, which brought Marlene Dietrich to fame, is set in a Tingeltangel rather than a satirical cabaret.

cabarets in East Berlin, 'but they deal with the abuses of a bureaucracy: a form of satirical criticism which is tolerated and even encouraged by the Communists. All-out political satire, on the other hand, would not stand a chance.'

John Wells recalled, 'I lived in Germany for a year in the 1950s, and arsed around a bit, and I used to go to a lot of satirical night-clubs – and so did Peter Cook. There was a direct influence of those. Peter went to Berlin and saw satirical night-clubs. I was absolutely amazed by it – no one had had them in England.'

During his last year at Cambridge, Cook found an ally for his scheme of opening a London cabaret club. The Footlights' treasurer, Nicholas Luard, had been at school at Winchester and had done his National Service as an officer in the Guards,[2] but had also spent a year painting in Paris, and had tasted its bohemian night-life. 'We'd both seen political–satirical cabaret in France and Germany,' recalls Luard. 'We felt an instinctive repugnance for the blandness and patronizing condescension of the Macmillan years … We had an idea, no more than a shadowy fragment of an idea, to open a little theatre in London where we could present the sort of satirical entertainment we'd seen abroad.'

Beyond the Fringe was fulfilling some of that hope, yet there were limits to what could be performed on the public stage, thanks to the powers of the Lord Chamberlain. 'Until one could escape his bloodshot gaze,' writes Jonathan Miller, 'there was no real hope of putting the last edge on the satirical scalpel. The privacy of a club offered a unique opportunity.' Cook, as usual, put it more bluntly: he wanted a place 'where we could be more outrageous than we could be on stage'.

The term 'The Establishment', which Cook adopted for his prospective club, had been coined a little while earlier by a *Spectator* columnist, Henry Fairlie, to describe the invisible web of (generally right-wing) power that controls British life more effectively than such public and open institutions as Parliament. The use of this name for a satirical night-club was, of course, intended to be ironic; though it transpired rather later that there was a further irony, in that members of the Establishment (in Fairlie's sense) became the club's chief patrons.

By midsummer of 1961, a few weeks after the London opening of *Beyond*

---

[2] Luard says of this: 'I did a very odd National Service. I was commissioned into the Coldstream Guards, but I spent most of my time with the Special Forces in Germany. I was one of a number of people who had been picked for being athletic and having special language skills (I'd had a Russian nurse when I was a child, and I spoke Russian well), and in the event of nuclear war we were to be left fifteen miles behind enemy lines, so that we could identify targets for the Allied forces. They would then allow you four hours to get out, before making a nuclear strike on the targets. And I spent some time in Germany on these exploratory exercises, to see how far you could run in four hours! It was a bit like the Civil Defence sketch in *Beyond the Fringe*!'

the Fringe, Cook had found suitable premises at 18 Greek Street, Soho, where the Club Tropicana ('All-Girl Strip Revue – Dancing to 3-D Sound') had recently been forced to close following a police raid. A considerable amount of cash was needed to refit and redecorate the place; Luard was able to put up most of this, using family money – his father was in the oil industry – and Cook generated an income for the project by soliciting subscriptions: three guineas for a year's membership, two guineas if paid in advance of the opening, and life membership for twenty guineas (life members received a free pin-up of Macmillan). Subscriptions rolled in, with several famous individuals not only subscribing but expressing their willingness to be mentioned in publicity as supporters: Graham Greene, J.B. Priestley, Yehudi Menuhin, Lionel Bart, Brian Rix of the Whitehall Theatre, Ben Travers (the elderly writer of farces), Gerald Gardiner QC, and – described as 'the prize' by the *Evening Standard* – Sir Isaiah Berlin.

Fleet Street gave the project plenty of sympathetic publicity. 'The Establishment aims to be London's first satirical night-club,' wrote a *Daily Mail* reporter.

Peter Cook outside 18 Greek Street, before its conversion into The Establishment.

To the seedy building…that used to house the Club Tropicana…it is bringing 'tough, accurate, and above all *funny* satire'…'We don't want it to be expensive,' said Peter Cook, 'because we don't want to have to play to the usual silly people.'…It may be that London will at last have a counterpart to San Francisco's hungry i, which launched Mort Sahl.

Indeed, the joke was going round that The Establishment would be a 'Mort Sahlon'.

Cook hired Sean Kenny, who had designed the set for the London *Beyond the Fringe* (and, far more memorably, for *Oliver!*), to plan the club's interior. 'No plush, nothing Caribbean,' reported the *Observer* in June 1961. 'Everything will be natural: wood, steel, glass, that sort of thing.' Besides the ground floor restaurant–bar, with a small stage, there would be an upstairs library with a tickertape news service and the current papers and journals, intended for 'members who simply want to spend a lunchtime talking rather than laughing about the fate of the world'. Cook and Luard – now officially 'Cook & Luard Productions' – provided themselves with an office; on the wall they hung a mask caricaturing Macmillan.

At the end of September, a few days before the opening, Cook held a press launch, wearing the mask for photographers. He explained that the targets of sketches in the club would range 'from Macmillan to Macmillan…It will not necessarily be left-wing…But because the Conservatives are…in power, it will, of course, be easier to attack what is there. Attacking the Labour Party at the moment seems a bit like robbing a blind man.'

There would be an hour's cabaret at 9.30 each night, performed by a resident company, consisting of 'John Bird, a Royal Court Theatre producer and an ardent Spurs fan; John Fortune, director of the 1960 Cambridge Footlights revue and a shark-fisher; Jeremy Geidt, star of *How to Fly an Aeroplane*, an instructional film for the RAF;[3] David Walsh, a rep actor from Canterbury; and Hazel Wright, who appeared in the London production of *Once Upon a Mattress*.'

On the strength of his Cambridge production of *A Resounding Tinkle*, John Bird, abandoning his Ph.D., had been given a trainee director's job at the Royal Court. 'I directed two shows there, one of which was *Brecht on Brecht* with Lotte Lenya – I was very, very frightened of her, because I was only twenty-two, but she was wonderful.' Nicholas Garland, who was then a stage manager at the Court, says, 'John was a brilliant director – he was assistant to Bill Gaskill, but in many ways I thought he was the better of the two.'

John Fortune had done plenty of straight theatre at Cambridge: 'When

---

[3] Geidt says this was Cook's invention: 'As far as I know, I never made any such film!' Nor has John Fortune ever fished for sharks.

John Bassett's membership card for The Establishment.

John Barton directed both parts of *Henry IV*, I played a small part and was his assistant director, which meant going to his rooms while he paced about and flicked ash off his long cheroots. There were a lot of good people in that – Ian McKellen, Derek Jacobi, Clive Swift.' The 1960 Footlights revue Fortune had directed was *Pop Goes Mrs Jessop* – 'a very Bristolian title', says Fortune, who hails from that city, where his father was a commercial traveller.[4] Cook was in the cast, and Fortune was fascinated by his way of inventing characters: 'You know Olivier used to start building up a character with make-up? Well, Peter usually started an idea for a sketch with the *name* of a character. The first thing I ever saw him do at the Footlights was about a woman called The Widow Speak (the widow's peak). The name would come first, and then the fantasy would start.'

Fortune emphasizes that *Pop Goes Mrs Jessop* – unlike its predecessor, Bird's *Last Laugh* – was entirely non-political:

---

[4] The family name is Wood; he changed it to Fortune, his mother's maiden name, to avoid confusion with the actor John Wood.

If somebody had said to us, 'Are you trying to be satirical?' we wouldn't have known what it meant. I wasn't a member of any political party. I'd flirted with Trotskyism, but only because I had a friend at Cambridge who said that if we joined the Trotskyites we could go down and live in some caves on Dartmoor, and there'd be lots of girls.

After Cambridge, Fortune had not intended to become a professional performer:

I'd had a wonderful English teacher at school, and I felt I wanted to do something like that, and I went to the Workers' Educational Association, and said, 'I want to bring D.H. Lawrence to the Nottingham coalfields and all that,' and they said, 'Certainly, we'll pay you £5 a week.' And then Peter said he'd had this idea of opening a club, and would I be interested, and he mentioned John Bird, whom I knew a bit, and I thought it was going to be more fun. Eventually I was paid £20 a week [at The Establishment], and my father was only earning sixteen, so I thought that was very good.

John Bird and Jeremy Geidt think it was £25.

Fortune explains that originally it was not intended that he and Bird should appear at The Establishment themselves:

John was working at the Royal Court, and Peter of course was still doing *Beyond the Fringe*, and the original idea was that the three of us would write the Establishment show, and I would direct it, and we'd get actors to perform it. And I did audition people for two days, at the Fortune Theatre, but we didn't really find anyone – except Barry Humphries, who had recently arrived from Australia.

I thought he was a genius. For his audition he came on the stage and started to measure out an imaginary body that was supposedly lying there, but it had very strange proportions, so that as he went on you began to imagine this monster. It was very funny and disturbing, and I thought he was wonderful, but there seemed no possibility that he would go in for ensemble playing.

Humphries describes himself in those days:

I was an awestruck colonial, not certain whether I was meant to be an actor, or what I was cut out to do. (I think when your whole youth is spent with parents saying, 'When are you going to grow up?' or 'What are you *really* going to do?', you worry about what you're cut out to do for the rest of your life.) I suppose I was a would-be satirist, because life in the 1950s in Melbourne, where I had grown up, was tremendously claustrophobic, and I was reacting against that in the Dadaist sort of things I did in my early days. And when I saw these London guys doing their satirical stuff, I thought, 'Yes, they're fellow spirits.' But Bird and Fortune kept on doing endless ad libs of their own, and I found myself being marginalized, not being asked to perform. So I drifted off.

Fortune continues, 'The only suitable person we found was Jeremy Geidt, who was a good straight man.' Geidt, some years older than Bird and Fortune, was an ex-public schoolboy who had trained in acting at the Old Vic Theatre School and then worked in rep. Fortune, who describes him as 'a jobbing actor', recalls, 'Jeremy's favourite bit of advice to me about performing – because in the end we decided we'd have to perform at The Establishment ourselves – was to wear a signet ring, and when you make your entrance, you rap it on the side of the door, and even on a Wednesday matinée in Blackpool the audience will sit up and take notice!' Bird says that Geidt was 'a boisterous, wonderful straight man, with terrific energy – he could hold the whole thing together'. Peter Cook once described him as 'great at falling over and farting'. Eleanor Bron, who joined the performing team a little later, wrote in her *Pillow Book*: 'There is no one to touch Jeremy for sheer relish in the matter of pouring forth filth.'

John Bird says that the decision to perform themselves at The Establishment was only *pro tem*:

> The people we liked wouldn't do it for the money, and the people who would do it for the money were no good. And Peter said, 'Why don't you do it?' And I'd never really performed, even at Cambridge, and I didn't think I was a performer. He said, 'Do it for a month or two until it gets going, and then we can get someone else.'

Early publicity for The Establishment promised that 'the boys will come in from *Beyond the Fringe* to perform at half-past midnight.' On the day before the opening of the club, the *Evening Standard* confirmed this: 'The *Beyond the Fringe* team will do the late-night show impromptu.' But Cook seems to have made no effort to see that this promise was kept. In reality, only the musically tireless Dudley Moore would commit himself – he was delighted to play late-night jazz in the basement with a bassist and drummer. Alan Bennett had to get back to Oxford on several nights a week, and a night-club was not really his scene. Cook tried to cover up his absence by telling the *Daily Express*: 'Alan Bennett is really behind the catering.'

Jonathan Miller agreed to appear in one of a series of short films, devised by Cook, that were to be shown between live sketches: a mock cigarette commercial, in which a surgeon operating on a patient with lung cancer has a cigarette in his own mouth. 'To help him concentrate,' says the voice-over, 'Dr Gatti smokes filter-tip cigarettes.' Jeremy Geidt also remembers 'two doctored wartime films of Hitler dancing outside the railway carriage having taken the French surrender, and a super one of Nazi storm-troopers marching back and forth to "The Lambeth Walk" '. George Melly observes that Cook was pioneering what we now call 'mixed media' by interspersing the live acts with these film clips.

Miller recalls making one live appearance on stage at The Establishment, possibly on the opening night, but it was 'rather humiliating – I fell absolutely flat. I can't remember what I did, but it was greeted with deafening silence. I thought, well, this is it – it confirms that I ought not to be going on with comedy.' Geidt says that Miller is underestimating his contributions: 'Jonathan appeared more than once – I remember we did a bit together about the Berlin police firing water cannons at rioters – and he didn't "fall flat".'

Cook had decided to recruit another performer for the opening night, whom he had not yet met, but who had a growing reputation. John Wells had won excellent reviews for his part in the 1961 Oxford Theatre Group Edinburgh Fringe show, *Late Night Final*. He had now left Oxford and taken a job teaching modern languages at Eton. 'People asked me to do the first night of The Establishment as a sort of second set,' Wells recalled. He came to the club a few days before the opening, meeting Cook for the first time among the builders' rubble. 'He was incredibly well mannered,' said Wells, 'very English and polite.' A sign had now been erected on the front of the building: 'LONDON'S FIRST SATIRICAL NIGHT-CLUB'.

*

The Establishment was to open on Thursday, 5 October 1961. The previous Sunday's *Observer* review section carried a front-page article on satire by Jonathan Miller. 'The Establishment,' he wrote, 'represents a research station in which we might see developed those weapons necessary for the final overthrow of the neo-Gothic stranglehold of Victorian good taste.' Miller developed this military motif:

> The ranks are drawn up and the air resounds with the armourer's hammer. When battle is joined one can only hope that blood will be drawn. That 'The Establishment' will be attacking from without rather than firing off pop-guns from within, for the entertainment of one big happy family.

But he admitted to doubts: 'The success of this project is seriously threatened by a subtle defence with which the members of "The Establishment" [in the Henry Fairlie sense, rather than the club] protect themselves against these new attacks. Cook is already somewhat disturbed by the number of applications for membership which bear the post-mark SW1.' Cook himself remarked to the *Evening Standard* that there were too many people joining from Kensington: 'These are the people he aims to attack, not to make laugh.'

In fact satire's audiences have always tended to come from the very section of society that is being satirized. For example *The Beggar's Opera* and Hogarth's sets of satirical drawings were sell-outs with the very beau monde they mocked, and a modern Hogarth, the German artist George

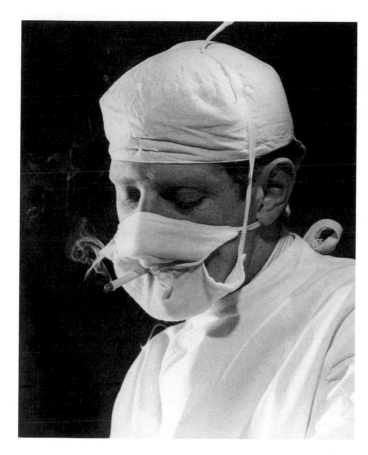

Jonathan Miller as a chain-smoking surgeon in one of the short films shown at The Establishment.

Grosz, who flourished during the Weimar Republic and exposed the tacky sexuality of 1920s Berlin, sold thousands of copies to the bourgeoisie who were his targets, even during the period of hyper-inflation when few people could afford to buy books. Even in the highly repressive USSR it was possible to observe that satire can appeal to those who were being satirized. The writer Vitali Vitaliev recalls of one Moscow theatre in the Brezhnev years:

> People went there just to hear something even mildly anti-Soviet, because the performances were very politically astute (by Soviet standards, of course). And what's interesting is that the Party *apparatchiks* loved going there. Usually half of the seats for every performance were booked by the Central Committee of the Communist Party! They liked jokes about themselves, apart from the stupidest ones. And now all these documents have been declassified from the Soviet archives, it turns out that even Brezhnev actually liked jokes about himself, and allegedly even invented some.[5]

[5] On the other hand Osip Mandelstam lost his life after writing a satirical poem in which he compared Stalin's moustache to a cockroach.

John Fortune says that the performers at The Establishment were embarrassed by Jonathan Miller's article heralding the club: 'I'm sure poor Jonathan thought he was doing the right thing, but it was disastrous to say we were going to tear everything down. As Peter used to say, "The heyday of satire was Weimar Germany – and see how it prevented the rise of Adolf Hitler!" ' Miller himself says that today the article makes him squirm. It inspired several letters to the *Observer*. Michael Spittal of Nottingham wrote that he had enjoyed *Beyond the Fringe*, but 'felt that this was not the stuff to make governments quake'; and W. James of London remarked that Miller and his companions were 'gentlemen' – 'the top people don't mind being "taken off" by *them*. I wonder if they would turn up at a club run by [Arnold] Wesker, with John Osborne doing a Mort Sahl.'

Four and a half thousand subscriptions had now been paid, and Cook was getting worried about space – he hoped that the members would be 'small enough to be stacked in tiers'. The London County Council had insisted that he spend £15,000 on what he called 'useless fire escapes', and he had also been obliged to take out insurance against libel suits. To the *Daily Express*, he pretended that the whole thing was a hoax: 'The first-night lot are going to find themselves playing bingo – there'll be nothing else for them to do.'

On the opening day, John Wells taught his last class of the afternoon at Eton, then slipped away to catch the London train. Arriving in Greek Street, he found a scene of indescribable chaos: 'Television arc lights blazed above the crush, rich girls in lovely diaphanous dresses wriggled and squealed in the crowd, their rock-jawed escorts bellowing above the din. "Hello, Jeremy! You going to Antonia's thrash on Thursday?" Satire was in, and they were damned if they were going to miss a second of it.'

Inside The Establishment, Wells found the atmosphere tense and exciting, an echo of Berlin in the 1930s: 'The harsh wooden décor, the clusters of spotlights, the little stage, the wooden tables, the committed cast running through their lines for the last time. The only thing that was missing, it seemed, was the harsh clatter of the fascist jackboots.' And then, as the audience was let in, boots were indeed heard; but they proved to be 'the elastic-sided boots affected at that time by the go-getting jet set. The fickle stripe-shirted heathen were mincing in to worship the incarnation of their latest graven image.'

So many people streamed in that the doors soon had to be shut. *The Times* reported next morning that 'angry members … who had arrived after 9 p.m. … formed a disconsolate queue … "We have been told to refuse admission to everybody or we'll lose our licence," said the commissionaire on the door.' Among those who had managed to get in was Alan Bennett:

The thing I remember is John Sparrow [Warden of All Souls] and I think Ian

Gilmour [Tory journalist and politician] being near me in the audience, and also Patrick Leigh Fermor trying to get in – he'd been to see *Beyond the Fringe*, and written us a fan letter. He couldn't get in, and he was passing a note through the door, trying to get in. And I remember the tables being extremely narrow, and the food not being very nice.

The noise was immense. 'To add to the confusion,' writes Wells, 'ludicrous parodies of pressmen lurched and belched about the bar. Somewhere in a corner, far away above the heads of the crowd, vainly trying to compete with the roar of conversation, the actors moved through their entertainment.'

In Bird, Fortune and Geidt, Cook had acquired a perfectly balanced trio of performers (of the others mentioned in the advance publicity, David Walsh

Dudley Moore as The Establishment's basement attraction.

does not feature in recordings made at the club, and seems to have left fairly soon after the opening night; John Fortune describes Hazel Wright as 'a good actress and a funny girl', but she seems to have been given little chance by the men to make a mark). When they performed in the USA some while later, John Bird was described in the *San Francisco Chronicle* as 'roly-poly' and John Fortune as 'a beanpole with an alarmingly dyspeptic stare', while Geidt was praised for a 'far-out leer [which] gave his material a masterful touch of insanity'. A more analytical description comes from Kenneth Tynan, who noted that Geidt tended to be cast as 'sweaty brutes and insensitive rogues'; that Fortune, 'a mop-shaped young man with tremulous lips', generally played males who 'come under the heading of Insecure Ruling Class'; and that Bird, 'the most gifted of the Establishmentarians', specialized in 'complacency, in smiles knowingly smiled and pipes portentously sucked'.

With considerable assistance from Cook, they had written an hour-long show, to be performed twice nightly. Fortune recalls that on the first night they started very late, 'because of everybody trying to get in; and sitting *on* the stage was Harold Hobson of *The Sunday Times*, with his gammy foot. So we went on and did the first sketch, which was about the Crucifixion, with Hobson just a few inches away – frightening!' This sketch has not survived, but Fortune describes it: 'The basis of the joke is that I'm Christ, and Jeremy Geidt and John Bird are the crucified thieves on each side of me, on their own crosses, which are slightly lower than mine, as in all the pictures. It was really about class – they spoke in working-class voices, but I didn't.' Peter Cook recalled Geidt and Bird 'objecting that Jesus was (a) higher up than they were, and (b) getting all the attention'. Geidt is able to reconstruct the opening from memory:

> FORTUNE: (*upper-class*) Eli, Eli, lama sabachthani.
> BIRD: (*Cockney*) Eh?
> FORTUNE: I said, Eli, Eli, lama sabachthani. Forgive them, Lord, for they know not what they do.[6]
> GEIDT: (*Cockney*) They bloody well know what they're doing all right, mate.

Geidt says, 'Bird and I went on complaining – "Why are you getting all the vinegar sponges and that?" – and about "that bint down there washing your feet".' Fortune says, 'The punchline was me explaining that the preferential treatment was because "I've got a very influential father".'

Cook gives this sketch as an example of the 'extremely bad taste [that] flourished at The Establishment'. Several other sketches performed at the club dabbled in blasphemy. The writer David Nobbs recalls contributing a

---

[6] Geidt remarks: 'Of course, "Eli, Eli," etc., means "My God, my God, why hast thou forsaken me?" but no one seemed to notice.'

The regular cast at The Establishment: Eleanor Bron in front of John Fortune, John Bird and Jeremy Geidt.

monologue that began: 'How do you do. My name is God, and I'm here tonight because I'm omnipresent,' and John Bird performed one which has the stamp of Cook's own authorship:

> Who is the only true, revealed, living God, eh? And I can give you the answer to that. *Me*. So let's have a bit more of the grovelling about on the ground, in abject veneration, and a bit less of the shouts of 'Go home and stuff your head'. And what about a few more of the unsolicited free gift, sacrifices and all that? It is written, 'Render unto Caesar that which is Caesar's, and render unto God all the loose change you happen to be carrying about.'

Jeremy Geidt remembers 'another religious one, called "Strangler Martin", which came from a newspaper report that some bishop had said that "capital punishment is welcomed by criminals as it gives them the chance to see the light and repent". I was a sweaty Strangler Martin, alone on stage:'

GEIDT: Ha, ha, ha! My name is Strangler Martin. Raping and strangling are my delights!
(*Knock on door. Enter* FORTUNE.)
FORTUNE: Good evening. I am the Bishop of Norwich.
GEIDT: Why don't you fuck off, you stupid old cunt?

'That was quite shocking then,' continues Geidt,

and I don't remember much more, except Fortune reading the parable of the Prodigal Son with the lights dimming, and me coming back on as a moved and changed Strangler who now welcomed his capital punishment. Oh, and I do remember asking the bishop. ''Ow is masturbation in the eye of Our Lord?' and Fortune delicately wiping his eye and replying, 'I'm not quite certain.' It was all in very bad taste.

In the spring of 1962 there was an Establishment sketch about the new, recently consecrated Coventry Cathedral, which replaced the one destroyed in Second World War air raids. Fortune played its architect, Sir Basil Spence:

First of all, of course, we owe an enormous debt of gratitude to the German people for making this whole project possible in the first place. Second, we owe a debt of gratitude to the people of Coventry itself, who when asked to choose between having a cathedral and having hospitals, schools and houses, plumped immediately (I'm glad to say) for the cathedral, recognizing, I think, the need of any community to have a place where the whole community can gather together and pray for such things as hospitals, schools and houses.

He then speaks about the huge Graham Sutherland tapestry of Christ in glory, hanging behind the high altar:

Now we come to Sutherland's great travesty – er, tapestry…It was of course woven by French weavers. They managed to amplify and magnify every single splodge of paint on Graham's original doodle. In fact if you look very closely at the bottom right-hand corner you can see an amusing pencilled message which reads: 'I hope this is all right – Graham.'…Lots of people coming into the cathedral and being confronted by this great work have immediately said: 'Jesus Christ!'

The Lord Chamberlain would have censored all these sketches, and John Fortune says that the *raison d'être* of The Establishment was to perform what he would have banned:

The fact that we were going to open a club, to get round the Lord Chamberlain, meant that we had to do something worthy of that. So in a way our subject-matter was dictated by that censorship. And we could have gone in two general directions, nudity-and-sex, or politics, being able to say rude things about our masters. And because we were too busy finding out about sex in our private lives, politics was the thing.

John Bird disagrees: 'The idea of the club wasn't really to do more outrageous things. It fitted the emerging Swinging London scene, and it freed you from the constraints of conventional theatre – you could have a tiny stage and no set, and the audience's expectations were different.'

Lavatorial humour occasionally featured. John Wells recalled Jeremy Geidt performing a sketch 'which you'd recognize now as being straight alternative comedy, about the difficulty of removing a piece of shit from the inside of a lavatory bowl by pissing on it. And it went down absolutely as you'd imagine – people were appalled. Filth! It had nothing to do with satire.' According to the journalist Peter Lewis, who was in the audience, it did: he recalls it as being about David Astor, editor of the *Observer*: 'I was rather disgusted by it. He ends up by saying: "The question I can never resolve is, whether the weakness of my pee is insufficient to dissolve the strength of my shit." The idea was to pillory Astor as the *bien-pensant* liberal editor. But God knows we needed one. Why attack somebody who's on the right side?'

How conscious were they of following in the European tradition of satirical clubs? 'Not at all,' says John Fortune, 'because none of us had any idea what they were like. I supposed I'd seen *The Blue Angel*, but that was all.' John Bird admits to some expertise in literary satire:

My favourite poet was Pope – and still is – and I'd done a lot of reading in the eighteenth century. But it couldn't be a model, because the context, the forms and the audiences were so different. And all the people I admired in the genre, from the classical satirists to Brecht, seemed to have worked on such an elevated level that one couldn't imitate them either.

Bird explains that the sketches were neither entirely written nor totally improvised: 'We didn't improvise in the way the Americans improvised, which was to get on stage without any preparation. We would sit round the table and think of jokes.' Cook was in his element in these sessions. 'He would start on some typical train of fantasy,' says Fortune, 'and after an hour or so we'd have to beg him to stop, because we were laughing so much.'

A reporter from *The Times*, who had squeezed into The Establishment on the first night, noted that 'subjects for satire in the first evening's programme included Mr Macmillan, Lord Home [the Foreign Secretary], Mr Butler [the Home Secretary], and Mr Jomo Kenyatta.' The Establishment version of Macmillan was much the same as Peter Cook's; one sketch (which has survived in recordings made at the club) has him appointing a new cabinet minister and then forgetting the man's name:

MACMILLAN [John Fortune]: I believe he was with Neville at Munich. He was
one of the people who helped to wring that agreement out of – of – what the
devil was the little fellow's name? He had a moustache. Anyway, this fellow
has been politically dormant since then.
IAIN MACLEOD [Jeremy Geidt]: Hitler.
MACMILLAN: What?
BUTLER: Hitler.
MACMILLAN: I'd never appoint *him*, don't be stupid.

Macleod, Chairman of the Conservative Party, also featured in a sketch in
which he proposes that the electoral system be replaced by market research:

Elections as such are a most unreliable means of estimating a government's
popularity…Get away from all this voting business, which is hit or miss…
Send these market-research firms out into the country, [into] a random area,
like South Kensington…interviewing people, with key questions like, 'Do you
want to go on in peace and prosperity with the Conservatives, or do you want to
chance it on four years of socialist botching up?'

On this occasion Macleod was played by John Bird. 'I wasn't a mimic,' he
says. 'I remember doing George Brown [a Labour politician] quite
frequently, and not making any attempt at imitation. It was only later, when
I started doing Harold Wilson on television, that mimicry became
necessary.'

On the other hand Bird's act as Jomo Kenyatta, seen at the first night of
The Establishment, was certainly an impersonation – though not of
Kenyatta, as Bird explains:

The voice was actually an imitation of Jonathan Miller imitating an African
politician. He and I had once ad-libbed a conversation between two Africans – I
can't remember where, when or why. And I used that voice for every African
politician, including Idi Amin, though he didn't talk like that at all – the only
one who did was Hastings Banda.

Rather oddly, the Kenyatta sketch at The Establishment took the form of
a radio sports programme:

LINKMAN [Jeremy Geidt]: Sports Report – and Saturday's big game is the top-of-
the-league clash between Tottenham Hotspur and Burnley. And here in the
studio to discuss the prospects of this match we have Jomo Kenyatta. Would
you like to stick your neck out and make a prophecy, Jomo?
KENYATTA: Yes. Ah shall be perhaps de first Negro man to be Queen of
England.
LINKMAN: No, Jomo, what I really meant was a prophecy of the outcome of the
Spurs–Burnley encounter. Odds-on draw, do you think?

KENYATTA: Ah'm already consolidatin' mah effective position as de first Negro prime minister of Great Britain, an' shall soon be rushin' on to de assumin' of even more gigantic powers as de Queen.

LINKMAN: Well, that is very interesting, Jomo, but what our listeners really want to know is whether you think super-Spurs can make it three in a row for the FA Cup?

KENYATTA: It's no use thinkin' dat de grabbin' of state control can be achieved without de gutters an' streets washin' about in a bit of white man's blood. What ah have in mind is de collectin' together of vast quantities of de poisoned spears, creepin' about in de night with dem, and den, swish swoosh, suddenly hurlin' dem into de livin' quarters of Buckingham Palace, where de Queen will be receivin' dem in de fleshy parts of her body and topplin' from de throne… So it will not be long before ah'm appearin' on de balcony of de Palace, dressed up in de crown and de ceremonial skirts of de Queen, wavin' an' shoutin' to de crowds below.

'Ah shall be perhaps de first Negro man to be Queen of England': John Bird as Jomo Kenyatta.

John Bird says that nowadays, of course, such a sketch 'seems very, very un-politically correct and racist. And a more serious objection, perhaps, is that when I came to do it with Amin, it made a seriously monstrous creature into an affable buffoon.'

John Fortune recalls that, on the first night, he and Bird also performed a sketch about abortion. In this, Bird (a businessman) has taken Fortune (a doctor) out to lunch in the hope that he will perform, or find someone to perform, an abortion, then illegal. The joke lies in his constant pretence that the unwanted paternity has happened to 'a friend of mine'. Fortune says that the sketch originated in 'Jonathan [Miller] saying that, as a doctor, he found that people were always saying "I've got this friend who – " when they were in trouble themselves.' The sketch ends with Bird explaining, 'Of course they'd love to be able to have the baby, but they just can't afford it... So they're willing to spend anything to get rid of it.'

John Wells made his first-night Establishment appearance at about midnight: 'I did a bit of John Betjeman, from the revue I'd done in Edinburgh, appealing for the preservation of a Victorian public lavatory.' Coming on stage with a cigarette-holder and a sherry glass, Wells's Betjeman informs his audience that Queen Victoria did not like this type of lavatory herself, 'because of the vibration', and goes on, 'Now you must admit it's jolly exciting... If we just push open this door, we are afforded a glimpse of the severe Doric pilasters supporting each pedestal, Shanks absolutely at his best, and the old oak accessories, mellowed with age...'

By the time that Wells had finished performing, 'I'd missed the last train back to Eton, so Alan Bennett put me up on his chaise-longue, and I had to get up at about five o'clock in the morning, and got back and found the house locked up – it was called a bachelor colony, where four or five bachelor masters lived. No way of getting in, and I had to change. So I got a brick and broke a window at the back, and got in, just had time to have a bath and get into a white tie, and started teaching at half-past seven.'

The following Sunday, the opening night was reviewed in *The Sunday Times* by Harold Hobson and in the *Observer* by Tynan. Hobson had not enjoyed himself sitting on the stage – he complained about the 'sardine spirit' in which people had been crammed in, and went on: 'The Establishment will certainly be more comfortable when it is less crowded: a state of affairs there should be no difficulty in bringing about if it continues with its present programme.' Jonathan Miller had 'recklessly' promised 'savage satire', but the most the show could offer was 'soporific charm'. Hobson had enjoyed John Bird's impersonation of Khrushchev, but was disappointed by a sketch in which Lord Home (played by Fortune) summoned two Foreign Office officials (Bird and Geidt) to decode an official telegram from Moscow. He felt that this gravely misrepresented Home; a curious reaction, since it was not a dig at Home at all – the point was the so-called experts' blustering attempts to cover up their almost total ignorance of Russian.

Tynan thought this 'the most brilliant number' of the evening, rightly describing it as 'a satire less on our foreign policy than on the complacency of jumped-up clerks'. But he too was generally disappointed:

> … the eighty-minute revue … is not really political cabaret, since that implies a more or less consistent ideology; it is a cabaret about politicians, among them Mr Macmillan, Mr Butler, Mr Ben-Gurion [Prime Minister of Israel], and the Bow Group [the moderate wing of the Conservative Party]. Snippets of doctored film are projected, sometimes hilariously, sometimes not. Such teeth as the script has are engaged more in nibbling than in biting …
>
> The noisiest applause by far came after an item parodying the aspirations of Jomo Kenyatta. This unsettled me; as did the audience, which was Liberal leaning to Tory, and the cast as a whole, which lacks the panache of its progenitors in *Beyond the Fringe*. I recommend the proprietors of The Establishment that no political cabaret can be accounted a success unless at least a quarter of the audience walks out in the course of the performance.

*

Two weeks later, the *Beyond the Fringe* cast was interviewed for a BBC radio programme by Wilfred De'Ath (who nearly forty years on would become familiar to readers of the *Oldie* for his picaresque adventures travelling the world without paying his hotel bills). As usual, Jonathan Miller announced that he was about to give up comedy and stick with medicine. To which Dudley Moore let out pained squeals of 'Oh! Oh!', and Peter Cook explained:

COOK: Dudley sees himself at the age of eighty, performing in a sort of ancient *Beyond the Fringe* cast.
MOORE: No, I don't – I always –
COOK: (*in an old man's voice*) Topical as ever! Just as good as it ever was!
MOORE: I always feel – almost guilty, when I hear Jonathan and Alan yearning to get back to their more academic pursuits.
BENNETT: Actually it's self-indulgence on our part, in a way, to be able to do this.
MILLER: (*interrupting*) It is, it's a sort of, you know, nostalgic. But this is bound to happen. In order to enjoy the luxury of having a successful revue, which has been produced because we are not strictly professional, we have to sacrifice in some ways some sort of measure of contentment, because we're going to be drawn back to those very things which have given us the advantages which have contributed towards the success.

Cook, of course, had absolutely no intention of quitting show business. The successful opening of The Establishment had finally closed the door to following his father into a Foreign Service career (in any case the 2–2 Cambridge had awarded him in Modern Languages did not meet the requirement). John Bird describes Cook's lifestyle during the months following the opening of the club: 'There was an atmosphere of open-topped cars, chic restaurants, fashion shows. And, just to fill up the time, he was performing in *Beyond the Fringe* every night.'

The Establishment continued to be crammed. Bird says that 'it was so fashionable that there were no empty seats, ever'. One evening he was shocked to see two empty chairs, but it turned out that someone in the audience had just had a heart attack, and they were quickly filled again. John Fortune remembers an evening when Randolph Churchill came:

> We were introduced to him after the first show, and he insisted on doing a piece in the second show. The Fleet Street columnist Hannan Swaffer had just died, and he got up on the stage and did a piece about Swaffer arriving in heaven. It was embarrassing, but also quite thrilling, the sort of thing you'd expect to happen in a 1930s satirical club. And Lord Boothby used to come, and I believe I met one of the Krays.

Nevertheless Fortune says that, after the initial rush of celebrities, it soon became predominantly 'a middle-class night out – all the men wore suits, and the women wore dresses'. John Wells confirms that 'most of the fashionable lunatics' soon disappeared from the audience. The atmosphere was *Guardian* readership: when the team performed a sketch poking fun at the anti-nuclear campaigner Pat Arrowsmith, a woman in the audience shouted angrily, 'That's not what you're here for.' Peter Cook alleged that she then 'hit me round the head with a handbag'.

Kenneth Tynan reviewed The Establishment again in the *Observer* after it had been open for three months, on 14 January 1962, by which time the cast were performing a new show. He noted that, after its early phase of 'grasshopper whimsy', the cabaret had taken up

> a more or less definable political position, somewhere far out on the antic left wing of the Liberal Party; in other words, its attitude is one of radical anarchism. It scoffs at the organization mind, whether Tory or Socialist (union leaders are slow-witted and company directors cold-blooded): in true Bergsonian style, it invites us to laugh, as free agents, at the spectacle of human beings who have become automata. It detests capital punishment …

Tynan praised the three principal performers, Bird, Fortune and Geidt, but continued:

> Despite the excellence of the cast, despite the astuteness of the anonymous author and his anonymous director, something is wrong with the show; some

essential is lacking. The girls are clever and personable, but they are not encouraged to be funny; in a curious way they are frozen out ... The jokes take on a glib, adolescent rattle ... And one misses that *sine qua non* of successful revue: a gripping, outgoing central personality for whose every entrance one waits and on whose every word one devotedly hangs ... At The Establishment we smile; we may even laugh; but we are never transported.

The obvious person to take this central role was Peter Cook, and on some evenings he did perform, doing an impromptu solo spot, often a mimicry of someone he had just been talking to in the club. Nicholas Luard used to watch him 'studying them as he talked to them ... Afterwards, in swift, incisive and achingly funny sketches ... he'd re-create them.'

Tynan mentioned 'girls' in the plural. Besides Hazel Wright, who appeared in some of the sketches, a singer, Carole Simpson, performed satirical songs with lyrics by Jay Landesman and Christopher Logue. Tynan described these as 'sub-Brechtian' lyrics with 'sub-Weillian' music, but Carole Simpson defends them: 'They were just as good as Brecht and Weill.' When the show went through yet another revamp in the late spring of 1962, Hazel Wright left the cast and her place was taken by Eleanor Bron.

After Cambridge, and John Bird's student production of *A Resounding Tinkle* in which she had played opposite Peter Cook, Bron had opted for the business world, and joined the personnel department of the Delarue Group. 'But then John lured me to The Establishment, and my parents didn't really mind me becoming a performer, though I had to warn them about some of the things I'd be saying on stage.' She describes her family as 'middle-middle class'; her father was a music publisher and they lived in Edgware, and she was the first of the family to go to university, after an education at North London Collegiate School.

John Wells, who performed with Bron somewhat later, on television, says, 'She just was fantastic fun to work with, because she would go anywhere, or invent or lead you anywhere, in the same way that Peter would.' Asked if she felt that the satire boom was an almost exclusively male preserve, Bron says, 'No, but I was less interested in politics than things like class and the relationship between the sexes.' This was reflected in a sketch in the new show that quickly became one of the favourites at the club. Bron describes it as 'the boy seeing a girl home after their first date ... loops and convolutions of sexual embarrassment, trying to get to the point, any point'. The 'boy' and 'girl' are actually a couple of middle-class graduates in their mid-twenties, like Bron and Fortune themselves; indeed Peter Lewis rather cruelly describes the sketch as 'type-casting':

BRON: It was awfully sweet of you to see me all the way home. How are you going to get back, though? It's nearly one o'clock.

FORTUNE: Well, I can walk, you know.

BRON: Where do you live, John?

FORTUNE: Lambeth.

BRON: But good heavens, I can't possibly let you walk all that way home.

FORTUNE: Well, er –

BRON: Why don't you come upstairs, and I could ring for a mini-cab or something? ...

(*They go up to her flat.*)

I used to share it, but it's so much nicer being on one's own. You know, one can really be one's own – mistress ... Have you read any Martin Buber at all? He's a German philosopher, he writes a lot about relationships between – one human being and the next. There's a wonderful essay of his in which he says that two people having a conversation – it's not necessarily a dialogue at all, but most often it's two separate monologues, running along side by side. And he says that lovers – lovers don't talk *to* each other, rather *at* each other, in a kind of perpetual self-glorification. D–d–do you think that's true?

FORTUNE: Yes, I do. I think that's the great thing about Martin Luther, don't you? ...

This study in mutual embarrassment and sexual hesitation was the sort of territory that had been explored in America by the comedy duo of Mike Nichols and Elaine May.[7] To what extent were Fortune and Bron aware of that? 'Not very much,' says Fortune. 'I'd heart Mort Sahl, but it was somebody who'd already watched my thing with Eleanor, at The Establishment, who got us to listen to Nichols and May, and it was very interesting to discover that other people were doing that sort of thing.' Bron, however, says she had heard Nichols & May records some while before joining the cast at The Establishment.

Alan Bennett recalls Bron performing another sketch there: 'I can remember Eleanor saying, "I'm pregnant, I'm pregnant," and John Bird saying, "Oh, don't be so silly, it's just a balloon." "It's not, I know it's not a balloon – I'm pregnant, I'm pregnant." "Oh, for goodness' sake," and of course it is a balloon, and he pops it!'[8] Compared to the self-conscious young couple, this seems merely zany, but Bron explains that it is meant to

---

[7] Mike Nichols and Elaine May, born in 1931 and 1932 respectively, began performing together when students at the University of Chicago. Their improvised or semi-improvised sketches were about relationships and conflict between the sexes, ranging from a Jewish mother phoning the grown-up son who is desperately trying to be independent of her, to a man in a hurry trying to get some sense out of a robotic female telephone operator. Ned Sherrin saw them perform in America: 'I remember they opened with one with the husband coming home to a suburban home, and it's "Hi, honey" right through to mixing the Martinis, and when she walks into the room he realizes he's come to quite a different house, but that's what happens in every house so nobody would notice.'

[8] Bennett's memory is totally accurate. The sketch survives on the recording of one of The Establishment's shows in New York.

John Bird and Eleanor Bron.

highlight 'the failure of one person to pay proper attention to the needs of another'.

Also dating from Bron's arrival is the only sketch from The Establishment to have survived on paper, because Cook submitted it to the Lord Chamberlain – though no one knows why (the play examiner blue-pencilled it extensively). Two young Hampstead socialists, Jane and Julian, and a smooth advertising executive, Toby, are trying to persuade an old-style North-Country Labour politician, George, of the need to change the party's style (with only a little adaptation, it could be the 1990s and the birth of New Labour):

TOBY: You need an image with a broader appeal…Well, we've found that the most successful image and certainly the most exploitable instinct in people is – let's not mince our words about this – is sexual…I've been associated with a most successful campaign of advertising for Mackeson stout. I don't know whether you know it or not.

GEORGE: Oh yes. 'There's promise in a glass of Mackeson.'

TOBY: Yes, well, you see the sexual allusions there immediately, of course… the picture of the tall thick stem of the glass with the frothy creamy head on top…We used it very successfully in the 'Unzip a Banana' campaign…

GEORGE: So all these slogans are sexy, are they? …I mean things like, you know, 'the mint with the hole'.

TOBY: Never thought of that. Yes, you're quite right.

GEORGE: So you think that's what we need for the Labour Party, is it? ... 'Unzip
   a Labour councillor'.
TOBY: Yes, er – there's not quite the *promise* there, is there?
GEORGE: Or – 'There's promise in Dick – er, Dick Crossman.'
TOBY: No. I don't think so ...

Although he had failed his audition for The Establishment, Barry
Humphries took out membership of the club, and was often to be seen
propping up the bar after his night's work as the undertaker in Lionel Bart's
Oliver! He says he 'always felt a little apart, a little excluded' from the Peter
Cook circle. 'Peter himself was always an uncomfortable person to be with.
There was this endless stream of jocosity; some of it was very funny, but
some of it was worryingly endless, incessant. He always erected a barrier of
words between himself and anybody else. And you couldn't really get
through to him at all.'

Humphries notes that, besides being patronized by 'girls with green
fingernails, who all said "Soopah", which was then the fashionable epithet
of approbation', The Establishment became an occasional haunt of such
literary and artistic Fitzrovians as Julian Maclaren Ross and Francis Bacon,
'but they didn't appear frequently, because sitting still and watching
comedians doesn't really go with the sort of serious drinking that was their
habit'. As to the acts, Humphries says that the midnight spot – occupied on
the first night by John Wells – was generally given to 'new acts, usually wags
from the great universities', and recalls the evening he saw an
'unprepossessing fellow' deliver a 'none-too-hilarious monologue about the
Royal Barge accidentally sinking into the Thames. "He looks like a
Methodist minister's son," I thought ... How was I to know then that David
Frost *was* a Methodist minister's son?'

Jeremy Geidt says that, in the summer of 1962, Frost, then totally
unknown, briefly stood in for John Bird: 'He was terrified – or so it seemed,
as he was so totally unrelaxed, and stiff as a board, that he fell off his chair,
and did Sean Kenny's modular stage some damage.'

Around the time that Eleanor Bron joined the Establishment cast,
Nicholas Garland was imported from the Royal Court by John Bird to help
direct the sketches. 'It wasn't really directing,' Garland explains. 'They
would ad lib the sketches in rehearsal, and I'd take notes, and we'd pick out
the best bits.' He recalls one of his favourites:

It was a sketch with the two Johns as a couple of men boasting about how many
times they'd had sex with a woman in one night. One of them says, 'Three, four,
five, that's nothing,' so of course the other one claims to have done it even more
often, and finally they reach some absurd figure: 'I once had this Turkish girl,
and she was fantastic – must have been fifteen or twenty times.' Whereupon

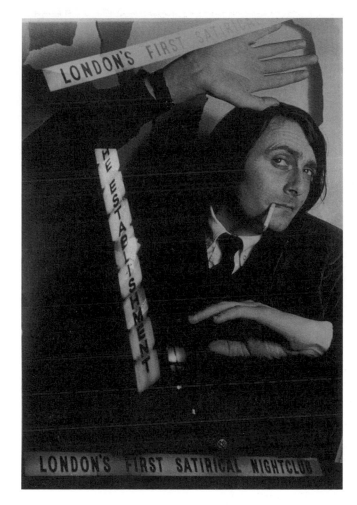

Barry Humphries makes his first UK appearance at The Establishment: 'When I saw these London guys doing their satirical stuff, I thought, "Yes, they're fellow spirits." '

they both go off absolutely aghast, each believing the other, and insanely jealous at what *he* seems to have managed!

Meanwhile Dudley Moore was quietly achieving a spectacular number of sexual conquests simply by playing the piano in the basement of The Establishment each night; Cook recalls that he was invariably 'surrounded by the best-looking birds in London'. Among other musical acts, there were occasional appearances by the surrealist band the Alberts; Cook claimed that their exploding harp had rendered a member of the audience unconscious.

On the wall of the bar, changed each week, hung a giant topical strip-cartoon, about sixteen feet long. This was the work of a tall, tough-looking, militantly left-wing artist named Roger Law. Peter Cook had known the future co-creator of *Spitting Image* since Cambridge. 'I come from East Anglia, the Fens,' Law explains, where I'd been brought up on a diet of comics, and I got a scholarship to art school in Cambridge. I was taught there by Paul Hogarth, who was quite radical, and he introduced me to *L'Assiette au beurre*, 'The Butter Dish', which was a magazine of caricatures and cartoons published in Paris at the turn of the century. They satirized everything, especially lawyers and doctors, and I got very excited by it. I was interested in George Grosz, too, and I decided that I would love to be a caricature-satirist.

Nicholas Garland recalls Law's strip-cartoons at The Establishment as 'this series of bloody great drawings by Roger – very good – like a Chinese wall newspaper'. A typical one featured Sir Roy Welensky, the white Prime Minister of Southern Rhodesia, metamorphosing into a pig.

The club kept its promise of opening in the daytime. John Wells recalls 'a reasonably good and cheap lunch, good films in the afternoons, a picture gallery in the bar on the first floor'. Cook disposed of the upper rooms to his friends. The photographer Lewis Morley, who had taken publicity shots for *Beyond the Fringe*, rented a studio on one of the upper floors, while on another Sean Kenny set up a theatre design and architectural practice. Cook also had the idea of publishing a magazine based on the club. Then, one evening, Christopher Booker, who had been at Shrewsbury with Richard Ingrams and his friends, and whom Cook had known at Cambridge, turned up in the bar of The Establishment waving a yellow quarto-size pamphlet. He explained that this was the first number of a satirical journal that he and some other people were putting together. 'I was actually very annoyed,' said Cook. 'I'd wanted to start a practically identical magazine – then bloody *Private Eye* came out and I was really pissed off.'

4

....

Fortnightly lampoon

Beyond the Fringe had hit London in Richard Ingrams' third and final year at Oxford. 'I didn't think the *Fringe* was anything all that special,' he says. 'It was just like the kind of thing the rest of us were doing – undergraduates in sweaters making silly jokes.' But he admits that it showed him and his friends 'that it was possible to sell university humour (the word "satire" had not yet been invented)'.

That summer, 1961, several of the Ingrams group were involved with the Oxford Theatre Group revue at the Edinburgh Fringe. *Late Night Final* was largely written by John Wells, and the cast also included Ingrams and Andrew Osmond. 'I thought Wells was much funnier than Alan Bennett,' says Ingrams loyally. The notice in the *Scotsman* shows how much the show was influenced by *Beyond the Fringe*:

> Staging is good and deceptively simple. A beginning which makes use of all the late-comers' shufflings and whispered excuses. An ending which gets everyone on their feet to sing the National Anthem ... In between comes the satire ... The targets are more or less the battered stock few – television, Lord Beaverbrook, the Bow Group, flogging, modern ballet.

Wells's impersonation of John Betjeman caused no offence to his daughter Candida, who was in the cast. 'All the focus was on her, as the sexy daughter of the poet,' says Ingrams.

After Edinburgh, the gang broke up. Peter Usborne, who had founded *Mesopotamia*, went to New York and took what he calls 'a miserable job in a press bureau in the *Time–Life* building, slicing press cuttings out of newspapers with a steel ruler'. Andrew Osmond set off for Paris to improve his French, with the aim of taking the Foreign Office exam. John Wells went to teach languages at Eton; Paul Foot had already become a trainee reporter with the *Glasgow Daily Record*; and Willie Rushton continued to draw cartoons for *Liberal News* in London. Ingrams himself teamed up with another Oxford graduate, Jack Duncan, who had directed him in a memorable production of *Tamburlaine* at Oxford, to form what would now be called a theatre-in-education group. Calling it 'Tomorrow's Audience', they set off to tour the country's schools with small-scale travelling productions. Nevertheless, Rushton's idea that the gang should continue to produce a comic magazine lodged in their minds – or at least in Usborne's. From New York, Usborne wrote a letter about it to Rushton, who showed it to Christopher Booker.

After Shrewsbury, Booker had 'wasted my three years at Cambridge, though I did a lot of writing for magazines, and made friends with Peter Cook. I didn't take part in Footlights, but I watched them – I saw Peter doing his Macmillan sketch in a Footlights smoker.' Meanwhile he had been brewing up his own ideas about comedy: 'I remember sitting in a house in Highgate, listening to one of Peter Sellers' records. I'd hated *The Goon Show*, because it wasn't *about* anything, but when I heard Sellers' sketches – like his parody of *The Critics* – I thought, "*That's* good stuff, *that's* what I want to do."'

In 1958, two years before *Beyond the Fringe* was staged at Edinburgh, Sellers had made a ten-inch LP called *The Best of Sellers*, which satirized several features of the contemporary British scene. The rise of rock 'n' roll under the leadership of Tommy Steele was guyed in a mock-interview with a gormless 'Mr Iron'; bland cinema travelogues were mocked in a sketch called 'Balham, Gateway to the South' (written by Frank Muir and Denis Norden); the BBC's cosy radio programme for under-fives, *Listen with Mother*, inspired Sellers to appear as a sadistic presenter called 'Auntie Rotter'; the penurious aristocracy opening their stately homes to the public were represented by Sellers' Earl of Prun, fleecing them ruthlessly at his Bedside Manor; and an ageing Tory government, utterly out of touch with the populace, was caricatured in a 'Party Political Broadcast' sketch (by Max Schreiner) which anticipated – and may conceivably have influenced – Peter Cook's impersonation of Macmillan:

> POLITICIAN WITH DRAWLING UPPER-CLASS VOICE: My friends, in the light of present-day developments, let me say that I do not regard existing conditions lightly. On the contrary, I have always regarded them as subjects of the gravest responsibility, and shall ever continue to do so. Indeed, I will even go further, and state quite categorically that I am more than sensible of the definitions of the precise issues which are, at this very moment, concerning us all. We must build, but we must build surely.

The Best of Sellers was followed in 1959 by the 12-inch LP *Songs for Swingin' Sellers*, which included the spoof of the BBC's arts-review programme *The Critics* which Christopher Booker particularly remembers:

CHAIRMAN: [Sellers] Good afternoon. Today we have with us in the studio Newton Tweedsdale, art critic of the *Onlooker*; J. Wallace Larwood, book critic of the *New Politician*; and Faith Bradshaw, film critic of the *Sunday Sun*. This week we have all been to see the exhibition of paintings by August Straptoconicus Bonstard at the Royal Tate.

FAITH BRADSHAW: [Irene Handl] Oh, yes!

CHAIRMAN: Newton Tweedsdale? ...

TWEEDSDALE: [Sellers again] One can now detect in Bonstard's present work a certain, how shall I say, a certain *architectural* – yes, architectural, as well as lyrical quality of suspenseful secrecy, with regard to the brushwork. A sense of fossilized motion seems almost literally to *spring* at one, from some of the paintings ...

Booker was also very impressed by another kind of humour, that of Bernard Levin in his 'Taper' parliamentary sketch column in the *Spectator*. 'I felt,' he says, 'that I would like to do stuff like that, and do it about politics.' Meanwhile, leaving Cambridge, he tried his hand at investigative journalism:

I'd run up an enormous bill in my college, and I paid it off by getting a job labouring for three months on the M1 motorway, which was just being built – serious work, mixing concrete. When I came down from Cambridge, I wrote a piece for *Time & Tide* exposing the fact (which I'd discovered) that there were no plans to build any more motorways. It caused quite a kerfuffle, and I thought, 'I'll become an investigative journalist.' But I was turned down by everyone in Fleet Street, and I landed up working on the *Liberal News*, alongside Willie Rushton, whom I hadn't seen since Shrewsbury (I'd had no idea what Ingrams and the others had been doing at Oxford – it was another world). Willie was doing his cartoons for *Liberal News*, and I wrote lots of learned little pieces about such things as the Rent Act.

Recalling Usborne's letter to Rushton from New York, proposing that they think seriously about starting another magazine, Booker says, 'The real key figure in getting *Private Eye* off the ground was Peter Usborne. Willie and I sat around talking about it, but Usborne was the one who was absolutely determined.'

Usborne soon returned to England and found a job in a London advertising agency, Mather & Crowther. Booker told him he thought the new magazine should be called *Bent*, on the model of the American *Mad*, which he admired – with reservations: 'We were quite keen on *Mad* magazine,' Booker says, 'but it was too zany. It didn't relate to anything – it was all self-referential.' (Nicholas Garland, who directed some of the shows at The Establishment, recalls that he and John Bird 'had a lot of jokes in common which were based on *Mad* magazine'.)

Meanwhile Usborne's job in advertising familiarized him with the new printing process called offset lithography, by which plates could be made easily and cheaply, combining text and pictures on the same page. If necessary, an ordinary typewriter could be used for the text, cutting out the cost of typesetting and thereby hugely reducing a magazine's budget. Usborne recalls that he 'spent most of my lunchtimes standing in a telephone booth...looking up printers and trying to find out about lithography'.

By the autumn of 1961 he had assembled a team, which he lists as 'Booker, Rushton and a bit of John Wells, and Danae Brook' – a glamorous girl from the cast of the Edinburgh revue *Late Night Final*. 'We had got as far as meeting in the Bunch of Grapes [in Brompton Road, Kensington] and arguing about a possible title. I wanted to call it *The Yellow Press*. I'm a gimmick merchant, and I had thought of this yellow paper. But this was all premature as none of us had any money.'

Usborne believed that Andrew Osmond might have been willing and able to put up some cash, so he sent a telegram to him in Paris: 'MESPOT[1] RIDES AGAIN COME HOME UZ.' Osmond answered the call, although he has recalled that 'by the time I got back and had found which pub in Chelsea they had moved to, they had completely forgotten about the telegram. They were still arguing about the cover. Anyway I had £450 and I agreed to back them with it. I became the original Lord Gnome.'

Usborne says that Osmond's enthusiasm, and his pledge of cash (equivalent to several thousand pounds today) was decisive. The title still eluded them; among rejected suggestions were the *British Letter* (as opposed to French letter), *Tumbril* and *Flesh's Weekly*. When Richard Ingrams put in an appearance he said he wanted to call it *Bladder*, because this suggested both a jester and taking the piss; but Rushton was against it because his grandmother was suffering from a bladder disease. It was Osmond who won in the end: 'I had been looking at the Lord Kitchener recruiting poster. We would be putting the finger on people.' He thought of *Finger*. 'Then I looked at Kitchener's eye. I thought of *Private Eye*.' Ingrams says that 'by that time everyone was so bored with trying to think up titles that they fell in with his conviction that *Private Eye* was far and away the best idea'.

The meetings now became more serious, moving to Usborne's mother's house in Kensington (28 Scarsdale Villas) and the garden studio at the Ingrams family home in Cheyne Row. 'Everyone lived in Kensington, Knightsbridge or Chelsea,' says Ingrams, 'and the early *Private Eye*s have a flavour of that world.' Meanwhile Usborne had found an offset lithography

[1] The Oxford nickname for *Mesopotamia*.

press in Neasden that would reproduce the kind of layout they wanted, dirt cheap. They got to work.

'I pounded out words on a battered typewriter,' recalls Booker. 'Willie bent low with his pen over a drawing board, sucking away as he produced a stream of cartoons and illustrations before laying them out on sheets of card ...Happy hours punctuated by Willie's mother knocking at the door to serve us each with little trays of tomato soup and beer.' Eventually the first issue of *Private Eye* was ready. The camera-ready pages were taken to Neasden, printed on bright yellow paper, and brought back to Scarsdale Villas for collation and stapling. The date on the front was 25 October 1961, three weeks after the opening of The Establishment.

'When we produced the first *Private Eye*,' says Booker,

> I shyly took a copy into The Establishment to give to Peter Cook, and he was very nice about it, considering it was mostly a load of old rope. But we weren't trying to join a satire bandwagon. We didn't say, 'We've had the stage show, now there's the night-club, so let's produce the magazine,' because we'd already been thinking about it for the best part of a year.

*

The first issue of *Private Eye* – now fetching a collector's price of at least a thousand pounds a copy – looks like an extended Rushton cartoon. The overall visual style and layout bears his distinctive stamp, and the poorly typed written material (these were the days before Tipp-Ex correcting fluid) seems to be a mere adjunct to his hilarious drawings.

The first of these is on the top left-hand corner of the front page – a parody of the crusader-in-armour from the *Daily Express* masthead. *Private Eye*'s crusader, who to *Mesopotamia* readers was recognizably John Wells as 'Little Gnittie', looks down-at-heel and carries a bent sword. He was retained ever after, though they soon dropped the Rushton drawing in the opposite corner, a face with one eye closed but the other – presumably the private eye itself – wide open.

Beneath this masthead, the first issue carried a Rushton frieze of current public figures, including Macmillan; and beneath that came the first headline, done by Rushton with 'R Type', a predecessor of Letraset, which he remembered as 'terrible stuff like Sellotape': 'CHURCHILL CULT NEXT FOR PARTY AXE?' This lead article, supposedly the work of 'Pravdaman Edouvard Khrankschov' (a dig at Edward Crankshaw, leading commentator on Soviet affairs), reported on an upheaval in the Conservative Party resembling Khrushchev's famous denunciation of Stalin:

> Sensation follows sensation in the campaign to isolate the 'anti-Party group' inaugurated at the recent 22nd Party Congress at Brighton. The latest and most

startling move is Selwyn Lloyd's 'public confession' that he must 'share the blame' for the current economic crisis.

Perhaps more ominous, however, is the series of articles by new Party Boss and Praesidium Leader Ivan Macleod in the Party organ *The Sunday Times*, in which he is rehabilitating the reputation of ex-Premier Chamberlain.

Chamberlain was in the doghouse throughout the Churchill era, for his pre-war 'appeasement' policy at the time of the notorious Anglo-German Pact. The Munich Pact is now viewed in top Party circles as a heroic attempt to buy time from Hitler before a war which Chamberlain saw was inevitable.

Obviously this campaign can only mean further humiliation for the man who ousted Chamberlain, ex-Premier Winston Churchill, and all those associated with him. Premier Macmillan has already relegated many of those who rose to power in the Churchill era to minor diplomatic and industrial posts, but hitherto the Churchill Cult itself has remained virtually inviolate ...

Alongside this wildly unfunny piece was a boxed announcement:

YOU'VE BEEN SOLD A DUMMY
– of what we hope, after further experiment, will be a
weekly newspaper to appear regularly in the New Year.
IF YOU HAVE ANYTHING TO OFFER
money, advice, goodwill or even contributions
CONTACT THE EDITOR, PRIVATE EYE
28 Scarsdale Villas, London w8.

Incidentally, neither the editor nor the publisher was named anywhere in the first issue, which technically made it illegal.

On the second page came the supposed fourth instalment of a children's serial about the nuclear arms race:

Last week, you'll remember, we told you how to make a simple, old-fashioned atom bomb ... We'd been told by Uncle Mac[2] in Parliament that this wasn't at all dangerous. Well, now it seems that when the Russians do it first it can be just the teeniest little bit worrying. But never mind, Uncle Mac is taking every precaution ... I expect Daddy has told you what a super time it was in the war – so I think we might be in for lots of fun, don't you?

This page also carried the issue's one genuine news story – or at least a potential one:

What really was the true story behind the CUNARDER SCANDAL, described privately by one MP as 'the most disgraceful episode in British politics since the

[2] Derek McCulloch of the BBC radio programme *Children's Hour* was known as 'Uncle Mac', though of course this refers to Macmillan.

PRIVATE EYE

Vol I No I Friday 25th October Price 6d

CHURCHILL CULT NEXT FOR PARTY AXE?

Butler for Gambia?

by Pravdaman Edouvard Khrankschov

Sensation follows sensation in the campaign to isolate the "anti-Party group" inaugurated at the recent 22nd Party Congress at Brighton. The latest, and most startling move is Selwyn Lloyd's 'public confession' that he must "share the blame" for the current economic crisis.

Perhaps more ominous, however, is the series of articles by new Party Boss and Praesidium Leader Ivan MacLeod in the Party organ The Sunday Times, in which he is rehabilitating the reputation of ex-Premier Chamberlain.

Chamberlain was in the doghouse throughout the Churchill era, for his pre-war "appeasement" policy at the time of the notorious Anglo-German Pact. The Munich Pact is now viewed in top Party circles as a heroic attempt to buy time from Hitler before a war which Chamberlain saw was inevitable.

Purge

Obviously this campaign can only mean further humiliation for the man who ousted Chamberlain, ex-Premier Winston Churchill, and all those associated with him. Premier Macmillan has already relegated many of those who rose to power in the Churchill era to minor diplomatic and industrial posts, but hitherto the Churchill Cult itself has remained virtually inviolate.

(continued on page 2.)

YOU'VE BEEN SOLD A DUMMY – of what we hope, after further experiment, will be a weekly newspaper to appear regularly in the New Year.

IF YOU HAVE ANYTHING TO OFFER

money, advice, goodwill or even contributions

CONTACT THE EDITOR, PRIVATE EYE, 28, Scarsdale Villas, London W8.

contents

Harold Throbson interviews Sir John Feelgood
(see Arts)
*
Arts (see Belmondo)
*
Film Man Dead
(see Press)

Mainly for Children
(Part IV: Fallout)
*
And – revealing new serial starting this week – The Memoirs of an Ordinary Man
(see inside)

EDITOR

DENTAL HEALTH

BORE of the WEEK
(back page)

The yellow pamphlet that annoyed Peter Cook: 'I'd wanted to start a practically identical magazine – then bloody *Private Eye* came out and I was really pissed off.'

war?' Why did the Government promise £20 million of public money to a private company that was self-confessedly in bad shape, for a project that was doomed to ridicule? What was the real part played by Mr Bence, the obscure Clydeside MP? What happened to the plan to commission an £80 million carrier as a sop to the shipyards that didn't get the Q3 tender? Read the FACTS exclusively in 'The Vote Buyers' – a *Private Eye* enquiry, two weeks' time.

But when the second issue was published, there was no reference to this Cunard story. Booker admits that none of them had any idea how to do investigative journalism.

Mort Sahl had visited England in July – he appeared in a BBC television show,[3] and was rumoured to have been disappointed by *Beyond the Fringe* – and the first *Eye* complained about the pompous newspaper articles he had engendered:

> There ought to be a law about people who write about Mort Sahl. The jokes should be underlined, so that one can get to them quickly and skip the socio-economic analysis of 'The Function of Sick Humour in Our Society'. We should then be saved from the sort of guff dished up by that gallant hack W.J. Weatherby – the *Guardian*'s Man on Main Street – who had his bash the other day. 'Back home in the United States he certainly makes the British satirists, this side of the fringe or beyond it, seem a mild lot, for he spares nobody there, from the President downwards.'... On and on, for columns and columns...

This implicit support by *Private Eye* of *Beyond the Fringe* was confirmed by a column headed 'Press', which quoted, without comment, from two reviews which had appeared in the same magazine, a few months apart:

> '...all we got was a narcissistic display of cleverness, with Jonathan Miller confirming an earlier tendency to pull faces... the satire was not sufficiently cynical... many targets were attacked; all were obvious, all had been previously assaulted...' *About Town*, July 1961

> 'Quite as good as we all say it is, if not better.' *About Town*, November 1961

None of the articles in the first *Private Eye* was signed, but John Wells recalled that he was the author of a mock-interview between two well-known theatrical figures. Like the arms-race serial this began in the middle; for, like *Parson's Pleasure* (and to a lesser extent *Mesopotamia*), *Private Eye* was spoofing the whole genre of magazines and journalism:

[3] Which Ned Sherrin describes as 'a fuck-up by the Light Entertainment department. They put him into a theatre, with dancing girls, and he looked awfully uncomfortable.'

Harold Throbson interviews Sir John Feelgood (cont. from p. 39)

F: I was also paid for it. (*Laughing*)

T: What about the famous all-male production of *The Dream* in 1910?

F: With Mungo Rolff; a quite remarkable man. He's dead now of course; but I remember visiting his widow in their little cottage at Abinger in 1939 when everyone else, you remember, was talking about the war and mobilization and things, and she delighted me with a charming anecdote about St John Parts.

T: Ah yes – dear St John! ...

Alongside this was a musical column, a piece in the manner of Beachcomber written by Ingrams:

RECOGNITION FOR MUZJIC?

Next year sees the anniversary of the marriage of Hermann Mousjäk, the late Latvian composer. To commemorate the event a festival of his works is to be organized at Bognor Regis by the Earl of Driftwood.

Our Musical Correspondent writes:

Muzack's work is little known these days except to a very few of us, myself for instance. Most people agree that the bulk of his music is vulgar and almost all of it is heavy, and in places bad. But, as Lord Driftwood has pointed out in his foreword to the Bognor brochure, this is no reason why the public should not be asked to listen to it, even if they find it boring. We are in danger, he adds, of only listening to music that we like.

There was also a review of an imaginary French film called *Qu'est-ce que tu penses de Princess Margaret?*, directed by 'Jean-Luc Gauloise' and starring an actress called Gitane. The back page was headed 'Bore of the Week', and was an attack on *Punch* in the form of an interview with Mr Punch himself, who was asked about his staff: 'Oh, much the same, you know. Still got Figgis the librarian, for instance – been with us since 1899 – checks the jokes to see whether they've been in before.' This was accompanied by a Rushton spoof of a typically unfunny *Punch* cartoon. 'The decrepitude of *Punch*,' writes Patrick Marnham in his history of the first twenty-one years of *Private Eye*, 'was a constant inspiration to the editors of the new paper, who intended to provide their readers with everything that *Punch* had ceased to attempt decades before.'

*

According to Richard Ingrams, the opening issue of *Private Eye* and its two immediate successors – also on yellow paper – were 'almost entirely the work of Booker and Rushton'. Booker says: 'I've probably written more words for *Private Eye* than anyone else, over the years, though no one would ever know that, because I'm regarded as a shadowy figure.' Patrick Marnham says that the initial print order was for 300 copies, while Ingrams gives the figure at 500, adding that they were 'sold in fashionable restaurants like Nick's Diner and cafés like the Troubadour where bearded CND men gathered to listen to folk songs'. Whatever the true figure, very little money changed hands.

Distribution was the responsibility of Andrew Osmond, who owned a Mini and (in Marnham's words)

> set out for the part of London he knew best – the South Kensington coffee-bar strip. That was the favourite stamping ground of Osmond, Booker and Rushton and that was where they tried to sell their paper. It was the land of striped shirts and hair lacquer where, after games of rugby and squash, public schoolboys faced up to grim reality and each other's sisters. Osmond took his copies to cafés in the Gloucester Road and Earl's Court, such as the Troubador, a CND stronghold.

Osmond admitted that, though the first issue had a cover price of sixpence, there were few takings:

> I would put a stack out in some likely spot with an honesty box. Later on I came back. The copies were always gone and the box was always empty. We did not mind. We decided that if we could live the way we had lived at Oxford we would have found supreme bliss.

Many copies were deliberately given away. Candida Betjeman (now Candida Lycett Green), who in the autumn of 1961 had a day job at *Queen* magazine, recalls that in the evening she would help staple copies of *Private Eye*, then get out her address book and post as many as possible to friends. The first person she persuaded to take out a subscription was one of her father's oldest friends, the artist John Piper. 'I expect he was just being kind,' she says.

> I suppose I did do quite a bit off the back of my father, who has always been an extraordinary passport to making things work. So that once we had Osbert Lancaster saying that *Private Eye* was funny – which happened very early on, thanks to my dad – then we were doing quite well.

A copy was also sent to Kenneth Tynan, who replied with a letter of encouragement, and to *The Times*, which ran a short article on it:

> The first copies of a magazine called *Private Eye*, edited from London by a group of recent Oxford and Cambridge graduates, have been published. The staff, mostly former writers for the Oxford undergraduate magazine *Mesopotamia*, are waiting to see how the sales go before launching the magazine as a national weekly next year. *Private Eye* concentrates on satirical comment.

*

The second issue, dated 7 November 1961, had a front-page headline referring to the birth of Viscount Linley, son of Princess Margaret and Lord Snowdon, which had taken place just as the USA had announced it would resume nuclear tests in the atmosphere: 'MEGATON? NO, IT'S A (6lb 4oz) BOY!!' This issue led on a character assassination of the Foreign Secretary, Lord Home, whom it described as 'the Berwickshire bleatnik...the little grey Home of the West...The sad truth is that this latter-day Halifax-figure is the last caricature of importance in our public life to have learnt his politics in the age of Munich...but he's such a nice chap.'

On the second page, a piece about the city of Leicester refusing to buy a Henry Moore sculpture included an unashamed borrowing of Beachcomber's Captain Foulenough, who was supposedly offering the mayor of Leicester cut-price works of art. The second Bore of the Week was the Liberal leader, Jo Grimond, and amid some supposed telegrams of congratulation to the *Eye* on its first issue came: 'PARDON US, OUR SHOW IS SLIPPING – The Establishment.'

The editorial team was now identified, in somewhat schoolboy fashion: 'This issue was compiled by W.G. Rushton, R.R. Ingrams and C.J.P. Booker, and published by Andrew Osmond...CORRESPONDENCE, WRITS, MONEY should be addressed to The Editor...'

It was Peter Cook who suggested to Booker that the *Eye* might start putting speech bubbles on photographs. Booker believes Cook got the idea from the American magazine *Sick*, though it was apparently invented – or at least first used in print – by an American 'photo-cartoonist' called Gerald C. Gardner. The front of the third *Private Eye* (30 November 1961) used the device to parody the typical 'Christmas issue'. It featured a pouting model – the *Eye*'s own Danae Brook – in a Santa Claus costume, and the bubble emerging from her mouth read, in Gothic type, 'Ad Majorem Dei Gloriam'.

Like *Beyond the Fringe* and The Establishment, the *Private Eye* team felt that it was acceptable to mock black African politicians. The third issue of the *Eye* included an exam paper for them: 'You can imprison some of the people all of the time and all of the people some of the time, but if you imprison all of the people all of the time who will be left to hail you as the Great Liberator? Discuss.' Meanwhile the Berlin Wall, which had been erected in August, featured as the third Bore of the Week:

> Yes, in diplomatic circles it's all the rage – the new, so-easy-to-do Wall Game, back in fashion for the first time since the good old days of Antoninus 'Balbus Amat Juliam' Pius. The rules? Just kids' stuff. No more frosty diplomatic notes or stuffy breaking off of relations. Nowadays, if you want to keep 'em out, wall 'em out. And is it a wow? The Game's gone down so well in Berlin that they've already started on their second.

By the time the third issue was finished, Booker, who again had written most of it, and Andrew Osmond, who was still trying to sell it almost single-handed, were beginning to feel they had had enough. But Rushton was still committed – not least because *Liberal News* had sacked him – and Usborne decided to go to Paris to get the advice of the editor of *Le canard enchaîné*. Complaining that it was difficult to unearth 'inside' news stories, he was told by his French opposite number, 'We…survive by getting the hot potatoes from our friends in power… You will have to wait until you are all aged forty [when] your friends in government will…come into power.'

For two months there were no issues; then, in early February 1962, a new-look *Private Eye* was loaded into Osmond's car. Printed on white paper in a slightly larger format, it had a front cover showing a photo of the Albert Memorial in silhouette, with the figure of Prince Albert clearly visible. This was captioned: 'BRITAIN'S FIRST MAN INTO SPACE – ALBERT GRISTLE AWAITS BLAST-OFF'. To it, Rushton had added a drawing of Queen Victoria with a speech bubble in which she was saying, 'Ho ho very satirical.'

The photo was credited to Lucinda Lambton, and the second page identified the current team responsible for this 'Fortnightly Lampoon', as the *Eye* now called itself:

> Editor, typist: Christopher Booker. Art editor, catering manager: William Rushton. Business Manager: Peter Usborne. Proprietor, driver: Andrew Osmond. Half-secretary: Candida Betjeman.

And on the back page: 'Published by Andrew Osmond, Pressdram Ltd, at 28 Scarsdale Villas, London W8, and printed on off-set litho by Huprint Ltd, Cricklewood, London NW2.' Marnham explains that 'Pressdram was simply the name of a ready-made company which Osmond had purchased for £26 "from a bloke in Fleet Street" '.

Though Osmond was identified as the real publisher, the *Eye* had now invented a fictitious press baron as its supposed owner. 'This is a great day for PRIVATE EYE,' wrote 'Lord Gnome' in the new issue:

> Our Advertising Section…makes its bow…I sincerely hope to see the day when PRIVATE EYE consists of nothing but a feast of advertising – with no distracting editorial matter whatsoever. Only then – when the true potential of the new Section has been realized – will PRIVATE EYE be in fact a paper fit for all generations.

This issue was indeed the first to carry real advertisements. It was explained that, to identify them as 'non-satirical', they would be 'surrounded by a black border' (to which Rushton had added the face of a landlady saying: 'Sorry, we don't take black boarders'). The advertisers included Ingrams's Tomorrow's Audience theatre company, which was performing for one night at the Royal Court, and several pubs, coffee bars and restaurants in Kensington, Chelsea

The first cover to boast a speech-bubble.

and Soho (including the Bunch of Grapes, where the *Eye* had been born); also The Establishment, which had generously taken a half-page advertisement: 'Britain's first satirical night-club announces a special reduction for students …' The black borders were certainly needed, because the artwork in the ads was by Rushton, so that they looked exactly like the rest of the magazine. His other contributions in this issue included a full-page comic strip, 'Carry on Breathless', a parody of British film comedies.

This issue brought a perceptible widening of subject-matter, and the jokes were getting much funnier. A medical column advised the man in the street how to recognize the symptoms of smallpox: 'Slight headache, and a sore throat for about 24 hours, followed by death.' A transport column portrayed the country as paralysed with traffic jams and railway failures. 'This Monday Dr Beeching [head of the rail services] stayed in bed. When asked how he had got there a spokesman for British Railways claimed, "Oh, I couldn't possibly tell you that, could I? Otherwise we might have everybody doing it." ' The 'Bore of the Week' was now the *Observer* – a do-it-yourself version: 'Colour may be applied without discrimination – but remember that the basic hue of all editorial material is Hampstead Pink.' The back page was a *Which* guide to the 'next Tory Leader'; among the candidates it had tested was Lord Home: 'On removing titles we were surprised to find nothing inside.'

Another peer, Lord Rank, head of Rank Xerox, was alarmed to discover that one of his companies, Huprint, had agreed to print this scurrilous little magazine, and the *Eye* was forced to find a new printer. An enterprising music-printing specialist, John Thorpe of Wembley, agreed to take it on, and the fortnightly order was optimistically increased to 5000 copies – far more than Osmond could distribute in his Mini. However, a van driver for *City Press*, John Harkness, agreed to drop bundles off when he called at newsagents. The country's biggest chain, W.H. Smith, absolutely refused to stock the *Eye*, which retaliated by renaming the company 'W.H. Smugg'.

Given that the *Observer* had been lampooned in the fourth issue, it was generous of it to give *Private Eye* a rave review later that month, on 18 February 1962:

> An engaging eight-page fortnightly called *Private Eye* has just entered the newspaper war, with a circulation of over 4000 and an emblem of a crusader with a bent sword. It is almost impossible to obtain, except at a few eccentric shops and at 28 Scarsdale Villas, Kensington. It is run by a disorganized staff just down from Oxbridge, helped by eight pretty girls. Its twenty-four-year-old editor, Christopher Booker, describes it as a 'British *Canard enchaîné*', or 'our answer to Roy Thomson' … [4]

[4] The Canadian magnate who in 1962 owned a group of newspapers including *The Sunday Times*.

The business manager is Peter Osborne [*sic*], who works in advertising ('We'll have to attack it and him soon,' says the editor) ... Booker ... is a liberal ... but the others are politically unaligned. Their hero is Michael Frayn ... Their main job, they feel, is to attack hypocrisy and inefficiency.

Sales were now sufficient for Osmond to feel able to pay small salaries to Booker and Rushton – £5 a week, subsequently raised to £7 10s – while Usborne decided to risk leaving his advertising agency. But an advertisement for subscriptions in the fifth issue hinted that the magazine was under-capitalized:

PRIVATE EYE COMPETITION

£50,000 AND CONSOLATION PRIZES

Yes! – for only £50,000 you can buy PRIVATE EYE, Britain's latest satirical dance craze, lock, stock and barrel ... CONSOLATION PRIZES – to each person who sends in 10/-, a SIX-MONTH subscription to PRIVATE EYE ...

Booker recalls that one offer did come in:

Within six issues, we were being approached by Michael Heseltine. This creepy figure and his sidekick gave lunch to Willie and myself, and I think Usborne. We'd just done a parody of one of his magazines, *About Town*, which was all about the new-style London, and Hezza wanted to buy us out so he could have an eight-page *Private Eye* section in every issue of it. We said 'Thanks for the lunch' and shook our heads.

Michael Heseltine confirms this: '*Private Eye* was very short of money. We had discussions but they came to nothing.'

They had no such compunction about accepting help from a Welsh publisher of soft pornography named Gareth Powell, who offered to take over the distribution and sell the *Eye* nationally. While this was being discussed, he provided the magazine with an office in Neal Street, Covent Garden – Ingrams recalls it as 'cavernous'. Issues 7 to 13 (March to June 1962) were published from Neal Street, and Osmond recalls, 'We never paid a penny's rent. All we had to promise was to lock it up at night because of the insurance ... Then one night someone forgot ... and Gareth Powell kicked us out.'

According to Ingrams, the circulation had now reached 15,000 (Osmond thought it was 18,000), 'and subscribers ranged from Lady Violet Bonham-Carter to several inmates of HM Prisons. But the magazine was nowhere near to paying its way. A further injection of cash was needed and Osmond for reasons best known to himself was eager to leave to join the Foreign Office.' Osmond explained, 'I was very worried about money ... I was utterly exhausted. I seemed to spend half the night doing the accounts and used to fall asleep at meals. The only thing I needed was a buyer.'

Willie Rushton looking like a frightened rabbit alongside a self-assured Christopher Booker, in early 1962, just as *Private Eye* was catching on.

The obvious people were Peter Cook, still flush with the success of The Establishment, and his business partner Nicholas Luard. Cook had already been the subject of a full-page lampoon in the *Eye*, the first in a series of modern fables entitled 'Aesop Revisited'. This one told how the young satirist 'Jonathan Crake', who becomes famous by mentioning the Prime Minister in the revue *Short Back and Sides*, opens a 'satirical night-club in Fulham', but ends up as a drunken bore who steals his jokes from back numbers of *Punch*. Aesop's victims in the following weeks included television arts pundit Huw Wheldon, editor and presenter of *Monitor*, lampooned as 'Hew Wellbread the omniscient compère of *Minotaur*'; Arnold Wesker, who became 'Ambrose Weskit the Worker's Playwright', and drama critic and columnist Bernard Levin, 'Bernard Unleaven'.

Luard was keen to buy the magazine, but he says that Cook was not: 'I don't know whether Peter was jealous of it or something, but at that stage the idea didn't appeal to him.' So Luard himself paid £1500 for 75 of Osmond's 100 shares in Pressdram Ltd. 'I had just enough left to be able to afford it,' he explains. Osmond kept most of his other shares, but gave a few to Peter Usborne and to Gareth Powell. He also generously handed half of the £1050 profit he had made on the deal to Rushton, Booker and Usborne. This was partly to assuage his guilt: 'I left them feeling that they wouldn't survive and feeling slightly treacherous.' Nevertheless he soon realized that the *Eye* was a winner – and in the most unlikely quarters: 'I had passed my Foreign Office exam and had to face the final board … As I walked in they all turned up a copy of *Private Eye* and said, "Are you responsible for this?" and tittered. I knew then I was in.'

5

·····························

Balls to the lot of them

'So,' writes Ingrams, 'Booker, Rushton and I and our two secretaries Mary Morgan and Elisabeth Longmore (who later became Mrs Ingrams and Mrs Luard respectively) moved round to The Establishment.' Luard had decided to house *Private Eye* temporarily in the club; meanwhile he sent out hundreds of copies of the latest issue of the magazine to Establishment members. Ingrams recalls that Luard summoned the *Private Eye* staff into his office one by one to give them job interviews, before becoming their employer.

The move was in late June 1962. Ingrams recalls, 'We produced two or three issues in the waiters' changing room.' The only access was via the stage, so that it was impossible to enter or leave the office if a performance was in progress. Also the waiters and waitresses kept coming in to change.

Among the latter was a girl newly arrived from Australia, Carmen Callil, the future publisher. 'I was working downstairs, where they played jazz,' she recalls,

> and I was always trying to dart upstairs to see the show. Nobody could drink without eating, so I had to serve people with ageing sandwiches. Dudley Moore used to play a heck of a lot. But my major preoccupation was what was going on in the kitchen. As I recall, there was a tremendous kerfuffle because the chief cook was in love with one of the other blokes, and I think he attacked someone with a knife. The *Sturm und Drang* in there was much more interesting to me than any of the official entertainments.

Despite their awkward working conditions, the *Eye* team immediately enlarged the magazine's format and number of pages, while Luard engaged a professional designer to revamp the cover. Issue 10 had stated that Booker was the editor; but issue 11 (dated 18 May 1962) read: 'Editorial Board: Christopher Booker, Peter Cook, Richard Ingrams, William Rushton.' Ingrams' and Jack Duncan's theatrical project, Tomorrow's Audience, had collapsed. They had over-reached themselves by mounting the first production of Spike Milligan's and John Antrobus's eccentric play *The Bedsitting Room* at a theatre in Canterbury. Willie Rushton had played the lead – Lord Fortnum of Alamein, who following a nuclear holocaust turns into the eponymous bedsitting room – and Ingrams had appeared in what he calls 'the very minor role of a rubber mackintosh man'. Kenneth Tynan praised it in the *Observer*. 'Unfortunately,' says Jack Duncan, 'we only got 1 per cent of 1 per cent of the box office,' mentioning names of those he considers to have cheated Tomorrow's Audience. Ingrams lost about £3000 of his own money: 'I put what I'd inherited into it, and it just ran out.' Regretfully, he gave up the theatre and applied himself full time to *Private Eye* – where it soon became apparent that he and Booker could not achieve a comfortable working relationship.

Luard recalls their 'constant quarrelling'. They differed hugely in character and appearance. The *Observer* described Booker as 'tense, desperately short-sighted [and] bespectacled, with bantering talk and a mauve-striped shirt', whereas Ingrams was 'modest, bear-like ... a big fellow with a cave-man look'. Although Ingrams seemed to treat writing *Private Eye* – like everything else he did – as a joke, and gave the impression of lazily freewheeling, he was quietly and steadily productive. Booker took it much more seriously. He says that he and Ingrams differed fundamentally in their view of the magazine:

> I was saying, 'This has got to be a satirical magazine, dealing with what's happening now, particularly politics, essentially with a serious purpose.' But Richard and Willie wanted something much more Goonish. There was also a rift between the 'Let's go to the pub' school and the 'Let's get it right even if it means not going to the pub and staying to rewrite what we've just done.' Willie had been prepared to work very long hours when it was just him and me, but when Ingrams arrived he went over to the pub faction.

Andrew Osmond recalled that tension had become evident even before he himself left the *Eye* – 'everyone was suffering greatly from Booker who was terribly highly strung' – and Ingrams claims there were Booker outbursts involving torn-up drafts, even 'smashed telephones'. Booker responds, 'This story about my tearing things up has become folklore. It probably didn't happen more than a couple of times. What I was doing was insisting that more time be devoted to the task.'

There were political differences too. Booker claims that by this time he had moved away from the Liberalism in which he had been brought up – 'I'd given up the Liberal Party as soon as it became fashionable' – and points out that he was writing the *Eye*'s parliamentary sketch in the persona of 'Eric Buttock', a gibe at the liberal MP Eric Lubbock. ('Buttock' wrote in the

Molesworth style: 'Old mac, he's hed of Skool as if you didnt kno, hav been studying the press with grate interest during the parst few dais. he hav been very woried about staing on as Hed of Skool and wondring how he could do it … it doesnt look as if hes going to be Hed of Skool much longer wotever he do … ') But Booker remained essentially Liberal, whereas Ingrams had voted Tory in the 1959 Election but was now describing himself as a socialist, and Rushton, if anything, was a Tory anarchist, who declared, 'We've got to put the Tories in and then bash 'em.'

The Booker–Ingrams tension was to some extent relaxed when Peter Cook, wandering into the waiters' changing room and dropping his guard against the *Eye*, began to make suggestions. This gave the magazine an injection of what it had badly needed since the beginning – inspired comedy (neither Booker nor Ingrams was a truly original humorist). Cookish letters soon began to appear in its pages:

> Sir,
>
>   I was delighted to read in your columns the obituary notice of my late wife, Lady Lettuce Gusset. However, I would like to point out that in her declining years my wife became pregnant by the then Vicar of St Botolph's-in-the-Marsh. I am extremely grateful to you for omitting to mention this fact. Had it been made public, it would undoubtedly have caused great distress to our whole family.
>
>   Your obedient servant,
>   H. Gusset

Sir Herbert Gusset was just one of the cast of original comic characters that, under Cook's influence, the *Eye* now began to create. Rushton had already invented the name Lunchtime O'Booze. At first a Catholic priest, he was soon recast as a Fleet Street hack, and a full page was devoted to his attempts to break into Gordonstoun, the Scottish public school to which Prince Charles had just been sent:

> Surrounded by a two-fold 12-foot-high electric fence, patrolled by Gestapo-trained bloodhounds, Gordonstoun is a challenge to any honest reporter.
>
>   I personally accept the challenge. The Duke of Edinburgh has used regrettable language about me, smacking more of the Tar than of the Consort, but I bear him no grudge. Though as I sit here in Elgin's Station Hotel, along with several of my colleagues, nursing a broken leg and an arm bitten to shreds by the Gestapo-trained bloodhounds, I must confess, as the locals say, 'I hae me doots.'

O'Booze was soon back, this time reporting on the strange case of Mrs Norita Vole of 29 Thornton Crescent, Staines, who had given birth to the Earl of Gosport:

One morning the editor of *Debrett* received a phone call from Fitzpestle, Master of the Balls ... 'The Earl of Gosport has been born to a commoner in Staines. This creates a dangerous precedent ... I think we should get down to Staines right away.' ... Imagine the scene in Thornton Crescent at the arrival of ... a coach drawn by three dappled beefeaters and an understudy from the Ministry of Works.

John Wells recalled how Cook would throw out ideas which others then wrote up:

It was just fantastic being there with him, to the extent that, when I look back through the pieces that Peter had thought of, I really regret having succeeded in getting any of my own jokes into them – something of mine that struck me as funny at the time, but now I can see that it tears away from Peter's originality.

However, Christopher Booker emphasizes that it was (and still is) a fundamental principle of *Private Eye* to devise everything collaboratively: 'That's even true of the cartoons, where the idea may come from someone else than the cartoonist. And actually Peter Cook has been given the credit for several things that were my ideas, such as the cover showing Enoch Powell (at the time of his racist speeches) with his hands wide apart, saying: "Some of them have got them *that* long." '

*

When the *Eye* moved to The Establishment, Wells was still teaching at Eton – despite the attempts of Ingrams and Rushton to dislodge him:

My idea was to take the job for a year, and then find some writing job in London. But Richard and Willie nearly fucked up that scheme by appearing there. There was I, ludicrously dressed up in white tie and gown, mooching along Eton High Street, returning the respectfully raised fingers of the boys, and suddenly this ridiculous horse-drawn vehicle appeared. It was some sort of barouche that you could hire at Windsor station, which Willie had taken, and there was a roar of 'Hello, Fat Jack! We thought we'd come down and polish off Wells's booze.' They stayed the evening, and drank everything I had, and said they had a proposition to put to me. They'd been offered a cabaret spot at a place called the Room at the Top in Ilford, on top of a furniture store called Harrison Gibson, and they absolutely assured me that no one would be aware that I was teaching at Eton, and why didn't I come along and join them?

The impresario behind the cabaret was Willie Donaldson. Ned Sherrin guesses that he was looking for another hit like *Beyond the Fringe*, but Donaldson says that the idea had come from the shop's owner: 'The silly man who owned the place came and asked if I would put on a cabaret there.' When Rushton and Ingrams asked Wells to join them in the cast, which would also include the young East End actress Barbara Windsor, Wells initially said no:

> But we had a lot to drink and I suppose I finally said OK. And I signed a contract with Donaldson and a man called David Conyers (Ingrams always referred to them as Con and Don). And then I realized what I'd done, and went to see Robert Birley [headmaster of Eton], and said, 'I'm in this terrible mess, because I've agreed to do a cabaret, and I'm sure somebody will find out that I teach here.' And he said, 'You must extract yourself from it.' So I went to see a very posh firm of Eton laywers, and they looked at the contract and said, 'You can't get out of it.' If Donaldson and Conyers had been half human, they'd have let me off it. But they said no.
>
> There was a dreadful marmalade-haired publicity man, who said, 'I can assure you there will be nothing in the press.' And it got a lead article in the *Daily Mail*, saying 'Eton Master Peddles Smut in the East End', and it was really deeply embarrassing. It wasn't smut. It was monologues I'd done in Oxford. One was General Montgomery having plans to become President – doing a General de Gaulle – which had just one risqué phrase in it, which was 'piss off', and that was the so-called 'lavatory humour'. And I did John Betjeman and a couple of other things.

Ingrams thinks the show was a failure – 'We really got the bird, from all those East End types, who hated it' – but Wells felt more positive about the experience:

> Once I'd gritted my teeth and went through with it, it was very enjoyable. The Kray twins came to see it [Barbara Windsor lived with one of their underworld cronies, Ronnie Knight], and Barbara developed a crush on Ingrams, and he had no idea at all, didn't notice. God knows why we did it in Ilford. It was the muckiest end of the East End. There was obviously some vast con-plot we knew nothing about, intended to promote the Harrison Gibson department store.

As to the content of the show, Ingrams says, 'We just did our old sketches from the old revues, I think,' and Rushton confirmed this: 'Ingrams did his John Gielgud impersonation and said "fuck" ... and I did Harold Macmillan.'

However, there was some new material, written by Stephen Vinaver, a young American ex-patriate who later became a key contributor to *That Was The Week That Was*. Ned Sherrin gives a summary of his career:

> Stephen came over here with a revue he wrote with [the composer] Carl Davis, which they'd done in America. It went to the Arts Theatre. Fenella Fielding was in it, Carl played, and Stephen directed it, and had written it all. And it was very successful, and he stayed on and occasionally directed – he directed Sandy Wilson's sequel to *The Boy Friend*. Not very well. He was very good at directing

Satire meets the East End: John Wells with Barbara Windsor in the Room at the Top cabaret, 1962.

one-person shows, or tiny shows; organization wasn't his thing. He did a very good act for Annie Ross at The Establishment.

Carl Davis confirms all this. He and Vinaver had been at college together in America. 'Stephen was a brilliant lyricist,' he says, 'and a wonderfully engaging person.'

Ned Sherrin was at the Room at the Top show, talent-scouting for the television satire show he was planning. He recalls it as

a very odd evening. It was one of those places patronized by Essex Man, in his fledgling state – he hadn't become defined yet. It was a characterless room at the top of a characterless store. Some of the cast were being highly amusing, but plainly much to the puzzlement of the punters. But at least it turned up Willie Rushton. That's where I saw Willie for the first time.

John Wells continues:

Despite the publicity, I went back to Eton next half. Robert Birley said that some of the Fellows had asked that I should be sacked, but he thought I was a very good schoolmaster, and he was going to get me to teach German to the Sixth Form. And I was so overwhelmed by this that I couldn't very well resign in the summer, as I'd intended. So in fact the whole thing landed me with another year at Eton.

Meanwhile, to protect the good name of the school, Wells began to use a pseudonym when contributing to *Private Eye* – 'Campbell Murdoch' (Campbell being his middle name). For a while he wrote an *Eye* column called 'In the Courts', which was very much in the Peter Cook style:

> 103-year-old Mr Justice Dribble, who retired last year after delighting the Press Gallery for many years with the viciousness and capricious savagery of his judgments, returned yesterday to the scene of his former triumphs…He… ordered counsel for the defence, Mr Maurice Israel, to be deported to Botany Bay, and the usher, Mr Arnos Grove, to be clapped in the stocks. He was then wheeled from the court beaming serenely, to have his robes changed.
>
> Mr Dribble was appointed to the Queen's Bench at the unusually early age of eighty-one, and is now one of the three oldest judges in the country, the others being Lord Chief Justice Sir William Bootle (117) and Sir Horace Plumfodder (Deceased).

*

On 8 July 1962 the *Observer* reported:

> The satire industry is booming. Following the recent merger of *Private Eye*, the fortnightly lampoon, with The Establishment night-club in Soho, the club are now preparing to extend their empire. They plan, among other things, to open a New York branch; to produce a *Private Eye* strip-cartoon book (published by Weidenfeld) for Christmas; to start a restaurant in London made of converted railway carriages, satirizing British Railways food; and to launch a weekly shilling magazine about entertainment, called *Scene*.

The report alleged that Nicholas Luard's favourite among these projects was the satirical restaurant. Young men dressed as gnarled railway waiters would serve such railway menus as Brown Windsor soup followed by lamb chops and jam rolls, but the food would be impeccably cooked. Painted scenery on rollers would rush past the windows, and when the lavatories were flushed they too would reveal the passing rails. Today, Luard admits that this was never a serious idea – 'merely one of Peter's teases' – but the press swallowed it, and about a year later, the columnist Alan Brien wrote that his worst nightmare would be receiving an invitation to London's first satirical laundrette.

The magazine *Scene*, however, was a perfectly serious proposition, and it soon became a reality. Luard assembled a team to write and run it, including the young Tom Stoppard, who contributed theatre reviews, and the first issue appeared on 14 September 1962. Its fashionable design and coverage of all the arts and show business now look like an early attempt at *Time Out*. Even before it emerged, *Private Eye* disloyally mocked it as 'SCONE – the new all-hip weekly paper devoted to all branches of the catering trade'.

The *Observer* noted that a total of sixty-two people were now employed by the various enterprises at 18 Greek Street, with Luard at the centre of the web: 'Smooth and twenty-five, he works in a large untidy office backstage at the club, with debs, Negroes and others moving in and out to help.' Ingrams later described Luard as 'the Brian Epstein of the satire boom... the only satirist to wear a suit'.

Rushton disliked assembling *Private Eye* at The Establishment: 'It was usually full of the very people it was targeting, all these people roaring with laughter and saying, "That's damn true about old Cyril." ' Moreover Luard was trying to amalgamate the *Eye* with the club, or at least to achieve some sort of flow of ideas between them, and the *Eye* team was firmly resisting this.

'Naïvely,' explains Luard, 'I brought the Establishment cast and the *Eye* team together for idea-exchanging working lunches.' John Wells recalled that the lunches, held on the first floor of the club, were tense affairs, with the *Eye* team warily eyeing The Establishment's cast – John Bird, John Fortune, Jeremy Geidt and Eleanor Bron:

> The two factions sat on opposite sides of the room, crouching on low stools, and eating as best they could off even lower tables in front of them. 'The Establishment' sneered across at us, despising us either because we wore waistcoats, or in Ingrams's case because he kept his trousers up with string, which they considered 'eccentric'. We naturally sneered back at them, though I can't quite remember why.

Luard soon realized that these 'Satirical Lunches' were doomed to failure, for more profound reasons than Wells suggests. 'The Establishment group,' writes Luard,

> state and scholarship-Cambridge educated, thought the *Eye* lads were greedy, ambitious and supercilious... The *Eye* contingent found the Establishment boys and girls flint-hard, down-market, even threatening... The *Eye* people... gloried in boozing, braying, and throwing up in pubs... The Establishment team ... worked, drank coffee, discussed F.R. Leavis, and played poker for relaxation.

Jeremy Geidt comments: 'Actually we (me anyway) did drink quite a lot. I expect the *Eye* boys were better at throwing up.' Ingrams says, 'We didn't really get on with Bird and Fortune. Jeremy Geidt was more relaxed, but Bird and Fortune took it all terribly seriously.' Bird denies this: 'Willie Rushton always said that I sat there dressed entirely in black, and looking very severe. I don't remember it like that – if anything, I had the feeling that *Private Eye* had their own thing, and they didn't see any point in this cross-platform.' And Fortune says:

> I've read a memoir saying there was no love lost between the two sides. I don't remember any of that at all. But I can honestly say that, though I loved Willie Rushton, and worked with him a lot (Ingrams I don't really know), for some reason I have never read *Private Eye* – I didn't when it started, and never since.

Christopher Booker has a simple explanation for the failure of the two sides to communicate: 'The two Johns don't come from a public-school background, and Ingrams and Rushton did give off a very strong aura of that.'

Meanwhile *Private Eye* was acquiring a number of highly talented new contributors. The young Ralph Steadman began to send in eccentric drawings, the first being a page of Plastic People who could supersede real human beings – 'a reject from *Punch*', Steadman recalls, adding that he and his friend Gerald Scarfe, who also started to contribute to the *Eye*, were much affected by George Grosz: 'He was probably the prime influence on us both; we realized that was where the acid was, and we wanted acid in those days.'

There were occasional *Eye* pieces by Spike Milligan, who claimed that (being Irish) he had lost his British rights of nationality because of a recent Act of Parliament, but later reported: 'I have been granted Welsh Citizenship, provided I stay on a mountainside and only say "Baa".' And the *Eye* began one of its most successful and longest-running features in the summer of 1962 when Christopher Logue compiled the first of his 'True Stories' columns, a series of unlikely, hilarious news items culled from the world's newspapers.

There were occasional lapses of editorial judgement. The nineteenth issue contained a comic article about homosexuals allegedly by 'Dr Jonathan Miller', called 'The Hounding of the Pooves'. Though it was an obvious hoax, Miller sent a furious note beginning, 'You stupid bloody irresponsible cunts'. He has claimed to hate everything that Ingrams stands for: 'We've always got those leather-elbowed thugs like Richard Ingrams, making sure we don't bring too much sensitivity into the country.' Ingrams himself is aware of this apparent antipathy – 'Jonathan Miller thought that *Private Eye* was anti-Semitic and fascist,' he says. However, when interviewed for this book, Miller denied that he had any underlying objection to Ingrams or *Private Eye*:

> I was simply annoyed that they called me 'Doctor', because I was very eager to get back into medicine, and in those days there was an absolute ban on doctors

mentioning their names in public *as doctors*. The 'Pooves' piece was actually rather funny – it was illustrated with Victorian engravings of people doing life-saving, sitting astride recumbent drowned figures, and the captions described this as 'Pooves at their deadly job'. Later on, when I started doing things like *Monitor* on television, *Private Eye* pilloried me as a pontificating gas-bag. I came to epitomize their notion of pseud.

It was occasionally necessary for the *Eye* to print an apology. By an odd twist, the first was to Lady Pamela Berry, wife of the owner of the *Daily Telegraph* and mother of Adrian Berry who had founded *Parson's Pleasure*. The *Eye* had alleged that she was the author of a speech that sneered at 'niggers, beatniks, Angry Young Men'. But as yet, nobody sued. Consequently, as Ingrams puts it, there was a 'tendency...to go to yet greater lengths to shock people'.

The thirteenth issue reviled the Home Secretary R.A. Butler as 'A FLABBY-FACED OLD COWARD' for not acting on his principles but bowing to the majority, adding, 'What's more, he's such a flabby-faced old coward he won't sue us.' Ingrams says this was 'hailed by some as, at last, a return to the fruity free speech of the eighteenth century'. Yet Kenneth Tynan felt that *Private Eye* was not yet fulfilling its satirical promise. He wrote to it: 'When are you going to develop a point of view?'

Although the *Observer* reported, in its article of 8 July 1962, that the *Eye* now had a circulation of 17,000, it expressed the same doubts as Tynan:

> Underneath all this business enterprise, how deep is the satire?...Behind the ferocity, there is a certain Oxbridge cosiness...A lot of their output, as with *Beyond the Fringe*, is very funny – but it certainly doesn't always spring, as they claim, from a heartfelt disgust at society.

No such claim was being made by Booker, Ingrams and the others. *Private Eye* was indeed developing a point of view, but it was neither political nor motivated by disgust. It was the ability to perceive and laugh at the absurd in almost all forms of authority, creed or institution, irrespective of such considerations as political parties. There was no savagery in the laughter, and no expectation that the lampooning would change anything. Indeed there was a certain relish that things should be so crazy, an ironical enjoyment of society's hypocrises and self-deceptions rather than any sort of campaigning for improvement.

Items in the magazine that seemed at the outset to satirize authority from a left-wing viewpoint might suddenly take a sharp turn to the right:

> Mr Butler today announced to the House the findings of his Official Enquiry into accusations of police brutality during last Sunday's anti-nuclear demonstrations in Trafalgar Square.

'I have never been arrested myself,' he said with a smile, 'and I can give you every assurance that our policemen are wonderful.'

The Report was prepared by Superintendent Acorn, who was also one of the chief witnesses before the Enquiry.

Said Ted Snivel, a member of the Committee of 100, who suffered a bruised ankle during the demonstrations, 'The British police are a lot of murdering Fascist swine.'

Labour came in for as much abuse as the Tories. 'I am one of the new, young, dynamic Labour MPs,' announced a character in a strip-cartoon in July 1962.

I support Mr Gaitskell on everything. That is to say I am both in favour of the Common Market and against it. I both support the independent deterrent and oppose it. I support the principle of public ownership, of course, but I am against it in practice. But on one thing, at least, I am quite uncompromising. When Labour gets in, I want a job.

Indeed the whole of politics was presented as beneath contempt, a subject that interested only the Tory-dominated press and not the public:

TORIES SNATCH BIG LEAD POLL SHOWS

In answer to the question 'If your vote had to decide whether the country was to be subjected to five years' disastrous rule by the Socialists, wouldn't you vote Conservative?' a sample poll of seven housewives replied:

Con.	Lab.	Lib.	Get Lost, Mate.
39%	18%	26%	75%

The remainder were divided equally between those who said 'I'm a good old-fashioned radical' and 'No more encyclopaedias today, thank you.'

Much of the mockery was achieved by the simple device of distorting an individual's name. Novelist-turned-pundit C.P. Snow became 'C.P. Snurd'; Marcello Mastroianni, star of *La Dolce Vita* and other trendy European films, was transmuted into 'Masturbani'; Ian Fleming turned – once again – into Ian Phlegm; and the author of *Look Back in Anger* and *Luther* was renamed 'John Osbore'. Being a bore was the greatest offence in *Private Eye*'s book – and, as in the *Salopian*, being a 'pseud'. By the end of 1962 this word had become part of *Eye*-speak: 'Pablo Picasso is 100 today…Lotte Krapp of the Musée Pseud in New York talks about the most richly creative artist of our time…'

This amused contempt for almost everything carried the danger of philistinism, and of failing to attack serious issues seriously. The *Eye* was certainly guilty of the former, though its habitual mockery of intellectuals and the arts did lead to some valuable puncturing of pretentiousness as the trendy 1960s got under way. And it was capable of making the most serious of points in the most comic of fashions.

A cartoon in an early issue showed a mini-skirted girl telling her hip-looking lover: 'Nigel, I think we're going to have an abortion.' As it happens, Booker was in favour of legalizing abortion, Ingrams against it, but they were united in their attacks on hypocritical attitudes. In August 1962 the cartoonist 'Trog' (Wally Fawkes) contributed a drawing in which a doctor tells a pregnant woman: 'I'm sorry, but the ethical position is quite clear. Thalidomide was a legal prescription, but what you suggest is an illegal operation.' The same issue contained a mock letter protesting against the abortion of foetuses known to have been damaged by this drug:

> ... any human life is a gift from God, and therefore sacred (except in wartime). In my opinion, these abortionists are guilty of the murder of innocent children and should therefore be liable to capital punishment ...
>
> Secondly, you are quite forgetting the immense advances that have been made by science in enabling these children to overcome these handicaps ... I myself have known of a child, born limbless except for two thumbs on its right shoulder, which, after years of devoted care from its mother, learned to smile and to perform simple tasks – even to feed itself. Many of these children actually benefit from the difficulty of overcoming their handicaps, growing up into very wonderful people.

This was satire in the best tradition, recalling Swift's *Modest Proposal* (1729), which suggests that the Irish poor should make money by fattening their children and selling them to be eaten by the rich. The magazine's overall attitude was neatly summed up in a phrase in the issue of 6 April 1962: '*Private Eye* says, "Balls to the lot of them." '

*

That same month, Peter Cook gave the cast of The Establishment a holiday and brought over the American comedian Lenny Bruce. His real name was Leonard Schneider, he was a dozen years older than Cook, and he had been brought up in a blue-collar Jewish household on Long Island. 'To me,' he writes in his autobiography,

> if you live in New York or any other big city, you are Jewish. It doesn't matter even if you're Catholic; if you live in New York you're Jewish ... My conversation ... is usually flavoured with the jargon of the hipster, the argot of the underworld, and Yiddish.

Bruce had managed to get discharged from wartime naval service by persuading the medical board that he was a compulsive transvestite. Later, he worked a charity scam by dressing up as a priest. By 1960 he had become a big name in stand-up comedy on the American night-club circuit, but the following year he was twice arrested, for using narcotics, and for obscenity (the word 'cocksucker') in his stage act. He was found not guilty on both counts, but this was only the beginning of a series of conflicts with the law.

In the spring of 1962, Peter Cook persuaded the Home Office that Bruce's drug-taking days were over; but when he collected Bruce from Heathrow, he found him 'an absolute, shambling wreck. I thought, Jesus, what have I got on my hands?' Nicholas Luard describes Bruce as 'fragile, sick, white-faced … and immensely gentle'.

Kenneth Tynan came to The Establishment to watch Bruce's opening night:

> Clad in a black tunic sans lapels, as worn by the late Pandit Nehru, he roamed out on stage in his usual mood of tormented derision; ninety minutes later there was little room for doubt that he was the most original, free-speaking, wild-thinking gymnast of language our inhabited island has ever hired to beguile its citizens.

Carmen Callil abandoned her customers in the basement and came up to hear him: 'He was completely wonderful. Watching him was one of the things that changed me from being a little convent girl from Melbourne.'

Lenny Bruce.

Tynan jotted down some of the topics that Bruce touched on that night: 'The smoking of marijuana should be encouraged because it does not induce lung cancer. Children ought to watch pornographic movies: it's healthier than learning about sex from Hollywood… Publicity is stronger than sanity: given the right PR, armpit hair on female singers could become a national fetish.' Jonathan Miller was there too, and Tynan writes that Miller 'agreed with me… that if *Beyond the Fringe* was a pinprick, Mr Bruce was a bloodbath'.

Miller says he watched Bruce night after night – 'I spent about four nights a week at The Establishment, because my wife was doing hospital house-jobs at the time, and therefore was working overnight' – and became friends with Bruce:

> I remember helping him once to mainline when he was taking heroin, I think tightening the tourniquet on his arm. He was enormously gentle, like some frisky goblin, and there was something enchantingly evangelical about him; he was really rather like some secular preacher.

John Fortune says much the same:

> Lenny Bruce stayed with me. Next to Peter Cook, he's the most remarkable person I've ever met. He had more charm than anyone I've ever known; he just made people love him, after a very short time, like five minutes. The first thing he said to me was, 'Where am I going to get some heroin today?' Yet he was incredibly fit – he'd been a Marine, and he was lean and strong and looked terribly healthy, and just as long as he could get enough heroin he was fine. I'd never met anybody who took drugs, and have a natural revulsion towards it – I'm squeamish about needles – but such was his charm that he made you think it was like listening to Beethoven quartets.

Fortune used to watch Bruce's act every night:

> It was a bit like Peter – the way these accretions would attach themselves to the basic routine, further and further reaches of fantasy. And it made us feel that we and our material were very juvenile by comparison.
>
> People would walk out – you'd hear a wife whispering to her husband, 'If he says *that* word once more we're going,' and Lenny would come out with another 'fuck', and sure enough they'd go. But the wisdom of what he'd do with that word! He'd say things like, 'If somebody says to me "fuck you", that's a compliment – fucking's the most wonderful thing. Now if they said *un*-fuck you – !'

In his introduction to Bruce's book *How to Talk Dirty and Influence People*, Kenneth Tynan confirms that the audience at The Establishment was stunned by him:

Scarcely a night passed without vocal protests from offended customers … The actress Siobhan McKenna … noisily rose to leave in the middle of Bruce's act; it seems she was outraged by his attitude towards the Roman Church. On her way out Peter Cook sought to remonstrate with her, whereupon she seized his tie while one of her escorts belted him squarely on the nose … A few days later a brisk, pink-faced sextet of young affluents from London's stockbroker belt … sat, half-heartedly sniggering, through jokes about money-making, sexual contact with Negroes, onanism as an alternative to VD, and genetic hazards proceeding from fall-out. Suddenly Bruce ventured on to the subject of cigarettes and lung cancer. At once … the brisk, pink stockbroker host sprang to his feet. 'All right,' he said tersely, 'Susan, Charles, Sonia! … *Cancer!* … All out!' And meekly, in single file, they marched out through the door.

Bruce's 'cancer' routine has been preserved in a sound recording:

I've been thinking about what the ad companies are going to do. Well, they're not going to stop selling cigarettes. I can't knock them for that, 'cause everything is profit-motivation, so what are you gonna do, man? What they'll probably do, the ad companies, is make it hip to have cancer. They'll make cancer a status symbol in the community. They'll start with soft-sell advertisements, guys talking in two-minute spots, you know: 'Say, Bill, haven't seen you in a couple of years. You really look great!' 'Why shouldn't I? I've got cancer!' 'Are you kidding me, Bill? Well, that's terrible.' 'Terrible the way you see it, not the way I see it. I was making about twenty-five hundred dollars a year selling shoes at home. Now since I got cancer – you never see any slob with cancer! Who has it? Doctors, lawyers, and judges! So I started thinking at home, the rich people are keeping it away from us with those charity drives they have.' 'And it's really good for you?' 'Certainly is.' 'Well, that's wonderful! How do you get it?' 'Chesterfields!'

John Bird says he learned something crucial from Bruce:

John Fortune and I had become quite hostile to the Establishment audience, because they were the kind of people we thought we were attacking – the Guards officers and their dollies. And I remember Lenny saying to me, 'This is wrong – these people have come to see you. And whatever they're like, you have to assume that they're on your side.' And he was right – when you attack people, they resist it, for the obvious reason that they feel, 'Those people up on stage think themselves morally superior to me – and I'm paying good money.'

Nicholas Luard says that, by the end of Bruce's month's engagement at The Establishment, several newspapers were demanding shrilly: 'Get this vile creature out of Britain and do the country a favour.' Tynan describes this as 'the conservative press baying at his heels'. Bruce himself writes that he had 'had a lot of fun in England – although I didn't get laid once'.

A highly successful year for British satire

The *Private Eye* team was now in demand from newspapers and magazines. They guest-edited the 'Atticus' column in *The Sunday Times*, and contributed a page to *Queen* magazine, and in May 1962 Ingrams was invited to become the theatre critic of *Time & Tide*. His first article was partly about a new satirical revue which had arrived in the West End, *England Our England*, by Keith Waterhouse and Willis Hall. 'The revue,' he wrote,

> is primarily concerned with Northern working-class people and with their attitudes to many aspects of the Affluent Society. *England Our England* is satirical in the best sense of the word in that it cocks a critical eye at a whole society and not just a lot of well-known figures ... Roy Kinnear, a splendidly ebullient person, heads the cast ... The whole ethos of Centre 42 [a left-wing arts group headed by Arnold Wesker] is disposed of when Murray Melvin as a builder sings an absurd folk song about the building of the Rotherham Comprehensive School, but this is done without a mention of Centre 42 or Arnold Wesker ... This is certainly the most pointful, most entertaining revue since *Beyond the Fringe*.

In the same article Ingrams declared himself unimpressed by Lionel Bart's new show *Blitz* – 'What sets out to be a great British saga degenerates into a great Jewish splurge' – and in the following weeks he was scathing about most shows that he had seen, including Arnold Wesker's play about National Service, *Chips with Everything*, which he called a 'crude allegory'. He ignored an editorial warning about his negative attitude, and by the end of June he had been sacked; whereupon *Private Eye* launched a readers' competition to get the maximum number of bogus letters into *Time & Tide*. In all, fifteen slipped past the editor's watchful eye, and the highest total was achieved by Roger Sandell of Southall, with three. *Private Eye* printed this one by him:

SHOULD THE QUEEN MOVE?

Sir:

   I am a Canadian and feel that, should Britain enter the Common Market, the Canadian Government should invite the British Royal Family to move to Canada, a country where the twin ideals of Queen and Commonwealth are still respected.
   R.M. Dobell.

The *Eye* commented: 'Unfortunately in almost every case the bogus letters were less ridiculous than the real ones.'

By the end of 1962 a rival to *Private Eye* had appeared, printed in tabloid newspaper format and called *Relax*. Edited by one Albert Vajda, it claimed that Macmillan, Gaitskell and the Liberal leader Jo Grimond had been invited to join its editorial board. Macmillan was depicted as a sexy pin-up, and there was a spoof annual report on the 'British Steal Industry'. But most of the humour was of the bedroom sort, on the level of *Tit Bits* – 'A PESSIMIST thinks every woman is immoral; an OPTIMIST hopes she is' – and *Relax* disappeared after a few issues.

Christopher Booker, Richard Ingrams, Willie Rushton and (seated) Nicholas Luard, photographed by Jane Bown at the height of the satire boom, in 1962.

The *Observer*, which described *Relax* as 'an inept new "satirical" magazine…modelled to some extent on *Private Eye*', had by this time climbed on the satire bandwagon itself. At the end of May 1962 it announced that the penultimate page of its Weekend Review would become a 'satirical page', to be called 'Almost the End'. In the first issue, Peter Cook provided the caption for a strip-cartoon drawn by Roger Law, who was providing the giant topical strips for the bar at The Establishment. This one depicted Hugh Gaitskell, who was regarded as having abandoned most of what Labour stood for, telling his fellow Shadow Cabinet member George Brown, 'Do stop calling me "Brother". It reminds me so much of the Labour Party.' Beneath this was the first in a new series of columns by Michael Frayn, who had transferred to the *Observer* from the *Guardian*:

> It gives me great pleasure to be here today (*said Sir Harold Sidewinder, the well-known chairman and man of opinion*) to declare this airy and comfortable new *Observer* satirical department open. I know the staff are young and keen and ready to send up anything and anyone without fear or favour, in the best traditions of British public service. I am sure that the beautiful way in which their premises are laid out will be an inspiration to them to send up even more higher…
>
> I even made my own small contribution to helping the movement on its way. 'Highly satirical,' I wrote of Ken Nocker's first novel…Ken told me later that until he read those words he had absolutely no idea he was doing anything but entertain people. Today, as we all know, Ken is Satirical Adviser to Spyros Stereos's new film epic of the Book of Jeremiah…
>
> Whatever new idea is taken up in the *Observer* today will infallibly find its way into *The Sunday Times* tomorrow. And once *The Sunday Times* has espoused the cause of satire, is there any force on earth which could prevent it from taking its place in our national cultural mausoleum? I look forward with confidence to *The Sunday Times*'s serialization of the comprehensive collection I have edited, 'Four Thousand Favourite Gems from our Satirical Heritage'.
>
> Then, who knows? A Royal Academy of Satire? The launching of a public subscription to prevent *Beyond the Fringe* from going to America by purchasing it for the nation?…
>
> With distinguished young satirists appearing on emergency television programmes to rally the country behind them with parodies of Harold Macmillan…there's a heroic new age opening before us.

Frayn stayed with the *Observer* for some while, whereas the Cook and Law strip-cartoon ceased at the end of July, thereby depriving 'Almost the End' of most of its satire. Frayn had joked about it, but it was perfectly true: *Beyond the Fringe* was going to America.

The Observer's new satirical page ⋗ ⋗ ⋗ ⋗ ALMOST THE END

You know I like you immensely, George . . .

and admire the way you support me . . .

No one could call me snobbish, George, but do stop calling me Brother . . .

It reminds me so much of the Labour Party

The first of the shortlisted satirical strips in the *Observer*, May 1962 – written by Peter Cook, drawn by Roger Law.

*

As soon as a transfer of the show to Broadway was mooted, all four insisted that in America they would require a considerable pay rise: from £75 to £750 per week, plus a percentage of the box office. This was agreed on, and the search began for replacement performers at the Fortune Theatre, since the West End production was to continue with a second cast. Among those auditioned were Richard Ingrams and John Wells; but in the end the parts went to Bill Wallis (as Bennett), Joe Melia (as Miller), Terence Brady (as Cook) and Robin Ray, replacing Moore, whom he had already been understudying.

Cook's dream of opening a 'New York branch' of The Establishment now came a step nearer reality. He and Luard arranged that, while *Beyond the Fringe* was on a brief pre-Broadway tour of American cities, the cast of The Establishment should go over there too, their places in Greek Street being filled by performers from American satire clubs. So John Bird, Eleanor Bron, John Fortune, Jeremy Geidt and the singer Carole Simpson found themselves booked for a season at Chicago's Second City.

None of them had been to America before. 'We are in a goldfish bowl,' wrote Bron in her diary,

> and our hosts are cats ... occasionally scooping one of us out, in quite a friendly way, to examine us from all angles, before putting us back in the water so that we can go on behaving for their amusement. Most of them, though not much older than us, are on to their second marriage, or at least going through their first divorce. They don't ask, 'Are you married?' or, 'Are you engaged?'; they ask, 'Have you been married?' They are amazed that the three boys like girls. They thought practically all Englishmen were homosexuals, but especially actors.

As to the creation of their satirical material, Bron noted:

> The Second City actors work differently from us. We sit round a table for the most part and decide on a topic, usually political, find a situation to contain it and then think up jokes to suit. They start with characters first, then situations, and they immediately get up and improvise from there. What emerges can be funny, unplanned and organic in a way that our work rarely is (except perhaps a sketch I do with John Fortune about a boy and a girl on a date) and their comment is social rather than directly political. Because of that they don't have such a hard time finding material for the girls.
>
> They suggested we do a workshop with them to try out their methods and we did have a go, but we were all far too self-conscious. We feel marooned without our jokes to hang on to; without them we don't trust the scenes to become funny. We have neglected our instincts perhaps – we try too hard.

The show that the Establishment cast gave in the USA opened with Bron as the Queen, who seems to be under the delusion that America is still one of the colonies: 'You have continued to progress by leaps and bounds. Perhaps one day you may even be able to stand alone, entirely without the prop and support of Mother England.' The Chicago audience loved this. 'It was a period when America thought that everything British was new, radical and charming as well,' says John Bird, 'and I suppose, because it was British, we were not considered dangerously subversive.' Carole Simpson says they found the audiences 'so polite' compared to Greek Street. A review in the *San Francisco Chronicle* a year later, when they appeared at the most famous comedy club in the States, the hungry i in San Francisco, shows how well they could go down with American audiences. It begins by praising

> the devastating brilliance of their satire … The 90-minute revue … was written by the cast and Peter Cook … Interspersed among the skits are jazz ballads of social significance, delivered with deadpan decisiveness by [Carole] Simpson … Superb use was made of some terrifyingly funny film clips … The show is performed with shaggy, conversational informality, reminding one of improvised theater … There are merciless attacks on … such well-known figures as Prime Minister Macmillan, President Kennedy, President de Gaulle, Queen Elizabeth, the Communist hierarchy, British Labour leaders, ban-the-bomb pacifists, Laotian patriots and sex maniacs. In other words it is a sweeping, malicious and sneering commentary on the madness and chaos in our present world, some of it in questionable taste, but most of it intelligent and perceptive enough to be utterly breathtaking …
>
> Miss Bron – perhaps my favorite in the group – is a statuesque brunette with wildly expressive eyes, whose impersonation of a Cuban exile was uproarious, particularly when she explained that Castro's revolution could not possibly succeed because 'the Cubans don't like to be dragged into the streets to be shot

down for Leninism. They prefer to return to the good old days of being shot down for no reason at all.'

Beyond the Fringe was first seen in America on 8 September 1962, in Washington DC. 'Even though many thought the evening "frightfully British",' reported a correspondent of the London *Sunday Times*, 'I have rarely heard a Washington first-night audience in such constant convulsive laughter…Hardly a word of the original version was changed…' In fact there were a few alterations, including the dropping of 'Steppes in the Right Direction' (the National Anthem opener) in favour of a sketch featuring 'The Star-Spangled Banner', which included some jokes about America:

> DUDLEY: Isn't there a very serious colour problem over there?…I gather the Negroes are sweeping the country.
> JONATHAN: They are. It's one of the few jobs they can get…
> DUDLEY: Isn't there a lot of poverty in America?
> JONATHAN: Yes, there is, but luckily it's all been concentrated in the slum areas. It's beautifully done. You'd scarcely notice it.

The show reached the John Golden Theater, New York, at the end of October 1962, just as the Cuban missile crisis had erupted. Back in London, *Private Eye* suggested that Fidel Castro was about to attack the USA with 'Fagots [sic]…or Pooves, as they are known in this country…bearded little men…wearing swimming trunks…The [spy] pictures show very clearly the characteristics of the Fagotus Cubanus Castratus, or lesser bearded poove…' In New York, *Beyond the Fringe* made no reference to the crisis, but the critic of the *New York Times*, Howard Taubman, wrote next morning: 'In a time of peril try laughing. Look in on *Beyond the Fringe* and try not laughing.' Alistair Cooke told *Guardian* readers in Britain that the cast had 'repeated the *coup de théâtre* of their 1961 London opening. And there is hardly a review this morning that is less than delirious.'

Alan Bennett writes that the show's transfer to America 'put…an end to my dwindling hopes of becoming a historian'. In any case, as he told a reporter at the time, he had 'slightly gone off Oxford', and wanted to return to Yorkshire, perhaps to open a bookshop. Miller was still declaring that he wanted to retire from the stage; he said he was now 'tending to turn away from straight medicine', and wanted to be 'a sociologist, with a bit of creative writing on the side'. In New York he attended Sociology lectures at Columbia University. Later in the show's American run, he announced that he would be joining the *New Yorker* as a television critic: 'I don't want to do ordinary reviewing of the past week's programmes. I'll probably discuss things like American concepts of law, commercialism, big social ideas as refracted through the medium of television.'

Scarcely had *Beyond the Fringe* opened on Broadway than Bird, Bron, Fortune and Geidt, still in Chicago, received a message from Cook that he was going to open an American version of The Establishment in New York. 'He'd found a really nice place on East 54th Street,' recalls Bird, 'some American partners, money…I suppose he'd been in New York about a fortnight, must have got bored with just being a sell-out on Broadway.'

Cook's chosen premises were a run-down night-club, the El Morocco on 154 East 54th Street. This was quickly refurbished, and renamed Strollers Theatre Club; a visitor described it as 'a very corny-looking version of a Gay Nineties music-hall with old theatre posters plastered around a very jazzily painted ceiling'. The Establishment cast's opening night there, 23 January 1963, was as much of a social event for fashionable New York as the opening of The Establishment had been in London.

Luard had told the *Observer* that the American Establishment would present 'a satiric view of English life – and also look…satirically at American life through British eyes'. One sketch mocked Britain's lesser role in the American–British military partnership. Bird, as the British Defence Minister Peter Thorneycroft, tells an interviewer (Geidt) about the recent Cuban missile crisis: 'We in the British government were in the fortunate position of being informed in advance of the Cuban manoeuvres – about three and a half minutes in advance, but we *were* informed, through the good offices of the CIA – the Cuban Invasion Agency.' Geidt asks him what he thinks Kennedy's next move over Cuba will be, and he answers, with reference to the widespread discrimination against black university students in the USA: 'It would be much simpler if Dr Castro were a Negro. Then they could just persuade him to enrol for a university here.'

John Fortune recalls that he and his colleagues had been shocked by American racism:

> When we were opening in New York, the manager said, 'Listen, I know you need a band, and we don't have a lot of money – I wonder how you feel about working with black musicians? I can understand if you don't want to, but there's a piano player who's really quite good, and his name is Teddy Wilson.' I was passionate about jazz, and it was as if someone had said, 'The interior decorator is going to be someone called Picasso.' We had months with Teddy, and I became a great friend of his. Moreover all the great jazz musicians who were playing in the neighbourhood would drop in and listen to his sets, and sometimes sit in too.

The Thorneycroft sketch also highlights the feebleness of British defence plans – Thorneycroft explains that the latest missile has a range of only a hundred and fifty miles, but it might be useful for suppressing 'trouble in

Scotland'. Turning to Berlin, Thorneycroft admits that problems have been caused by the Wall,

> which is in some places eight or ten feet high…and this of course completely knocks out our missiles. They simply haven't got the height, you see…We are developing a number of new techniques to combat this – for example, the so-called Ladder Technique, which involves placing ladders against the Wall, carrying the missiles up and throwing them over.

Asking to be given a map of Berlin so that he can show the location of Checkpoint Charlie, Thorneycroft is instead given one of the world. 'Good God,' he exclaims in surprise, 'isn't Russia enormous?'

Peter Cook supplied The Establishment's New York show with a monologue in which a blind man addresses the audience: 'Good evening. I am blind…I am reading this message…on the wonderful system known as Broille – I'm sorry, I'll feel that again.' Much material was repeated from the London Establishment shows, including Bird as Jomo Kenyatta and the Bron–Fortune duologue about the couple failing to go to bed together. However, according to John Fortune, one item speedily vanished from the running order:

> On the opening night in New York, we did the Crucifixion sketch, and the next morning the reviews couldn't have been better. So we all arrived at the club to celebrate, drink champagne before the show, when these two men appeared – the biggest men you've ever seen, in homburgs and overcoats. And they said, 'We're from Cardinal Spellman's office, and you know that sketch you did last night about the Crucifixion? You won't be doing it tonight.' And being young and radical and satirical, we said, 'Certainly – we certainly won't be doing it tonight.' And we never did it again.
>
> It wasn't just cowardice. To perform cabaret in New York you have to get a licence from City Hall, and there just wasn't any way we could have got round that.

Jeremy Geidt remembers the incident rather differently:

> There may have been big men from Cardinal Spellman's office, but what I recall is that we were taken to some police HQ office and told to cut the Crucifixion because complaints had been received. Actually it was a bit scary as they seemed to have bulky files on us. (Maybe mine was so big because I'd been seeing someone called Jan Graham, who worked for the Foreign Relations Committee in Washington, and had for-your-eyes-only security status. She's now my wife.) But we invited the cops to come back as our guests, and they did.

Bird recalls similar trouble occurring on the political front:

I remember how efficient the Kennedy machine was at putting the lid on anything that hinted at his sex life. We'd picked up rumours about it – the press knew lots, but had a tacit agreement that they wouldn't print anything. And one night I threw in some oblique reference to it, on the lines of 'There are things you can't do when you've got a bad back', and the very next day our manager got a call from one of the Kennedy aides, saying, 'If that joke is repeated, the club will be closed down.'

Reviewing the New York Establishment show in the *New Republic*, Robert Brustein praised Peter Cook as the show's 'invisible mastermind', and described the cast as 'very talented in an unpolished sort of way; the writing is always literate and intelligent; and the atmosphere invokes that admirably jaded cynicism which has become the characteristic tone of the world's dissenting and disaffiliated young'. In 1969, discussing Stanley Kubrick's film *Dr Strangelove*, Brustein remarked on the similarity of its conclusion – 'a series of nuclear explosions... which flower soundlessly while a female voice croons "We'll Meet Again" ' – to a sketch in The Establishment's show. Jeremy Geidt says, 'This refers to Carole Simpson's last song, "Sitting Around", which she sang while riots and the like were projected behind her on film, ending with a lovely mushroom cloud.'

*

Meanwhile, during October 1962, *Private Eye* had celebrated its first birthday. The press coverage was enthusiastic. 'Though they calculatedly defame at least half a dozen people in every issue,' claimed *The Sunday Times*,

not a single libel action is in sight... Stirling Moss [the country's most famous racing driver] has rather taken the wind out of their sails. After their recent strip-cartoon, which described him as a 'boring little man, interested only in cars, money and sex in that order', readers wrote to say that they were outraged and appalled. Then Stirling Moss himself rang up – he wanted to know if he could use the cartoon as a Christmas card.

The *Eye* itself celebrated the anniversary with a mock company report from 'Satirical Holdings Ltd':

Lord Gnome stated that the closing year had been a highly successful one for British satire and for the Company in particular, in view of their virtual monopoly. 'Our expansion has been continuous,' he said, to loud cheers, 'and you will be extremely pleased to hear that almost all the Satire manufactured in the last year, notably by the Establishment and Fringe groups, has now been exported to the United States. This, of course, offsets our imports of crude satire from America which have proved so invaluable to our production line.'

A typical page of Willie Rushton drawings in *Private Eye*.

A few weeks before the anniversary, in August 1962, the *Eye* had acquired its own offices a few doors from The Establishment, at 22 Greek Street, above a betting shop and strip club. Sales were still increasing; the so-called 'Christmas issue', published in mid-autumn 1962, sold 46,000. Even this was material for lampooning:

> The latest figures…show that *Private Eye* has a circulation of 21,975 among Class 'F' readers…the lowest socio-economic grouping of the population: occasional labourers, MPs, Beaverbrook journalists, meths drinkers, drama critics…

In the month of this lampoon, August 1962, Malcolm Muggeridge, former editor of *Punch*,[1] had some sharp words about the satire boom in the *New Statesman*:

> Hard hearts and coronets throng the Establishment Club; *Private Eye* sells like hot cakes outside the Ritz; and the youthful performers in *Beyond the Fringe* survey in their appreciative audiences the living targets of their wit. The lash falls on willing shoulders, and evokes cries, not of pain or outrage, but of delight.
>
> The pleasure that is taken in contemporary satire by its victims necessarily raises certain doubts about it. Can it really be an effective antiseptic when there is absolutely no hurt?…Lenny and Mort, after all, are surely for the rich. The poor like *Coronation Street*.

Muggeridge also suggested that, while Swift's eighteenth-century satire had risen out of 'the furious indignation which lacerated his heart', and even twentieth-century cartoonists such as Low and Vicky looked contemptuously at the follies of mankind 'in the vain hope of correcting them', the creators of *Private Eye* were merely unruly children to whom

> authority is a schoolmaster, who, when his back is turned, can be pelted with paper darts and mocked with mimicry and funny faces. Such subordination can easily be laughed off; boys will be boys. With Swift it was different. He understood too well what he was attacking. When his trumpet sounded, the walls of Jericho really did tremble.

Moreover (concluded Muggeridge) the modern world was so 'inherently absurd' that one need not be inventive in order to ridicule it. 'The camera, not pencil or brush, is the young satirist's instrument.' Moreover, most of his targets crumbled long ago. 'He is rooting about in the rubble of an already blitzed citadel, advancing upon positions long evacuated.'

[1] In his biography of Muggeridge, Richard Ingrams writes that when Muggeridge and Claud Cockburn were both at *Punch* in the mid-1950s they had discussed starting a new satirical magazine 'which would be genuinely satirical and independent of all the commercial pressures they were then working under. Then the *Eye* had come along in answer to their prayers.'

As Luard had promised, the *Eye* published a book for the Christmas market. Called *Private Eye on London*, it was a rehash of some of the year's best items, linked by 'Little Gnittie' wandering through the capital city, just as he had through Oxford in *Mesopotamia*. The *Eye* also produced its first gramophone record, on the *Mesopotamia* model, with Ingrams, Wells and other regular contributors reading out another pick of the year's items, with sound effects. It could be ordered from Greek Street for twelve shillings and sixpence, and was described as 'Harold Macmillan Sings'. The final item on the second side was a recording of Macmillan himself reciting the old popular song 'She Didn't Say Yes, She Didn't Say No', to which musical accompaniment had been added. Solicited by the *Eye* for a comment, his wife, Lady Dorothy, replied, 'We haven't heard it. We have no gramophone.'

Christmas was also marked by Booker, Rushton and Ingrams being invited to contribute a satirical section to the seasonal edition of the *Spectator*. This took the form of an alphabetical guide to 'Modern Culture'; for example:

> K is for KEN. Ken is the Grand Old Man of British theatre criticism. He is thirty-five. He is a brilliantly savage critic. When he started he was brilliantly savage about everything. Then he discovered John Osbore ... He is no longer brilliantly savage. When the next Great Breakthrough comes he dare not miss it.

The *Eye* also claimed that it had been invited to contribute to television:

> The BBC has rashly handed over *Panorama* next week to the staff of *Private Eye*. The three-hour programme will include The Poet [Christopher] Logue in an exclusive interview with the Dalai Lama on 'Tibetan Satire Today'; Mr Peter Cook will chair a discussion between Sir Herbert Gusset and Mr Eric Buttock MP on 'The Newt: Its Position in the Common Market'.

This was in August 1962. A month later, a spoof BBC spokesman told *Eye* readers:

> We're right on the trail of all the latest trends with our forthcoming satirical programme *Saturday is Satire Day* – a sort of expanded, two-hour version of that frightful, that is to say delightful little cartoon satire that Bernie Levin's doing for us at the moment on *Tonight*. Absolutely no holds barred, of course, within the framework of the libel laws, good taste, and the producer's sense of humour – we're going to let these young chaps really let their hair down – we're even going to let them take off some of our own programmes ...

Although the spokesman was spoof, what he said soon proved to be absolutely true.

PART THREE

'The BBC moved in on the act'

1

A mixture of News, Interview, Satire and Controversy

It began with John Bird and Peter Cook. 'Peter and I were developing the idea of a television satire show based on The Establishment,' recalls Bird, 'with a certain amount of stuff to be done actually in the club, in front of the audience, and bits on film. And we wrote quite a lot, and had talks with Stuart Hood and Donald Baverstock, and they made encouraging noises.' Baverstock, then Assistant Controller of Programmes, Television, is described by his younger colleague Alasdair Milne as a 'wild, voluble Welshman with [a] broken nose…Ideas tumbled out of him in a flood…' Hood, a more sober BBC career man, was Controller of Programmes, Television.

Oddly, Baverstock said nothing about his conversations with Bird and Cook to a young BBC TV producer called Ned Sherrin, who was working on a plan for a late-night Saturday show. However, Bird was on Sherrin's list of possible linkmen. 'The next thing I knew,' says Bird, 'was Ned Sherrin ringing up and introducing himself, saying: "The BBC are thinking of doing a satire show." And both Peter and I felt they'd taken the idea from us.'

Sherrin invited Bird to lunch at a restaurant near the BBC TV studios, Bertorelli's on Shepherd's Bush Green. 'We had a long lunch,' writes Sherrin,

> and John, although guarded about committing himself to the show, was an invaluable new sounding-board for me as I tried to formulate my own ideas…I said that we were trying to construct a programme with a particular character for a particular time on a particular day of a week that was nearly over. We wanted to purge the memories of the week that had been, shrug and look forward to the next. John echoed and modified the Shell advertising slogan[1] in murmuring, 'That was the week that was.' It leapt at me as the perfect title.

---

[1] A famous advertisement for Shell petrol in the 1950s showed a fast car whizzing past a garage mechanic whose head twists so fast to watch it that it looks like two heads. He remarks admiringly, 'That was Shell, that was.'

Bird has no recollection of this: 'But Ned is so convinced about it that I'm reconciled to the idea.'

Sherrin, then aged thirty-one, the son of a farmer in the West Country, had done National Service in Austria with the Royal Corps of Signals, read Law at Oxford, and been one of the first graduates to join Britain's brand-new commercial television service, which began broadcasting in 1955. He had gone to ATV in Birmingham, where he showed considerable nerve at handling tricky live programmes. These included a series he had dreamed up called *Paper Talk*, in which a tabloid journalist called Douglas Warth challenged public figures in confrontational live interviews. 'Douglas engaged in wild attempts to provoke the unprovokable,' recalls Sherrin. 'He showed childlike joy at hearing Norman St John Stevas say "masturbation".' Sherrin soon learned from this that 'it is much better for your programme to be mentioned on the front pages of newspapers than in columns of television criticism'.

In 1957 he moved to the BBC to direct the cameras on its new early-evening magazine *Tonight*. Invented to fill the space between teatime children's programmes and the beginning of evening broadcasting (which had previously been left blank, from about 6.00 to 7.30 p.m., so that parents could get their offspring to bed), *Tonight* was the first British television programme to treat news entertainingly and slightly irreverently. Joining it, Sherrin found himself in charge of forty-five minutes of live television, five days a week. His own interests lay less in current affairs than in revue and musical theatre. While at Oxford he had assembled and produced several light-hearted shows, and he was now trying to create musicals with Caryl Brahms, a colourful writer and critic twice his age.[2] Consequently his own contributions to *Tonight* tended to be on the show-business side. He recalls that he 'scanned the obituary columns keenly and the moment I saw that someone had gone to the great Tin Pan Alley in the sky I would chase up the well-known songs he had written'. He would then book two young actor–singers, Millicent Martin and David Kernan, to 'coo the songs at one another'.

Meanwhile *Tonight* made some cautious forays into the edges of satire.

---

[2] Caryl Brahms (1901–1982), born Doris Caroline Abrahams, was a ballet, opera and theatre critic. She teamed up with a White Russian bridge expert, S.J. Simon (originally Skidelsky), to write a series of comic novels, beginning with the whodunnit *A Bullet in the Ballet* (1937). Sherrin had approached her in 1954, wanting to turn the Brahms–Simon novel about Shakespeare, *No Bed for Bacon* (1941), into a musical. (The 1999 film *Shakespeare in Love* bears a striking resemblance to this book.) Simon had died in 1950, and Brahms suggested that she and Sherrin collaborate on the adaptation. Sherrin describes her appearance as 'dark, tiny, with a very prominent nose on which she permanently perched large dark forbidding spectacles. Her pouter-pigeon figure and thrust-forward chin matched her combative approach to life.' She became a key contributor to *That Was The Week That Was*.

Sherrin recalls 'attempts to dramatize Michael Frayn's very funny columns in the *Guardian*', but says that

> the effect of fleshing them out with actors was invariably to transform them into nudging and winking…We [also] attempted a genuine television strip-cartoon…'Evelyn'…Bernard Levin wrote her and Tony Hoare devised paper scenery and paper clothes for the main stars, who were Prunella Scales as Evelyn and Ronnie Barker as the irascible Uncle to whom she posed unanswerable questions.

Dennis Potter may have been thinking of these elements of *Tonight* when he wrote in his *Daily Herald* television column, in the autumn of 1962, that the BBC's version of satire had, so far, been 'as harmless as a punch from a broken-down flyweight at the end of a gruelling fight'. Yet the BBC's internal rules at that time made it virtually impossible to broadcast anything more biting. Sherrin recalls that a small pamphlet, the *BBC Variety Programmes Policy Guide for Writers and Producers*, put shackles on all comedy – even though it had been issued in 1948 and never updated. 'There is an absolute ban upon the following,' it proclaimed:

> Jokes about –
>   Lavatories
>   Effeminacy in men
>   Immorality of any kind
>
> Suggestive references to –
>   Honeymoon couples
>   Chambermaids
>   Fig leaves
>   Prostitution
>   Ladies' underwear, e.g. winter draws on
>   Animal habits, e.g. rabbits
>   Commercial travellers

The *Guide* was less prohibitive when it came to politics:

> We are not prepared in deference to protests from one Party or another to deny ourselves legitimate topical references to political figures and affairs, which traditionally have been a source of comedians' material. We therefore reserve the right for variety programmes in moderation to take a crack at the Government of the day and the Opposition so long as they do so sensibly, without undue acidity, and above all funnily.

However, 'We must bar altogether…anything that can be construed as personal abuse of Ministers, Party Leaders, or MPs…[and] anything which can reasonably be construed as derogatory to political institutions.' Not surprisingly, in this climate, BBC television comedy in early 1962 played it very safe, with such programmes as *The Charlie Chester Music-Hall*, *The Charlie Drake Show*, a sitcom series starring Eric Sykes and Hattie Jacques, and the innocuous *Comedy Playhouse*. There was nothing on television – either BBC or ITV – even half as subversive as the Goons.[3]

By the beginning of 1962, the *Tonight* team was empire-building. Their show ran from Monday to Friday, but they were also casting an eye at the late-night Saturday slot, and Sherrin was dispatched to America to look at chat shows. He was already well versed in American satire, having been on an earlier BBC trip there to talent-scout among the new wave of American comics. He watched Mike Nichols and Elaine May, and Mort Sahl, and came back 'an unstoppable authority on the new American humour whenever I found half a chance to bore someone with my new knowledge'.

He did not feel that the American talk-show format would be right for the BBC; its success depended almost entirely on the host and guests, whereas the *Tonight* team was looking for something that could be 'structured, edited and controlled'. Meanwhile, even though the content of the programme was undecided, Sherrin started to look for performers.

He visited The Establishment on a night in April 1962 when Lenny Bruce was dealing with a drunken heckler:

> The joker stood up and, swaying, managed to enunciate clearly enough for all to hear, 'Why don't you tell an English joke?' There was a long, pitying pause before Lenny Bruce said – as kindly as he could – 'But you *are* an English joke.'

Bruce was out of the question, but in two other venues – Quaglino's restaurant, and the Blue Angel club, which was in a Berkeley Square basement – Sherrin watched a young performer called Lance Percival, who had appeared in John Bird's revue *Here is the News*. Percival, great-grandson of a bishop and an old boy of Sherborne public school, had developed the skill of improvising calypsos on any topic, and seemed ideal for the new programme. From the strange evening at the Room at the Top in Ilford, it was Willie Rushton that Sherrin picked rather than Richard Ingrams or John Wells. An 'automatic choice' was Millicent Martin, already very used to having songs thrown at her at the last minute on *Tonight*.[4]

Sherrin began to put his ideas on paper. He described the proposed late-

---

[3] Before the arrival of *TW3*, the late-night Saturday slot was occupied by sport. Other popular programmes included *Juke Box Jury*, *What's My Line?* (in which contestants guessed people's jobs by what they mimed), *Dr Finlay's Casebook*, *Dixon of Dock Green* and *Maigret*. In other words it was all very cosy.

[4] Born in 1935, Millicent Martin trained at the Italia Conti stage school and appeared in the chorus of West End musicals, before being picked for solo roles in *The Boy Friend* (Broadway production) and *Expresso Bongo*.

night show as 'a new sort of revolutionary programme ... a mixture of News, Interview, Satire and Controversy', and, in another memo, as 'an experimental two-hour mixture of conversation, satire, comedy, debate and music'. But who was to be the compère? It was at this point that Sherrin lunched with John Bird, whom he had seen and admired at The Establishment.

'Ned said, would I be the linkman,' recalls Bird. 'But I'd already agreed to go to America for a couple of months with The Establishment, and I felt I couldn't pull out of that – I didn't necessarily want to anyway. So Ned asked if I could suggest anyone else. Well, I was sharing a flat with David Frost.'

*

'It is hard to convey just how "ordinary" he seemed in those days,' writes Christopher Booker, describing David Frost at Cambridge, where they were freshmen together. In his first year, Frost had quickly attached himself to Peter Cook, whose style – the Goonish names and voices – he would imitate in his own cabaret turns, without (says Booker) ever getting them quite right: 'Compared with Cookie, he seemed like a little amateur trying to imitate this force of genius.'

In Booker's and other people's invariably mocking recollections of Frost as an undergraduate, there is an element of public-school contempt for an ambitious grammar-school boy ('There was a lot of snobbery among the whole group,' remarks Barry Humphries). Frost's suburban accent regularly comes in for gibes; John Wells claimed that the Old Etonian actor Jonathan Cecil once congratulated Frost on 'that wonderfully silly voice' that he used in cabaret, only to discover that it was his real one.

In his own memoirs, Frost gives no hint that he was treated with contempt at Cambridge, but his description of his arrival there does convey the kind of breathless *naïveté* that is implied in other people's accounts:

> The first night I spent at Gonville and Caius College, on Saturday, 27 September 1958, was only the second night I had ever spent away from my parents. I had arrived at five that afternoon ... and by six I felt as if I had lived there for years ...
>
> The Societies Fair at the beginning of that Michaelmas Term could not have been better timed ... Two of the larger stalls were for *Granta*, the university's general arts magazine, and the Footlights ... I remember thinking, 'God, I'd love to edit that, and I'd love to run that.'

He eventually achieved the editorship of *Granta*, and the secretaryship (though not the presidency) of the Footlights.

All his Cambridge contemporaries agree that the key to Frost's personality was ambition. Indeed, Booker claims that it was the only genuine element in his character:

David's most obvious quality was [that] he simply wanted to be amazingly famous for being David Frost…In fact he has unusual gifts – superhuman energy, compelling charm, an extraordinary memory for faces, great personal generosity. In all these respects, his eulogists, such as Bernard Levin, are completely right. What they forget to add is that the bad fairy who came late to the christening decreed that all these gifts should be used only to serve one end, David's peculiar ambition to be world-famous simply for the sake of being world-famous … That is why the most fitting epitaph on Frost's career remains, alas, that coined as long ago as 1967 by Kitty Muggeridge, when she said, 'Frost has risen without trace.'

This relentless ambition can hardly have been inherited from his father, a Methodist minister who was obliged to serve wherever his church posted him. Between David's birth in 1939 and his arrival at Cambridge nineteen years later, the Frosts lived in many small towns in southern England and the Midlands. Improbable as it may seem, David for a while seemed inclined to follow his father's calling. He writes that an evangelical rally conducted by Billy Graham 'made a real impression on me', and just before going up to Cambridge he became a lay preacher. But at university – where he arrived without doing National Service[5] – his enthusiasm was soon diverted into the fashionable channels of journalism and cabaret.

'Although he never produced anything very remarkable,' Booker writes of his work in these fields at Cambridge,

> Frost worked at it all so hard – at his sketches and little bits of journalism, at being everywhere and knowing everyone – that in that highly competitive world, he soon became a kind of affectionately regarded joke. He was so dogged and so open about his desire to 'get on' that … he was impossible to dislike.

Booker recalls the occasion when 'a group of his fellow cabaret artists arrived at Great Yarmouth to find posters announcing "DAVID FROST presents The Cambridge Footlights" – of which he was at the time only a very junior member'.

By the time he left Cambridge in the summer of 1961, Frost had secured a traineeship with the London-based commercial television company Associated Rediffusion. He also got himself an agent and, in the evenings, began to perform his own version of what he calls 'the new wave of satirical comedy' in various London clubs. 'David did some nights of cabaret at the Blue Angel,' recalls his flat-sharer John Bird,

---

[5] Frost writes, 'I…won a place [in December 1956] at Caius for the Michaelmas Term of 1959, after National Service. As it turned out, it was later ruled that undergraduates would do their National Service after their time at university and not before, and then while I was at Cambridge National Service was abolished altogether.'

and the thing about him is he's someone with complete self-belief. He'd come home from the Blue Angel, and I'd ask how it had gone, and he'd say, 'Oh, fine,' and then he'd describe what to me sounded like a nightmare – some drunk interfering with his act, or what have you – but David always saw himself as coming out of any situation triumphantly. And I envied him that.

Because he was working nightly at The Establishment, Bird had never been able to see Frost's Blue Angel act, 'but I suggested that Ned [Sherrin] should go and have a look at it – though I had no idea that he'd get the job on Ned's new programme'.

Frost says that, at the Blue Angel, he was ad libbing as Macmillan: ' "Ask me about any subject," I invited the audience. "What about the Queen?" someone shouted. "The Queen is not a subject, I replied."' Christopher Booker had seen this at Cambridge, and recalls that it was cribbed from Cook: 'When Cook introduced a "Macmillan Press Conference" cabaret act, to wild acclaim, Frost quickly had a pale version of his own.' Sherrin, not knowing this, was impressed:

> He was adept at provoking questions from his audiences and at the improviser's knack of changing gear from an unpromising premise to a position which enabled him to bang home a prepared joke as an apparently spontaneous answer. At the time I was still hoping that there might be room in the programme for some improvised comedy in the American manner of Nichols and May and Mort Sahl, and in the way in which the Establishment group were experimenting... At any rate it was clear that David was informed and enthusiastic and could think quickly on his feet. I arranged to lunch with him soon after, quite sure that I had found a valuable member of the supporting cast.

At the lunch, Frost seems to have persuaded Sherrin that he should not only perform in the new programme but present it – or at least co-present the pilot. He had made a few appearances in front of the cameras at Associated Rediffusion, introducing an occasional series of short programmes on the new dance craze, the Twist; but this was hardly enough experience to qualify him to handle an elaborate new live show with an untried format. As insurance, Sherrin also recruited, as second presenter, the far more experienced linkman, Brian Redhead, who had worked on *Tonight*.

The pilot was arranged for Sunday, 15 July 1962, to be recorded in front of a 'small and select audience'. Not content with co-presenting, Frost now began, in effect, to co-produce. 'He was tirelessly inventive and energetic in helping to shape and colour the programme,' writes Sherrin, adding that he particularly valued Frost's contacts with the current and recent Oxbridge cabaret stars, who could be enlisted as writers.

Sherrin wanted the programme to have a Brechtian style of presentation and décor, with no attempt to disguise the studio walls ... and cameras moving in and out in full view. The last-minute nature of the news content meant that cameras must at some time be seen inadvertently, so I decided that we might as well see them intentionally from the beginning.

Frost says that 'the casual let-it-all-hang-out style of Ned's camera work, with cameras in shot' was a help to the performers, creating a setting as informal as a college smoker:

> In a situation where you can see the back wall of the studio, the cameras and the sound boom, the performer can suggest the essence of Harold Macmillan two minutes after another quite different sketch, without having to be made up for twenty.

Sherrin is wary of claiming originality in his use of the bare studio – 'The opening credits of ITV's *Armchair Theatre* had always shown just that,' he says – but it was *TW3* that popularized the idea, and George Melly (in his cultural history of the period) regards it as immensely influential on the pop culture of the later 1960s:

> ... a great deal of pop's televisual language came out of Ned Sherrin's satirical shows ... Sherrin virtually invented the new TV brutalism: the scaffolding, the sound booms blatantly probing towards the speakers instead of jerking guiltily out of sight when picked up accidentally, and especially the cameras roaming around like purposeful Martians: the machinery as part of the spectacle it's responsible for.

The first pilot of *That Was The Week That Was* was recorded on the evening of Sunday, 15 July 1962. Though John Bird had turned down the chance to link the programme, he and the others from The Establishment had agreed to perform several sketches in the pilot, on the assumption that they would soon be back from America and could take part in at least some of the series, if it went ahead. Their material that evening included a semi-improvised sketch called 'Utyligenesis' which they had been performing at The Establishment:

JEREMY GEIDT: Utyligenesis, you may remember, is an idea of Sir Julian Huxley's, whereby he considers that one could create a race better than the race we already have ... Exactly how do you feel about Utyligenesis?

ELEANOR BRON: Well ... could you explain what it is, actually?

GEIDT: Utyligenesis, I think, can be best described as Artificial Insemination by VIPs ... One would be artificially inseminated by people at the top of their profession ...

BRON: But you see, I'm not married.

GEIDT: That's quite all right, that doesn't matter at all.

BRON: Is that all right? It's just sort of theoretical, is it? You mean, I don't actually have to – ? Oh, goodness!

Peter Cook was supposed to join Bird, Bron, Fortune and Geidt for a sketch called 'Panel Game'. Sherrin writes, 'My memory may be playing me false, but I recall some small drama during the recording as to whether Peter Cook would turn up or not – in the end he decided against an appearance.' However, Willie Rushton delivered a monologue (written by Frost) that was very much in Cook's style. Two days earlier, Harold Macmillan had announced a Cabinet reshuffle, and Rushton played a retiring Tory minister, 'Sir Arthur Trench-Foot', who had been in the Cabinet since the Munich crisis of 1938. Cook's influence was also notable in a sketch written by Johnny Speight, set in a hotel, in which a Grole-like nuisance pesters one of the guests.

There was a topical sketch on the new Telstar satellite station, and a piece adapted from one of Michael Frayn's *Guardian* columns in which instructions on using a public telephone box were given in Chinese style:

> Insert four pennies. If no have four pennies, take silver dollar along nearest smoking tube merchant humbly beg change. Smoking tube merchant unhumbly reply no change given for electric talker. Go eventide news scroll merchant, buy unwanted eventide news scroll. Return with change to public use electric talker. Find member public electric talking. Go teahouse, seek solace heavenly tea. Return public use electric talker, find no man electric talking. Feel encouragement. Find have given heavenly teahouse all heavenly pennies. Feel delicate Chinese melancholy...

Frost did his press-conference improvisation, but possibly not as Macmillan, since Rushton had been designated the show's Macmillan impersonator. 'It's my only impersonation that people have ever actually recognized,' Rushton said some years later, 'so I'm very grateful to the old bugger – but then I had voted for him, so I think he owed me something.' Millicent Martin sang the show's title song, with words by Sherrin and Caryl Brahms, who would supply fresh topical lyrics each week to Ron Grainer's theme tune; and at the end Lance Percival performed an ad-lib calypso commenting on things that had occurred during the programme.

Sherrin had planned two non-sketch items: an after-dinner-style conversation between the three people named by Kenneth Tynan as the best talkers in London; and a spot called 'Invective', featuring Bernard Levin. Besides his fame as drama critic and parliamentary sketch-writer, Levin had made a name in argumentative live discussions on *Tonight*, and in the new programme Sherrin wanted him to confront a series of people with whom he disagreed violently.

The after-dinner conversation, which featured George Melly, actor Harold Lang and film director Seth Holt, was a disappointment, mostly because they had been given the gloomy topic of 'human unhappiness'; but the Levin 'Invective' proved the most successful item in the programme. Levin was ranged opposite a group of lady members of the Conservative Party, who wore what Sherrin calls 'their traditional hats'. No record survives of what was said;[6] the ladies afterwards complained that Levin had made them a laughing stock, but Frost remarked that they needed no such assistance.

The pilot had been planned to last a generous two hours, and overran by a further half-hour. During it, Millicent Martin left to go on holiday to Spain, and Rushton claimed that she had arrived there before it finished. Frost says that 'by the end the audience of seventy or eighty were on the edge of their seats, not so much with excitement as with the sheer pressing inconvenience of having to sit for so long'.

Showing the recording of the pilot to his bosses, Sherrin emphasized that it had been an experiment: 'The object was not to produce an immediately transmittable show.' Donald Baverstock was very impressed by Frost's performance – 'Frost is a winner,' he noted – but he thought the improvisatory style of the team from The Establishment 'uncontrollable', and recommended that they should not be used again. Sherrin strongly disagreed, but in any case Bird, Bron, Fortune and Geidt were setting off for America, uncertain as to when they would be back.

Among others who watched the recording was Grace Wyndham Goldie, the formidable Head of Television Talks and Current Affairs, to whose department *Tonight* and Sherrin belonged. He remarks that Mrs Goldie was 'not without humour, but only in the sense that the equator is not without ice if you ship in a refrigerator'. In her memoirs, she writes that she found the pilot 'amateurish in its endeavours to seem casual, and politically both tendentious and dangerous'. She gave no encouragement to Sherrin to continue with the project, and it might have died at this stage if competition had not suddenly arisen.

David Frost was still on the payroll at Associated Rediffusion, and when word of the BBC pilot reached his employers they immediately proposed to make a satire programme of their own, with Frost as presenter. When in turn the BBC management heard of the Associated Rediffusion plans, they decided to press ahead with *That Was The Week That Was*. 'The competitor is going to attempt a light-hearted review of the week every Thursday in the

---

[6] Unfortunately the 16mm film on which the pilot was recorded has disappeared. John Bassett, who was in Sherrin's production team, confesses that he took it to his old school, Bedales, to show to the boys, and it never came back again. 'Oh, so that's where it is,' says Sherrin.

autumn quarter,' grimly noted the BBC's Controller of Programmes, Stuart Hood, on 3 August 1962. Sherrin was given the go-ahead for another pilot.

Frost decided to remain loyal to the Sherrin project, turned down the Associated Rediffusion offer and was consequently sacked from its staff. 'From then on,' he writes,

> I was full-time at Lime Grove,[7] sharing an office with Ned as we worked on the second pilot. By now we had become *de facto* joint editors of the programme, and we spent much of the time … lunching writers … and trying to boil down the ingredients that we thought had worked on 15 July … That period was really the making of *TW3*.

Among the lunched writers were Keith Waterhouse and Willis Hall. Then in their early thirties, they had known each other since schooldays in Leeds, and had begun to collaborate when they adapted Waterhouse's novel *Billy Liar* for the stage in 1960. On *Tonight*, Sherrin had used some material from their revue *England Our England*, which Richard Ingrams had praised in *Time & Tide*. 'We were summoned to Lime Grove,' recalls Waterhouse,

> that cluster of more or less condemned terrace houses knocked together[8] that was the home of some of the BBC's best output (interesting how the more ramshackle the premises, the more stimulating the product) … Mrs Wyndham Goldie, who had the demeanour of a magistrate about to impose a stiff sentence for shoplifting, talked a good deal about German cabaret … David Frost talked about his pension insurance, advising Willis and me, ten years his senior, that it was never too early to start. Ned Sherrin told his theatrical stories. As Willis and I left the table we casually agreed to contribute to the show whenever we got an idea. In the event, we wrote for every single edition of *TW3* from the first to the last.

Sherrin had been impressed by the chubby comic actor Roy Kinnear's performance in *England Our England*, and booked him for the second pilot, which was recorded on 29 September. A group of barristers came along to be Bernard Levin's target for abuse. Brian Redhead did not come along; he had been dispensed with, for Frost was now to be sole presenter.

Christopher Booker, who was soon to work with him on the programme, grudgingly allows that Frost now displayed extraordinary skills:

> Frost was never by any stretch of the imagination a 'satirist' (indeed he scarcely held passionate views on anything) but … it was impossible not to be impressed

---

[7] The former film studios in Shepherd's Bush which were the main BBC Television premises until the opening in 1960 of Television Centre, about half a mile away. Lime Grove was retained for some years thereafter as an extra production facility (*Tonight* and *Panorama* were broadcast there).

[8] Waterhouse is referring to the Victorian villas adjacent to the studio building, which housed BBC offices.

by … his extraordinary, intuitive feel for television itself. In the studio, he was instantly, nervelessly at home, as if the very presence of cameras and lights gave him an extra charge of confidence and energy.

This time Baverstock, Mrs Goldie and the other BBC executives decided that Sherrin (and Frost) had got it roughly right, and he was given a starting date of just under two months' time. Meanwhile Baverstock made a note of the programme's objectives – or, rather, of the BBC's anxiety not to be accused of climbing on the satire bandwagon:

> This programme does not spring from a desire to get in on the 'satirical vogue'. The word 'satire' will not appear in the programme or be used in connection with it in our publicity. The *raison d'être* of the programme as we see it lies elsewhere. Many of the elements in the programme will be seen as satire by viewers and critics. But it is a term we cannot use ourselves as a guide to action in producing the programme. It is too vague.
>
> The general run of serious television programmes is helping to make people more and more earnest about the world and its doings. Week in week out the public breathes, and we foster, a kind of philosophy of concern, goodwill and public spiritedness on a massive scale … Not surprisingly, a large amount of this communication goes on in language that is colourless, obscure, stale and devitalized. It all adds up to what Mary McCarthy calls 'the slow drip of cant'.
>
> Late on Saturday night people are more aware of being persons and less of being citizens, than at any other time of the week. It is therefore the best time to hang this contemporary and vague 'philosophy' on the hook in the hall, to relieve the pressure of earnest concern and goodwill which presses down on us for the rest of the week. There should be room in this programme for prejudice, for cynicism, for Juvenal's 'sacred indignation'.

The BBC's aim, in other words, was higher than that of the 'satire boom' – no less than to revive satire of the quality of Juvenal's. This was a tall order for an organization that did not permit jokes about lavatories or 'immorality of any kind'. At no time in the history of satire had anything satirical been commissioned and promoted by any kind of public body or bureaucracy, let alone one as august as the British Broadcasting Corporation, with its anxious cabals of Heads of This and Controllers of That, sending each other curt, tense little inter-office memos.

The real impetus, of course, would come from the writers and performers; and Frost emphasizes that *TW3*, or *TWTWTW*, as the new programme was soon nicknamed, did set out with a mission:

> We did not come to *TW3* with a specific agenda or political programme. We were not further examples of what the newspapers called 'the Angry Young Men'. We were the Exasperated Young Men – exasperated by Britain's recurring

failures, by hypocrisy and the shabbiness of its politics … There was no danger
of running short of material.

To be more specific (Frost continues), the aims were dual: first, to break
open what he calls the 'traditional *cordon sanitaire* of sanctimony' that in
1962 still surrounded public figures; and second, to treat the television
audience as mature adults with independent minds, and not just *hoi polloi*
who accepted orders from officialdom: 'We kept coming back to the way
that audiences in Britain were underestimated by so much of television, and
by so many of the newspapers and advertisers.'

Sherrin stresses that, before it began, no one expected *TW3* to win vast
numbers of viewers: 'It was late-night, ghetto television which would
probably only attract a fringe metropolitan audience.' Millicent Martin,
offered a contract for the first series, was unhappy to have to turn down a
pantomime engagement in Bromley, since *TW3* seemed nothing special to
her. She said later, 'If I'd known I was part of an era, I'd have taken more
notice.'

Meanwhile Dennis Potter wrote in his *Daily Herald* TV column, a month
before *TW3* began, on 20 October 1962, 'ITV are … mounting a late-night
satirical spot optimistically entitled *What the Public Wants* … The BBC
have also announced plans to stage a similar late-night show … I hope these
new programmes will get away with murder. The "new" humour, whether
sick or savagely satirical, is at least pungent and provocative – qualities
desperately needed on the TV.'

2

....

'Live' as hell

'That Was The Week That Was,' sang Millicent Martin, into the lens of Camera 4 in Studio 2, Television Centre, live at 10.50 p.m. on Saturday, 24 November 1962.

> That Was The Week That Was
> It's over, let it go.
> But what a week it was –
> On the Stock Exchange the tea shares hit an all-time low.

The song was illustrated with headlines and photos from the week's news stories to which the Brahms–Sherrin lyrics alluded:

> A Time Study group's asking questions at Court,
> And who'll get his finger out when they report?
> At Brussels Ted Heath has the world at his feet –
> He got tariff reductions on kangaroo meat.
> Sir Keith Joseph's lady gave the homeless a break:
> They called to protest, she said, 'Let them eat cake!'[1]

Even today, viewed through the fog of an ancient 'telerecording' (originally made on 16mm film), the first edition of *TW3* looks startling. The production style is unbelievably casual. Cameras wander in and out of shot; indeed sometimes Sherrin, as director, seems more interested in showing the studio equipment than the performers. Frost, Rushton and the rest of the team read some of their lines off autocue, and deliver some from memory, but when seated at the long desk which became one of the

---

[1] Prince Philip had shocked the nation by using *risqué* language about slackers – he said they should 'pull their fingers out'. As Lord Privy Seal, Edward Heath was responsible for negotiations concerning Britain's projected membership of the European Economic Community. A deputation of the homeless had marched to the residence of Sir Keith Joseph, Minister of Housing and Local Government, where his wife had given tea to the fifteen children among them.

A Lewis Morley shot of a rehearsal during the first series of *That Was The Week That Was*; on the far right is cartoonist Timothy Birdsall, who died before the second series.

programme's trademarks they tend to glance openly at scripts. Millicent Martin invariably delivers her complicated songs with ultra-professional polish, but the other performers frequently fluff words and look at the wrong cameras. However, none of it matters. Indeed the lack of polish, the fact that nobody seems worried about delivering a smooth performance, puts the emphasis where it should be, on the material.

The challenge for the performers was immense, and Willie Rushton recalls fortifying himself before transmission:

It was produced under Talks, which meant that we were protected from the very jealous members of Light Entertainment who didn't like us at all. But we also got trolley-loads of drinks, being Talks – there was a wonderful piss-up before and after the show, which you wouldn't have got with Light Entertainment. Mrs Reynolds was the magnificent lady in green who served the drinks before and afterwards, and knew everybody and looked after them, and was, I think, a major influence – she did make sure you were relatively sober by the time you got on. And the studio audience were served with the most appalling mulled wine, served by girls in black fishnet stockings. And it was 'live' as hell – it was very exciting.

As Millie Martin finishes the first chorus of the title song, the picture switches to Frost, who utters his first words on *TW3*: 'There's a one-eyed yellow idol to the north of Kathmandu,/With a little Chinese rifle in 'is 'and.' Recalling this, he comments, 'Scarcely the stuff of which revolutions are made, but in its reference to current Chinese designs on India it was topical and got a respectable laugh.'

Besides presenting and appearing in sketches, Frost had now persuaded Sherrin to let him write some of the material, and had arranged for the BBC to hire Christopher Booker to help him – Booker was, after all, the editor of *Private Eye*, and this would strengthen *TW3*'s satirical credentials. It was agreed that they would co-write a political opening sketch each week. The first was a parody of television's coverage, a few days earlier, of an East Anglian by-election:

DAVID: By-elections in Central Dorset and North Suffolk, so first of all over to Lance Percival in the market place in North Suffolk.

The *TW3* cast in rehearsal: Frost, Rushton, Martin, Kinnear and Percival.

LANCE: Well, this is Lance Percival in the market place in North Suffolk and now I return you to the studio.

DAVID: Well, thank you, Lance Percival, and now straight back to Lance Percival...

This was crude stuff compared to the Waterhouse and Hall sketch that followed it – and which Sherrin thought the best topical piece in the first programme. Legislation had been passed to allow soldiers to be candidates for Parliament, and the writers fantasized about the army itself becoming a political party, with Roy Kinnear as a squaddie in battledress giving a party political broadcast:

What is our policy? It is as follows. Right? No. 1: Commonwealth.

Our Shadow Secretary for Commonwealth Affairs is Provost-Sergeant Macmichael, J., who has done extensive tours of the Commonwealth and is in fact married to a wog bint. So what Jock does not know about these hot countries is not worth knowing; get your knees brown, Lord Home.

No. 2: Afri'a. Our Shadow Colonial Secretary, Signalman Cooncy, who is himself an Anglo-Banglo, proposed to go on a goodwill mission to all these nignog countries and chat up the blackies as if they was man to man. As Signalman Cooney so shrewdly puts it, you've got to live with the darkies, therefore you might as well look as if you was good mates – and I endorse this policy.

Policy No. 3: Common Market. I would like to introduce to you tonight our European expert, Fusilier Geordie Woolerton...He outlines our Common Market Policy quite simply and succinctly: You cannot trust the Krautheads. Also, if the price of a bottle of lager at Helga's Bar, Windelstrasse, is indicative of Common Market trading, you can stuff it...

Next came what Frost describes as 'a mock tribute to Norrie Paramor, for ten years Artists and Repertoire Manager of Columbia Records, which had been inspired by a comment made to me some months earlier by George Martin'. Martin, who worked for the rival EMI, had pointed out that Paramor was in the habit of putting his own songs on the B-sides of potential hit singles, and the *TW3* 'tribute' gave an airing to these sub-standard numbers. Sherrin says that Paramor was furious at the exposé. But the Paramor style was already on its way out; this was the month in which the Beatles (produced by George Martin) entered the charts for the first time with 'Love Me Do'. Jonathan Miller sees a connection between the Beatles and *Beyond the Fringe*: 'We had the same timing as the Beatles and challenged the same conventions...In a way you could say that the Beatles were satirical, or at least sceptical.' This is borne out by an interview with Paul McCartney in the *Evening Standard* for 2 February 1963 in which he

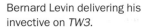
Bernard Levin delivering his invective on *TW3*.

said, 'Our humour is based on anything that other people don't laugh at – death, for instance, or disease.'

The victims of Bernard Levin's invective in this first transmitted *TW3* were a group of men working in public relations, a profession Levin despised. Pat Williams in next morning's *Sunday Telegraph* wrote, 'Bernard Levin, in unarmed combat, took on and wonderfully insulted a crew of public relations representatives. They may have thought they had come to a party but they ended up at a massacre. Certainly the discussion was far more serious and naked than others on the topic we have heard on more "serious" programmes.'

Thirteen years later, Levin wrote of *TW3*:

I don't know why – I don't think any of us could say – it was such a happy experience for all who took part. If I had to guess, I would have named Ned as the chief reason; he has an altogether exceptional talent for human juxtaposition, and assembled the participants with a skill that brought out the best (or, as the complainers would say, the worst) in them all. Certainly I do not believe that anyone in the team failed to feel the same intense satisfaction at a shared experience that I remember so vividly myself ...

It was not the things we did on the programme I was remembering, but the hours we passed in each other's company off the studio floor; padding in and out of each other's dressing rooms; eating and drinking at the magnificent running buffet in the green room, presided over by the imperturbable and motherly Mrs Reynolds; unwinding at dinner.

Among the other items in the first *TW3* was a 'quickie' written by Richard Ingrams, about the fact that the film of *Mutiny on the Bounty* had cost £7 million, which was 'six times the cost of the whole British Navy for the year in which the Mutiny happened':

CHRISTIAN: Look, sir. What's that, sir?
BLIGH: My God, cameramen. Thousands of cameramen.

There was also a sketch about a spate of newspaper articles on pre-marital sex, with Millicent Martin and David Kernan singing a parody of the current pop song 'Love and Marriage'. In the script, it begins:

> Sex before Marriage,
> Sex before Marriage,
> Goes on everywhere from Hull to Harwich.

In rehearsal, 'Sex' was changed to 'Love', possibly by Mrs Goldie's deputy, Alasdair Milne, who had been set to keep a discreet but close watch on Sherrin and *TW3*.

A last-minute addition to the first programme was a young cartoonist, Timothy Birdsall, who could draw skilfully live on camera. Frost had known him at Cambridge, and he was now contributing to *Private Eye* and the *Spectator*. Frost recalls that 'he had appeared in our office on the Friday with some sketches about Identikit. As we talked, the sketches grew into a dialogue which we scripted together on the spot. This became our regular way of working.'

The first Birdsall–Frost piece exposed the ludicrousness of the Identikit way of picturing criminals. Later Birdsall appearances included 'How to Draw Your Own Political Cartoon', and 'A Day in the Life of a Cartoonist', who has the sort of experiences he invents for his characters. Sherrin writes, 'Birdsall…almost by accident…pioneered his own brand of illustrated monologue with a lightness and pertinence unique among television illustrators.'

Quite a lot of material in the first edition of *TW3* was repeated from the second pilot, including a sketch Peter Cook had written in his Cambridge days, and which had subsequently been used in the Edinburgh *Beyond the Fringe*. It parodied the 'product placement' advertising shows which were then still seen on ITV, soap-opera-like programmes in which merchandise

The 'Jim's Inn' product placement sketch which concluded the first edition of *TW3* on 24 November 1962: (left to right) Roy Kinnear, David Frost and Lance Percival.

was mercilessly plugged. It was a classic piece of Cook, performed by Lance Percival, Roy Kinnear and Frost (in an imitation Peter Cook voice) as Jim the barman:

> NIGEL: Where did you come by this suit?
> BASIL: Old Nige's face is going to be a picture when he hears that my suit was picked up at our old friend, Arthur Purvis of Gorleston ...
> NIGEL: And look at these shoes ... They can't have cost a penny under £167,000.
> BASIL: Well, as a matter of fact, Nige, they did. They cost exactly a penny under that sum. The reason why he's able to run a line like this is, of course, that Purvis, and Purvis alone, has the courage to use violence on his workers.
> JIM: Yes, he cudgels them into greater efforts every year. I was talking to Arthur the other day and he said that all Purvis's electricity is provided by women rushing after bread on treadmills.

Frost ended the sketch and the first *TW3* by calling 'Time, gentlemen, please'. The programme had overrun, and, turning to the camera, Frost remarked that members of the Lord's Day Observance Society must be reaching for their pens, 'as the BBC is in danger of going into Sunday broadcasting'. He delivered a final political gag, about Chancellor Adenauer of Germany saying, 'I am old enough to be your Führer'; then the credits rolled as the band, led from the piano by musical director Dave Lee, reprised the title song.

*

As soon as the first show had come off the air, the cast climbed into taxis and went off to the fashionable King's Road to celebrate into the small hours in a restaurant called the Casserole. The next morning, Frost and Sherrin met again, at the Kenya Coffee Bar in the same street, 'and we shared a feeling of anticlimax', writes Sherrin.

> Everything had gone as well or better than we expected. There had been calls of outrage and we had had congratulatory messages. However, what we wanted was notices. Suddenly and miraculously David came upon a review by Pat Williams in the place we least expected it – the back page of the *Sunday Telegraph*.

Frost remembers this 'moment of pure joy ... It said everything that we could have prayed for':

> LATE-NIGHT TV SATIRE HITS TARGET
>
> Without reservations, *That Was The Week That Was*, the BBC's first late-night satirical show, is brilliant. It based itself securely on the week's events, repeating and expanding on its idiocies, invectives and near-libels.
>
> It did so with intelligence and dislike ...
>
> Much of the material was written by the experts in this sort of thing: Peter Cook and Michael Frayn.[2] All of it was uncompromisingly 'in' ... Best of all was a manic sketch of 'Jim's Inn' ...
>
> This is the first late-night show I have seen on television which uses the licence of the late hour and the smaller audience to be adventurous both visually and in its material ... If the pattern does not ossify into a formula, then for the first time it seems reasonable that one should need a licence for a television set; it can be as lethal as a gun.

Monday morning brought more rave reviews, including a double-edged one from Peter Black in the *Daily Mail* – 'David Frost, the anchor man, established himself as what you could call the first anti-personality on TV' – and a characteristically overwritten one by Dennis Potter in the *Daily Herald*:

---

[2] Frayn does not seem to have contributed to the first *TW3*.

Satire – or how to laugh when something is gripping your throat – is getting a foothold in the most unlikely places nowadays. Even Auntie BBC … is having a go …

One or two items fell flat, as is inevitable in an opening programme, but more than enough blows thudded home for the purple bruises to be counted.

The *Daily Sketch* reported: 'Only five viewers phoned the BBC to complain about the programme and eighty-three phoned in congratulations.' Viewing figures were soon available; the BBC executives had hoped that *TW3* would have at least a million viewers, but Audience Research reported that the first edition had been watched by three and a half times that number, very high for a show starting so late in the evening. A memo soon arrived in the *TW3* office from Kenneth Adam, Director of Television: 'D. G. [Director-General] says that he wants there to be no delay in his offering warmest congratulations to all those concerned with the production of *This [sic] Was The Week That Was* last Saturday night.'

Hugh Carleton Greene, Director-General of the BBC from 1960, was the younger brother of the novelist Graham Greene, six and a half feet tall, moon-faced and rather donnish in manner, but more liberal than most of his predecessors or successors. 'I was delighted,' he said (some years later) of the first edition of *TW3*; 'the programme sprang fully armed into life – almost every item seemed to be on the ball, and I thought, really we have achieved something.' After leaving Oxford in 1933, Greene had joined the Berlin office of the *Daily Telegraph*, and his five years in the German capital had left him with a very favourable view of the possibilities of political cabaret. Willie Rushton recalls, 'Whenever he [Greene] was asked about satire, he always said, "I remember Berlin in the thirties," which was obviously the big experience of his life.'

Sherrin was delighted with the way that Frost had coped with fronting a live show for the first time: 'His curious classless accent, sloppy charcoal suit and over-ambitious haircut concealed a man who had come into his kingdom with a bound … He responded happily to the pressures and … rarely made errors, except in sketches.'

Frost's failings as a comic performer in 'Jim's Inn' had been noticed by Jack Duncan, Richard Ingrams's former partner in his theatrical venture, Tomorrow's Audience. Duncan had joined *TW3* as an assistant director. 'I was unemployed,' he explains.

> *TW3* had just done a pilot, and Ned was finding that rehearsing the sketches, as well as working with the writers, was proving a bit too much, and he wanted someone who could take that over. (I thought for years it had been Rushton who'd suggested me, because I'd given him his acting break in *The Bedsitting Room*. But Chris Booker then said it had been him.)

Ned would give me the sketches, and I would cast them, rehearse them and have them ready in a suitable form on the Saturday morning. Rehearsals were very informal – we used to rehearse in a room in the Executive Suite at Television Centre, and there was no marking the floor or anything like that. The cast usually managed to do some learning of the material; the autocue would be there on the night, but you can't do sketches staring at the camera.

Millicent Martin agrees that the autocue was best avoided:

The music for my songs came on the Thursday, the lyrics came on the Friday, and I performed them on Saturday! It was no good using autocue; in those days it couldn't run fast enough to keep up with the jazz songs, because it was a big roll of paper, which would tear if it went too fast.

Lance Percival, who calls Jack Duncan a 'brilliant' director, describes the different talents of the cast. Sherrin had now signed up a young North-Country actor, Kenneth Cope, who was appearing in *Coronation Street*, where he was playing Jed Stone. 'I suppose,' says Percival,

people were meant to think that we were bright young things fresh from university, like *Beyond the Fringe*, but in fact David Frost was the only one with a degree. Roy Kinnear was the real actor of the group, and could get into any character, though Ken Cope was pretty versatile too. Millie Martin was an experienced actress, but she was mostly doing the singing. Willie Rushton was playing himself, and I was doing funny voices. David was rather separate from us – we'd mix together socially, but not so much with him. And Ned kept the writers in an entirely different compartment. We didn't meet them at all. And we usually didn't see what they'd written till Friday morning.

Ken Cope did not get his script till Friday night, when he arrived in London from a week's work on *Coronation Street* in Manchester. He remarks that he and the others did not necessarily understand all the nuances of what they were delivering. Christopher Booker, too, emphasizes that the *TW3* performers were mostly not 'real' satirists:

Up to that point in 'satire', if people went on stage, they were doing their own lines. So there was an integrity to it. But here you had people who were not in a million years 'satirists' (apart from Willie) uttering other people's words with varying degrees of success. In a way, it was the old revue world hitting back at satire.

Jack Duncan says that Frost's desire to appear as a satirical all-rounder caused a certain amount of embarrassment:

In the first programme, Frostie appeared in a sketch ['Jim's Inn'], and he was dreadful. Also he obviously wanted to direct the sketches himself. So I went up

TW3 songstress Millicent Martin: 'The music for my songs came on the Thursday, the lyrics came on the Friday, and I performed them on Saturday!'

to Ned and said, 'I don't want Frost in any more sketches. He's not an actor.' And I never had him in any more sketches – which was good for the programme, because it turned him almost exclusively into the front-man journalist, which it needed. Though Ned let him go on doing monologues – I never directed those.

In a newspaper article a few weeks after the show had begun, Sherrin wrote of Frost's compèring style:

> He seems to me to have a unique ability to switch from wild comedy to straight narration. He is, incidentally, the first of a new sort of television performer, coming straight from school or university into the studio and absorbing cameras and cue cards and inlay and overlay and run-up and feedback as the basic tricks of his first trade.

George Melly sees Frost's *TW3* compèring as more than slick professionalism; he reckons that it potentially changed the whole persona and image of the television presenter. 'Sherrin's "invention" of David Frost,' Melly writes,

> was another stroke which was later to turn out to pop's advantage … In the early heady days of *TW3* he stood out as the first compère who, instead of helping to

keep the children from becoming over-excited, seemed determined to make
them behave even worse.

And Bernard Levin writes, in his book on the decade, 'Perhaps David Frost
grasped earlier than most the quality of the Sixties.'

While *TW3* was arriving in a burst of glory, Associated Rediffusion's
Thursday-night satire show *What the Public Wants* came and went almost
unnoticed. It began on 25 October 1962 at 11.12 p.m. and ran for half an
hour. The *TV Times* announced:

> The programme will be a weekly dose of virulent, unrestrained satire. Backed
> by swinging jazz from the Tubby Hayes Quintet, the members of the cast –
> Chris Bryant, Allan Scott, both Canadians, Dorothy Bromley, Aubrey Woods
> and Clemence Bettany – will be looking at people, from a race-rioter to the
> Prime Minister, at subjects from the Common Market to the space race.

Philip Oakes, who was the programme's script editor, says that a talented
team of writers was assembled, but it quickly transpired that, unlike the
BBC's Charter, the Television Act which had governed ITV since its
inauguration specifically ruled out 'any offensive representation or
reference to a living person'. The consequence of this (says Oakes) was that

> they appointed our very own censor, some lady from the pay office or something
> – she certainly wasn't anything to do with television – and, poor woman, she
> had to adjudicate on things which were due to go out that night. They were
> mostly political and sexual things that she censored, none of which struck me
> as very serious, but it caused a certain amount of hell, because we had nothing
> to replace it, and there was sheer panic.

Cast member Aubrey Woods has similar memories of 'terrible trouble with
the legal department – we were scarcely allowed to mention anyone in
public life who was actually alive. And, probably as a consequence, I can't
remember a single one of the sketches, though I think it was really pre-
Beyond the Fringe in style, slightly naïve.'

What the Public Wants ran for two months, ending on 20 December 1962.
A few days later the *Sunday Telegraph* reported that Granada Television
had been piloting a satire programme called *Man Bites Dog*, but had now
'turned it in, realizing it couldn't get away with it in terms of the Act'. The
BBC had therefore succeeded in the face of its rivals' failure. Giving an
interview many years later, Hugh Greene claimed much of the credit for
this, alleging that his own liberal vision (and German experiences) lay
behind *TW3*:

> I had the idea that it was a good time in history to have a programme that would
> do something to prick the pomposity of public figures; I've always had a

considerable degree of confidence in the power of laughter. I thought it would be healthy for the general standard of public affairs in the country to have a programme which did that. *How* it did that was, to my mind, not my affair. All I did was to start talking about this idea, to start putting it in people's minds. So far as a programme format was concerned I didn't have anything in mind – I *did* have in my mind the political cabaret in Germany; I hadn't known it in the Weimar Republic, but it still did exist in the first years of the Nazi regime.

*

The second edition of *TW3*, on Saturday, 1 December 1962, opened with a political sketch by Frost and Booker surveying the likely successors to Harold Macmillan. Considering the Home Secretary (a highly unpopular figure), Frost told viewers:

> Never forget Mr Henry Brooke, the Quiet Man of British Politics – quiet, indeed, silent. Particularly since he came successfully through this week's Soblen debate. As one correspondent said later, 'It just shows that if you're Home Secretary you can get away with murder.'

Booker explains that this refers to the death of Dr Robert Soblen: 'The American, who had been convicted of spying, attempted suicide while being taken to America, ended up in a London hospital with Mr Brooke insisting that he be deported the moment he was in a fit state and then managed to

Ned Sherrin directs Willie Rushton as a *TW3* Dixon of Dock Green.

repeat his suicide effort with greater success.' The 'murder' accusation was strong stuff by BBC standards, especially since its guidelines forbidding 'personal abuse of Ministers' were still in force.

TW3 was still using up material accumulated for the pilots, some of it from Frost's collection of old Footlights scripts. Three of these, used in the second edition of the programme, were by John Cleese. 'David was then the only person in England who knew who I was,' says Cleese. 'I was only paid £4 a minute for the ones that were used on *TW3*, but someone kindly inflated the amount of time they supposedly took, so that I got £24 for one that had really only lasted four minutes.' One of them was a parody of a popular scientist giving a television talk full of meaningless statistics: 'Three hundred and seventeen light years, or just under the distance that an ordinary rhinoceros, running at 18 miles per hour, would travel if he ran for 148 million years.' The second Cleese script was an episode from an incomprehensible TV thriller serial, much like the 'Ian Phlegm' parody in *Parson's Pleasure*. The shortest and most effective of the three was a quickie about the increasingly tarnished reputation of the police – as Frost puts it, 'Dixon of Dock Green was no longer [their] sole public image':

> LANCE *enters in policeman uniform.*
> ROY: Good evening.
> LANCE: Evening, sir. (*He beats* ROY *up.*) Just a routine enquiry, sir.

Jack Duncan says that, during the run of *TW3*, he himself was beaten up by two plain-clothes policemen in Hampstead, after he had made a cheeky remark to them.

Commenting on the second *TW3*, the *Daily Telegraph* reported that there had been '37 complaints from viewers', some of whom had objected to 'ribald remarks' in a monologue delivered by Kenneth Cope as yobbish professional cricketer. It ended with him holding up a pair of cricket balls: 'Any ignorant git that says different is talkin' a load o' these.' Again, this was strong stuff by current BBC standards.

On the day that the third edition was to be transmitted, Saturday, 8 December 1962, the *Daily Herald* published a feature on *TW3* by its arts reporter, David Nathan, who visited the team in their Lime Grove office:

> Before it was taken over by the BBC the bay-windowed terraced house … must have been highly respectable. Now it is the home of the programme that is keeping 5 million Britons out of their beds until after midnight … Three large desks are crammed into what was once the back parlour … Behind the one with the two bottles of cough medicine sits Ned Sherrin … a large man in an aggressively striped shirt. Opposite is David Frost … At the other end is one of three overworked secretaries …

The *TW3* cast at the opening of the second series, in September 1963: (right to left) David Frost, Lance Percival, David Kernan, Al Mancini, Millicent Martin, Kenneth Cope, Robert Lang, Willie Rushton and Irwin C. Watson.

In and out flow associate producers, associate editors, researchers and people who have ideas they find vaguely amusing and think might be useful. Among them John Bassett, who got together the *Beyond the Fringe* crowd...'We call him the Father of English Satire,' explained Frost kindly.

Bassett was receiving a retainer of £30 a week during the London run of *Beyond the Fringe*, which he attended assiduously ('I must have seen the show about eight hundred times') but he earned nothing from the American production. 'From the springboard of that show,' he says,

> I should have had a fantastic career. And it took an awful lot of adjustment to realize that I didn't have the talent. I thought that, after coming to London with a show like that, somebody would say, 'Let's get hold of the guy who made it work.' And I sat around waiting for that to happen. And was surprised when it didn't.

He had hoped to be selected for the replacement cast when the original four went to America. Instead, as Alan Bennett puts it, 'He was edged out by the Albery management. We should have stood up much more strongly for him than we did.'

Meanwhile Bassett had joined Granada Television as a trainee director, soon moving to the BBC where he worked on *Tonight*. 'Then Ned very kindly took me on for *TW3*,' he says self-effacingly. 'I think I was a big disappointment to him – but I'm an affable, nice fellow to have around! And I did organize the music, and edited the graphics to fit it.' Sherrin praises Bassett's contribution: 'He knew lots of jazz musicians, which wasn't really my field, and brought them in to compose for us.'

David Nathan's article described Frost and Sherrin talking to the show's writers on several telephones at once, discussing topics for the next edition. 'Both men shy at the word "satire",' Nathan reported.

> 'It's sort of adult chat,' said Sherrin, 'the kind of intelligent comment you find in the best conversation. We are not trying to shock. It's simply the kind of thing one says to one's friends at a time like eleven o'clock on a Saturday night. It has some shock effect simply because it has never been said on television before.'

John Wells has made the same point:

> Again, as in *Beyond the Fringe*, the basic innovation was that people were talking in the same way when the cameras were on them as they did when the cameras were not ... The impact on viewers who had not seen manifestations of this kind before was clearly very great: the fact that it appeared in the BBC made it stunning.

Wells contributed only one sketch to the first series of *TW3*. Unlike most of the show's writers, he came to the studio to see it being broadcast:

> Ned asked me up to the gallery to watch, and I've never been so impressed. I've watched a great many television directors working, but he was with every single camera, anticipating the next move, and I remember thinking it was like being on the deck of a battleship.

Sherrin admits that he was having to begin work very early each morning:

> The only way to cope was to get in about 6.30 a.m. After about a couple of hours of working through the post – all kinds of people were sending in scripts – I would go up to a gym which was very fashionable in Notting Hill Gate, for a bit of health-freakiness, and then get back when everybody else was arriving, about ten. This meant that later I could go up to the Café Royal and meet people who were writing for the programme.

David Nathan described the third edition being assembled:

> Sherrin was talking [on the telephone] to Willis Hall, who, with Keith Waterhouse, writes a sketch a week for the show. 'Are we going to have "Shoddy Goods" this week?' he asked. Frost was on the phone in a flash. He listened. Then said: 'Good, super' (he is very fond of 'super').

While Nathan listened, 'Shoddy Goods' was dropped, and a taxi was sent to collect another Waterhouse and Hall sketch, 'This Wonderful World', a parody of a John Grierson documentary series.

Keith Waterhouse recalls that taxis played a significant part in the writing process:

> Willis and I tended to write our *TW3* sketch at the last minute on Friday morning, when the BBC would send round a taxi to whisk it over to Lime Grove for the cast to learn and rehearse for the following evening. Sometimes, if inspiration faltered, we would hear the cab meter remorselessly ticking away in the street below even as we wrestled with the final lines. The fashion at the time for sketches without blackout punchlines was put down to the influence of *Beyond the Fringe*; I am inclined to think it was often more to do with the impatient presence of a cab at the door.

David Nobbs, who wrote for *TW3*, at first solo, then with Peter Tinniswood, has similar memories of taxis playing a big part in the process:

> Peter and I once wrote a complete sketch on a Saturday morning, sent it by taxi, and saw it performed that night. And on Saturdays we would regularly scurry back to our disgusting flat in Narcissus(!) Road, West Hampstead, from White Hart Lane and the joys of watching Danny Blanchflower to write a few last-minute topical 'boffos' for David Frost. The taxi would arrive mid-evening and the one-liners would go out a couple of hours later before anyone had had a chance to realize how awful they were.

Though Nathan's article did not mention it, Sherrin encouraged Nathan himself to offer material to the show, remarking that many of the *TW3* writers seem to work best in pairs. Nathan went back to the *Herald*, co-opted his neighbour in the office, Dennis Potter (who had worked in television before joining the *Herald*), and they began to work on scripts – this being some while before Potter wrote his first television play. Their first contribution, in the edition of 5 January 1963, was an exposé of hypocrisy about the former Labour leader Clement Attlee, who, on his eightieth birthday, was being revered by the very people who had disparaged him in his prime.

Christopher Booker's writing partnership with Frost was working well. 'I would have some idea for a sketch,' says Booker,

> and we would then talk it through for an hour or two; most of the jokes came from me, but … at a certain point he'd say, 'Right – I think we've got enough now'; and I would just go to a typewriter and sit down, and he would virtually dictate a script – he had an amazing gift for putting a sketch together in a way that would work on the air.

Booker was struck by the way in which the huge success of *TW3* had
changed Frost's manner, indeed almost his physique:

> Suddenly, at the age of just twenty-three, he had entered a magic new world –
> expensive restaurants, taxis, newspaper interviews – where every day was like
> a royal progress through a wash of compliments ('loved the show', 'super', 'bless
> you')...The transformation in him was remarkable. He even looked physically
> broader.

*

David Nathan's excitement about *TW3* was fully justified by the third
edition (8 December 1962) – the one he had watched being compiled. Most
of the scripts commissioned for the two pilots had now been used up, and for
the first time the show began to respond fully to the week's news. As the
Daily Sketch put it, with a tastelessness worthy of the *Sun* thirty years later,
the programme 'H-bombed its way into its third edition'.

The American elder statesman Dean Acheson had been denigrating
Britain's post-imperial world status: 'Britain is not quite as important in the
world as she used to be...Britain has lost an empire and not yet found a role.'
Millie Martin referred to this in the opening song: 'Dean Acheson says we're
played out and can't fight/Let's keep quiet and count three while we think,
"Is he right?" ' (Christopher Booker says that of course he was: 'The truth
was too obvious to be denied.') Willie Rushton then appeared as Macmillan,
on the hotline to President Kennedy: 'About this Acheson thing, Jack. It's
Harold here. (*Pause.*) Harold Macmillan. (*Pause.*) M–A–C–M...' There was
also some film of the real Macmillan on his return from Moscow, edited in
such a way that his words became repetitive nonsense.

Roy Kinnear, in the role of a tobacconist, delivered a monologue
responding to the news that, in a year in which the dangers of smoking had
become fully clear, cigarette sales were higher than ever:

> For forty-three years now I've been selling carcinogens...There's always
> somebody trying to spoil your pleasures...Why, if we tobacconists closed down
> you wouldn't have no independent British hydrogen bomb. If you look at it...
> impartially, twenty thousand deaths a year from lung cancer is a small price to
> pay for the liberty of the subject *and* a nuclear stockpile.

This monologue was the work of yet another writing duo, both on the staff
of the *Daily Mail*: Peter Lewis, who had given *Beyond the Fringe* a rave
review in Edinburgh, and Peter Dobereiner. Lewis recalls:

> I'd been friends with Dobereiner since the *Daily Express*. At the *Mail*, he was
> then a chief sub-editor and caption-writer. We read about this new programme,
> and wrote to Donald Baverstock, saying, 'Why don't you get in a few journalists,

like us?' Ned Sherrin told us to send stuff in right away. We went to the second pilot, to see what it was all about, and then we started.

In those days, journalists didn't get the chance to say things which might rock the boat, so *TW3* was a great opportunity. Each Tuesday, Ned would ring up one or other of us, and discuss what was going on in the world, and what might happen by Saturday. At first, I said we'd post him whatever we were writing, but he said: 'Don't do that! The BBC will take *weeks* to get it to me – I'll send a taxi.' So a taxi would arrive on Thursdays and tick away while we finished.

In the edition that included the Lewis–Dobereiner tobacconist monologue, the Norrie Paramor treatment was given to songwriter Lionel Bart, by means of an anthology of old-time songs interspersed with the 1960s hits which Bart was alleged to have plagiarized from them – all performed live with great panache by Millie Martin, David Kernan and Willie Rushton. (Kernan remarks on 'the folly of youth, to go live to millions of people after almost nil rehearsal, when you don't even know the tune, let alone the words!') Sherrin recalls, 'Lionel was in America when it was shown, and shortly afterwards he came back and went to the cinema, where the trailer for his film musical *Sparrers Can't Sing* was showing, and as his name came up on the screen the entire audience burst into laughter, and he couldn't understand why.'

The Second Vatican Council had just ended in Rome – as the opening song noted, it had 'authorized vernacular translation,/For this is the age of *mass* communication'. Hilariously, the *TW3* cast, dressed as a group of cardinals, sang 'Arrivederci, Roma'. There was also a sketch by author and journalist Quentin Crewe parodying the mendacious advertisements in which the South African government had been trying to justify apartheid and the house arrest of black activists:

> Dear me! In Africa, you see, words like 'house' have quite a different meaning. Until recently the Bantus didn't even have houses, never knew the word. So, as you can imagine, house arrest gives people a sort of prestige – a status symbol …

For the first time, Bernard Levin attacked just one person, Charles Forte, the hotel and catering supremo. On camera, with all the aggression of a prosecuting barrister, Levin described Forte's company as 'lazy, inefficient, dishonest, dirty, complacent, exorbitant – but disgusting just about sums it up', and asked him, 'Why is the catering at London Airport a major national disgrace?' He continued, 'I'm terribly sorry to have to tell you, Mr Forte, but I ate your bacon and eggs at lunch today, and the bacon tasted of nothing but salt, and I had to ask three times for a glass of wine, and the plate was cracked.'

Forte smiled gamely throughout the encounter, but he had to endure several minutes of attack from Levin before he was allowed to say a word, and the studio audience was manifestly on Levin's side throughout. Moreover the confrontation soon ran out of time and ended in mid-air, without Forte having had a proper chance to defend his reputation. A few days later his solicitor wrote to the BBC to complain of what they called a 'vicious and unwarranted attack', and to protest that when Forte tried to reply he was 'constantly interrupted'. In response to this, Alasdair Milne, in an internal memo, wrote a vigorous defence of Levin:

> Mr Forte…was originally invited as one of a group of restaurateurs and hoteliers, but towards the end of the week we decided to limit [it] to one man… I myself briefed [Forte] before the programme…pointing out to him that…he could expect some fairly frank talking…He said that he was perfectly prepared for this…and…was quite capable of looking after himself…Mr Forte knew he must expect a vigorous debate and that was what he got.

The 8 December programme was also memorable for a couple of Frost news items. He told viewers that Reginald Maudling, Chancellor of the Exchequer, had ended a brief interview with a group of the unemployed by remarking, 'I've got work to do if you haven't.' This was also the week in which a fifty-four-year-old woman civil servant at the Central Office of Information, Barbara Fell, had been sent to prison for two years for passing a number of utterly innocuous though technically classified documents to her Yugoslav lover, a press attaché at his country's embassy, even though he was pro-West and anti-USSR. Frost remarked sarcastically to the cameras that, with Miss Fell in prison, 'we can all sleep more safely in our beds tonight'.

Up to now, the press had shown only a mild interest in *TW3*, but the 8 December edition whipped up a storm of news stories and editorial comment. The *Daily Mail*, reporting that the BBC had received 443 complaints about this edition, summarized viewers' complaints:

> RELIGION was ridiculed – a small harmony group of Cardinals sang 'Arrivederci, Roma'…THE PRIME MINISTER was insulted – one of his TV recordings was distorted. BERNARD LEVIN…was rude to Mr Charles Forte… And a 'blue' sketch about open fly buttons…also brought criticism.

This sketch – one of the most famous in the history of the programme – was one of a series of two-handers for Millicent Martin and Roy Kinnear, scripted by Stephen Vinaver, the young American who had written for the Room at the Top cabaret in Ilford. He became *TW3*'s specialist in jazz-style lyrics for Martin, which he wrote to fit recorded instrumental solos by celebrated jazz musicians (his friend and collaborator, the composer Carl Davis, says that he got the idea for this from the jazz singer Annie Ross, who had done the same thing both solo and as part of the vocal trio Lambert,

Hendricks and Ross).[3] In the sketch, Martin points out that Kinnear's fly is open, and he protests, 'You want to stamp out any individuality I've got... You're so bleedin' bourgeois.' The effect of the sketch was reinforced by Lance Percival's improvised calypso, which followed it. When the audience was asked to suggest subjects for the calypso, a man called out, 'Open your fly'; Percival responded by suggesting – in song – that the man should open his own. Sherrin recalls that Donald Baverstock had been worried about the 'propriety' of this sketch, and it had been held over for several programmes. 'It is difficult to believe today that it ... caused alarm and some of our earliest accusations of smut-peddling.'

The *Daily Mail* seemed to be taking sides with the complainers, yet it mentioned that Levin was its drama critic; and Philip Purser in the *Sunday Telegraph* said he had recognized several journalists' names in the programme's closing credits. Fleet Street itself was creating much of *TW3*. This had now become deliberate policy by Sherrin and Frost. 'Old-style revue-writers are no good,' Frost told the *Observer*. 'We've got to get at the basis of a subject – *journalists* are what we like.'

David Nobbs was among those whom Sherrin had recruited from a reporters' room. 'When the programme began,' he writes,

> I was working as a reporter on a North London weekly of bizarre character, called the *St Pancras Chronicle*. I used to write my *TW3* sketches in office time, on the office typewriter, and a taxi would fetch them, usually from Hampstead Magistrates' Court, where I seemed to spend most of my time (professionally only).
>
>   Later Peter Tinniswood, my great friend and former colleague on the *Sheffield Star*, joined me and we wrote everything together. Every week we would ring Ned and tell him our ideas. There would usually be two. He would say he loved one and hated the other. We would send them both. Almost every week he would do the one he'd said he hated and not do the one he'd said he loved.

Among other papers commenting on the 8 December *TW3*, the *Observer* remarked approvingly that its satire was 'less inbred than that of *Private Eye*', but declared itself shocked by the singing cardinals sketch, which it described as 'near blasphemy'. The *Daily Telegraph* devoted a leader to the programme:

> Satire is an intimate thing between a few gifted artists and small audiences, best sampled at the Fortune Theatre [home of *Beyond the Fringe*]...But when it is poured into licensed channels, such as BBC late-night television, it can work like new wine in old bottles. There is, moreover, the temptation, since millions

---

[3] Vinaver went back to the USA in the mid-1960s and died before the end of the decade, in his early thirties.

Harold Macmillan took *TW3* in his stride:
'It is a good thing to be laughed over – it is
better than to be ignored.'

view it, to insert propaganda in the form of satire. This is a reproach that is sure
to be levelled against Saturday's programme *That Was The Week That Was*. For
it guyed cardinals, distorted a film of the Prime Minister to a point beyond
ridicule, and made a questionable comment on the judgment in the Fell case.

Obviously wit cannot be processed. Satire eludes, nay it thrives on
censorship. Its best subjects are pompousness, hypocrisy and abuse of power.
But in a country such as Britain, tolerant to the point of faineance, it may
sometimes be easy to overdo the gibe at authority. And whereas the real satirist,
who plays to a keenly critical audience, is kept on his mettle by their reactions,
the TV performer, divided from them by the screen, is in danger of lapses of
taste. The public may either squirm in their seats, or switch to another channel.

Private Eye's first allusion to *TW3* was a spoof of this leader, in the form
of a Rushton cartoon of a Tory buffer saying: 'I'm all for the BBC's new satire
show – let the young chaps let off a bit of steam and all that – but tampering
with films of the P.M. and making him look a doddering old idiot is going a
bit too far – the viewer might quite easily think it was the real thing.'

Judging by its correspondence column, the *Telegraph*'s readers did not
share the leader-writer's view of *TW3*. 'Let us be thankful,' wrote one, 'that,
at last, there is at least one television programme offering adult and

stimulating entertainment'; and another asked, 'Why should such speech or writing be enjoyed only by the minority who can either obtain or afford a seat at the Fortune Theatre or a table at The Establishment Club?' A third said he had indeed squirmed in his seat, but 'with laughter and admiration'.

The *Telegraph* also reported that the Postmaster-General, Reginald Bevins, had asked for the script of the 8 December edition of *TW3*, presumably on account of the tampered film, and had said, 'If I find that there was anything said or done which appears to call for enquiry on my part I shall take the matter up with the Director-General.' But nothing further was heard about this, probably because Macmillan himself had written Bevins a note which demonstrates that, behind the old-fogey façade, his response to the satirists' parodies of himself was wise and sophisticated: 'I hope you will not, repeat not, take any action about *That Was The Week That Was* without consulting me. It is a good thing to be laughed over – it is better than to be ignored.'

3

....

The death of deference

David Frost writes that, after the 8 December 1962 edition, 'TW3 was definitely in orbit.' Indeed, its jokes were already becoming self-referential. In the next edition, on 15 December, Waterhouse and Hall provided Roy Kinnear with a monologue in which an old-style comedian of the Max Miller generation desperately tries to catch up with the satire boom:

> David Frost, eh? 'Though the frost was cruel!' I knew his brother, Jack Frost. Oh, he's vicious, is David. I'm not saying he's got a cutting tongue but he's the only man I know who doesn't have to slice his bread before he eats it. No, but seriously, David, you're doing a grand job and it's a great pleasure and privilege to be working on your show tonight.
>
> Work, eh? Half a million unemployed... Still, we don't want to get maudlin about it, do we? Maudling? Get it? Maudlin, Mr Maudling. No, but seriously, boys and girls, he's doing a grand job.

Frost says that, later in the same programme, he found it 'irresistible to add the words "Seriously though, he's doing a grand job" to political jokes that were already in the script. I probably only used the phrase half a dozen more times in the rest of the series, but it stuck.'

Britain's dwindling international status was referred to again in this edition, in a sketch in which the US Defense Secretary, Robert MacNamara, tells his British counterpart, 'We in America have always had the highest regard for British craftsmanship – you make the buttons – we'll press them.' This became a recurrent TW3 theme; in one programme, Frost ironically read out a list of 'the colonies we've still got – Fiji, Mauritius, Swaziland, the New Hebrides Condominium...'

A letter to the *Daily Telegraph* shortly before the 15 December edition expressed the hope that TW3's satire would be politically even-handed:

> I am sure it would be a great mistake for Conservative supporters to become too

outraged by these attacks on our party. At the same time we shall certainly
expect the programme to transfer its taunts to our opponents from time to time.

Maybe in response to this, Waterhouse and Hall wrote an anti-trades union
sketch, featuring a group of workmen quarrelling over what to do about a
hole in the road, since each belongs to a different union. The next edition
had a sketch mocking Labour's uncertain policies ('We're in favour of
nationalization in principle, but against in practice'). Jack Duncan
emphasizes that *TW3* was not consistently left-wing: 'We had no
campaigning motives, no political beliefs.' Indeed Gerald Kaufman, who
was recruited to the *TW3* writing team in a later edition, remarks that Ned
Sherrin 'was a Tory then and is a Tory today, a very committed
Conservative'. Sherrin says this is true, and adds, 'It helped me to be
impartial about the whole thing.'

The Queen's Christmas broadcast featured in the edition of 22 December,
in a sketch by an Oxford research student, John Albery,[1] about the
Archbishop of Canterbury and the Prime Minister censoring what Her
Majesty has written. Reviewing the programme, the TV critic Philip Purser
felt uncertain whether the speech itself was being mocked, but the *Daily
Telegraph* was certain it detected 'irreligious and cynical undertones' in this
item, while in the Commons, the Conservative MP for Twickenham had
already asked the Postmaster-General to ensure that *TW3* 'cease making
references to the Royal Family and religion'. He declined to do any such
thing. It was, however, announced that Hugh Greene had forbidden *TW3* to
tamper again with news film. The programme's response was to show some
doctored film of Frost himself ludicrously repeating the words, 'There is to
be no more tampering with film.'

A frequent note of complaint by callers to the BBC was that Bernard
Levin's confrontations usually degenerated into undignified shouting
matches. In the 15 December programme he tried to provoke a group of
farmers, whom he attacked for being over-subsidized and lazy, addressing
them as 'peasants'; unlike their predecessors on the show, they virtually
shouted him down. Sherrin cheerfully admits that all he and Levin hoped to
do in this slot was 'have a bit of fun, get up somebody's nose – it was baiting
rather than debating'.

Meanwhile Fleet Street continued to keep a regular score sheet of the
number of pro- and anti-*TW3* phone calls to the BBC during and after each
edition. Reporters and columnists gloated if the number of complaints was
high, and if it had fallen off they sneered that this was a sign of 'diminished
interest'.

On 29 December came *That Was The Year That Was*, in which Philip

[1] He eventually became Master of University College, Oxford.

Purser spotted no fewer than three jokes borrowed from back numbers of *Private Eye*. This was the edition that brought in Gerald Kaufman. 'A script arrived from him out of the blue,' recalls Sherrin. 'His name … meant nothing to me at the time. He was working as a writer and researcher on the *Daily Mirror* and he had plainly watched the "exposé" items on the programme carefully.' Kaufman confirms this: 'I was visiting Leeds for the weekend and watching television in my parents' flat on Saturday night … I watched [the] topical sketches with interest and, what is more, with a certain degree of annoyance. I was certain I could do better.' He decided to offer an idea given him by Hugh Cudlipp, editorial director of the *Mirror* group: a demonstration of how frequently the 'Cross-Bencher' political column in the *Sunday Express* had erred in its predictions. 'Accordingly,' continues Kaufman,

> the following Monday morning, I telephoned BBC Television and asked to speak to the programme's producer, Ned Sherrin … To my astonishment I was instantly put through to him. I outlined my (or, actually, Cudlipp's) idea and without hesitation he commissioned a sketch based on it for his next programme.

Kaufman's sketch showed that 'Cross-Bencher' was indeed often ludicrously wrong:

> WILLIE RUSHTON [as Cross-Bencher]: '1 July. Cluster round now, all you hopeful Tory backbenchers. I bring you the news you so anxiously await. It concerns the big Government reshuffle which everyone has been expecting this month. And what is my news? There won't be one.'
>
> KEN COPE: 13 July. Macmillan carries out biggest-ever Government reshuffle …

And so on.

Since 8 December the programme had been concluding with a round-up of the next morning's Sunday papers, already in print by the time *TW3* was ending. This was thanks to Clement Freud – as Sherrin explains:

> Clement, who had been running cabaret at the Royal Court, offered to do this. He used to go and hang around the vans at the back of Fleet Street, and cajole papers out of the delivery men, because in those days the newspapers thought it was awful to have their stuff seen or read out on the television the night before – they assumed it would kill people's desire to read it in the morning. That sounds unbelievable when you think of the way they rush them down to *Newsnight* now – but in those days it had to be very covertly done.

Frost recalls that, on this occasion, it was natural to look at what 'Cross-Bencher' had written for the next day's *Express*: 'What predictions had he made this week? One stood out: "Despite his mysterious minor illness,

Hugh Gaitskell is on the way to recovery. In no time at all he will be fit and back at work again." ' In view of Cross-Bencher's track record, Frost's ad-lib response to this was to look at the camera and say, 'Sorry, Hugh.' Unfortunately this proved horribly accurate, for three weeks later the Labour leader was dead.

The right-wing newspapers continued to tut-tut over the programme. On 22 December, a *Times* leader muttered about 'glib little exhibitionists', and a few days later the *Sunday Telegraph* pontificated:

> There are dangers in indiscriminate knocking. Good ideas, worthwhile institutions, well-intentioned people with the right ideas but the wrong style are already going down in the shooting. And an anti-Establishment establishment seems to be growing, which cannot take maverick opinion... Indeed, as the 'movement' grows the result could be the worst sort of anarchy.

Sherrin recalls that 'there used to be letters in the *Telegraph* saying, "Can't we have constructive satire?"' Yet both *The Times* and the *Sunday Telegraph* allowed their television critics to praise the programme. Philip Purser was one of its most loyal fans, and the anonymous reviewer in *The Times* judged most of *That Was The Year That Was* to have been 'very funny indeed', singling out Roy Kinnear as a 'splendid underestimated comic actor'.

Hugh Greene, meanwhile, felt the programme was improving. After the edition of 5 January 1963, Kenneth Adam told Stuart Hood: 'D. G. says he has not laughed as much before as he did on Saturday... He found the note of geniality in some of the humour (the diaries sketch, for instance) particularly pleasing.' This was a whimsical, *Punch*-like item by Lewis and Dobereiner, picking out some of the curious information printed at the front of diaries. But the memo reported that Greene '*does* think we must put off, at least for some time, the Lord Chancellor item which was re-raised last week'.

Ned Sherrin explains:

> I wanted to examine the career of Sir Reginald Manningham-Buller ('Bullying-Manner' in Bernard Levin's phrase for the *Spectator*), by now Lord Dilhorne, the Lord Chancellor, not a lawyer I admired. The first script which I commissioned was caustic, amusing and wild; and at about the same time I got a warning from Hugh Carleton Greene that it would be politically inadvisable to consider Dilhorne as a target. Disappointed, I filed the script and waited...

Meanwhile senior BBC staff were quietly noting the objections to *TW3* in right-wing quarters. One R.D. Pendlebury reported on 11 January 1963 that he had had lunch with a member of Conservative Central Office, Howell Thomas, who had many individual complaints, but their policy at the moment was to play it down as far as possible in the hope that it would either die a natural death or (he hinted) drop such a clanger as to incur a major libel action. He said that many of the people he knew would feel happier about it if its targets occasionally included such things as CND, *Tribune*, Khrushchev and so on. Being anti-Establishment was one thing, but it was hard to swallow a programme whose general line was so consistently extreme left-wing, socialist and pacifist.

The next day, Frank Gillard, Controller West Region, reported that a member of his regional council, Colonel W.Q. Roberts, Land Steward to the Duchy of Cornwall, had written to him:

> Personally, I am completely against all this carping at authority in an age when the young seem to have little respect for the Establishment ... In my view these broadcasts are only encouraging lack of respect among young people of school or university age, and I cannot see what earthly good they do, albeit they are devilishly clever in parts.

*

Scripts were now tumbling into the *TW3* office from all quarters. Kenneth Tynan contributed a piece suggesting that all the headlines in the popular press were the work of the same person, 'an excitable middle-aged woman in thick tweeds and an advanced state of manic depression'. Two young television playwrights, Alan Plater and Jack Rosenthal, teamed up to write a sketch on the growing unemployment figures. The thirty-year-old novelist and academic Malcolm Bradbury sent a poem, modelled on Rupert Brooke's 'Grantchester', about the trend for northern writers to come south – where they wrote about the north:

> Ah God, to see the branches stir
> Across the moon, at Manchester ...
> Those Yorkshire moors, that pelting rain,
> Those daily tea-cakes with John Braine.
> Those back-to-backs, that outside bog at
> The garden end that Richard Hoggart
> Recalled so well. But now we're wealthy,
> We'll stick to Bournemouth, where it's healthy.

Bradbury, who supplied other scripts to *TW3*, recalls the 'enormous euphoria' the programme caused, 'as if the great British log jam was being broken at last. All my age group was carried away by it, week on week, and it did have an important effect in changing views of – and deference towards – politicians and institutions generally.' Keith Waterhouse remembers Edward Heath saying, at a *Punch* lunch, that he blamed *TW3* for what he called 'the death of deference'.

Bradbury was an established writer, who had already been contributing parodies and literary satires to *Punch* and the *New Yorker*. The script that proved to be the most controversial item the programme ever screened was the work of two actors with no literary credentials. One of them, Charles Lewsen, had approached Sherrin at the outset of *TW3* in the hope of joining the programme's cast. There was no room for him, but he was encouraged to write for it, and Sherrin handed him an idea that seemed promising but which had failed to get written up satisfactorily: a consumer guide, in the manner of *Which*, to the major religions of the world.

Lewsen co-opted another actor, Robert Gillespie. 'My own religious background was nil,' Gillespie explains,

> except that I was born in France, and there was an English community in Lille, where we lived, and I remember harvest festivals. And for a very brief time, after we came to Britain, I went to a Catholic school. And Charles Lewsen is Jewish; so between us we'd had experience of the Anglican Church, Catholicism, and Judaism.

Their 'Consumer Guide to Religion' began by explaining that 'three basic tests' had to be applied to each religion: 'What do you put into it? What do you get out of it? How much does it cost?' First came Judaism:

> This is the oldest religion we tested … What do you get out of it? Membership of the oldest club in the world … and we particularly liked the guarantee of Eternal Life through the Messiah or Saviour who will take responsibility for all your guilt – when he arrives …
>
> We next tested the Roman Catholic Church … What do you put into it? Belief in One Only God-head operating on a troika basis … Belief in the Infallibility of Giovanni Batista Montini, now known as Paul the Sixth … We must stress here that the idea that the Head (or Pope as he is called) claims infallibility in all matters is a fallacy. The Pope cannot tell you which television set is best … He can only tell you which television programme you cannot watch …
>
> Jesus Christ has already undertaken personal responsibility for the consumer's misdemeanours. This gives extra support. And the confessional mechanism is standard; it operates as an added safety-factor to correct running mistakes, making Salvation almost foolproof.

Similar treatment was meted out to Protestantism, Islam and Buddhism – and for good measure to the secular religion of Communism ('its Chief Prophet appears to have no background in the industry at all'). The sketch ended by recommending, as the best buy, the Church of England – 'a jolly good little faith for a very moderate outlay'.

Sherrin showed the sketch to Alasdair Milne, and said he would add some introductory remarks emphasizing that what was being mocked was not the faiths themselves, but the churches' increasing tendency to use worldly methods of selling their wares (scarcely true, but an ingenious get-out). Nevertheless the 'Consumer Guide' was nearly axed. On the day it was going to be transmitted, Saturday, 12 January 1963, Kenneth Adam decided to look in on rehearsals, and said he would prefer to have it cut. However, Milne had already given it the green light, and BBC protocol discouraged Adam from countermanding a decision that had been made by the proper person. 'It is a good example of the protective umbrella which Milne and Baverstock held over the programme,' writes Sherrin, 'making it much easier to operate with freedom underneath.'

That evening, Frost delivered the monologue skilfully to camera, in front of blow-ups of photos of typical representatives of each religion. Immediately he had finished, the telephones started ringing, and not just at the BBC – which logged a record 246 complaints about the sketch, but also 167 appreciations. Someone told the press that Frost's father was a Methodist minister, and Frost says that 'having a pack of Fleet Street tigers on the phone, all trying to put words into his mouth, then printing them if he so much as paused for a second before denying them' was 'a new experience' for his father.

Sure enough, Mr Frost was widely (mis)quoted as disapproving of his son having delivered the monologue, and many papers gleefully seized the latest opportunity to denounce *TW3*. 'Do you believe a man's religion should be mocked?' cried the *Daily Express*. But Peter Simple in the *Daily Telegraph* took the same line as Sherrin: 'As I understood it, the intention was not to mock at religion, but to mock at the idea that religion is a product.'

Clergy all over Britain were divided. An Anglican preacher in the Isle of Man told his congregation, 'If we were 100 per cent Christian we would storm the BBC building and make it drop this horrible programme.' The Bishop of Swansea and Brecon, in a letter to Hugh Greene, described the sketch as in 'deplorably bad taste, and gratuitously offensive to many viewers'. But a Catholic priest wrote to Sherrin, 'It was very good and the sort of people who complain will all be converts.' Frost had a phone call from a vicar in Surrey asking what was the current score of complaints versus congratulations, and saying he was 'giving a sermon in favour of *TW3*'.

The 'Consumer Guide' was mild stuff compared to a book written within the Church of England which was published two months later, *Honest to God* by John Robinson, the Bishop of Woolwich. This shocked the faithful by rejecting belief in a personal God, 'a kindly Old Man..."up there" '. Moreover Ned Sherrin, far from wishing to unsettle religious convictions, describes his own religious position as 'wet Church of England conservatism', and says he has always made his Communion once a month. 'On the whole I feel comforted by it and I put in a few requests each month.

I don't waste my time on trying to formulate a concept of God. I have observed far brighter people than me trying to do just that and failing.'

Despite the 'protective umbrella' the BBC was trying to hold over *TW3*, the 'Consumer Guide' perceptibly harmed the programme's image with the BBC hierarchy. Hugh Greene, till now its stout defender, wrote to the Bishop of Swansea and Brecon, 'In a satirical programme of this sort one is continually walking the tightrope and sometimes one falls off. I personally agree that this was a fall.' Donald Baverstock sent his more junior BBC colleague Alasdair Milne an ominous memo:

> This note is not concerned with the arguments for and against including the 'Consumer Report on Religions'. There were strong reasons for thinking that this item did have a place in the context of this programme. I would be happier about it, however, if the programme as a whole had been better. In my opinion it was the worst yet.

Baverstock grumbled that the edition had overrun by twenty minutes, and was particularly upset by a sketch about a young professional footballer, played by Kenneth Cope, which (Baverstock said) merely 'showed that there are a lot of people in this country who talk in a vulgar accent and with obscene gestures' – the footballer tells people to 'get stuffed' and makes V-signs. Baverstock complained that, while *TW3* was busily attacking other people's values and beliefs, the writers and performers themselves had only 'muddled standards and cheapjack values'. He went on:

> This is the point that worries me most. If we are asked, 'By what right do these people attack as they do?' we have to be able to point to the programme and say, 'By right of the programme's fairmindedness, its quality, its style and the consistency of its own values.' Judging [by] last Saturday's programme, I for one cannot make this defence…
>
> It must now be reaffirmed to Sherrin that the Corporation's restriction on the use of swear words, blue jokes and obscene gestures applies… to this programme as it does to all others. You must inform him immediately that he is henceforth expected to consult with you on all matters of programme content in detail and with complete candour. It is his responsibility further to inform you of all last-minute alterations to the script wherever they are likely to be questionable… The length of the programme henceforth should be taken to be 50 minutes.

Unaware that the BBC's commitment to satire was already weakening, young people and schoolchildren[2] all over Britain were switching on *TW3*

[2] In the edition of 9 February 1963, Frost sarcastically invited any children who might be watching to send in a hundred-word précis of a complicated legal wrangle then going on between the Boulting brothers (film producers) and the cinema technicians' union. Next week he told viewers, 'We were surprised to find how many thousands of children seem to stay up this late on Saturday, and take in what's going on.'

religiously every Saturday night, and were being profoundly affected by the programme's cynicism. Tim Rice, who was an eighteen-year-old public schoolboy when *TW3* began, recalls its 'incredibly daring new outlook on politics. I was one of the people deeply affected by this wave of satire, as a schoolboy, and it was quite shocking. I remember teachers saying, "It's all so terribly destructive. This sort of thing won't last." But of course it did, and it's changed attitudes to politics ever since.'

4

....

Sick jokes and lavatory humour

'It is sad, but not surprising,' wrote Sherrin in an article on *TW3* a month after the 'Consumer Guide to Religion' row,

> that so many of the subjects dealt with have outraged people, but already the sort of speech that we favour is beginning to be accepted...Those of us who work on the programme hope that a point of view emerges even if it isn't overtly stated.

Strikingly, the article had been commissioned by one of the papers that had been most critical of *TW3*, the *Sunday Telegraph*.

Sherrin did not identify that point of view, but went on to praise his performers, especially Millicent Martin:

> [She] impresses continually with her versatility, her musicianship, her ability to master incredibly difficult words and tunes at very short notice...The men who work with her are constantly asked what makes her so attractive and have evolved a stock answer – 'Her earthy sexuality'.

He also mentioned that the viewing figures had now reached 'between 11 and 12 million people', and that 'nearly 200 people' had now contributed material to the programme, while 'thousands' of other people were sending in unsolicited sketches. According to the *Daily Mail*, the figure was 'around 500 scripts a week', and it was John Bassett's job to vet them.

In fact most of the programme was still being written by the core team of regulars; and despite the row over the 'Consumer Guide', much of it was not really satire. For example, in the next programme (19 January 1963) only two items could have been described as truly satirical. One was a Gerald Kaufman mock-tribute to thirteen MPs who had never made a speech in the Commons:

> Salute Sir Norman Hulbert, Tory MP for Stockport North...Sir Norman is Chairman of Associated Motor Cycles, last month he hit out at ton-up boys [motorcyclists who rode at 100 mph] because of 'the noise they make'. No one

could hit out at Sir Norman for this reason, the only noise he has made in the House since the Election has been to ask a question about naval survival rafts…

Sitting today in his office in the House of Commons, Kaufman says of this sketch: 'It entailed an enormous amount of research, and it was the one that made an impact here, with silly Members of Parliament getting up and trying to get it referred to the Committee of Privileges.' Sir Norman Hulbert did indeed attempt to protest in the Commons, but was virtually laughed out of the chamber.

The other truly satirical item in this programme was Millicent Martin singing a bitter-sweet lullaby inspired by news of a steep rise in illegitimate births: 'Go to sleep, my little baby… /The world is full of bastards just like you.' Surrounding these pieces were a sketch about that winter's great freeze-up, discussed in the manner of *Juke Box Jury* ('Well, two of you seem to like it – what about you, Jet?' 'Cool, man, real cool'); a Waterhouse and Hall parody of the true-crime television programmes by Edgar Lustgarten; a song about a girl who dislikes her lover's nose; Timothy Birdsall drawing the *Mona Lisa* in sixty seconds (and singing 'When You're Smiling' as he finished); and the whole cast performing a sketch about a trade-union go-slow in a circus. None of these items would have seemed out of place in a pre-*Beyond the Fringe* 'intimate revue'. Indeed, writers who belonged to that world were now infiltrating *TW3*. A song in the edition of 28 January called 'Anyone for Tennis?', which suggested that actors were getting tired of appearing in sex-and-kitchen-sink dramas, was the work of that very pre-satirical writer Sandy Wilson. Sherrin had even approached Noël Coward – and got a very quick 'No'.

Two days after this edition, the *Evening Standard* suggested that the show's novelty was wearing off:

> *That Was The Week That Was* … is already beginning to go damp. Last Saturday's programme was one of the worst yet. It was too long, too self-consciously clever and, worst of all, neither very funny nor biting… It has been grossly overrated, and the oldest jokes gilded with praise because they are new to television.

A week later, 'Peterborough' wrote in the *Daily Telegraph*: 'In really advanced circles, I hear, the smart thing is now to switch off *That Was The Week That Was* before the programme has had time to have been.'

Richard Ingrams was no longer contributing. 'I'd done quite a few things for *TW3* with Jack Duncan,' he says. 'I seem to remember doing little films.' He had also written a studio piece for Willie Rushton as a French Dixon of Dock Green, in which 'Evening, all' became 'Bonsoir, tout le monde'. 'But they didn't like me,' says Ingrams. 'I don't think Ned approved of me. It was a good thing, because it would have left *Private Eye* without anyone to run it.' Sherrin has no memory of Ingrams writing for the show, but remembers him 'appearing occasionally as an extra – and I didn't think he was a conspicuously good performer'.

Ingrams writes somewhat scathingly of *TW3* as 'the climax of the Satire Boom, when the BBC moved in on the act'. Like many people, he simultaneously despised and admired Frost – though few would have dared to say so in such patrician language:

> There was something ungentlemanly about a man who was so obviously on the make. His astonishing industry ran counter to the spirit of public-school amateurism which characterized *Beyond the Fringe* and *Private Eye*. At the same time there was a strange charm about his barefaced ambition which was somehow endearing.

Elsewhere, Ingrams recalls, 'For a short time I went to Frostie's flat and wrote scripts, but then I had a traumatic experience…and ceased to contribute.' The trauma was caused by Frost retiring to sit on the lavatory while they were having a script conference, and continuing the discussion with the door open.

Ingrams also regretted that 'the lure of the telly with its fat cheques' was tempting Booker and Rushton away from *Private Eye* – and that they were taking what would have been *Eye* material with them. The cheques were indeed fat: Booker, who had been earning £15 a week at the *Eye*, received 80 guineas per edition of *TW3*. Rushton and the other performers were on a sliding scale of between 40 and 100 guineas, and Frost, who had initially received £135 (*sic* – the BBC swung between guineas and pounds), was soon given a raise to £180. Waterhouse and Hall shared £70 for each of their scripts, but the other writers were given much less – around 10 to 12 guineas per sketch – and even Caryl Brahms received only £25 for the consistently brilliant topical lyrics she wrote for the title song with Sherrin (who was still on a fairly meagre BBC salary, with no extras). 'Somehow, I was excluded from the pay roll,' writes Ingrams rather bitterly, 'though Mary [Morgan, whom he had married on the day that *TW3* was first broadcast] and I used to go along regularly on Saturday nights to the BBC's TV Centre…where something like an enormous cocktail party would be taking place.'

In February 1963 the *Eye* carried a double-spread mocking the BBC's claim to have reformed its 'Auntie' image; a cartoon showed Frost leering at the camera and saying: 'But seriously, viewers, we think the BBC's doing a grand job.' On the desk in front of him lies a script, on which is written: 'Dave, please try and use this, I need the money. Chris.' This mockery of Booker and Frost cannot, however, have been very heartfelt, since the cartoon was drawn by their *TW3* colleague Timothy Birdsall.

At a BBC Controllers' Meeting on 12 February 1963, Kenneth Adam reported that the Director-General wanted *TW3* to be 'curtailed in length';

moreover 'the question of a replacement during the summer was being considered'. Later that month an anonymous columnist wrote in *Time & Tide*: 'I think it needs shortening and shaping ... More, too, of the set-pieces such as the bold item on religion which caused such an uproar ... I would like to see *TWTWTW* ... much bolder.'

So far, the Royal Family had escaped close attention from the programme, but a sketch on 16 March mocked the style of broadcasting royal occasions. This was the monologue that Barry Humphries had watched Frost perform at The Establishment – indeed it had become Frost's party piece, in the days between Cambridge and *TW3*:

> The Royal Barge is, as it were, sinking. The sleek, royal-blue hull of the Barge is sliding gracefully, almost regally, beneath the waters of the Pool of London ... Perhaps the lip-readers amongst you will know what Prince Philip, Duke of Edinburgh, has just said to the Captain of the Barge ... And now the Queen, smiling radiantly, is swimming for her life. Her Majesty is wearing a silk ensemble in canary yellow.

It had been written at Cambridge by Ian Lang, who eventually became a Conservative MP in Margaret Thatcher's government and rose to be Secretary of State for Scotland and then Trade Secretary. Now Lord Lang of Monkton, he explains how he came to write satire:

> It started when I saw *Beyond the Fringe* when I was an undergraduate at Cambridge. It was like a blinding flash of light – the funniest thing I had ever seen in my life – and I immediately went home and started writing sketches myself, and joined the Footlights. Later, I auditioned for the replacement cast of *Beyond the Fringe*, when they all went to America. I didn't get it, but Clement Freud booked me for a season of cabaret with a pianist friend, Tony Branch, at the Royal Court Theatre Club.
>
> The 'Royal Barge' sketch had been banned from a Footlights revue by the Lord Chamberlain, but it wasn't an attack on royalty, but on the bland pomposity of Richard Dimbleby's BBC commentaries on royal occasions. And my belief about satire is that it works best if there's an underlying respect for the institutions that are portrayed, and the satire is, by today's standards, gentle.
>
> I did a few more pieces for *TW3*, and one or two of my things were used in later satire programmes. In those days I think I was only conservative with a small 'c' – I had no political ambitions. But later, I came to feel that writing satire, and attacking or undermining institutions, was ultimately a very negative approach. And my switch to politics put an end to it for me. I first became a candidate in 1967, but I didn't get in till 1979.

Sherrin admits that Lang's 'Royal Barge' sketch was fairly soft stuff: 'None of our items dealing with the Royal Family had the cutting edge that those with political or religious content sported.'

The *TW3* audience was still vast – Jack Duncan says, 'It was wonderful going into the pub on Sunday morning and seeing people doing the previous night's sketches,' and Ken Cope remembers that 'West End restaurants had to install TV sets on Saturday nights, otherwise there'd be no one there' – but inevitably the programme's shock value was now diminishing, simply because viewers now knew what to expect. After the 'Consumer Guide', no offence could be caused by Frost's adaptation of the Ten Commandments to fit the *mores* of gutter-press journalists:

> Thou shalt have no other gods before fee … Thou shalt not take the name of the Lord thy Boss in vain … Thou shalt not omit adultery … Thou shalt not bear false witness against thy neighbour; look what happened to *Private Eye.*

This referred to the *Eye*'s first libel case. Randolph Churchill had sued them on account of drawings by Rushton which showed him presiding over a team of hacks writing a ludicrously bowdlerized biography of his father. The case was dropped after a retraction was published.

Nor was there an outcry when the opening of London's first skyscraper hotel, the Hilton in Park Lane, was marked on *TW3* by Al Mancini (a recent recruit to the cast, described by Caryl Brahms as 'an Italo-American zany'), dressed as an American preacher, delivering a parody by Lewis and Dobereiner of the Book of Genesis:

> In the beginning there was darkness upon the face of the earth and there was no iced water. And Hilton said, Let there be iced water, and in every bathroom pipes ran with plenteous iced water and Hilton saw that it was good …
>
> And Hilton said, Behold I have given unto you the London Hilton containing everything meet for your needs: a view into the garden of your Queen, yea, and a library wherein you may read Hilton Milton and 850 Hilton menservants and maidservants smiling Hilton smiles, which they smile saying not cheese, as other men, but saying Hilton Stilton.
>
> But the people were a stiff-necked people who would not drink of the iced water … And Hilton was exceeding wrath and departed with a gnashing of teeth to beget the Athens Hilton which begat the Moscow Hilton which was called the Comrade Hilton which begat the Pisa Hilton, which was called the Tiltin' Hilton which begat the Tel Aviv Hilton which was called the Hilton Schmilton … And it came to pass that the Hiltons covered the face of the earth and there was a great flood of iced water and the darkness was greater than it was in the beginning.

The programme in which the Hilton piece was broadcast (20 April) attracted considerable press attention, but not for the sketches. Bernard Levin's weekly ideological confrontations (with, among others, Randolph Churchill and Lionel Bart) had continued to be aggressively controversial, and when in this programme a member of the audience tried to punch Levin on the jaw it was assumed that he objected to something Levin had said on the programme – ironically that evening the Levin confrontation was with a group of pacifist Aldermaston marchers. In fact the assailant was the husband of an actress whom Levin had reviewed scathingly in the *Daily Mail*. The floor manager, Peter Chafer, aided by Frost, removed the man, and Levin resumed his discussion, quite unshaken, with the words 'Can we concentrate on non-violence?' (Levin writes that many years later he and his would-be assailant 'met in Dublin on a rainy day and made it up over tea'.)

One of the few sketches in the spring 1963 programmes to have the bite of the 'Consumer Guide' was 'Henry Brooke, This is Your Life', in which the Home Secretary (played by Rushton) was confronted by the victims of his decisions – or indecisiveness:

> And so, Henry, to this week and the case of Chief Enahoro, the Nigerian opposition leader who has asked for asylum but whom you are sending back to danger and almost certainly death … You've changed your mind – as you did over the Vassall witnesses and Carmen Bryan.[1] And you've ignored the spirit of British tradition to please another government – like Soblen. Your policy, Mr Brooke, has been one of trial and error. Their trials. Your errors.

Ned Sherrin writes of this sketch:

> When people ask what practical effect *TW3* ever had on politics this is the only example to which I can point with some certainty. I am convinced that Henry Brooke's subsequent election defeat [in 1966] was materially affected by it. Certainly Edward Heath was of that opinion, inveighing against it for some ten or fifteen minutes at a rumbustious *Punch* luncheon.

The 'Vassall witnesses' featured in the case of William Vassall, a homosexual civil servant who had been gaoled for spying. There had been much searching for sexual innuendoes in some innocuous letters between him and a superior, and the playwright Peter Shaffer made this into one of *TW3*'s best sketches:

> SENIOR OFFICIAL: (*reading a letter*) 'To Mr Jenkins.' Good. None of that 'dear' nonsense. (*Reading again*) 'Pursuant to your letter –' *Pursuant*?
> JUNIOR OFFICER: It's the usual phrase, sir.
> SENIOR OFFICIAL: I don't like it. The word has an erotic penumbra. Take it out …

In another programme, there was a memorable two-line exchange on the same topic, between a pair of judges: ' "What do you give these homosexual johnnies?" "Half a crown and an apple, generally." '

---

[1] For the Vassall case, see below. Carmen Bryan was a Jamaican girl who had been given a six-week prison sentence for shoplifting goods worth £2. Brooke said he was going to deport her under the new Immigration Act, then changed his mind.

Homosexual acts were not made legal – and then only between consenting male adults – until 1967. 'One was a little worried,' says Ned Sherrin, who is gay, 'because one didn't want to be arrested and sent to prison. But apart from that [being gay] has never bothered me.'

Hugh Greene was in the studio audience on 20 April, bringing as a guest Reginald Maudling, the Chancellor of the Exchequer. Sherrin writes that it was 'fashionable' for distinguished visitors to drop in. (He recalls that 'George Brown came, and was seen laughing his head off, and the Tories asked for a sort of right of reply to this, and I was told that Reggie Maudling was coming. Sure enough Hugh Greene brought him, but said, "In no circumstances must he be photographed," so dear old Reggie sat there expecting to laugh and show what a good sport he was, and I'd been given firm instructions not to show him at all.') Yet it had now been decided that the first series of *TW3* would end the following week, after a run of five months. Kenneth Adam told Alasdair Milne that the Director-General 'thought it was only right to give them a rest in order that they should not over-tire themselves'. Greene had been misquoted in the press as saying that the *TW3* team were 'tired'. In fact the 20 April programme contained one of the programme's best-ever items.

In recent weeks there had been various sketches about the Bomb, Civil Defence and the secret fall-out shelters to which the country's top people would retreat while the rest of the population were left to die; but the most

David Frost conducts the guns and bombs in one of *TW3*'s finest sketches.

effective anti-war piece, on 20 April, was entirely wordless. Dressed in white tie and tails and holding a baton, Frost conducted not a piece of music, but the sounds of war – gunshot and the detonation of an ever-louder series of bombs.

A week later, *TW3* bowed out of its first series in sparkling form. A series of racial killings in the American South inspired lyricist and drama critic Herbert Kretzmer (then at the *Daily Express*) to provide a superbly ironic song for Millicent Martin and a group of mock Black and White Minstrels:[2]

> I wanna go back to Mississippi,
> Where the scents of blossoms
> Kiss the evenin' breeze.
> Where the Mississippi mud
> Kinda mingles with the blood
> Of the niggers who are hangin'
> From the branches of the trees...

There were also predictions of the news stories that would occur during the programme's summer break: 'May 23rd. Christine Keeler appointed Conservative Party's Chief PRO...June 13th. Christine Keeler becomes Conservative Party Chief Whip.' Rumours about this model's relationship with Tory Cabinet minister John Profumo had begun to filter through a month earlier, and *TW3* had alluded obliquely to it when Millicent Martin sang a verse of 'She Was Poor But She Was Honest':

> See him in the 'Ouse of Commons
> Makin' laws to put down crime
> While the object of his passion
> Walks the streets to hide her shame.

Martin had also delivered a David Nathan–Dennis Potter monologue as a model, reclining in a négligée and dark glasses:

> I was on first-name terms with top politicians and we often had discussions which went on far into the night...It has been an interesting and exciting life and though I am temporarily broke I am sure that one day my luck will turn again. Especially with all the information I am ready to spill if it doesn't.

The next issue of *Private Eye* went a little further, carrying a cartoon

---

[2] Sherrin recalls: 'I had a lot of work to persuade Herbert Kretzmer to write a song a week for us. He'd just done "Goodness Gracious Me" for Sophia Loren and Peter Sellers, and it seemed to me that anybody who could do that could write funny songs. But he needed an awful lot of persuading that he could.' (*The Black and White Minstrels* was, in retrospect, a highly politically incorrect, long-running television song-and-dance show, with white male singers performing in blackface. There were frequent close-ups of 'Mammy'-style wide eyes and splayed white-gloved fingers.)

depicting Macmillan as a debauched Roman emperor which included the
words 'Per Wardua ad Astor' – a reference to rumours that a fashionable
osteopath, Stephen Ward, had procured girls for Profumo and the smart set
at Lord Astor's country home, Cliveden. This drawing (which also featured
David Frost as the court satirist 'Juvenile') brought Ward himself round to
the *Eye* with the words, 'I see you know everything' – which of course they
did not. (What they did know came largely from journalist Alan Brien, who
was renting a cottage on the Cliveden estate.) Booker was out of the office,
and though Ward seems to have hoped that if the *Eye* printed his own
account of the affair, it might save his skin, Ingrams and Rushton were able
to make little of the tangled tale he told them.

After the closing credits of *TW3* on 27 April, Millicent Martin and Roy
Kinnear ended the first series as a suburban couple watching the programme
at home. 'It was satire, wasn't it?' says Kinnear uncertainly. 'Mucky jokes.
Obscenity – it's all the go nowadays.' Frost writes that the BBC hierarchy
was now becoming more concerned about the programme's sexually risqué
jokes. For example, a Tory MP's demand that the Attorney-General should
prosecute Henry Miller's *Tropic of Cancer* for obscenity inspired a *TW3*
sketch highlighting *double entendres* in apparently harmless works of
literature, such as *Peter Pan* – the passage where Peter teaches the children
to fly: 'It looked delightfully easy, and they tried it, first on the floor and then
on the beds.' Another sketch featured innuendoes in sports writing: 'As
John's fingers stroked the ball, all the subtlety of his fingers attacking that
impregnable fortress...' Frost admits that the programme had become 'a
wall-to-wall festival of *double entendres*', and Michael Frayn has written
scathingly about its habit of going for 'mildly dirty jokes', the kind of
'stagnant cliché' that *Beyond the Fringe* had seemed to banish for ever. It
was probably this rather than the attacks on politicians that led BBC
management to impose on *TW3* the indignity of yet another pilot before it
began its second series in the autumn.

*

In the *People* newspaper, 'Man of the People' welcomed *TW3*'s summer
break, under the headline 'Goodbye to a Gang of Low Schoolboys'.
Reporting that 'at least 12 million' had watched the 27 April edition, he
branded them 'bemused, deluded dolts'; while in his parish magazine, a
Church of England vicar, the Revd John Culey, complained that the
programme's devotees were revelling in 'an apparent victory of evil over
good'. Millicent Martin seemed to Mr Culey 'a repulsive woman', while
Bernard Levin was 'a thick-lipped Jew boy'.

Frost, who found the 12 million figure 'thrilling', alleges that he was now
regularly receiving letters from proud parents asking what training their
children needed to become satirists. Sherrin, who claims to have had one

Macmillan Confesses

IN RECENT MONTHS, BRITAIN HAS BEEN ROCKED BY A SERIES
OF SCANDALS INVOLVING MANY OF THE LEADING FIGURES IN
POLITICS AND SOCIETY. THE VASSALL AFFAIR. THE ENA-
HORO SCANDAL. THE PROFUMO CRISIS. THE DUCHESS OF
ARGYLL DIVORCE. IN ALL OF THEM CABINET MINISTERS
WERE INTIMATELY INVOLVED.

And running through all these scandalous sensations, they
all had one thing in common.

Only one man in Britain was in a position to know the innermost
truth of all these events.

Only one man was in a position to cover up for his friends.

HAROLD MACMILLAN

Today 'Private Eye' starts publishing the full, exclusive confessions
of 70-year old Mr. Macmillan, the humble crofter's grandson who
rose to become on intimate terms with many of the most famous
and fashionable names of our time.

Among the questions Mr. Macmillan has fully and frankly
answered in this sensational 'Private Eye' series

O Why I consistently lied to the House of Commons
over the years

O What I told Jack Profumo when he first came to me
with the truth back in March

O What I told the Security Boys they could do with themselves when they first came to me with the truth back
in February

O Why I always think I can get away with it

Little did I know, in those happy days back in 1957 when I at last
attained my life's ambition - to be Prime Minister of Britain -
how tragically and terribly the whole affair was going to end.

As I first walked into Number Ten, on that cold January day,
everything looked bright for me. From my humble origins
I had risen to be accepted in the highest ranks of society.
By skilful manoeuvering at the time of the Suez crisis, I had
achieved the highest honour my countrymen can bestow.
Little did I foresee how I was to betray that honour so
grossly over the next seven years - until the final
humiliation of my resignation!

The letter that fell into the hands of 'Private Eye' six months
ago. Because we are gentlemen, we returned it, at once, to
Mr. Macmillan (although keeping a photostat copy simply for
our files.)

Dear Jack
In great haste and because I can't
get a reply from your phone
(Must have a word with Reggie
about that !!!)
Please be careful what you get
up to if we play our cards right
no one need ever find out
about us
Let it be our own precious
secret which no one else
need even know
Love M

How the country was to be consistently betrayed by my lies
and evasions.
How so many of my friends
were to have their names
dragged in the mud of public
contempt and degradation.
How my Government was to
become notorious throughout
the world for its incompetence,
laxity and vile corruption.
Little did I foresee , at that
time, how every one of my
policies - such as they were -
would collapse in disaster
through mismanagement and
lack of conviction. And that
eventually the little children
would run through the streets,
howling execration at my
name and tweaking without
mercy my already ludicrous
moustache.

Scarfe.

THE HAPPY DAYS

NEXT WEEK: I flirt with Russian official 'Mr. K.' and am
invited to Moscow - Henry Brooke lets me down - the night
I was thrown over by de Gaulle - Henry Brooke lets me down
again - the day I told Lord ▮▮▮▮▮▮ that I preferred 'a
real MAN' - Henry Brooke lets me down for the last time

Private Eye adapts the Christine Keeler photo for its own comment on the Profumo affair.

such letter himself, writes that *TW3* was still trying to avoid the 'satire' label: 'I had a sixth sense that it would rebound, and it did ... I was chary of using a label that we could not, and frequently would not want to, live up to, except in the sense that the original Latin, *satura*, means hotchpotch.'

To Sherrin's amusement, Frost had chosen to spend part of the break performing in variety theatres. Sherrin caught up with him in, 'of all places', Weston-super-Mare, where also on the bill was the old-style North-Country comedian Al Read. 'Watching [David's] hopeful clowning alongside Al Read's contained, confident, immaculate act,' writes Sherrin, 'was a powerful reminder of an older school of professionalism.'

Frost recalls that the Profumo affair 'finally unravelled' during the summer. On 4 June 1963, John Profumo admitted that he had lied to the House of Commons, and resigned; on 8 June, Stephen Ward was arrested for living off immoral earnings; and then Christine Keeler's confessions began to appear in the *News of the World*. A bewildered Macmillan tried to hold together his collapsing government.

The photographer Lewis Morley, who had his studio on an upper floor of The Establishment, was commissioned to take nude shots of Keeler by a company that proposed to make a film about the scandal. She came to The Establishment but, though she had agreed to the proposal, proved reluctant to take off her clothes. 'The film company representatives,' writes Morley,

> insisted on her carrying out their contractual requirements. There was an impasse which I solved by clearing the studio of people, including my assistants. 'If it's required for you to pose naked,' I said to her, 'then we can do it, without showing what they want to see. Take off your clothes and sit back to front on that chair. Most of you will be hidden but you will have carried out their conditions.'
>
> I turned my back while she stripped and straddled the chair. Then I shot off a roll of film in a matter of minutes, asked her to get dressed, and that was the end of the session.

The picture was stolen from Morley's studio, published in the *Sunday Mirror*, and flashed around the world. Morley subsequently photographed David Frost and Joe Orton in the same pose.

Christopher Booker was on holiday, and Ingrams and Rushton decided to hand over an entire issue of the *Eye* (9 August) to Claud Cockburn, who before the war had edited his own scandal sheet, *The Week*. Cockburn was living in a remote corner of Ireland, and had hardly bothered to keep in touch with the news, but (with the assistance of Alan Brien, who describes Cockburn as 'hardly an operator to pass anywhere unnoticed, with a lanky frame wrapped in a horse-blanket overcoat, a hairy mask of a face, a mouthful of teeth like crowded tombstones, all wreathed in a new-bottled

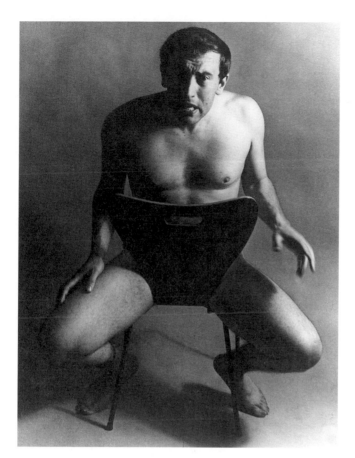

David Frost standing in for Christine Keeler.

Scotch mist') he dashed off an *Eye* that was far more brilliant and scandalous than any of its predecessors.

Written not in the magazine's usual funny voices, but as furious polemic, it floated a rumour that Stephen Ward's death by an overdose during his trial at the beginning of August was not suicide but murder – 'bumped off by the police'. In passing, Cockburn named the head of MI6, Sir Dick White, giving his home address and telephone number, and for good measure he also linked the name of Harold Macmillan's wife Lady Dorothy with Lord Boothby, with whom she had been having a discreet affair since 1929. Cockburn then went back to Ireland, leaving Ingrams and his colleagues to face the consequences – the chief of which was an abrupt rise in the circulation of *Private Eye*, to about 90,000.

*

Meanwhile *Beyond the Fringe* was still playing to full houses in New York. There had even been a presidential visit to the show. Peter Cook alleged that the nuclear button had been installed backstage, just in case John F.

Kennedy had felt like blowing up the world during the performance, and claimed that the secret servicemen sent to check out the theatre before the Kennedys arrived had failed to notice a prop handgun he had placed prominently on his dressing-room table.

The *New York Herald Tribune* for 11 February 1963 reported the event:

> Last night ... the Kennedys took in *Beyond the Fringe*, the British satirical piece lampooning world leaders. In the opening scene ... the targets of the satire were ... Macmillan and ... Khrushchev ... The audience howled, but Mr Kennedy, diplomatically, remained silent and unsmiling ... At one point [Cook] referred to the Cuban crisis as America 'trying in your own way to emulate our splendid effort at Suez'.

Alan Bennett recalls that 'the Kennedys came backstage after the show'. Afterwards,

> Jackie Kennedy asked us to have supper with Adlai Stevenson [American ambassador to the United Nations], and I was just too petrified to go. And the invitation came twice, and both times I said no, I was ill ... My stomach's always been my weak spot, just a totally nervous thing ... I felt I was about to be sick always. So that any formal meal just filled me with terror ... I just actually thought I'd throw up over Adlai Stevenson.

Bennett suspects that something might have developed between Cook and the First Lady – he has a memory, when the presidential party came backstage, of 'Mrs Kennedy absently stroking Peter's hand as they chatted'. Meanwhile (adds Bennett) Dudley Moore was finding American girls even more responsive than British: 'Dudley's ... performance on stage was often merely a perfunctory interruption of the more prolonged and energetic performance going on in his dressing room.'

As word of the huge success of *TW3* crossed the Atlantic, Cook became furiously resentful of what he saw as Frost's and the BBC's appropriation of his own plans for a television show. Miller felt the same: 'And then it all got taken up by *fucking* David Frost, who took it *seriously*. Before you knew it, satire had become a routine, and you could even see it on the BBC.' Speaking more coolly about this today, Miller says:

> We [*Beyond the Fringe*] were undergraduate comedians. The reason why it turned out to be as 'satirical' as it was thought to be at the time was just simply that we were not Shaftesbury Avenue denizens – we were people who could make allusions to other things, and obviously had our own eye on society, and thought there were some absurd, ludicrous things. But it was rather affectionate, most of it. There was no vicious hatred in anything we did, I think.
>
> In contrast, the people who followed on from us rather opportunistically took up the idea of it *being satire*, and then explicitly promoted it. Once it was

labelled 'satire', people took the bit between their teeth, and then raced in the direction of what they thought was a satirical goal. Frost in particular saw that it was fashionable, and pushed it like mad. One of the reasons why Peter Cook was so bitter about him was that he really took advantage of Peter's absence in New York to do this.

Cook had his chance for revenge when Frost, who had come over to America during *TW3*'s summer break, joined him and the *Fringe* cast at a house in Fairfield, Connecticut, which belonged to the show's American producer. Although scarcely able to swim, Frost jumped in the pool – and got into difficulties. Cook said that at first he thought, 'Ah, ho ho, David is making a satirical attack on drowning,' but then realized it was serious. Long afterwards, at Cook's memorial service, Alan Bennett told the congregation, 'The only regret he regularly voiced was that … he had saved David Frost from drowning.'

John Bird met Frost in New York, and was amazed at the change in his status:

I hadn't seen David since he'd co-anchored that fairly disastrous pilot for *TW3*, and when he came to New York only a few months later he'd obviously become a kind of national hero. I've seen a few recordings of it since then, and he was certainly very, very good, much better than I could ever have been.

Nicholas Luard had been left in charge of the London end of The Establishment. From New York, Cook sent him suggestions for performers. Some were disastrous; in this category, Luard remembers Barry Humphries 'simpering and whimpering in sequinned dresses'. Ned Sherrin watched this too, and recalls that in those days the future Dame Edna was 'slightly pathetic … clad in a homespun brown dress'. Humphries says he was given 'the amazing fee of £100 per week … The reaction of audiences and critics confirmed my worst fears … I wondered if I could ever look Peter Cook in the eye again after that.' However, Nicholas Garland says that Humphries was 'a huge success' with a discerning few: 'We immediately began talking to each other in Barry-style Australian.'

Cook had also recommended the comedian Frankie Howerd, whom he had seen giving a comic speech at an *Evening Standard* awards dinner. Howerd's career was at such a low ebb that he was thinking of giving up show business and running a pub. Cook suggested to him that he should appear at The Establishment – 'I was absolutely petrified,' writes Howerd, 'for the previous artist there had been Lenny Bruce' – and Luard eventually booked him for a month's solo spot in September 1962. Howerd did what he always did in an emergency: he telephoned the best writers he could think of, who in this case were Johnny Speight and the duo of Alan Simpson and Ray Galton, and asked for ideas. They decided that Howerd should base his

Frankie Howerd.

act on the truth, that he was an essentially old-style comedian who might be out of his depth in The Establishment.

Luard says that his performance was marvellous – 'winsome, roguish, naughty, and in some strange way genteelly menacing with his lisp and his flapping hands' – and he played to packed and wildly enthusiastic houses. Ned Sherrin came on no fewer than three evenings to witness this triumph, and booked Howerd for a *TW3* appearance on 6 April 1963. Again, Howerd decided to base his act on being a fish out of water, plus some comments on Chancellor of the Exchequer Reginald Maudling's Budget, which had been announced a few days earlier. Sherrin was fascinated to discover that Howerd's apparent spontaneity was the fruit of intensive rehearsal, with only a few 'oohs' and 'ahs' added in performance: 'We hired a rehearsal room for a week, during which he paced and paced, and broke off to phone every scriptwriter he knew – Johnny Speight, Took and Feldman, Muir and Norden, and God knows how many more.'

On the night, Howerd came on as the last item, and began by looking at his watch:

About *time*. I've been waiting a hell of a time to get on. It's *twenty-five to twelve*! I thought I'd have to have another shave before I got on. Still, I enjoyed bits of it. I mean, the bits I *understood*...

Before I start this little lecture, I thought I ought really to explain what I'm doing here in the first place, because as you perhaps know I'm usually associated with variety – music-hall – and I'm not usually associated with the sophisticated wags and wits, these youngsters, I'm more sort of Billy Cotton, me, and I thought I would apologize – (*he reacts to a laugh in puzzlement*) – has someone dropped something? Never mind, I shall drop a few tonight, so don't worry. That's what they call ad libbing – you don't usually get that on *this* programme...

I was at the hairdresser's, you see, placing a bet, with Teasy,[3] and under the next drier was this familiar face...It was David Frost, you know, the one who wears his hair back to front. (*Big laugh.*) No – no – please, please. He'll want more money – he's earning enough as it is...So anyway, he obviously recognized me, he said, 'Hello, Tom, I wonder if you'd like to come round and do us a turn.' I said, 'Well, I – I' – I thought if I stuttered long enough he might mention money. The lips were pursed...

So I came along and saw the producer, this Ned Sherrin. Nice man. Underneath. (*Laugh.*) No – no – please. And of course he *confronted* me. He said, 'I want you to address the nation on the Budget.'...I know what he wanted. He was expecting a diatribe of viciousness and satire...Of course, that's not me... I'm more the lovable kind of comedian, you know. (Well, don't take a vote on it.) Anyway these days you can't be filthy if you haven't got a degree. (*Big laugh and applause.*)...

Since the programme was open-ended (Baverstock's 50-minute limit had not, after all, been imposed) it was possible to let Howerd continue for as long as he liked. 'There was nothing coming on afterwards,' says Sherrin, 'so nobody minded. And no commercials were going to cut him off, which was what had thrown him on ITV, because if it was going well he'd need to over-run, but they had to keep to a tight schedule. I could just see him relax.' He continued for nearly a quarter of an hour, and finished to enormous applause. It was one of the highlights of the entire run of *TW3*, and it restored Howerd's career quite literally overnight – as he writes in his autobiography, he now found that he had become 'a cult figure on a national scale'. All thought of buying a pub was abandoned.

Lenny Bruce was booked by Luard for a return to The Establishment in April 1963, but it never took place. The press had continued to campaign against him, and when he flew into Heathrow on 8 April he was detained by

---

[3] 'Teasy-Weasy' Raymond, the society hairdresser, who had been sparring with Bernard Levin in this programme.

Gerald Scarfe's *Private Eye* comment on the banning of Lenny Bruce.

immigration officers acting on the orders of the Home Secretary, who perhaps was looking for a satirist victim after 'Henry Brooke, This Is Your Life', which had been broadcast two weeks earlier. They strip-searched him and sent him back on the next flight. Brooke announced that it was 'not in the public interest' to admit Bruce into the country, on account of his 'sick jokes and lavatory humour' – a phrase that *Private Eye* used on its masthead in its next issue.[4] Peter Cook tried, but failed, to arrange for Bruce to be smuggled back into Britain via Ireland.

Bruce described the whole experience in one of his stand-up routines:

I actually flew to London and was rejected...They kept me overnight in [a] cell...Then I got back to Idlewild [now JFK airport]...and...was taken into a private room where I was stripped and internally searched...What if you get a hard-on? 'All right, take your shoes off now and – what the hell's the matter with you?...A damn weirdo – getting a hard-on at Customs...Cut the silliness...' 'I'll try, sir, but – it's never done this before. I guess it's nerves... Could you gentlemen go out while I make it go away? Oh, here, I know what I'll do, I'll put it in the wine basket and I'll carry it.'

[4] *That Was The Week That Was* featured a spoof photograph of Bruce becoming an honorary Doctor of Letters, describing him as 'the man who won fame using four of them at a time'.

Bruce was busted for obscenity again in New York in April 1964, and a year later he was declared bankrupt. Drug abuse broke down his health, and in August 1966 he died.[5]

The failed attempt to bring Bruce back to England cost Cook & Luard Productions a considerable amount in legal fees, and they had also advanced most of Bruce's fee to him. Their showbiz magazine *Scene* ran out of money and ceased publication in the month of Bruce's non-appearance at The Establishment, April 1963, and the club itself began to go on to the rocks. As Harry Thompson puts it in his biography of Cook, 'Thickset gentlemen began to pay courtesy calls, pointing out the immense structural vulnerability of a satirical night-club to accidental damage.' Willie Rushton recalls that 'most of the waiters were lifting all the money', and John Wells writes that the staff 'proved incapable of keeping out fighting drunks who came reeling in from vice-ridden Greek Street; there were bottle fights, the staff turned out to be fiddling the management blind'.

Wells resigned from his Eton job in July 1963, with considerable heart-searching, 'because I had had a fantastic year teaching the Sixth Form German. In many ways, even now, I feel it might have been sensible to have remained a schoolmaster. Schoolmasters are very valuable people, and comics aren't.' During the following months he was occupied with writing and trying to launch a musical of an Agatha Christie whodunnit, living with his parents – 'My father was then the Rural Dean of Bognor Regis.'

On 23 September 1963, a few days before *TW3* returned after its summer break, Cook & Luard Productions was put into voluntary liquidation, with debts of nearly £66,000. The *Guardian* reported that The Establishment would nevertheless continue to operate 'in the same old satirical way' under a Mr Raymond Nash, who 'was said to be experienced in running clubs', and had made a deal with the creditors.

The original cast of The Establishment was still performing in New York, and had also toured Canada with great success (Jeremy Geidt recalls performing to full 2000-seater theatres). 'We would have stayed on,' says John Fortune,

> but we had a visit from this man called Raymond Nash. His argument was that the London club was going downhill, and had been mismanaged by Nick Luard, and only another show from us would revive it. And Eleanor was getting a bit homesick, and in the meantime in New York I'd married [an American], and my wife was keen to come to England. And we did come back, and did one more show, at the end of 1963, for about a couple of months.

[5] The moral climate was changing so fast that only a year after his death his stand-up material began to be published (as *The Essential Lenny Bruce*) and in 1971 Julian Barry's biographical play about him, full of Bruce's routines with their four-letter words, opened on Broadway.

Nash put out an announcement:

> On November 4th, the return of The Establishment's original company from a
> brilliant year in New York to open in a new production. So come and join John
> Bird, Eleanor Bron, John Fortune & Jeremy Geidt in THE MUFFLED REPORT ...
> Jazz in the basement. Late-night talking and drinking in the theatre bar.
> Gaming on the first floor. Mingle with renegade nuns, unfrocked prime
> ministers, and plain-clothes policewomen posing as both.

'Gaming on the first floor' indicated the direction in which Nash was taking
the club.

Although Cook no longer co-owned The Establishment, he had helped the
cast write *The Muffled Report* – indeed in a letter to David Nathan at the
Daily Herald he described it as 'the new show I wrote'. He contacted Nathan
to complain that the press had mostly ignored it. (An exception was Alan
Brien in the *Sunday Telegraph*, who described the evening rather
sarcastically as 'a sentimental occasion for old satire hands who can
remember the time when David Frost was the most famous man in Britain'
– in other words, satire was no longer the latest fashion, though *TW3* was
still running.) Nathan wrote back to Cook giving the reason:

> The fact is that The Establishment while you have been in America has
> acquired an unsavoury reputation. It is difficult to see how an entertainment
> which takes upon itself the right to criticize society can operate within a
> framework which is more open to criticism than its targets.

This was a polite way of saying that the club was now largely in the hands of
gangsters.

Lewis Morley, who still had his photographic studio in the building,
describes Nash as having an 'underworld aura', with a bodyguard called
Speedy who carried a gun. 'It quickly became obvious that we couldn't go on
working there,' says John Fortune.

> It was too frightening – these were very hard men. Raymond Nash was Lebanese
> or something, and he was Muslim, and didn't drink, and insisted that his lads
> didn't drink, and they went to the gym all the time, so that if you brushed past
> them it was like making contact with the wall!
>
> One evening we were doing a show, and Raymond was standing at the side,
> and there was some sort of City young man who heckled us, and we loved that.
> That was what it was about. But Raymond Nash just walked across to him, and
> I've never seen it outside films – he just took him by the lapels and lifted him
> with one hand, at arm's length, and just carried him out. And one of the waiters
> was in the lobby, and told us that Nash put him against the wall, and forced two
> fingers up his nose and broke the septum. And there was blood everywhere, and
> an ambulance – it was dreadful.

John Bird recalls the incident vividly. 'I felt particularly responsible, because it had been a drunk in the audience, and I said, "I'm not going on again till that man's taken out." And he was taken out and done over.'

The Establishment lingered on for a little. 'Side-effects from extra-mural activities like gold smuggling and sundry criminal affairs hastened its demise,' writes Lewis Morley. 'The *coup de grâce* came when Nash himself was arrested in Japan. The club passed into other hands. It was sold, lock, stock and barrel, to a Mr Jones, who turned it into a private "club", by which time 18 Greek Street had turned full circle. I shifted my studio...' In the autumn of 1965 John Wells noted, 'It's now a gambling club; the sign about satire has been taken down, and it reads simply "Dine and Dance till 3 a.m."'[6]

*

Nick Luard, who was deeply upset by the club having failed in Cook's absence, had resigned from their other joint enterprise: 'I handed over my *Private Eye* shares to Peter... [who] became the *Eye*'s owner. There was little else to be picked up from the debris, and I went off to Spain in search of new and warmer pastures – to travel, explore and write.' He wrote thrillers and travel books, and his wife Elisabeth became a cookery writer.

A few days before the liquidation proceedings, Nicholas Tomalin reported in *The Sunday Times*:

> *Private Eye* is safe now from any financial troubles of The Establishment night-club, as it has a new owner. Peter Cook has bought 80 per cent of the shares, and makes it very clear that there will be no chance of the magazine suffering.
>
> At the same time, the editorial board has changed. Christopher Booker, whose name once led all the rest in the editorial credits, has gone for good. 'I went off for two months' holiday,' he tells me. 'And two days before I returned I received a letter from Ingrams and Rushton saying my services were no longer required.
>
> 'After two years building up the magazine it seemed rather curious treatment. I admit we have always had disagreements, but the letter came as a great shock.' ...
>
> Says Ingrams: 'Willie and I probably were a clique, two against one. Perhaps the letter *was* rather abrupt. It was a difficult decision, but general opinion in this office was for it.'

Booker's holiday, taken at the end of the first series of *TW3*, was in fact his honeymoon. He had married into the aristocracy, his bride being the daughter of Lord Glenconner – the future novelist Emma Tennant. She was on the rebound from a short-lived marriage to Sebastian Yorke, son of the

---

[6] In 1999 comedy came back to 18 Greek Street – now a bar called The Boardwalk – with a show calling itself 'The Establishment', featuring a number of alternative-style comedians. Recordings of Peter Cook were played to introduce the show.

novelist Henry Green, and had met Booker when Ken Tynan's wife Elaine Dundy had taken her to sit in the *TW3* studio audience. 'I have met a satirist,' Emma Tennant writes in her memoirs, 'and I decide then and there to ally myself to this new movement...I am a part of this scintillating, dangerous new world.'

John Wells attended the Booker–Tennant wedding, and recalls it as an 'absurd' event featuring two singing transvestites: 'They were called Rogers and Starr, and their most popular number was "Would you like a lick of my lollipop,/Would you like a suck of my stick?" It seemed to bode ill for a normal marriage. And it didn't last very long.' Indeed, Emma Tennant writes that she soon found that she and 'Mr Booker' (as her five-year-old son from her first marriage insisted on addressing him) had 'almost nothing in common', and she managed to ditch him by moving flats and leaving him behind in the old one. But in the summer of 1963 they were still married, and honeymooning at Glen, the Tennants' Scottish baronial castle; Booker had begun to write a book – which became *The Neophiliacs* – and intended to return to the *Eye*, as well as *TW3*, in the autumn.

The problems of the Ingrams–Booker working relationship had never been solved, and were now compounded by what Ingrams saw as Booker's near-desertion of the *Eye* for the BBC's fat cheques; also maybe his resentment of Booker's society marriage. 'Booker got terribly taken up with the telly, having this trendy wife' is how he puts it today, though chronologically speaking the telly had preceded the wife. Ingrams contacted Peter Cook in New York, and obtained his agreement as *Private Eye*'s new owner that Booker should go. 'The reason why Willie and I fell out with Booker,' Ingrams says today, 'was that he was very indecisive, and he could never finish anything, which when applied to a magazine made things difficult. We would be sitting around at half-past eight at night, waiting for him.' Nicholas Garland, who by this time was having drawings printed by *Private Eye*, says, 'Booker had a kind of preachy quality, and that's what Ingrams didn't like.'

Booker says he was 'horrified' to have the *Eye* snatched from him, and claims that 'Richard's ambition to be editor was very considerable'. But he adds, 'I'm sure they found it a relief not to have me around, driving them to their task.' The swift demise of his marriage was due at least in part to the sacking; Emma Tennant writes that it was 'a blow', and that she soon realized that Booker and his pals had the same social ambitions as anyone else – that 'satirists are really *Telegraph* readers in disguise'.

*

Ten days before *TW3* was due to return to the nation's screens after its summer break, Stuart Hood, the Controller of Programmes, made a statement at a press conference which came like a slap in the face to Sherrin and Frost.

First (he said) the show was to lose its freedom to overrun, which had been possible because no other programme followed it. 'The programme will be 50 minutes long,' announced Hood, 'and there will be a programme after it.' He continued by implying that it had overstepped the mark politically:

> We have seen what the mistakes were and it will be my hope that the mistakes which there were will not be repeated. This does not mean it will not continue to act as a gadfly, and when a gadfly stings you it hurts. But I hope it will sting accurately, and the proper people, and I hope it will not give offence in unnecessary ways.

He did not specify who 'the proper people' might be.

Having implied that *TW3*'s satirical claws would be blunted, Hood turned to the matter of what the Home Secretary called lavatory humour. 'The programme,' he told the press conference, 'was criticized towards the end of the run for smut, and this is something which we will be keeping a very sharp look-out for ... The element of "smut" will be omitted.'

Frost writes that he and Sherrin were furious. 'It was such a gift to our enemies. You don't label yourself with a pejorative word like "smut".' Sherrin had not expected this aspect of *TW3* to be attacked:

> We had never really worried about 'smut'; it was not a very important feature of the programme. We were not particularly conscious of it nor, I think, were most of our viewers. However, once [Hood] had lit the blue touch-paper political opponents realized that they could stand well away and watch. A wave of reaction gathered momentum.

Even if the programme had given particular emphasis to sex, this was in tune with popular feeling. The contraceptive pill, first made available in American in 1960, was soon contributing to a feeling of sexual liberation in Britain. An article in *Time* magazine observed of the changing British attitude to sex:

> On the island where the subject has long been taboo in polite society, sex has exploded into the national consciousness and national headlines. 'Are We Going Sex Crazy?' asks the *Daily Herald*. 'Is Chastity Outmoded?' asks a school magazine for teenagers. 'Are Virgins Obsolete?' is the question posed by the solemn *New Statesman*. The answers vary but one thing is clear: Britain is being bombarded with a barrage of frankness about sex.

As a BBC staff member, Sherrin was not supposed to talk to the press. Nevertheless he told the *News of the World*, 'I don't think we have had smut in the programme.' The *Daily Express* pounced on this in an editorial:

> First Mr Stuart Hood, the Television Programme Controller, says that the smut will be cut out of the programme ... Then the show's producer denies that there

was ever any smut. The impression given is that the programme will continue as before. Mr Hood must tell the BBC's bright young men that they do not have a licence to behave as they please. He should say that either they mend their ways or else they do not return to the screen.

Frost says that an additional insult was the BBC's choice of programme to follow *TW3* on Saturday nights. B.A. Young made this point in *Punch*:

> Why the BBC has so evidently decided to harass the opening of the second season of *That Was The Week That Was*, after having earned such adulation for having introduced it last year, is simply one of those minor mysteries about the Corporation that it may never be given to us to understand... And so we see the programme planners robbing *TWTWTW* of the charm of its unpredictable duration and its basic requirement of being the last programme of the week and packing it into a firm schedule before – I can hardly believe it – *The Third Man*.

Frost suggested to Sherrin how they might sabotage this scheduling: they should discover the plots of *The Third Man* – repeats of a third-rate 1959 series loosely based on the famous film written by the Director-General's brother – and at the end of each *TW3* Frost should read them out, giving away the endings. 'Ned loved the idea, though both of us thought that all hell would break loose when we tried it.'

It was in this atmosphere that a *TW3* pilot was recorded on 22 September, a week before the first actual programme. The cast's mood was sombre for another reason: in June, Timothy Birdsall, whose on-the-spot cartooning had become one of the programme's most popular features, had died of leukaemia at the age of twenty-six.

The report of Lord Denning's judicial enquiry into the Profumo affair had just been published, and the pilot opened with Millicent Martin singing:

> That Was The Week That Was,
> Macmillan always reads in bed,
> This week the Denning Report,
> But he'd have done much better with a Trollope instead.

At which point Willie Rushton leaned into the shot and said severely, 'We'll have none of that smut on this programme, I'll have you know!'

This line was cut when the programme came back on the air the following Saturday (28 September 1963). The first edition of the new series opened where the first series had left off – with Martin and Kinnear as the suburban TV watchers:

ROY: What's on next, love?
MILLIE: (*consulting the* Radio Times) Nothing... Well, nothing to suit our taste. *That Was The Week That Was...*

ROY: Don't tell me they've fetched that back ... Bum and po! Take your knickers
off! They did it every week – without fail!

MILLIE: Will they say it again?

ROY: They've got to. If they hope to make a comeback. They've set a standard
now. They can't disappoint the British public.

Frost says that this summed up the team's feelings about the BBC's
'incipient Grundyism'.

The opening political sketch was a series of spoof reviews of the Denning
Report, but the next item was a far more effective comment on the Profumo
affair and the report – a photo-montage of its main characters in various
poses and situations, to a soundtrack of Frank Sinatra singing 'I Could Write
a Book'. The rise of the Beatles was celebrated in a musical number called
'The Liverpool Sound' ('Yes! The Beetle [*sic*] Boys are crawlin' everywhere'),
and the black comedian Irwin C. Watson, whom Frost and Sherrin had
spotted in America, did an impersonation of Jomo Kenyatta (now President
of Kenya) much in the manner of John Bird. John Mortimer contributed a
brilliant little monologue in which a judge (played by the actor Robert Lang)
demonstrates that the root cause of divorce is marriage: 'Abolish
matrimony and the divorce rate would soon fall; you don't have to be a
mathematical genius to understand that.' (Mortimer says he thinks *TW3*
was 'very important – nobody had really laughed at politicians before, and it
liberated us all from having to be respectful'.) Bernard Levin attacked a
puritanical Tory MP, Sir Cyril Osborne, who told Levin, 'Take sex out of
this show and you've nothing left!' David Kernan sang a Herbert Kretzmer
song about the failure of Pope Pius XII to resist the Holocaust:

> Does it matter if some German Jews
> Aren't dying in their beds?
> For Hitler fights for Jesus
> And he's fighting back the Reds.

Frost concluded the evening by telling viewers that, though *TW3* would
be followed by *The Third Man*, they might be wanting to go to bed, so here
was the plot to save them the trouble of watching it: 'The plane, which
Harry Lime says crashes, hasn't really, and Marta, the fascinating girl spy, is
in fact working for the enemy.' Frost writes: 'The audience greatly enjoyed
this little piece of in-house sabotage, though Ned and I were convinced it
would be a one-week phenomenon.' In fact he was allowed to get away with
it again for the next two episodes, after which Hugh Greene personally gave
orders to scrap the repeats of *The Third Man* and let *TW3* finish the evening,
open-ended as before.

Two days after the first edition in the new series, Sherrin wrote to the

BBC's legal department, enclosing a script: 'I am very anxious to do Lord Dilhorne this week. Can you please tell me which specific sentences you would advise me not to use.' Sherrin was still trying to take a swipe at the Lord Chancellor, and he enclosed a script. The legal department passed it to Hugh Greene, and then sent word to Sherrin that the Director-General 'does not think it right to broadcast the Lord Dillon [*sic*] item'. Kenneth Adam, Director of Television, had more to say about this to Alasdair Milne:

> D. G. [Director-General] and I feel that we must drop this one once and for all ...
> D. G. and I feel we must lay off these prolonged personal attacks unless there is great topical provocation ... Dilhorne is out.

Censorship was also now being exercised with regard to Bernard Levin's confrontations. His guest on 5 October was the Labour front-bencher Ray Gunter, and James Callaghan had also been invited, but Kenneth Adam wrote to Stuart Hood two days after Levin and Gunter had jousted on screen:

> Please note that the Board of Management has ruled that there should be no invitation to front-bench members of the House of Commons of any party by *TWTWTW*. The Levin confrontation is thought quite unsuitable for such members of either the Government or the 'Shadow Cabinet'.

Meanwhile Kenneth Tynan responded to the BBC's fuss about 'smut' with a spoof of a letter to *The Times*, read out by Kenneth Cope in the 5 October edition:

> Dear Sir,
>   I hope I am not a prude, but I feel compelled to lodge a protest against the recent outbreak of violence and sexuality in dreams. Many of my friends have been as shocked and sickened as I have been by the filth that is poured out nightly as soon as our eyes are closed. It is certainly not my idea of 'home entertainment'.
>   Night after night, the most disgraceful scenes of perversion and bestiality are perpetrated in the name of 'freedom of expression', though I would call it licensed smut-peddling. In the past week, for instance, I counted six rapes, one of them involving a woman old enough to be my mother (indeed, I thought at the time it *was* my mother), and several sadistic orgies in which grotesque and appalling liberties were taken with members of the Royal Family.
>   Things have come to a parlous state ...

There was plenty of other material of this calibre; nevertheless Sherrin and Frost felt discontented. Sherrin describes the first four shows of the second series as 'dull ... stilted and self-conscious'; Christopher Booker calls them 'slipshod and lifeless' and recalls that *The Avengers* on ITV was becoming the new craze with viewers; Frost agrees that there was a general feeling in the air that *TW3* was not performing up to its previous standard... There certainly had not been an unforgettable humdinger of a show in the first few weeks of the second series. But there had not been a new Profumo affair either. Perhaps people's anticipation had been built to a point where it was impossible to fulfil.

As Sherrin puts it, quoting Cole Porter, the public's love affair with the show had been 'too hot not to cool down'.

On 9 October, Kenneth Adam drew to the Director-General's attention what he called a 'shrewd' review of the opening of the new series in the *Daily Herald* by one of *TW3*'s writers, Dennis Potter. It was headlined 'NOW THE SHOCK HAS GONE OUT OF SATIRE-DAY NIGHT':

> Saturday night can once more be pickled in vinegar. *That Was The Week That Was* – its hour-long anarchical sprawl cut back to a mere 50 minutes by nervous planners – came back to BBC screens with the old outrageous mixture of wit, rudeness, cruelty, smut, and sheer exuberance. A year ago on this page I welcomed the first show with a joyful but incredulous stupefaction. On Saturday, of course, the shock was gone. A bomb explodes only once... This time there was an almost cosy air of self-congratulation between performers and viewers as the predictable swipe about Marples [Minister of Transport] tumbled hard upon a predictable snigger about Macmillan...

Potter, who seemed to be cutting *TW3*'s throat and therefore to some extent his own as one of its writers, then did a volte-face and praised the programme's continuing strengths. However, Kenneth Adam summed up Potter's review as arguing that 'audience and performers now form a kind of club, and there is no longer the same power to shock the initiates' – which was evidently Adam's own opinion. Michael Frayn made the same point during 1963 in his introduction to the newly published text of *Beyond the Fringe*:

> Once [satire] had annihilated the convention, to go *on* mocking the so-called Establishment has more and more meant making the audience not laugh at themselves at all, but at a standard target which is rapidly becoming as well-established as mothers-in-law. To do this is not to undermine but to confirm the audience's prejudices, and has less in common with satire than with community hymn-singing – agreeable and heart-warming as that may be. It's also much less funny.

Yet it was on the day after Adam had written his memo that the Director-General – making no reference to Frost's sabotaging of *The Third Man* – decided that *TW3* should once again be the final programme on Saturday evenings. The BBC had not yet given up faith in it.

5

....

The party's over

On Saturday, 12 October 1963 came the chance for the 'humdinger' that *TW3* needed. Harold Macmillan had told the Conservative Party Conference at Blackpool that he was resigning as Prime Minister, at the age of sixty-nine. In fact the programme treated his going gently; the actor Robert Lang recited an affectionate elegy by Caryl Brahms ('O Squire, who once had England for your village/The time has come to render up your lease'), and Willie Rushton as Macmillan sang 'The Party's Over' – 'very sweetly and very touchingly', recalls Sherrin. Lance Percival adds that Rushton was very sad at Macmillan's departure, 'because he lost a very good part'.

This edition considered the candidates for 10 Downing Street on the Tory front bench, referring to them as 'Drab Butler' (R.A. Butler, known as 'Rab'), 'Reginald Middling', and 'Swine' (Lord Hailsham, whose family name was Hogg), and suggesting that 'A year that started with Profumo/Could even end with Premier Home-oh'. Sure enough, it was announced shortly before the next edition (19 October) that the new Prime Minister would be Lord Home, the Foreign Secretary, who would resign his title and become Sir Alec Douglas-Home. (An earlier *TW3* had joked about how Home got this job: '[He] joined the Cabinet when that classical scholar and grammarian, Harold Macmillan, approached on the grouse moor by a messenger with the query, "Who are you going to make Foreign Secretary?" replied, "You mean *Whom*." ')

The popular choice would have been Butler, whose opinion-poll rating was more than four times higher than Home's. Frost writes that most people of his age were furious that 'the Conservative Party appeared to have learned nothing from recent events', and had picked an apparently undistinguished aristocrat without even a seat in the Commons. Sherrin calls the choice of Home 'retrograde', and says that *TW3*'s sketch about it was 'the nearest I got to mounting a personal pulpit'. Although the writing of it was undertaken –

at the last minute – by Christopher Booker, and the piece was to be delivered by Frost, it was Sherrin himself, a disillusioned Tory, who provided the idea.

He describes the piece as in 'a measured Disraelian style', and Frost explains it as 'Benjamin Disraeli writing a letter to his latest successor':

> My Lord:
>
> When I say that your acceptance of the Queen's commission to form an administration has proved and will prove an unmitigated catastrophe for the Conservative Party, for the Constitution, for the Nation, and for yourself, it must not be thought that I bear you any personal ill-will … Let it not be thought that your inheritance of an ancient and anachronistic title, through no intention of your own, should in itself be regarded as in any way an obstacle to your possession of an even higher honour …
>
> Your bleak, deathly smile is the smile today not of a victor – but of a victim. You are the dupe and unwitting tool of a conspiracy … of a tiny band of desperate men who have seen in you their last, slippery chance of keeping the levers of power and influence within their privileged circle …
>
> You have always drifted with the tide – the tide of appeasement, the tide of Suez … You have foreseen nothing. You are qualified only to do nothing …

During the first series of *TW3*, responsibility for censorship had been in the hands of Alasdair Milne. Now, at the instigation of Hugh Carleton Greene, the more senior – and far more uptight – Grace Wyndham Goldie had largely taken over the role. In her memoirs she writes:

> The Director-General had summoned me and said that I must take personal responsibility for *That Was The Week That Was*. He would make himself available on the telephone at any time for consultation … I was dismayed. I felt as if I was being asked to ride a tiger … The crunch always came on Saturday afternoons … Milne was not always available to attend rehearsals. In that case I did. And if he did attend and found that an item which we had agreed was doubtful was still being included, he telephoned me. I went across to see it, and if I felt necessary to do so I consulted the Director-General.

On this occasion she passed the script to Greene. 'I remember standing in the hospitality room,' says Christopher Booker, 'with the show due to go on the air in two hours' time; and getting a call from Hugh Greene … explaining why he thought certain passages ought to be taken out.' They duly were; nevertheless the remaining text was still strong stuff. Sherrin admits that 'no such savage attack on a politician had previously been delivered on BBC Television', but adds that its 'inelegant' performance by Frost himself (dressed and made up as Disraeli), as the last item in that evening's show, 'went some way to sabotage the Disraelian panache and blunt its cutting edge'. On the other hand, at the end of the monologue, Frost dropped the

Disraeli persona and put in a remark which shocked many people more than the sketch itself: 'And so, there is the choice for the electorate; on one hand Lord Home – and on the other hand Mr Harold Wilson. Dull Alec versus Smart Alec.'

Wilson, chosen as Labour leader after the death of Gaitskell, had already been caricatured by *TW3* as 'New Instant Wilson...makes your Party go with a swing – 6 per cent to the Conservatives'. Now, the Disraeli monologue whipped up the largest protest the programme had yet received; according to Frost, there were 'more than six hundred phone calls of complaint, and only sixty of congratulation'. Douglas-Home himself made no public comment, but some years later he said in a radio interview:

> The only time I think I really felt that lampooning went over the edge was during – do you remember? – *The Week That Was* [*sic*], David Frost's first programme, which was 'satire'. And I think pretty poor satire. And indeed it faded out, and hasn't been resurrected. So I think that probably the public didn't really like it. But the drip of it, every week, that year I was Prime Minister was pretty tiresome.

His memory was at fault: *TW3* was to last for much less than a year of his prime ministership. Frost says that the immediate reaction to the Disraeli speech in the BBC hierarchy was 'not discernibly positive...In retrospect, that item was probably the death-knell of *TW3*.'

In order to gain a seat in the Commons, Douglas-Home now had to put himself up at a by-election in a safe Tory seat, Kinross in Scotland. Five days after the Disraeli piece, Controller of Programmes Stuart Hood warned Sherrin that the BBC Legal Department 'tell us that it would be an infringement of the Representation of the People Act if any reference *at all* were to be made to the Kinross By-Election in *That Was The Week That Was*. This is harsh but it is the Law.' Sherrin knew this was nonsense. 'Of course we will not mention the Kinross By-Election,' he replied,

> but I do think it was worth pointing out to the Legal Department that throughout the last session...we made constant, long and specific references to many by-elections and staged comprehensive, detailed and in some cases extremely funny sketches about them. I am wondering if the threat of arrest is hanging over me.

The next *TW3*, on 26 October, made no reference to the by-election. There were a few mild jokes at Douglas-Home's expense, but just as many at Harold Wilson's. The script also included a Waterhouse and Hall sketch about Lord Baden-Powell, inspired by the opening of the 1963 Boy Scout *Gang Show*. Played by Lance Percival, Baden-Powell tells two fellow officers at Mafeking that, if he survives the war, 'I'm going to start taking a

serious interest in young lads … Little chaps of about twelve or thirteen.'
One of the officers remarks, 'He'll get fifteen years.' In the climate of
anxiety, even this old joke seemed too much to *TW3*'s minders. The sketch
was dropped, and Grace Wyndham Goldie reported to Huge Carleton
Greene:

> [Milne] had said to me over the telephone … that he thought the Boy Scout
> item … should go … When I went to the rehearsal in the evening, however, I
> found that it was proposed, after all, to include it. [Milne] explained to me that
> he had changed his mind about the sketch, because of the way in which it was
> being played. The central character, Baden-Powell, was played with simplicity,
> sincerity and directness, and he felt that this meant that it was the others who
> were made to look foolish, not Baden-Powell.

Amazingly, Goldie believed this. 'Nevertheless,' she continues,

> I felt that the phrases which I have underlined … still meant that it had
> unsavoury overtones … and I did not think we should transmit it on grounds of
> taste. Both Ned Sherrin and [Milne] disagreed … but … the sketch was removed.

Greene's reaction is not recorded; but it seems that his patience was further
stretched, maybe because much of his weekend was now taken up with
anxious phone calls from Goldie about *TW3*.

Unbeknown to Sherrin and his team, Greene was now having to defend
himself from a barrage of attack from his Board of Governors and the BBC's
General Advisory Council, most of it caused by *TW3*. At a meeting on 10
October the Governors expressed 'anxiety' about the programme, and said
they thought it had become dull and lacking in new ideas. Greene would not
be drawn on its future, but said it would be kept under review. Two weeks
later, at the General Advisory Council, one of the members described it as
'offensive, undergraduate, potentially venomous, increasingly humourless
and creating too many difficulties'. Greene was beginning to feel the strain,
as he admitted in a private letter:

> I think this is one of the most difficult years I have ever had. Things had been
> going too well in the previous three years, but 1963 has been the year of
> criticism and of quite bitter attacks on the sorts of things I've been trying to do.

By the next meeting of the Board of Governors, on 7 November, he had
decided to take action about *TW3*. He told the Governors that at the
General Advisory Council the programme 'had recurred as a subject of
criticism', and said he himself had come to feel it was a 'gigantic red
herring', which was diverting attention from the real achievements of the
BBC, and prejudicing the public response to serious programmes on
important but difficult social themes. Very senior staff, including himself,

were having to devote themselves to 'weekly consideration of the script in detail'. The minutes continue:

> Under this firmer control the programme's own perceptible decline in vitality was likely to be accentuated, and there was a strong case for ending its run before spring 1964. The fact that 1964 would be a [General] Election year, and one of hot political argument and acute sensitivity, seemed conclusive in that the political balance which had to be achieved by the BBC at such a time was inherently impossible in *TWTWTW*...He had therefore come to the conclusion that it was strategically right to take the programme off, and tactically right to choose the end of the year as the moment to do so. There would be protests from the public over what would be seen as BBC cowardice, but the political considerations gave a firm basis for reply. There would be internal difficulties of staff morale, which made it highly desirable to emphasize the BBC's high opinion of the programme as a new concept in broadcasting. The timing of the announcement, and the security arrangements which would precede it, were critically important...
>
> The Board noted D. G. 's recommendation that *TWTWTW* should end with the year, and unanimously approved of it.

The following spring, Greene told Kenneth Harris of the *Observer* that it had been 'an absolutely personal conclusion of mine that *TW3* should be taken off the air...and when I told the Board it came very much to its surprise. It decided I was right and endorsed my conclusions.' *Private Eye*'s version (printed soon after the news of the axing became public) had Greene saying:

> What happened was that the Board of Governors never liked the programme but they kept quiet so long as everyone else seemed to like it. Once it became fashionable to say it wasn't any good, they came out into the open and then I, being the weak-kneed old *Daily Telegraph* buffer that I am, decided to pack it in.
>
> What I really wanted was something reminiscent of Berlin in the 1930s; now that I've stopped it, I feel I have at last re-created that atmosphere.

Apart from the concluding joke, this was pretty close to the truth.

Talking many years later about his decision, Greene put the blame on others:

> Sir Arthur fforde, the Chairman of the Board of Governors, was a sick man; he was a very liberal-minded man, but didn't have the strength to keep as close a hold on the feelings of the Board as he would have done otherwise. Sir James Duff, the Vice-Chairman – an excellent man – was a bit old-fashioned in his attitudes on the 'smut' angle, and I knew that he was getting particularly

worried about it. I began to be worried lest there should really be a row on the Board of Governors, and lest Sir James Duff might resign. I came to the conclusion that it was in the interests of the BBC that the programme should come to a premature end.

At the time of the axing, the *Birmingham Post* alleged that Greene had taken the decision following a conversation with the Assistant Postmaster-General, Ray Mawby, who had conveyed to him the government's wish that *TW3* should end. This was strenuously denied by the BBC; but the Disraeli monologue may well have stirred the government into something more active behind the scenes than mere resentment.

An additional factor must have been the BBC Charter, which had technically expired in June 1962, though it had been extended for two years by a White Paper. Greene must have been concerned to do nothing that would impede the government's agreement to a new long-term Charter. Backstairs discussions about this (probably involving Mawby) were going on at the time of the announcement that *TW3* would end, and in this context it is easy to understand the Director-General's anxiety that one late-night programme, however popular, should not distort the government's opinion of the BBC. Sure enough, a few weeks after the announcement that *TW3* would end, a White Paper was published proposing a new Charter securing the BBC's future for no less than twelve years. This was passed by Parliament the following summer.

Rather strangely, it was not until five days after Greene had told the Governors that the programme would end that Kenneth Adam drafted this press statement:

> The BBC announces that the present run of *That Was The Week That Was* will end on December 28th 1963, and not continue, as had originally been intended, until the spring. This decision has been taken for one reason only; 1964 will be General Election Year…and as controversy grows over issues which the electors will be called upon to decide…the political content of the programme, which has been one of its principal and most successful constituents, will clearly be more and more difficult to maintain. Rather than dilute that content, and so alter the nature of the programme, the BBC thinks it preferable that *TWTWTW* should continue as at present until the end of the year, and then cease. [Whether it will return after the General Election is a matter for later decision in the light of programme needs, but] the BBC has no intention of abandoning permanently the kind of satirical commentary on current affairs represented by *TWTWTW* … The BBC wishes to emphasize that in deciding to curtail the run of the programme for the reason given, it has not done so because it has ceased to have confidence in the *TWTWTW* team, or because of any recent events.

The words within square brackets were crossed out before the statement was issued on 13 November.

Frost describes the announcement as 'a stunner', and over the following week the BBC received more than seven hundred letters of protest, many of them expressing disbelief in the official reason for axing the programme. A typical response was: 'Election year? Tell that to the Marines.'

Sherrin decided to play it coolly, and Mrs Goldie was able to reassure the Director-General that he was 'as usual, perfectly calm and highly reasonable'. When a reporter did manage to get a quote out of him, it was very mild: 'I think we would have been needed more in 1964 than ever before.' Frost took a similarly calm line with the press: 'It's a compliment. I'm delighted the show is being taken seriously.'

As to the politicians, Sir Cyril Osborne, the Tory backbencher who had appeared in the Bernard Levin spot, said he was 'damned pleased', and alleged that he had received 'hundreds of letters' supporting him after his confrontation with Levin. The Labour Leader, Harold Wilson, issued a statement in support of the programme: 'I deplore this decision to abandon *TW3* for political reasons ... The Labour Party have enjoyed attacks made on itself equally with attacks on others.' Willie Rushton recalls that 'Dick Crossman ... was going round saying that if a Labour government came into power they couldn't put up with that sort of thing, and Harold Wilson told me not to worry in the least – Crossman was talking a lot of nonsense.'

Fleet Street columnists were incredulous at the BBC's behaviour. 'Have you ever in your born days heard of a more idiotic reason for an idiotic action?' wrote Dee Wells in the *Daily Herald*. The *Guardian* took a philosophical view, observing that, just as 'satire came in as a craze, like boots for women', it was now 'probably about to go out, much as boots will go out next year'. But it praised the programme for having changed attitudes for the better: 'Whatever its defects, *TW3* has done more than anything else to foster a healthy irreverence towards persons in authority. Some of this irreverence will surely outlive the craze – and may be the healthier for no longer being modish.'

*

'We had to do six more programmes,' writes Sherrin. The next edition, broadcast only three days after the announcement, began with Lance Percival as Alec Douglas-Home singing:

> Happy days are here, my dears,
> Auntie's put the clock back years.

Frost pointed out to viewers that, ironically, the first American edition of *TW3* had just been broadcast. 'It seemed to go quite well, but of course they may be in trouble next year – they have an Election.' NBC had just put out a pilot, with Henry Fonda in the Frost role.

Sherrin had hastily commissioned David Nobbs and Peter Tinniswood to write a 'Cancellation News', in which Frost announced the axing of other programmes thought likely to be dangerous in Election year: the children's puppet show, *Andy Pandy*, *The Black and White Minstrel Show* and the hospital series *Dr Kildare*: 'In a recent episode a young woman was shown in Labour pains. To comply with BBC regulations she should also have been shown in Conservative pains.' There was more bite in the Waterhouse and Hall sketch which followed the closing credits that night, and featured Frost in search of a job:

CLERK (Roy Kinnear): Occupation?

FROST: Satirist.

CLERK: Nothing in that line. They've been coming in all morning...It's gone out, has satire. I don't know what we're going to do with you. And sit up straight. Get your hands out of your pockets. We're the masters now.

The following Friday night, the *TW3* team was at the Dorchester Hotel to receive an award from the Guild of Television Producers (forerunner of BAFTA). 'As we arrived,' writes Frost, 'the news was just coming through from Dallas that President Kennedy had been shot...Ned and I took it in turns to find hotel phones in order to talk to our writers about how we could do justice to the news.' No one would have been surprised had the next night's *TW3* been dropped from the schedules; but Sherrin says the BBC executives, stunned by the assassination, had taken refuge in alcohol-fuelled grumbles that their news teams had not provided adequate coverage of the shooting and its aftermath. *TW3* went ahead, with Sherrin jettisoning all the comic material for a 20-minute straight-faced Kennedy tribute.

Frost and the cast described Kennedy as 'miraculous...an amazing man who seemed so utterly right for the job...a father figure...the dream come true'; Millicent Martin sang a song with the refrain 'His soul goes riding on'; and Dame Sybil Thorndike made an appearance to recite a poem by Caryl Brahms beginning 'Yesterday the sun was shot out of your sky, Jackie'.

Paul Foot describes this programme as 'sickeningly sycophantic'. It made a big impression at the time – the cast was even invited to America to give a live stage performance of it – but it now looks like a belated attempt to save *TW3* from the scaffold. However, there was no reprieve, and Grace Wyndham Goldie writes that, ironically, *TW3* 'disappeared in a blaze of conformist glory'.[1]

---

[1] *Private Eye* ignored the Kennedy assassination, apart from carrying a rather meaningless cover drawing of a statue of him, and printing a mock letter from 'Herbert Gusset' complaining about the BBC's television scheduling: 'I wanted to be alone and think things out in silence. Instead I was forced to turn on my television and watch the idiotic antics of Harry Worth. Yet another display of shocking bad taste by the BBC!'

Not quite. The final edition, on 28 December 1963, mostly played it safe, consisting chiefly of encores of the most successful sketches from both series – though a striking omission was the 'Consumer Guide to Religion'. However, after the closing credits Willie Rushton, in the role of the BBC commissionaire come to turn out the studio lights, briefly let viewers know what *TW3* thought of its masters:

> WILLIE (*sings*): That was the week that was,
>   It's over, let it go …
>   The D. G. is a fleabag,
>   He couldn't run a bus.

And Sherrin had had a more subtle revenge on Greene two weeks earlier. By chance, everyone who knew about the ban on the sketch about the Lord Chancellor (Lord Dilhorne, the Bullying Manner) was away that Saturday, and he slipped it 'deceitfully' (his own word) past Mrs Goldie. The work (in its final form) of Gerald Kaufman, the sketch ended by implying that Dilhorne had got the Lord Chancellorship because of his wife's connections. Greene had to write a grovelling letter to Dilhorne: 'I hope that you and your wife will accept my most sincere apologies …' It was a much more appropriate end to the first-ever British satirical television programme than the fulsome tribute to an American president who, had it been known in Britain, had been leading a far more scandalous private life than any of the half-baked British politicians *TW3* had lampooned.

PART FOUR

Everyone is a satirist

1

Swimming is out of fashion

Just as *TW3* was coming to an end, Jonathan Miller left *Beyond the Fringe*. He had intended to make films, but when he came back from New York and went for advice to Huw Wheldon at the BBC, he was offered the job Wheldon himself had held for many years, presenter–editor of the television arts magazine *Monitor*. 'After I'd done *Beyond the Fringe*,' Miller says, 'I had absolutely no desire to do it again at all. Even when I was doing it, I thought of it – as I think Alan Bennett did – as a brief episode, time out from something else.'

He was replaced in the New York *Fringe* by an English-born actor, Paxton Whitehead, and the show was re-launched on Broadway during January 1964, with some new material. This included a sketch about the previous summer's Great Train Robbery, written by Peter Cook and featuring him as a senior policeman giving a television interview:

> COOK: I'd like to make one thing quite clear at the outset – when you speak of a train robbery, this in fact involved no loss of train … They're very hard to lose, you see, being so bulky …
> BENNETT: Who do you think may have perpetrated this awful crime?
> COOK: We believe this to be the work of thieves, and I'll tell you why. The whole pattern is extremely reminiscent of past robberies where we have found thieves to be involved – the tell-tale loss of property, that's one of the signs we look for, the snatching away of the money substances – it all points to thieves.
> BENNETT: So you believe thieves are responsible?
> COOK: Good heavens, no! I feel that thieves are totally *ir*responsible.

Alan Bennett wrote himself a new monologue, the first he had done 'in a voice that was my own', rather than a comic impersonation. It was about 'death and its supposedly comic aspects in the North of England':

> After a few days, when the body's been consumed, they'll send the ashes down to the undertakers, and you go and collect them … You don't get them *all*, like –

you just get a selection … Mind you, you don't know that them ashes you get are
your ashes … For all you know, it might be a couple of copies of the *Yorkshire
Evening Post* that they burn up …

My aunt Maria Alice, she were in St James's at the finish, and I went to see
her; and she says … 'When I go I want to be scattered on the South Shore at
Blackpool.' And I says, 'They won't allow that … The municipality won't want
all them smuts blowing about there – it's a smokeless zone.'

The monologue anticipated Bennett's North-Country television plays and
Talking Heads; but it was not a success in New York, 'and when the revue
ended it was nearly ten years before I ventured to write about the North of
England again. So much for "being myself".'

The revamped *Beyond the Fringe* survived the loss of Miller by a mere
four months, closing in April 1964. Cook, Moore and Bennett returned to
Britain – where the original production was still playing in London, and was
to run (at the Mayfair Theatre, with various casts) for another two years.
Bennett was completely at a loss: 'I couldn't see myself doing anything
similar again … I wasn't confident of my ability to do anything by myself …
And I went back to Leeds, and thought, "Well, that was it." ' Peter Cook, too,
was disoriented. The previous autumn he had told David Nathan that he
had come to like America a lot, 'and I look forward to my return with mixed
feelings'. Now married (to Wendy Snowden, whom he had known since
Cambridge), with his first child born this year, he bought a big house in
Hampstead; but satire had suddenly gone out of fashion, and no one seemed
disposed to make use of his talents. Interviewed by the *Daily Mail*, he said
defensively, 'When people talk about the satire movement being over it's
like people saying that "singing is over" or "swimming is out of fashion".'
Later, he admitted that this had been a very difficult time: 'I came back [from
America] expecting to be enormously well known, and of course nobody
knew me from Adam.' Consequently he drifted to Greek Street and *Private
Eye*.

The Booker-less *Eye* was having a tricky time too. 'I do have to say that the
magazine went off terribly, as a result of my departure,' says Booker with
unashamed glee. There were several new recruits, including a cheerful
cartoonist called Barry Fantoni; but Peter Usborne, still the magazine's
business manager, recalls that Ingrams was finding it hard to keep it going:
'Richard [had] made himself effectively editor of the magazine, and he was
very nervous, sitting there alone with a little notebook, ringing people up
trying to find stories.'

Much of the editorial work was done in the Coach and Horses, the pub
down the road, whose landlord Norman Balon liked to be thought of as the
rudest barman in London. John Wells, who gravitated back to the *Eye* in the
spring of 1964 after giving up on his Agatha Christie musical, said, 'The

thing to remember, in view of Ingrams's later abstemiousness,[1] is that it was all edited from the boozer, and Ingrams was permanently pissed – feet on the table, saying, "Who shall we bash this week?"' A girl applying for a secretary's job on the magazine was sent to the 'Coach' (as it was known), where Ingrams and the others were watching the Test Match on television and paid no attention to her. 'Eventually Norman ... said, "You're here about the job?" and I said, "Yes." So he said, "You'll do," and I was hired.'

Most of the secretaries found Ingrams highly attractive; but he too was now married, and with his wife Mary he soon moved to rural Berkshire. This not only allowed him to adopt a congenial Chesterton–Belloc lifestyle – he became the organist at the parish church – but kept him away from London parties where he might have met the people the *Eye* was lampooning. A journalist noted, 'He finds himself disconcertingly unable to attack people after he has met them.'

Claud Cockburn's Profumo issue had inaugurated investigative journal-ism in the *Eye* (Cockburn returned as a co-editor the following summer, when he introduced the 'Colour Section', a page of brief scurrilous news stories). But during the winter of 1963–4 the *Guardian*'s prediction that satire was 'probably about to go out' came horribly true. Following the news that *TW3* was ending, the *Eye* suddenly became (as Usborne puts it) 'the last thing to be seen carrying'. Sales halved, and *The Sunday Times* wrote dismissively of the magazine as 'the last and dying echo of the satire boom'. The staff took cuts in their already meagre pay, and closure loomed.

Then one day in June 1964, for the first time in about two years, the magazine's owner appeared in the office – or, rather, in the Coach. So did Paul Foot, who after a spell on the *Glasgow Daily Record* had come south again and joined the *Daily Herald*. Entering the pub one day at lunchtime, to see his old *Mesopotamia* chums, Foot noticed

> this rather shy man at the table. 'This is Peter Cook,' Richard Ingrams was saying, and we shook hands. The conversation was stilted, almost formal, until suddenly something quite mundane seemed to click in Peter's mind and he said something ridiculous. We all laughed. The laughter seemed to jolt him out of his reverie. His eyes sparkled, his face broke into a mighty grin and he was off, leaping from one glorious fantasy to another – it was something about bees. He started to talk about bees and within about thirty seconds the entire table, and not just the table, but also all the pub around, clustered about and started to laugh. Every morning after that I scuttled through my work in the hope that I might inhale another gale of that infectious laughter.

Cook's latest 'bee' turn featured a zookeeper attempting to rescue a rare

---

[1] In 1967 Ingrams was told to give up drinking by his doctor, and immediately did so.

species of the insect which had become inextricably entangled in a lady's underwear.

Realizing that *Private Eye* was in real danger of closure, Cook immediately injected £2000 of his own, and coaxed further funds from friends and celebrities. 'If it wasn't for Peter Cook arriving from America,' says Barry Fantoni, 'we would simply have gone under.' Cook's most useful form of aid, however, was humorous rather than financial: he made the magazine funny again. Harry Thompson writes of this:

> He invented catchphrases: 'This man is a proven lawyer', and 'My lady wife, whose name for a moment escapes me', as uttered by the blustering writer of letters to the *Daily Telegraph*, Sir Herbert Gusset. He dreamed up topical jokes: in the wake of the collapse of the John Bloom package tour company, he put *The Raft of the Medusa* on the cover, with one of the cannibal survivors saying, 'This is the last time I go on a John Bloom holiday.' Bewildered, laughing, all Ingrams could do was write it all down as quickly as possible.

Cook wrote only one *Private Eye* series himself, 'Tales of the Seductive Brethren', featuring Sir Arthur Starborgling and Sir Basil Nardly-Stoads, who had taken a secret Masonic-type vow to 'seize hold of young women and clamber hotly all over their bodies'. But his style of humour was soon enriching almost every page of the magazine. Always an avid reader of newspapers, he had somehow spotted that the *Aberdeen Evening Express* had wrongly captioned a picture of Sir Alec Douglas-Home with the weird name 'Baillie Vass'. This became the *Eye*'s label for the Prime Minister, and Cook even led a readers' march to Downing Street pledging mock-support for the Tories with the slogan 'The Baillie will no fail ye!'

Cook also inaugurated the *Eye*'s first and most memorable comic strip. Barry Humphries explains:

> I had made a gramophone record which included the plaintive monologue of an Earl's Court Australian; a youth called Buster Thompson who huddled together with his mates in an Anglophobic ghetto, drinking Foster's Lager, a Melbourne-brewed beer, which in those days could be obtained only at one pub in London. Cook thought that a character like this, an Australian innocent abroad, would make a diverting comic-strip hero, and he introduced me to a New Zealand artist called Nicholas Garland.

'Buster Thompson' became 'Barry McKenzie', and the adventures of this naïve Aussie expatriate, written by Humphries and drawn by Garland,[2] first appeared in the issue of 10 July 1964. The hero had four preoccupations:

---

[2] Garland explains: 'I had trained in Fine Art at the Slade before I went to the Royal Court, and I'd had a few drawings published in magazines, including *Private Eye*. Eventually I told Peter Cook I wanted to be a cartoonist – I wanted to be Tim Birdsall – and Peter came up with Barry McKenzie.'

Barry Humphries.

searching the pubs of London for ice-cold 'tubes' of Foster's; ineptly pursuing 'Sheilas' (women); vomiting; and urinating. The chief appeal of the serial lay largely in its hero's peculiar euphemisms for these last two activities, most memorably 'chundering' for throwing up. Humphries has sometimes claimed that these are genuine Antipodean slang:

> Australians [have] an enormous vocabulary celebrating incontinence in all its infinite variety … 'shaking hands with the wife's best friend', 'pointing Percy at the porcelain', 'going where the big nobs hang out', 'shaking hands with the unemployed', and 'draining the dragon' … 'Chundering' [was] a term I had first heard at Melbourne University, and which was not in general currency.

Elsewhere, however, Humphries admits that many of these words and phrases were 'made up', and it seems likely that Cook played some part in the making.

When Humphries, lank-haired, saturnine, and in those days rarely sober, began to appear in the Coach and Horses, John Wells became fascinated by his excesses:

> Barry used to sit in the Coach when he was in one of the Lionel Bart shows, *Maggie May*, which he had to open as a one-man band. And anybody who works in the theatre knows that the sacred rule is that you have to be there for the 'half' [half an hour before curtain-up]. But, far from leaving the pub, *that* was when Barry used to start drinking seriously! The show was at the Adelphi in the Strand, no small distance from Greek Street, and he used to leave at about seven minutes to the curtain, blind drunk, running like the clappers. I was actually in

the audience one night, and the curtain went up, and he'd made it on stage but he was still putting on the harness!

Humphries confirms the truth of this, and remarks:

> In those days I was rushing round doing all kinds of things, and was also, as they say in Australia, 'in the grip of the grog'. Moreover, since I appeared only at the beginning and the end of *Maggie May*, I had a couple of hours to kill in between, so I would go off to a party in Hampstead, try to keep an eye on my watch, and get a taxi back to the theatre, where I had to put on elaborate character make-up before my reappearance. It was indeed sometimes a close shave.

Wells found Humphries's conversation 'absolutely memorable. I particularly remember one when it was coming up for my thirtieth birthday, and I said something about approaching the flat plateau of middle age. And Barry said, in gleeful tones, in his most exaggerated Australian voice, "But there's always the unexpected crevasse, the frayed and smoking rope, the diminishing cry ... !" '

*

David Frost had been participating in American television's version of *TW3*. Sherrin describes this with some amusement:

> It was beautifully American. Rather than expose their own bare studio, they built a set that exactly replicated ours, rendered in pastel shades – they even reproduced the ventilator pipes! And though it was called *That Was The Week That Was*, it went out at 8.30 on a Tuesday, which is quite a short week. And it was much more anodyne, very gentle.[3]

However, Frost was so keen to make a name in the States that he decided to commute between New York and London to take part in it – despite the fact that the BBC wanted him to front a successor to *TW3*, to begin after the General Election in the autumn of 1964.

Almost as soon as *TW3* had been killed off, it became (with typical BBC managerial perversity) a general assumption in the higher echelons of Television Centre that the corpse could be revived once the General Election was out of the way. The original idea, indeed, was to do it on a far bigger scale than the original – no less than five nights a week. Eventually this was reduced to Friday, Saturday and Sunday; but this was still three times the weekly airtime of *TW3*.

The Election, on 15 October 1964, had the expected result of bringing in Britain's first Labour government in thirteen years, under Harold Wilson;

---

[3] However, in 1968 American TV produced a show to equal the impact of the original *TW3*, NBC's *Rowan and Martin's Laugh-In*, a hectic succession of one-liners and repetitive catchphrases performed by a cast that included Goldie Hawn. Sherrin says he remarked to the *Laugh-In* producer, George Schlatter, that *TW3* seemed to have influenced it. 'He replied, "Influenced? We stole every fucking thing!" '

Willie Rushton writing a speech when standing against Sir Alec Douglas-Home in the 1964 General Election.

although the Tories very nearly held on to power. 'The Conservatives – under Alec Douglas-Home, for heaven's sake! – were only defeated by a Labour majority of five,' recalls Gerald Kaufman, who himself entered Parliament as a Labour MP six years later. *Private Eye*'s contribution to the Election included putting up Willie Rushton as a 'Death to the Tories' candidate at Kinross, Douglas-Home's own constituency, where he polled forty-five votes.

The Labour victory had been an implicit goal of the satirists – as Richard Ingrams puts it, 'Consciously or not, the satire movement had been working with Wilson' – so its achievement suddenly left the *Eye* bereft of its principal political function. 'As with Tony Blair in 1997,' continues Ingrams, 'people thought, "This is a new dawn, this is something wonderful and new." But Peter Cook wasn't taken in. He had a very clear view of politics, and he wasn't taken in by the Wilson dynamic. And I think "Mrs Wilson's Diary" was his idea.' This Pooter-inspired serial, illustrated by Rushton, began in the *Eye* on 30 October 1964, the issue immediately following the Election, with the Wilsons moving into 10 Downing Street and meeting the staff, including

> Inspector Trimfittering whose job is to protect Harold and be with him at all times. When after our Ovaltine (laced with Sanatogen) we retired for the night, I was surprised to find the Inspector lying between us. 'Don't mind me,' he said,

'just carry on as if I wasn't here.' I tried to but somehow I couldn't get to sleep with the Inspector snoring at my side. Harold tells me I will get used to him and I sincerely hope I will.

At first, Peter Cook co-wrote 'Mrs Wilson's Diary' with Ingrams – or, rather, improvised jokes which Ingrams hastily committed to paper. 'I don't remember Peter ever sitting down and *writing*,' says Ingrams. 'It seemed to me that he just extemporized, and if somebody was there to write it all down that was fine.' Later, John Wells took over as Ingrams's collaborator, explaining, 'We on the magazine pinch [Cook's] jokes and imitate his style so closely that people believe he has written it.' The 'Diary' often proved to be astonishingly close to the truth – as Cook put it, 'You make something up, and Downing Street begins to think…that people are leaking facts to you.'

Barry Humphries observes that ' "Mrs Wilson's Diary" turned out to be a collaboration between two men who otherwise had a somewhat uneasy relationship.' Wells has admitted that he never felt entirely comfortable with Ingrams at *Private Eye*, for reasons going back to schooldays – 'Salopian snobbery, a secret kind of feeling by Richard, Willie and Footie that, coming from Shrewsbury, they were a kind of crypto-Eton'. Moreover Ingrams and the others had begun to mock what they saw as Wells's social climbing. 'I think Princess Margaret must once have rung up *Private Eye*, in search of me,' Wells recalled, 'and said, could she speak to "Jawn"? Thereafter I was always "Jawn"!' Barry Humphries says that Wells began to be 'very snobbish and name-dropping – though he'd refer to his grand friends in a very odd fashion. He'd say, "Do you know who I mean by Kingsley Amis?" – even "Do you know who I mean by Princess Margaret?" '

2

I still think there is room for satire

John Bird proved a very capable impersonator of Harold Wilson in the new BBC satire show. This was optimistically titled *Not So Much a Programme, More a Way of Life*. Sherrin, who was once again producing and directing, was obliged to make no fewer than six pilots, causing Denis Norden to joke that David Frost had 'had more pilots than the average air hostess'. This betrayed an uncertainty about the show's nature and purpose, which became obvious when it was launched a month after the Election, on the inauspicious date of Friday, 13 November 1964.

So as to diminish the resemblance to *TW3*, Frost was to co-host with Willie Rushton and actor and writer P.J. Kavanagh. However, as Rushton puts it,

> Frost was determined in his heart of hearts that it should be his; and Kavanagh and I really didn't mind. Neither of us wanted to be on the programme. So we got elbowed to one side a bit; and in the end we were being paid £80 a show for doing nothing – it was the best job I ever had, except that it was driving me absolutely up the spout!

Kavanagh's account is much the same:

> Ned's plot was that I should replace David, but David hung around, not to be displaced (and not at all unpleasantly, just insistently; it was his world, not mine). I made some lovely friends, especially Willie Rushton, but rather hated it. Came back home one day and astonished myself by bursting into tears! So I resigned.

He and Rushton left the programme after a few weeks. Christopher Booker, who was writing for the new programme, remarks that Frost had 'worked himself (again not as originally intended) into the centre'.

There was a neurotic concern with finding a new format – 'Why does TV stick to this superstition of never repeating good ideas?' asked Peter Black in the *Daily Mail* after watching the first edition – and it was decided that the sketches would be interleaved with lengthy items of chat between people selected for their conversational powers. (Historian of television comedy Roger Wilmut writes, 'This was one of the first appearances in England of the now-ubiquitous "chat show".') Paradoxically the most popular of these talkers proved to be Patrick Campbell (Lord Glenavy), who had a severe stutter.

Sherrin admits that the first weekend of *Not So Much a Programme* was a 'fair disaster', and says that the series took many editions to settle down. Booker describes it as 'lumbering', and says it was 'padded out [with] "camp" little dance routines'. John Wells, writing soon after it had ceased, was equally scathing:

> There is certainly very little that is satirical about *Not So Much a Programme*, despite its origins. The fact that it made jokes about politicians, the fact that actors occasionally stumbled before the cameras using such amazing words as 'bum' and 'po', this was really only sugar on the pill. The real dose can be discovered in the opening lyric, written by Miss Caryl Brahms, a slightly earnest and rather sentimental humorist of the old school.[1] 'Not so much a programme, more a way of life,' it says, 'or a way of looking at the world. One eye open wide, one eye closed; and between the two the picture gets composed.' The viewer in other words is exhorted to come in and share the sophisticated view of things. One eye open for what Alan Bennett's clergyman calls 'all the good things of life', and one eye closed in a knowing wink: faith in cynicism.
>
> It just seems a pity that the educators can't respect the viewer's intelligence just a little more.

Wells himself contributed scripts to the programme, and eventually made his television début on it: 'The reason television came in for me was entirely due to physical deformity. I was writing a sketch with John Fortune and John Bird which involved Selwyn Lloyd, and Ned Sherrin said, "You have exactly the same-shaped mouth as Selwyn Lloyd." That was how I got in.' This was a sketch in which Lloyd, former Conservative Chancellor of the Exchequer and Foreign Secretary, was seen discussing Africa with Jomo Kenyatta, played of course by Bird – a regular figure on *Not So Much a Programme*: 'Good evenin'. Well, I always say, as in the words of an old proverb, he who is without stones let him throw himself into the glass house ... '

Equally regular was Bird's Harold Wilson impersonation. 'I'm not a mimic,' he says, 'but everybody can do somebody, and luckily I could do Wilson.' He feels that his version was closer to the truth than the suburban sitcom of 'Mrs Wilson's Diary': 'Theirs was very funny, but I don't think it

---

[1] Three singers were used in *Not So Much a Programme*: Barbara Evans on Fridays, Josephine Blake on Saturdays, and Cleo Laine on Sundays.

was really true'. On one occasion he had a chance to perform it in front of
Wilson himself:

> It was at a Press Club evening. He made a speech, and I was asked to do the
> cabaret – as him, of course – and since it was a politically sophisticated audience
> I said the things that they, the pressmen, knew Wilson knew and was thinking,
> but wasn't saying out loud. He'd been introduced to me at the beginning of the
> evening, and was very affable, but afterwards he didn't speak to me at all. So I
> was quite pleased.

John Fortune had now settled in Scotland, and appeared on only one of the
three weekly editions of *Not So Much a Programme*:

> I'd come down on the train on Friday night, and write something on Saturday
> morning, do it on Saturday night, and get the train back. The way the BBC
> worked in those days made that sort of thing possible – it was lavish. I remember
> one Saturday morning I was writing a sketch with John Bird, and we decided
> that we'd do something about a municipal statue. So at about eleven o'clock in
> the morning, when the designer came along and said, 'Is there anything you'd
> like for tonight?', we said, 'We need this gigantic statue.' 'How big?' 'About
> sixty foot high. You only need to see the legs – but they need to be about twenty-
> five feet high.' He said, 'That's fine.' Then at about two in the afternoon we
> realized that the sketch was going absolutely nowhere. And by this time there
> were twenty people working on these vast legs. So we had to think of some other
> way of using them! And we did a piece called 'The El Greco Fragment': 'It's not
> generally known that El Greco was also a sculptor. No complete sculpture by
> him exists today, but we do have these legs ... ' And of course we thought it was
> much funnier than the audience did, because of our botch-up!

Eleanor Bron often appeared as a character originally devised by Peter
Cook at The Establishment, a Conservative supporter with a *double
entendre* of a name, Lady Pamela Stitty, who somewhat ineptly defended
the former Prime Minister and now Opposition Leader, Sir Alec Douglas-
Home: 'I think people have been jolly unkind about Alec ... I do rather wish
that people could get a chance to see him in committee, because he is
absolutely staggering there – he's forceful and dynamic ... you really
wouldn't recognize him.' Bron also performed some more 'relationship'
duologues with John Fortune. 'The best thing I did with Eleanor,' recalls
Fortune,

> was a sketch in which we were in bed together, and said the same things
> simultaneously in perfect unison (which took a lot of rehearsal). It began: 'The
> thing I love most about you, darling, is that you *listen*.' And: 'I think it was Rilke
> who said, "Lovers should be the guardians of each other's solitude."' All

absolutely in unison. And I had a letter from a man who said, 'I'd like you to know that this sketch has succeeded in sending my wife into a lunatic asylum.' The word I liked was *succeeded*.

Not So Much a Programme was hopefully abbreviated by the BBC publicists to *NSMAP*, but not surprisingly this failed to catch on. From the outset the programme had a generally unfavourable reception from the press, who compared it with what now seemed the golden age of *TW3*. So did John Bird: 'I really felt that the thing was on a downward slide, that the high point of it had passed.' *Private Eye* swiftly dubbed the programme *NSMAPMAFCKUP*, and printed a cartoon of Frost leering at the camera alongside the programme's opening title: 'NOT SO MUCH A FROST – MORE A SHOWER OF SHIT'.

The *Eye* was now occasionally issuing floppy gramophone records, stuck to the front cover. The first, entitled 'His Master's Vass', came with the issue for 2 October 1964, just before the General Election; when removed, it revealed a photograph of Sir Alec Douglas-Home, seated on a lavatory, shouting: 'Put that record back AT ONCE!' A few weeks later the second, labelled 'I Saw Daddy Kissing Santa Claus', included Dudley Moore as a department-store Father Christmas:

> Yes, I've been Father Christmas now for many years. You know, I love to have those little boys sitting on my knee. Lovely! And in the evenings it's back to the house, up the chimney, thrusting my way up that sooty passage – ooh! Christmas comes but once a year, and so do I, ooh-hoo!

On the next floppy record, in the spring of 1965, Peter Cook did a devastating impersonation of Frost's whining voice as he tries to present *Not So Much a Programme*, with the rest of the cast making rude noises in the background, suggesting that the whole thing is utterly out of control: 'Hello, good evening, welcome, hello – I wonder if you could get the autocue moving a bit faster, please, ha ha! This evening we'd like to welcome some very welcome returnees, who are here again, to be with us once more ...' He gets Patrick Campbell's title wrong, and Campbell calls him an 'ignorant prick'. Other guests include 'the Warden of Arseholes'.

Highlights of later *Private Eye* records included Barry Humphries singing 'Chunder in the Old Pacific Sea'; Peter Cook as 'John Osbum' eulogizing a legendary music-hall performer called Arthur Cock, whose theme song begins 'When you're feelin' glum,/Stick a finger up yer bum ... /When you're feelin' grotty,/Stick a finger up yer botty'; Dudley Moore as Spiggy Topes, leader of the pop group The Turds; a song in praise of Neasden (recorded with the aid of The Alberts); and a genuine pirated recording of the infamous edition of the BBC schools' radio programme *Music and Movement* in which the lady presenter told children – in all innocence – how to play games with balls ('You don't know where I'm going to hide your balls'). Barry Humphries recalls that the records were made 'in a place called Magnagraph, a tiny downstairs studio off Rathbone Place. I always had the feeling that I was only a guest in the group, and could easily be edged out, or my contribution dropped.'

As the real *Not So Much a Programme* carried on, the sketches became almost crowded out by the chat. However, it did create one *TW3*-style controversy. This was over a sketch broadcast in the edition of 27 February 1965, in which a Catholic priest asks a Liverpool Irishwoman why, having already had fifteen or sixteen children, she does not appear to be pregnant again: 'Have you sinned, Mrs O'Hara? Have you been using those dirty black Protestant pills?' Reassured that she has not, he turns to the camera and says, 'We'll catch the Chinese up yet.' As the *Not So Much a Programme* format dictated, the sketch was followed by a serious discussion on the Catholic attitude to contraception, with the Catholic viewpoint represented eloquently by Norman St John Stevas, who appeared regularly on the programme. Nevertheless there were protests in both Houses of Parliament, and Hugh Greene issued an apology. A month later there were further high-level complaints when Bernard Levin, taking part in a discussion, described Sir Alec Douglas-Home as a 'cretin' and 'imbecile'; while a musical-comedy-style treatment of the Abdication was thought to have been in bad taste because the Princess Royal (sister of the Duke of Windsor) had died a few hours before it was performed. A day after this, Greene announced that, after the end of the series in April, *Not So Much a Programme* would cease. He added, 'I still think there is room for satire, but I am not sure we have the form right.'

Frost was in America when the news of the axing broke – this time without a public outcry – and Sherrin says that Frost's commuting 'double life' had made it hard for him to keep abreast of British news and opinion. (Sherrin alleges that on one occasion Rushton observed that Frost's open briefcase contained a file labelled 'Airport Quips': 'David had become an international traveller, and expected to be interviewed at every airport where he touched down.') Moreover, Frost seemed to want to operate under the American system, by which the star performer was served by the producer rather than vice versa. 'It was clear,' says Sherrin, 'that our careers were ready to go in different directions.' The BBC stipulated that Sherrin was to be allowed a third stab at a satirical show only if Frost (whose American *TW3* was also coming to an end) did not front it. Wisely, Frost swallowed the insult in silence – Christopher Booker says the BBC allowed him to give the impression that he had resigned of his own volition – and began to make plans for future programmes of which he would have full control.

*

At the end of 1964, while *Not So Much a Programme* was limping through its one and only series, the BBC began to plan a one-off television special featuring the talents of Dudley Moore. He co-opted Peter Cook, who had been making forays into television too; in the ITV show *On the Braden Beat* he made a weekly appearance as his Arthur Grole character, now renamed E.L. Wisty. Cook and Moore were both determined to avoid anything as unfashionable as satire, and their joint sketches in the show were built around one of Cook's absurd aristocrats, Sir Arthur Strebe-Greebling, and the Wisty character. Wisty (played by Cook), however, was now being featured in a beer commercial on the other channel, in which he assured viewers that if they drank Watney's Brown, they would be 'visited by lovely ladies in diaphanous nighties, coming into your room and dancing about'; so for the purposes of the BBC show, Wisty became simply 'Pete', and Moore was therefore 'Dud'.

Thus was born one of the great comic duos. Their first sketch, performed in the cloth caps, old raincoats and scarves that became their trademark, embroidered on the 'lovely ladies in diaphanous nighties' theme, with 'Pete' describing how he had been pestered by late-night visits from Betty Grable and Greta Garbo. Cook had held some of his best lines in reserve during rehearsal, so they were a complete surprise to Moore, who was soon spluttering with helpless laughter. So were the audience and studio crew, and Moore and Cook were immediately booked for six shows, to be called *Not Only... But Also* (not only Moore and Cook – or Cook and Moore, as it soon became – but also their guests). The fortnightly series began on 9 January 1965, and was an instant success; John Wells called it 'the most popular show on television... Peter was absolutely on a winning streak; all the sketches were funny, everything he improvised, the audience carried him along.'

Alan Bennett, who was still wondering what to do after *Beyond the Fringe*, was deeply disconcerted by his colleagues' sudden and enormous success in a different medium: 'I remember watching one of Peter and Dudley's shows and being terribly depressed... thinking I could never do anything as good as that... Jonathan was doing *Monitor*... I began to feel like the drummer who left the Beatles before they became famous.'

However, Bennett soon started taking his own tentative steps into television. Sherrin's third late-night show (starting on 2 October 1965) was to be called *BBC3*, with a format similar to *Not So Much a Programme*, Frost being replaced by the older and more urbane Robert Robinson. Bennett was invited to contribute whenever he wished, but with no obligation to do so each week. 'I used to work with John Bird and John Fortune,' he recalls, 'and we used to go in on a Saturday morning to prepare a sketch for the evening. And it was done live, in circumstances which would now terrify me.' John Wells has described the hazards of performing live:

After the *Fringe*: Cook and Moore as Pete and Dud – 'the most popular show on television,' said John Wells.

Ned had fitted us all up with autocue, and we got used to using it in sketches, which is desperate, and one of the most terrifying traumas I had was seeing a television camera rushing at me with the autocue broken and hanging loose, so that I couldn't see a word of the script. We'd rehearsed it, of course, but I only vaguely remembered it.

In one edition of *BBC3* on 29 January 1966, Bennett delivered a monologue about Virginia Woolf, which he afterwards adapted for his stage play *Forty Years On*:

Of all the honours that fell upon Virginia's head, none I think pleased her more than the *Evening Standard* Award for the Tallest Woman Writer of 1933, an award she took by a short neck from Elizabeth Bowen, and rightly, I think, because she was in a very real sense the tallest writer I've ever known. Which is not of course to say that her stories were tall – they were not. They were short.

Bennett also recalls 'a thing I did with John Fortune – I played the vicar and he played the boy, and there was a crucifix which doubled as a pipe rack, and I put my pipe into it, and there were questions in Parliament about this!'

John Bird continued to appear as Harold Wilson, in Gannex mackintosh and with a pipe clenched between his teeth:

Now I imagine you'll think it a bit peculiar for me to appear on such a gay and light-hearted programme as this. But, you know, I don't have to go on being prime minister for a living – I could always go back to being a socialist …

Now, I'll be frank with you; I admit, in the privacy of this television studio, that all is not well within the government. Some of my colleagues have not performed as I expected them to. Even worse, some of them have. But there are better prospects to come. This morning, for example, George Brown told me he had seen the Queen. Well, there it is – some people see snakes, some people see elephants; George sees the Queen.

The reputed alcohol intake of George Brown, the Foreign Secretary (which led to the invention of *Private Eye*'s euphemism for drunkenness, 'tired and emotional'), also featured regularly in 'Mrs Wilson's Diary':

Last weekend we had a big party at Chequers, our country house. All went well until, after our Ovaltine, Harold said, 'Well, comrades, it's ten o'clock and we were up till all hours last night as well. I think it would be appropriate to turn in.' Everyone agreed, except for George Brown, who had been a little edgy all evening. 'I think I'll just stay down here and have a little read,' he said, taking down the third volume of *The History of the World in Pictures*. Well, no sooner had we climbed into our Viyellas than there came a terrible crash from the direction of the library … When they reached the library, however, they discovered George reading his book. 'It's nothing, brothers,' he explained with a smile, 'the cocktail cabinet suddenly fell over. I think it must be some kind of Geisterpolt.'

Sherrin feels, with hindsight, that '*BBC3* was certainly the wrong title. We nearly called it *It's All Been Done Before*, in an attempt to pre-empt criticism, and I wish we had, instead of saving the phrase for the title song.'[2] He adds that 'people commented on "lack of bite" ', and Christopher Booker describes the programme as a 'watery relic' of *TW3*. Certainly the only row caused by it was not the result of a sketch. On 13 November 1965, during the course of a live discussion about stage censorship, Kenneth Tynan said, 'I doubt if there are any rational people to whom the word "fuck" would be particularly diabolical, revolting or totally forbidden.' Sherrin says that this first use of the f-word on television 'did everything for our viewing figures'. (Three years later, when censorship of public theatrical performances by the Lord Chamberlain had finally been abolished, Tynan devised the erotic entertainment *Oh! Calcutta!*, which brought nudity to the West End stage.)[3]

---

[2] Which began: 'It's all been done before,/But so have spring and summer,/We welcome them the more/That each is not a callow newcomer./It's all been done before/By Swift, who said it better…' (and so on).

[3] The initial idea for *Oh! Calcutta!*, which opened in New York in 1969 and London in 1970, came from Willie Donaldson.

There was more bite in David Frost's new BBC programme *The Frost Report*, which began on 10 March 1966.[4] Topical and political satire was carefully avoided, but each edition set itself a theme, and the sketch (written by Marty Feldman and John Law) in which the English class system was discussed by three performers arranged in order of height – John Cleese (upper class), Ronnie Barker (middle) and Ronnie Corbett (lower) – has a place in the comedy hall of fame:

> CLEESE: I look down on him (*indicating* BARKER) because I am upper-class.
>
> BARKER: I look up to him (*indicating* CLEESE) because he is upper-class; but I look down on him (*indicating* CORBETT) because he is lower-class. I am middle-class.
>
> CORBETT: I know my place. I look up to them both. But I don't look up to him (BARKER) as much as I look up to him (CLEESE) because he has got innate breeding.
>
> CLEESE: I have got innate breeding, but I have not got any money...

Particularly in its second series, *The Frost Report* gave opportunities to two young writer-performers recently graduated from Oxford, Michael Palin and Terry Jones. They also wrote material for yet another BBC attempt at live late-night Saturday satire, *The Late Show*, which ran for six months from 15 October 1966 (*BBC3* had ended the previous April). Sherrin had now gone off into film production, and Barry Humphries, who was in the *Late Show* cast, and appeared in one edition as 'Mrs Edna Everage', describes the programme as 'very uneven in quality' – partly because of the proximity of the bar of the BBC Club, 'a trap for people with my susceptibilities'. John Bird was still involved, but he describes *The Late Show* as 'not successful, even though they did it largely according to my specification – I got them to fetch American performers over, from Second City'.

The style of humour was now moving away from the would-be satirical towards the surrealism that would eventually come to the boil in *Monty Python's Flying Circus*. Humphries recalls a *Late Show* sketch about the Pre-Raphaelites that he wrote with Richard Stilgoe,

> in which the painter Millais, hearing a knock on the door, opens it to reveal a blow-up of Holman-Hunt's famous painting, *The Light of the World*. Holding a lamp aloft, Jesus's lips suddenly animated, and he delivered a well-known commercial for pink household paraffin ... The matter was raised in the House of Lords by the Archbishop of Canterbury.

---

4 Booker ascribes Frost's return to the screen to the celebrity breakfast which he hosted at the Connaught Hotel on 7 January 1966, with Harold Wilson among the guests: 'From then on he was "the man who invited the Prime Minister to breakfast". His career now took off like a rocket.' But in his autobiography Frost states that *The Frost Report* had been commissioned by the BBC the previous autumn.

Barry Humphries, John Wells and John Bird working on *The Late Show* in 1966.

Again, Alan Bennett made sporadic contributions; meanwhile, in January 1966, word reached the press that he was planning his own television show. Barry Norman was dispatched to interview him for the *Daily Mail* in his NW1 *pied-à-terre*:

> Across the darkening room Mr Alan Bennett shifted slightly in his chair and said, 'Would you like some more tea?' I said, 'No, thank you,' not because I didn't want any but because I knew he'd have to go and get it and I didn't like to disturb him … He said, 'I work about two hours a day. That's all I can manage.' The accent was broad Yorkshire, soft, relaxing. The splendidly prissy academic voice with which, about once a fortnight, he enlivens the sometimes hilarious proceedings of BBC3 is, like his legend, more or less phoney. 'Really, I'm a comedian among dons and a don among comedians. It's very uncomfortable, sometimes.' … As a bachelor he needs and wants little money and as a countryman he dislikes London and scuttles off to his home near Leeds whenever he can … 'Sometimes I think that if I don't do anything worthwhile in five years, I'll go back to teaching. It was very pleasant at Oxford, knowing one was going to see the same people every day.'

Bennett's series *On the Margin*, which began a six-week run on BBC2 on 15 November 1966, showed that, for all his desire to portray himself as a country mouse, he thoroughly understood smart London life. Its most substantial item each week was a serial-within-a-show called 'Life and Times in NW1', guying Bennett's neighbours in that postal district, who in those days were chiefly engaged in 'knocking through' their houses to create bigger rooms, and collecting junk to turn into *objets d'art*:

> NIGEL KNOCKER-THREW *is talking to* SAM *and* CLARISSA TOUCH-PACEY.
> NIGEL: Jane's up to her ears in ratatouille. Why don't I show you round the house?
> SAM: Christ, what are those? (*Two 'Spastic Children' statues with collecting boxes.*)
> NIGEL: Well, Jane saw them standing outside a shop. I mean, nobody was appreciating them really, they were just being widdled on by dogs, so she went down with the car one night and whipped them into the back. They've got a real Rauschenberg feel.
> CLARISSA: Oh yes, they are hideous, aren't they?

After *On the Margin* had finished, the Knocker-Threws were taken over – with Bennett's consent, and their name changed to the Stringalongs – by the cartoonist Mark Boxer, initially for a strip in the *Listener* and later in *The Times*, where during the 1970s they satirized the lives of trendy London media folk.

Bennett says that, despite the ground-breaking of *TW3*, he found the BBC extraordinarily stuffy:

> In *On the Margin* we were still trying to see how much we could smuggle past them. We had a battle even to mention knickers. Yet in a sense I relished that, because the audience knew there was a line the BBC drew, and when we were getting close to it there would be much more reaction from them. And it seemed to me that when *Monty Python* came along, they seemed to be able to say absolutely anything, like 'Oh, bugger' at the end of 'Spanish Inquisition' sketch. *Monty Python* was wonderful. But if there isn't a line drawn, you're deprived of a tool.

On the Margin was a considerable success, but Bennett then turned his attention back to live theatre, writing and performing in *Forty Years On* (1968), which he admitted was 'as much a revue as a play'. It surveys twentieth-century British cultural life through the multiple ironies of a play-within-a-play being performed by the boys of a traditional English public school. (John Gielgud created the role of the headmaster.)

Meanwhile, from the end of December 1967 to early March 1968, the BBC attempted yet another weekend satire show, *At the Eleventh Hour*. This time the initiator was Anthony Smith, then editing the current-affairs programme *Twenty-Four Hours*. He explains how it came about:

I had been producing a number of other programmes which had filled the Saturday-night satire slot, including a kind of debate between lawyers called *Your Witness*. The slot had been taken over for a while by Tony Palmer with a programme concentrating on rather recondite pop music, and the Current Affairs Department had been anxious to repress this. Paul Fox was ready to take on my proposal for an updated descendant of the Sherrin programmes.

It was all very tense, very enjoyable, and on my part rather incompetent, since I had never before produced a comedy show. But it was a very successful bit of talent-scouting – we had Richard Neville (fresh from *Oz*),[5] the first films ever of Stephen Frears, and Miriam Margolyes delivering monologues written by Esther Rantzen. Jeannie Lamb sang a song each week written topically by Ray Davies of the Kinks, Ned Sherrin (as ever) advised by telephone, and David Nathan wrote sketches.

Nathan, this time working without Dennis Potter, found *At the Eleventh Hour* much harder going than *TW3*. 'It became clear very quickly,' he says,

that Tony Smith did not have Ned Sherrin's eye for a performer. This had given us such roundly formed characters that within a few weeks the dialogue in our *TW3* scripts was not marked 'A', 'B' or 'C' but 'MILLIE', 'ROY', 'KEN', etc. The only performers I can clearly recall from *At the Eleventh Hour* were Miriam Margolyes, Richard Neville, creator of *Oz* magazine who did a weekly face-to-camera piece, and Alan Shallcross, who eventually decided that his place was behind the screen.

Shallcross, former undergraduate friend of Alan Bennett, had joined the BBC as a general trainee and was working in programme planning when Smith recruited him for *At the Eleventh Hour*. 'I had to leave the BBC staff to do it,' he recalls. 'And it only ran for a few months, and stranded me without a job.' Smith says that Paul Fox 'hated the programme and took it off as soon as he decently could'.

A year and a half later, in October 1969, the BBC began to transmit the first series of *Monty Python's Flying Circus*, which changed ideas about comedy as much as *Beyond the Fringe* had done ten years earlier. Its originality included constant mockery of the very medium in which it was operating, the television comedy show:

> *Lingerie shop set.* ASSISTANT *standing behind counter. At the side the* ROBBER *also stands waiting. They hum to themselves and waste time, looking at wristwatches; this takes about fifteen seconds. Cut to a letter on BBC stationery. The camera pulls back to show a grotty little* MAN *reading the*

---

[5] A typographically inventive 'underground' magazine famously prosecuted over an issue ostensibly edited by 'schoolkids', which included a graphic depiction of the sex life of Rupert Bear.

letter and sitting at a breakfast table in a small kitchen. His WIFE *is busying herself in wifelike activities.*

MAN [Michael Palin]: Ooh. Ooh.

WIFE [Terry Jones]: Oh, what is it, dear?

MAN: It's from the BBC. They want to know if I want to be in a sketch on the telly.

WIFE: Ooh. That's nice.

MAN: Well, I'm a plumber. I can't act.

WIFE: Oh, you never know till you try. Look at Mrs Brando's son next door. He was mending the fridge when they came and asked him to be the Wild One. What do they want you to do?

MAN: Well, they just want me to stand at a counter, and when the sketch starts I go out.

WIFE: Oh, that sounds nice. It's what they call a walk-on.

MAN: Walk-on? That's a walk-off, that's what this is.

(*Cut to the lingerie shop;* ASSISTANT *and* ROBBER *still hanging around waiting. A few seconds of this.* FLOOR MANAGER *walks on.*)

ROBBER [John Cleese]: (*Quietly*) Well, where is he, George?

FLOOR MANAGER: I don't know, he should have been here hours ago.

ROBBER: He bloody should have been ...

'Nothing makes me laugh more than *Monty Python*,' Alan Bennett told an interviewer in 1978. 'I just like the sheer silliness of it.' There were occasional echoes of the satire days. For example one *Python* sketch, 'Ypres 1914', aroused complaints for joking about the First World War, just as 'The Aftermyth of War' had in *Beyond the Fringe*; again, the defence was that the sketch was parodying not the war but the cinema's portrayal of it. A Terry Gilliam animation sequence in another edition made a joke out of cancer, just as Lenny Bruce had done – it was the story of a prince who ignores a cancerous spot which eventually kills him; the cancer itself survives, and gets married and lives happily ever after. The BBC objected, and 'cancer' was changed to 'gangrene' before transmission. Most obviously, *Monty Python* was out to shock, just as its satirical predecessors had been. The film *Monty Python's Life of Brian* (1979) followed in the steps of *TW3*'s 'Consumer Guide to Religion', not mocking Christ, but parodying the absurdities inherent in religious belief.

John Wells recalled that, even in the age of *Monty Python*, BBC Television was still making faint attempts at live topical comedy: 'We experienced a sort of after-life, in a series called *Up Sunday*.' Beginning on 6 February 1972 and running (with a break of some months) to 28 January 1973, this grew out of BBC2's *Late Night Line-Up*. 'We had an extraordinary degree of freedom on it,' said Wells.

We got Dickie Murdoch, Max Wall, Peter Sellers, who by that time was a friend – if I rang him up on Friday night he'd come along for a hundred quid and work all day Saturday. We did an *Inspector Poirot Investigates*, with Peter Sellers, John Fortune, and me as Hitler, and Percy Edwards (doing all his bird impersonations) as Poirot. 'As the murderer left the house, he heard the sound of the cuckoo…' And it was still being done live, like *TW3*, with dreadful disaster – like Vivian Stanshall as Father Christmas. He had a Barry Humphries-type bet in the bar that he'd drink a pint of Bloody Mary before he went on. And I lifted up the lid of a hamper, and he was meant to come out as Father Christmas. Instead of which, he flourished what was left of his Bloody Mary at the camera, and fell forward – it was a white studio floor – and cut his hand on the glass, and there was blood all over the studio.

3

Giggling into the sea

In his book *The Sixties* (1998), Arthur Marwick, Professor of History at the Open University, traces the social and cultural changes in Britain, Europe and America between about 1958 and 1974. He suggests that 'key features of the 1950s' included

> rigid social hierarchy; subordination of women to men and children to parents; repressed attitudes to sex; racism; unquestioning respect for authority in the family, education, government, the law, and religion, and for the nation state, the national flag, the national anthem; Cold War hysteria; a strict formalism in language, etiquette, and dress codes; a dull and cliché-ridden popular culture, most obviously in popular music, with its boring big bands and banal ballads.

In contrast, the 1960s were distinguished by

> black civil rights; youth culture and trend-setting by young people; idealism, protest, and rebellion; the triumph of popular music based on Afro-American models and the emergence of this music as a universal language, with the Beatles as heroes of the age; the search for inspiration in the religions of the Orient; massive changes in personal relationships and sexual behaviour; a general audacity and frankness in books and in the media, and in ordinary behaviour; relaxation in censorship; the new feminism; gay liberation; the emergence of 'the underground' and 'the counter-culture'; optimism and genuine faith in the dawning of a better world.[1]

[1] Although the Beatles' early singles were topping the charts during 1963, and the protest march on Washington DC which brought the black civil-rights movement in America to worldwide attention was in August of that year, the Stonewall riot, which marked the beginning of the equivalent movement for gay rights, was not until June 1969 (the year of the Woodstock flower-power pop festival), and Germaine Greer's pioneer feminist polemic *The Female Eunuch* did not appear until the following year. Nineteen sixty-eight was an *annus mirabilis* for the extreme left wing in Britain, when there was a certain amount of student rioting in imitation of the much more serious student–police confrontation in Paris; but in general the period 1963–9 was distinguished more by the mini-skirted consumerism of 'Swinging London' than by serious change in attitudes. Much of what we remember as 'The Sixties' actually happened in the early 1970s.

In the course of 806 pages, Marwick devotes precisely one paragraph to the satire boom, observing that *Beyond the Fringe* 'presented in witty and potent form the anti-Establishment ideas circulating velocitously in the late 1950s', noting that The Establishment Club gave a platform to 'the more adventurous elements from the youth sub-culture', and praising Hugh Greene at the BBC for supporting 'the first-ever television programme genuinely satirizing current affairs'. *Private Eye* is not mentioned. Marwick concludes the paragraph: 'The "satire boom" lasted no longer than the "New Wave" [of British films], but was, as it were, its junior partner in making public and explicit important changes in British attitudes and values.'

In contrast, the 'New Wave' films occupy twenty-five of Marwick's pages. Those he analyses include *Room at the Top* (1959), based on the John Braine novel, and the Keith Waterhouse–Willis Hall *Billy Liar* (1960), adapted from their stage play which in turn was adapted from Waterhouse's novel of the same title. 'The British New Wave,' writes Marwick, 'was…directly expressive of new social forces.'

So it was; but can Marwick be right to give it about a hundred times more space than he allocates to 1960s satire? 'Shurely shome mishtake,' as *Private Eye* often remarks. Marwick himself admits that 'Braine was a figure of the later 1950s', an Angry Young Man whose novel was somewhat *passé* by the time it reached the screen.[2] As it happens, Braine contributed several sketches to *TW3*, turning himself quite successfully into a satirist. 'I am a heterosexual,' declares the lonely-looking speaker of a Braine monologue which mocks the hypocrisies of the Vassall affair:

> There are few outward signs by which a heterosexual reveals himself…A heterosexual walks – or rather clumps in hobnailed boots and belted mac – alone. Not for him the joys of true comradeship; his energies are all spent in the pursuit of women. There is nothing he longs for more than a night out with the boys, but a night out in the boys – in the truest, deepest sense – is precisely what he can never enjoy. He is too busy making passes at the barmaid…
>
> It began early with me, at my public school…

As to *Billy Liar*, this engendered another *TW3* sketch, by Waterhouse and Hall themselves, mocking the clichés Waterhouse's novel and their jointly written play and film had helped to create. It was called 'What is a Northerner?':

> A Northerner is a scrap of humanity moulded by God in his own image, swathed

[2] Another 'Angry' novel, Kingsley Amis's *Lucky Jim*, had been bowdlerized out of recognition by the time it reached the screen in 1957. Although Jonathan Miller had been considered for the title role, it went to the anodyne Ian Carmichael.

in a cloth cap and set down in the Metropolis...He showed the world that beneath their simple cotton frocks even mill girls are stark staring naked.

The Northerner is a dreamer and a maker of films. He abolished insipid dialogue such as 'Anyone for tennis?' and replaced it with biting, incisive lines such as 'Would you like a cup of tea?'...Beneath every Northern watch-chain is a Southerner screaming to be let out.

Speaking personally, as someone whose fifteenth birthday fell in the year that *Beyond the Fringe* reached London, and who was nearly eighteen when *TW3* was taken off the air, it was they and *Private Eye* which gave me the sense that the rules of society were changing, much more than the handful of 'kitchen-sink' films, of which I was scarcely aware at the time. I have never seen *Room at the Top*, and I retain only a vague memory of *Billy Liar*. The 1960s films that influenced me were of a very different kind. Stanley Kubrick's *Dr Strangelove* (1963) had far more effect on my feelings about the nuclear deterrent than all the campaigning of CND, and Lindsay Anderson's *If...* (1968) gave vivid expression to the sense of revolution among young people which was then in the air.

As for *TW3*, I rarely failed to see it on Saturday nights – I particularly remember a rowdy teenage party (at least, rowdy by the standards of those days) coming to a silent halt while all we crowded round the set, absorbing every satirical word being delivered by Frost and company. At my public school (Marlborough) we began to copy the *TW3* style in our end-of-term revue; also the style of *Beyond the Fringe*, which I had seen with my parents. Abandoning the usual sets and costumes, we did a sketch about the BBC booklet that forbade jokes about lavatories and effeminacy in men (the BBC itself had tacitly abandoned these guidelines during the run of *TW3*). Our equivalent of Peter Cook's Macmillan impersonation was a brilliant parody of the headmaster's end-of-term speech written and performed by the future sports commentator Christopher Martin-Jenkins. The school film society screened some of the New-Wave films on Saturday nights, but in comparison they made very little impression, and certainly there was nothing in them we could copy.

Arthur Marwick devotes several pages to the cultural influence of John Trevelyan, Secretary of the British Board of Film Censors from 1958, whose liberal outlook permitted the 'New-Wave' films to be shown almost uncut. As it happens, John Trevelyan was my uncle. Some years later he talked to me about what he saw as his proselytizing liberalism in British cinema in the late 1950s and 1960s, and he certainly believed that his influence on the nation's changing *mores* had been substantial; but I do not think he would have expected to be given far more space in a cultural history of the period than Peter Cook, Richard Ingrams, David Frost and their colleagues.

Nowadays, most films, even from the 1960s, can be purchased or hired on videotape, and so are easily accessible to historians. In contrast, the remaining recordings of *TW3* are almost impossible to prise out of a remote department of the BBC, and are of appalling technical quality when you do get hold of them. The scripts can be read on fuzzy microfilm only in the BBC's Written Archives in a suburb of Reading. Understandably, few writers about the period have made the effort to do this. The early numbers of *Private Eye* are almost as inaccessible. Only *Beyond the Fringe* is easily available, in several printed editions and recordings. Consequently satire gets short shrift when people survey the 1960s.

The satirists themselves are inclined to belittle their achievement. 'I don't think we were more than marginally responsible for some of the changes that took place in the 1960s,' says Jonathan Miller.

> I think that we wouldn't have happened had there not been an ice-break quite a bit earlier – from about 1956, a gradual change in the political temperature. It was things like *Look Back in Anger*, which preceded us by four years, and also that convivial duffle-coated marching from Aldermaston to Hyde Park every year, and Suez; those all showed, to a lot of young people, that the ruling order, which had prevailed all through the Second World War, was cracking up.

Alan Bennett emphasizes that 1960s satire 'wasn't a crusade or anything like that. But you felt you were in the forefront of something.'

George Melly gives a much greater importance to the satire movement. 'Satire spanned the period between Rock and the Beatles,' he writes (by 'Rock' he means the early British rock 'n' roll of Tommy Steele), and he praises it for having handed on a 'licence for irreverence' to the pop culture which followed swiftly on its heels, and which dominated the later 1960s and the 1970s; indeed, it still dominates our lives today. But Melly also stresses crucial differences between the two:

> Satire's origins are Oxbridge, and it tends to find pop's incoherence and aspirations half-baked. To this day *Private Eye* remains hostile to pop culture, eager to jump on its pretensions and parody its solemnity ... Satire is ... moral in the old-fashioned sense. Its intentions are reformatory. It wants people to behave well. Pop really doesn't care about that at all.

In his book on the 1960s, *The Pendulum Years*, Bernard Levin considers the question of whether the various manifestations of satire were 'symptoms rather than causes' of the revolutionary cultural changes in Britain during the 1960s, and decides that they were both; which is probably a fair judgement. But another question remains.

Emma Tennant, writing of her brief marriage to Christopher Booker, remarks that the satirists were 'all male' (Eleanor Bron was the single exception),[3] and 'really *Daily Telegraph* readers in disguise'. Indeed in later life many of them, including Booker and Rushton, became *Telegraph* contributors. To what extent was their satire reactionary all along?

Arguably many of its earliest targets, such as Bennett's platitudinous preacher, were manifestations not so much of a corrupt or enfeebled old order deserving destruction as of the old guard pathetically trying to modernize itself in the age of television and rock 'n' roll. Peter Cook was not mocking Macmillan so much as the absurdity of an elderly aristocrat attempting to become a TV personality – his Macmillan sketch in *Beyond the Fringe* was called 'T. V. P. M.' *Private Eye* was the creation of a gang of ex-public schoolboys who had the deepest contempt for 1960s trendyism, which was largely working class in origin (many of its key figures, such as David Bailey, had working-class roots). *TW3* was the invention of a Conservative voter (Sherrin) and was fronted by an ambitious individual (Frost) who Bernard Levin forecast in 1970 would eventually get a knighthood. And of course the entire satire movement had its origins in two institutions that have always given the appearance of nurturing social change while in reality reinforcing the social *status quo*, the oldest universities in the country.

*

Private Eye, far from being 'the last and dying echo of the satire boom' as *The Sunday Times* called it in 1963, is its only true survivor. In 1991, on the thirtieth anniversary of its foundation, John Wells observed, 'It has run nearly as long as *The Mousetrap.*'

It has several times come near extinction. In 1966 a libel action brought by Lord Russell of Liverpool, who had been accused in the *Eye* of pandering to sadistic tastes in his Nazi war-crimes book *The Scourge of the Swastika*, resulted in a £5000 bill for the magazine, which in those days, says Richard Ingrams, was 'a colossal sum, far beyond our means'. Once again Peter Cook came to the rescue, arranging a mammoth charity matinée entitled *Rustle of Spring*. 'Even the much-maligned David Frost offered to perform,' recalls Ingrams, 'and was at once enlisted.'

By this time Christopher Booker – though still resenting the Ingrams coup against him – had returned to the magazine as a contributor. During 1965 Ingrams invited him to write a series of profiles called 'Pillars of Society', in which he singled out various fashionable idols for vicious attack. 'In his new manifestation,' writes Ingrams, 'Booker appeared as the sworn enemy of all that was new, dynamic and trendy – the Swinging London craze, Wilson's "New Britain"…and the cult of dynamism and technology.' This is a typical passage from one of these attacks by Booker:

---

[3] If one defines 'satirist' as someone who writes it as well as performs it. To the television-watching public, Millicent Martin was in the forefront of the satire movement.

A number of foreign observers have recently commented in awe on the extraordinary revolution that has taken place over the last ten years in the social life of Britain. 'London,' they remark, in what they hope to be the breathless vernacular of the times, 'has become the most switched-on city in the world.' They observe a country which, having lost an empire and any serious purpose, has given itself over more fully than any other to the wholehearted enjoyment of the delights and values of the 'consumer society' ... The English need concern themselves with nothing more than the right colour of their shirts, the latest record in the Hit Parade, the most amusing way to cook paella or the most up-to-date model of sports car. The values of Matthew and Thomas Arnold have been replaced in the New Britain by those of the Ad Lib [one of London's first night-clubs featuring a disco] and Carnaby Street ... A new aristocracy has arisen in Britain, that of the smart parasites, the photographers and model girls and dress designers and beat musicians.

(In contrast, Jonathan Miller looks back nostalgically on the heyday of Swinging London, recalling it as 'an enormously exciting mini-skirted place, with pretty girls, and fizzing irreverence, and there were smart clothes in the shops, and interesting plays, and England was rapidly modernizing itself'.)

Booker says that, once he was back in the *Private Eye* office again, 'I started to do a few jokes, and became part of the team – once more that shadowy figure, hovering on the edge!' He is still there today. But 'Pillars of Society' was only the beginning of a more sustained attack by him on the fashionable idols of the 1960s. In 1969 he published *The Neophiliacs*, an angry study of the decade which gave *Beyond the Fringe* and *Private Eye* only a few passing mentions, and made an astonishingly savage attack on *TW3*: 'If some of its material was witty and original, particularly the surrealist sketches by the cartoonist Timothy Birdsall ... much of it was amateurish, juvenile and completely stereotyped in attitude.' Booker sticks firmly to this view today: 'Tim and I used to look at each week's script and groan. I thought it was incredibly patchy, and I did dislike the lack of real commitment underneath. It was synthetic, and it had a heavy showbiz element.' Nicholas Garland says much the same: 'We watched *TW3* to see how ghastly it was – we were contemptuous of David Frost, and of the razzmatazz, and the fact that it wasn't anything like as interesting as *Beyond the Fringe*. It was crap – that was what I thought, though probably there was a lot of energy in it.'

Some of Booker's ire against the trendy 1960s can perhaps be explained by the swift break-up of his marriage to Emma Tennant. In the wake of this, and under the influence of Malcolm Muggeridge (himself undergoing a conversion), Booker had turned religious. 'He got very thick with Muggeridge,' says Richard Ingrams, 'and they both found God together.' At the end of *The Neophiliacs*, Booker dismisses the 'twentieth-century dream' of scientific and social progress and personal self-expression as a hollow fantasy, and contrasts it with what he saw as the life-giving power of 'the most powerful myth in the history of the human race...the story of Jesus of Nazareth'.

A different kind of conviction drove another key *Private Eye* contributor, Paul Foot, who left Fleet Street and joined the *Eye* full time in 1967. Foot had become an extreme left-winger during his period in Glasgow, and in the *Eye*'s 'Illustrated London News' page, originated by Claud Cockburn and now renamed 'Footnotes', he attacked the Wilson government for its failures to live up to Labour ideals. 'With Foot's invaluable help,' writes Ingrams,

> the information side of *Private Eye* now began to snowball...Starting with a few free-lancers and left-wing malcontents from the *New Statesman*, we began to build up a supply of sources. A regular Wednesday lunch was established in an upstairs room of the pub opposite the office [the Coach and Horses], to which we invited possible informants...*Private Eye* became a receptacle for all kinds of information which for one reason or other was being kept out of the papers.

This led to many triumphs of investigative reporting, including the uncovering of the Poulson financial corruption scandal in the North of England in 1970, the naming in 1979 of Sir Anthony Blunt as the 'Fourth Man' spy, and, in the same year, the bringing to trial of the Liberal Leader Jeremy Thorpe who was accused (but eventually acquitted) of conspiracy to murder his alleged lover Norman Scott. Paul Foot played a crucial part in the Poulson and Thorpe investigations, but his own politics were not taken very seriously by the rest of the *Eye* gang, and in 1972 he left to join the *Socialist Worker*. (He later wrote a column for the *Daily Mirror*, and after being 'constructively dismissed' by them, returned to *Private Eye* in 1993.) The *Eye* has never been consistently left-wing; its unnamed contributors have occasionally included Tory MPs, and Richard Ingrams voted Conservative in 1979, 1983 and 1987, abstained in 1992, and voted Liberal Democrat in 1997.

When he finally met Harold Wilson, at a Downing Street reception in 1970, Ingrams was amused to find him much like his fictional counterpart in 'Mrs Wilson's Diary'. 'Y'know,' Wilson said to him earnestly, looking round at the odd assortment of guests, who included Cliff Michelmore, Iris Murdoch and Morecombe and Wise, 'Jack Kennedy's parties at the White House had nothing on this!'

Edward Heath, whose Tory government replaced the Wilson administration between 1970 and 1974, was not considered worthy of a *Private Eye* diary, and the job of caricaturing him was left to cartoonist John Kent, in a strip called 'Grocer Heath and His Pals'. This nickname had been first attached to Heath by the *Eye* some years earlier, when he had been conducting Common Market negotiations about the price of groceries. The relentless use of a sobriquet has always been an *Eye* technique, all the more effective when the joke originated accidentally, as with 'Baillie Vass'. Harold Wilson soon became 'Wislon', on account of a typographical error in a newspaper – almost certainly the *Guardian*, which in those days was so erratic in its type-setting that it was said to have mis-spelled its own name; this is why the *Eye* has always called it the *Grauniad*.

Besides the nicknames there is the cast of invented characters, such as hardbitten woman journalist Glenda Slagg, Inspector Knacker of the Yard, and of course Lunchtime O'Booze, whose name mutates to fit the occasion; for example, reporting on the musical world he becomes Lunchtime O'Boulez. Also the catchphrases: 'Who he?' (which *New Yorker* editor Harold Ross used to scrawl in the margin of contributors' copy); 'Shurely shome mishtake?' (said to have been suggested by the 'sh'-for-'s' pronunciation of one-time *Daily Telegraph* editor William Deedes, but taken by most readers to indicate inebriation); and 'Ugandan discussions', meaning sexual intercourse. This originated at a party where an official from that country, discovered in bed with a woman journalist, was said by a spokesperson to have been holding discussions with her about his homeland.

A different kind of fictional diary, by Auberon Waugh, first appeared in *Private Eye* in the year of Heath's arrival at Downing Street, 1970. As his father Evelyn had done before him,[4] he portrayed himself as an extreme right-wing country gentleman of the highest social standing; a typical entry begins 'Sad and terrible news about my cousin, the Duke of Norfolk…' Waugh also had an inspired touch with insults, writing (for example) that Sir Michael Edwardes, chairman of the Leyland motor group, looked like 'a victim of forceps delivery'.

Though its contents often seemed as fictitious as Waugh's diary, the 'Grovel' gossip column, written from 1972 to 1985 by Nigel Dempster, usually offered readers nothing but the truth. Dempster picked up his tittle-tattle about the rich, titled and fashionable at first hand, since he belonged to the smart world he described. Before becoming a Fleet Street gossip writer, he had been a stockbroker, and he has twice married into the nobility. For a token fee, and the fun of it, he supplied *Private Eye* with gossip that his employers at the *Daily Express* and *Daily Mail* would not print.

---

4 Auberon Waugh says, however, that he did not read his father's diaries until Michael Davie edited them for publication; they appeared in 1976. The *Private Eye* Waugh column began as a spoof of a diary Alan Brien was writing for *The Times*.

In his book *Inside Private Eye*, the journalist Peter McKay, himself for many years a member of the *Eye* team, describes the difference in personal style between Dempster and Ingrams:

> Dempster wore expensively made suits, Turnbull & Asser shirts and Gucci shoes, while Ingrams stuck to his faded corduroy, Marks and Spencer shirts and mis-shapen walking shoes. They made a delightfully odd pair, chuckling at the corner table upstairs in the Gay Hussar.

McKay emphasizes that Dempster supplied *Private Eye* with much more than high-society gossip:

> Although most of his stories went into 'Grovel', he was always ready to assist on other leads that required his special knowledge of the rich and powerful – especially those facts about them that had not been widely publicized. It was he who had brought to the *Eye* the story that was to result in their most protracted and costly saga – the Jimmy Goldsmith affair.

In 1975 *Private Eye* ran a story alleging that the financier James Goldsmith was among those offering secret help to Lord Lucan, who had gone missing after trying to kill his wife. Goldsmith's response was to issue no fewer than sixty-three writs, served against the magazine's distributors (including W.H. Smith, who had reluctantly been stocking it for some while) as well as the *Eye* itself; those served on Ingrams and on Patrick Marnham – who had written the article – accused them under ancient law of 'criminal libel', which carried the penalty of gaol. Though rabidly right-wing, Goldsmith was being secretly encouraged by Harold Wilson, who had become eaten up by hatred of *Private Eye* for its exposure of the shady hangers-on who had characterized his second term of office (1974–6). The *Eye* staff took a 50 per cent salary cut to help pay the lawyers, and a 'Goldenballs' fund was opened for readers' contributions, which came in plentifully. After a series of nonsensical court hearings spread over two years, during which it became clear – not for the first time – that the judiciary were still suspicious of satirical magazines *per se*, Goldsmith suddenly offered to call off the case for a mere £30,000 and an apology. With hindsight, Ingrams says, 'I think Goldsmith was a great blessing to the *Eye* in terms of publicity. It made us front-page news.' Auberon Waugh remarks on Ingrams's 'genius at living with, and avoiding, libel actions. God knows how he did it, but he's a great survivor, and he knows what he can get away with.'

Far worse financial damage was done to the magazine in 1986 by Robert Maxwell, who managed to extract a third of a million pounds from the *Eye* after it had accused him of funding the Labour Party in the hope of getting a peerage. Revenge came when Maxwell died mysteriously at sea in 1991; the

Richard Ingrams and Peter Cook during James Goldsmith's court hearing, 1976.

Eye cover was a photograph of his burial with a speech-bubble from one of the pall-bearers saying, 'We're administering the last writs.'

Historian David Starkey has argued that, for all its campaigns against corruption, *Private Eye* is not satire: 'I suspect satire depends on verbal dexterity, and with the exception of the "Dear Bill" letters, which were very good, *Private Eye* isn't well written. It's simply gossip, innuendo and leaks.' These letters, purporting to be from Margaret Thatcher's husband Denis to his crony William Deedes (former Tory MP and editor of the *Daily Telegraph*), were once again mostly the idea of Peter Cook, when Thatcher came to power in 1979, but this time Ingrams and John Wells wrote them from the beginning. Ingrams recalls that Cook was now going into a decline:

> To my mind, it was just a straightforward case of alcoholism. Peter was a very, very nice and kind person who when drunk would become vicious and unpleasant. And he took it out particularly on Dudley [Moore], and broke up the partnership. His appearances at *Private Eye* grew less and less frequent. We never knew when he was going to come in, but he was always very welcome.

John Wells believed that the supposed author of the 'Dear Bill' letters objected strongly to the joke – 'Denis Thatcher was furious – thought we'd got him completely wrong' – and certainly Deedes protested about them. 'Neither Denis Thatcher nor I accept this impeachment,' he said in a radio interview. 'It's a little hard, after a struggle of half a century in politics and journalism, to find that you're really only known because you appear in some odd letter in a curious magazine.' However, Carol Thatcher, daughter of Denis and Margaret, writes in her biography of her father that initially he enjoyed the joke: 'Denis … became a keen reader of his fictitious epistles –

largely because so many people he met kept on referring to them, some under the impression that he was ghosting them himself.' She says he became annoyed only when they were published as a book, and people began sending copies to Downing Street for his autograph, expecting him to pay the return postage.

Wells recalls that, as with 'Mrs Wilson's Diary', there were suspicions in Whitehall that *Private Eye* had a mole in Downing Street:

> We were actually asked about this by someone at the Foreign Office, because we reported Carrington [the Foreign Secretary] throwing his briefcase over the filing cabinet, and saying he was fucked if he was going to sit in Brussels any longer with earphones strapped to his head, haggling about the price of beetroot. And apparently that had happened, word for word.
>
> And the other most extraordinary coincidence was after Mountbatten had been assassinated, and we had Denis playing golf, and he's followed to the first tee by Inspector Trimfittering, with his trousers too short and his socks hanging down. And Denis says he has to have tight security, now that Mountbatten has been assassinated, but he's not going to be followed round by such a figure. Well, it turned out after we'd published it that Denis had indeed been playing golf with Willie Whitelaw, and he was followed on to the green by a security man, and he'd refused to go on playing because the man was 'improperly accoutred'. Extraordinary, but I think that, once you get on to a wavelength, you pick it up.

Like 'Mrs Wilson's Diary' before it, 'Dear Bill' was turned by Wells into a successful West End play, under the title *Anyone for Denis?* Wells himself appeared as Denis, and the Thatchers came to see the play. 'My mother *loathed* it,' says Carol, 'though she told an interviewer through gritted teeth that it was a "marvellous farce".' Carol adds that, by this time, her father had begun to play up to the role invented for him by *Private Eye*:

> I remember one time at a charity lunch he was asked, 'Mr Thatcher, what on earth do you actually do with your time?' And Denis said, 'Well, when I'm not completely pissed, I like to play some golf.' Now in the beginning he would never have said that. This was acting 'Dear Bill'.

Ned Sherrin observes that, whatever Margaret Thatcher thought of all this, she herself was the ultimate beneficiary: 'The "Dear Bill" letters made her more human, because if this nice old buffer could live with her, then she couldn't have been all bad.'

*

When Ingrams resigned as editor of *Private Eye* in March 1986, he explained that he was tired not of writing and editing it, but of wasting time in lawyers' offices. Three years after he had departed, the wife of the Yorkshire Ripper was awarded an unbelievable £600,000 over an *Eye* allegation that she had taken money from a journalist. This was reduced on appeal to a tenth of the amount, which soon flooded in from *Eye* readers.

Ingrams picked his successor, Ian Hislop, a junior member of the staff, as autocratically as he had ousted Booker twenty-three years earlier. A group of objectors which included Auberon Waugh and Peter Cook (who was, after all, the proprietor) held a rebellious lunch at which they decided that Peter McKay, who had been on the *Eye* payroll part-time for eleven years and had a wealth of Fleet Street and gossip-writing experience, should have the job instead of Hislop. However, Cook got so drunk during the meal that, when he arrived at the magazine's office to make this announcement, he instead beamingly confirmed Hislop's appointment with the words 'Welcome aboard!'

There have been criticisms that, in its years under Hislop, *Private Eye* has brought off fewer big exposés than in the past. But Harry Thompson argues that this is inevitable, since the rest of the media have increasingly followed *Private Eye*'s example: 'Today every newspaper and news magazine is looking for the big story that will bring down the government.' Certainly Hislop's handling of the death of Diana, Princess of Wales, was as iconoclastic as anything in the Ingrams days. The edition of the *Eye* published the day before her funeral (5 September 1997) began with an editorial mocking the hypocrisy displayed by the press ever since news of the fatal car crash had broken the previous Sunday:

> In recent weeks (not to mention the last ten years) we at the *Daily Gnome*, in common with all other newspapers, may have inadvertently conveyed the impression that the late Princess of Wales was in some way a neurotic,

John Wells, West End playwright – author of *Mrs Wilson's Diary* and *Anyone for Denis?*

irresponsible and manipulative troublemaker... We now realize as of Sunday morning that the Princess of Hearts was in fact the most saintly woman who has ever lived... We would like to express our sincere and deepest hypocrisy to all our readers on this tragic day and hope and pray that they will carry on buying our paper notwithstanding.

In its next issue (19 September) the *Eye* reported that two retail newsagent chains, T&S and Alldays, had refused to sell the previous one on the grounds that it was disrespectful towards the Princess, and that W.H. Smith had initially decided not to sell it, though they had then changed their minds. (One distributor asked the *Eye* if the issue had been 'cleared with the Palace'.) The 19 September issue published six letters of protest from readers about the *Eye*'s response to the death – with phrases such as 'grossly offensive' and 'total and complete tastelessness' – and twenty-six of support. 'The biting satire mined rich veins of double-think,' wrote one reader. Another asked, 'Who else will criticize the press? They sure as hell won't do it themselves.'

*

Early in 1979, a few months before Thatcher led the Tories to power, a thirty-three-year-old life-insurance salesman and former disc jockey named Peter Rosengard was on holiday in Los Angeles, where he went to a club called the Comedy Store. 'When we left the club, I said, "I must open a place like that in London."'

Like Peter Cook eighteen years earlier, he headed for Soho – still predominantly a district of strip-joints – and booked a room in the Nell Gwynne club for one night a week. 'A lot of people thought I was crazy to open there. "Who wants to go to Soho at midnight on a Saturday to a sleazy strip-joint to watch a bunch of amateur comics?"'

Amateurs were what he had in mind, first-timers who would devise fresher comic material than the tired clichés of television and the northern clubs. After the brief flowering of *Monty Python* (in three series, between 1969 and 1973) the 1970s had been a comparatively barren time for television comedy, with the notable exception of John Cleese's short-lived masterpiece *Fawlty Towers* (two short series in 1975 and 1979). Political satire had all but vanished, and viewers were left with Mike Yarwood's deft but harmless impersonations of politicians ('I got through a lot of raincoats playing Harold Wilson,' Yarwood writes in his memoirs). There was more daring in Johnny Speight's sitcom *Till Death Us Do Part*, which began in 1966 and ran through the 1970s. Speight describes the (anti-)hero of *Till Death Us Do Part*, the working-class right-wing racist Alf Garnett, as a 'satire' on 'all those bigoted, illiberal chauvinists and... xenophobic half-wits that plague us':

ALF: Where d'you get this meat? ...

ELSE: It should be all right – it's best English lamb.

ALF: English? How d'you know it's bloody English?

ELSE: Cos it said so on the label.

ALF: Label! They can put anything on labels these days. Can't go by bloody labels. I mean, blimey – they could put English labels on Pakistanis, couldn't they? But it wouldn't make 'em bloody English, would it?

George Melly has praised Speight for having 'probed, with an admirable contempt for our sensibilities, into the social sores and abscesses which we have tried to ignore in the vain hope that they might cure themselves'. However, Warren Mitchell, playing Alf, soon discovered that much of the programme's audience were unaware they were watching satire: 'One chap came over to me saying, "I'm glad you had a go ... at the coloureds." I told him, "You stupid so-and-so, I was having a go at you." '

Soon after Thatcher's Election victory, the BBC sitcom *Yes Minister*, by Jonathan Lynn and Antony Jay, began to mock the impotence of a typical Cabinet minister, showing him as the puppet of his civil servants; but it

Ian Hislop and Peter Cook in 1990.

carefully avoided references to Thatcher and her real-life Cabinet. Meanwhile one satire show descended from *TW3* had quietly established itself – on radio rather than television. BBC Radio 4's *Week Ending*, a Friday late-night compendium of topical sketches, repeated on Saturdays, began in 1970 with David Hatch producing and continued till 1998 (when it was dropped not for political reasons but because Radio 4 was being replanned). Harry Thompson, who produced it for a while, caricatures the typical *Week Ending* writer:

> After the great dinosaurs of the satire boom were brought down, some little sharp-toothed rodents of the left had been busy burrowing away in the corridors of Broadcasting House. *Week Ending* writers' meetings were surely the only public gatherings in Britain boasting an absolute majority for the Socialist Workers' Party – with the possible exception of the National Union of Teachers' conference! I never quite knew whether these ragged creatures had been driven leftwards by the unendurable hardship of trying to live on BBC writing fees, or whether they were so committed to their cause that they'd actually volunteered for penury, just to try and get their message across. If the Labour Party was attacked, it was always for not being socialist enough, and the crime of actually being right-wing was so heinous that merely to point out this evil-doing was usually enough.

Exaggerated as this may seem, John O'Farrell, who served an apprenticeship on *Week Ending* before going on to write for *Spitting Image*, closely fits Thompson's stereotype. In his autobiographical book *Things Can Only Get Better*, a witty memoir of what it was like to be a fervent young Labour supporter during eighteen years of Tory rule, he explains:

> Writing left wing satirical sketches seemed to fit in very well with the ideologically pure image I had of myself…Who knows, I thought, perhaps people would be influenced by things Mark [Burton, his writing partner] and I wrote and be persuaded by the rightness of the left's cause. As if the C2s in the West Midlands marginals were all sitting round waiting to hear what Radio 4's *Week Ending* had to say before they voted: ''Ere, Brian, coming down the polling station to vote for Maggie?' 'No, hang on there, Kev. Cos whilst I was polishing my Sierra, I was listening to this satirical sketch about the budget done like an episode of *Star Trek*. And although it made me laugh, it made me think as well. It's Labour for me this time, and no mistake.'

Despite its almost propagandist left-wing slant, *Week Ending*'s style was fundamentally old-fashioned: a series of topical sketches with punchlines, and (at the end of the programme) a bulletin predicting the next week's news. Peter Rosengard wanted something far more anarchic for his Soho comedy club, and he advertised in *Private Eye* and the *Stage* for aspiring comedians. The *Private Eye* small ad read: 'COMEDIANS WANTED for new comedy and improvisation club opening W1. Call Peter Rose ... ' (Rosengard had temporarily trimmed his surname.)

'My first mistake had been to put my ad in the *Stage*,' Rosengard writes. 'I'd been besieged by every out-of-work Butlins Redcoat in Britain ... Also a lot of semi-pro northern club comics sent me their glossy eight-by-ten photos.' At last there walked in 'a stocky, tough-looking young man in a leather jacket with a Liverpool accent. He'd seen my ad in *Private Eye*. His name was Alexei Sayle and five minutes later, after a brilliantly surreal and hilarious monologue involving a violent encounter in a cake shop, I knew I'd found my compère.'

Sayle had more in common with Aristide Bruant, Frank Wedekind and Bertolt Brecht than with Peter Cook, Jonathan Miller or David Frost. Born in 1952, he was the son of a railway guard, and after leaving school he had studied art, done odd jobs and co-founded a Brechtian cabaret troupe. His stand-up act was distinguished by a ranting style, the speed of his attack and the liberal use of four-letter words – hallmarks of 'alternative comedy', as the new wave soon became known.

One of Sayle's set-pieces was a portrait of the average London working-class male, whose natural loquacity was somewhat hampered by the limited supply of swear-words:

> Turn it up, knock it on the 'ead ... shit–piss–cunt–fuck–bollocks ... wanker, wanker, wanker ... Cortina! Millwall – fuckin' Millwall! ... Jean-Paul Sartre – what a fucking cunt, eh? What a fucking cunt old Jean-Paul Sartre is, you know what I mean? We fuckin' *hate* him round our way – you know why? Cos he knows fuck-all about the Cortina, that's why.

It might seem from this that the motto of alternative comedy was 'anything goes'. In fact it was always left-wing, and strictly governed by political correctness, with a particular ban on any material that might be thought racist or sexist.

Physically a big man, Sayle made no attempt to ingratiate himself with his audience, commenting on this, 'Dudley Moore used to say he did comedy to get out of trouble because people used to pick on him – I used to do comedy to *make* trouble, because I was big anyway, I could look after myself, and I used to do comedy just to be irritating.'

He proved an excellent compère at the first night of London's Comedy Store – Rosengard had decided to copy the American name – on 19 May 1979. The event strongly recalled the opening of The Establishment eighteen years earlier. 'I'd sent out over three hundred invitations,' Rosengard recalls. 'The club was only licensed to hold a maximum of a hundred and twenty people, but I was told that most people probably wouldn't want to come. They all did and it was packed.' However, there was one crucial difference from Cook's club: the social mix of the audience. Rosengard describes them as 'from all walks of life – students to dockers, lords to dustmen'.

For the first night he had amassed no fewer than twenty-three amateur comedians, including Tom Tickell of the *Guardian*, who described the occasion the following Monday:

> Have you heard the story about the dentist, the caretaker and the journalist who turned into comedians on Saturday night? Mr Peter Rosengard believes you have not. He claims that the Comedy Store, which he opened with a flourish of champagne in Soho this weekend, is the first place in Britain where almost anyone who believes that they have hidden dramatic talent can go through their patter for up to ten minutes on a stage, in front of a live audience.
>
> There are, however, safeguards. If the compère or anyone else decides that enough is enough, or the hidden talent should remain concealed, a vast gong is struck and you depart – to be replaced by the next performer, just as desperate to catch the eye of a passing television producer in search of a new and original talent…
>
> How did the twenty-three aspiring comedians react? This one kept telling himself that his script was not that bad…We were due to start at 10 p.m., or certainly by half-past or anyway when *Nationwide*'s television cameras were ready and the lights were fixed. The club itself, above a strip-club and close to a massage parlour, was filled to capacity, with standing room only – and not much of that…The pace got faster, the audience got drunker, and baying for each act to end almost before it had begun. A beautiful act from a pair from Footlights at Cambridge – and many others – just did not stand a chance. This particular Daniel could only be grateful that he met the lions before they got hungry.

The failure of the Footlights duo was significant. Harry Enfield, who was eighteen when the Comedy Store opened, writes that until then 'it seemed to young people that to do comedy you had to have been in the Cambridge University Footlights or the Oxford University equivalent. Then the Comedy Store opened…and…*anyone* could get up and try to be a comic.' However, the operative word on that first night was 'try', and another press reporter commented, 'All Rosengard has to do now to make the Comedy Store a success is find some comedians.' This was not easy. 'I kept trying to get well-known comedians to come down to try out new material,' Rosengard recalls,

> but their agents weren't very enthusiastic…Then some new and very funny people started to appear…Soon we had a nucleus of half a dozen regulars who

were tremendous. Within six months they were joined by two brilliant double-acts ... Rik Mayall and Adrian Edmondson ... and ... Peter Richardson and Nigel Planer.

The next significant recruit was a twenty-two-year-old Manchester University drama graduate. Ben Elton came from a middle-class family – 'My dad's an academic, my mother's a teacher, so I suppose I had quite an academic background' – but his style was as hectoring, aggressive and sexually explicit as Alexei Sayle's. 'What I don't like is nudie sunbathing,' runs a typical Elton routine. 'A lot more women nudie sunbathe than men – this is true – now, there's two reasons for this: the first is your average dick – and believe me, lads, they're all average. Well, mine's not, mine's fucking enormous.' This gets a big laugh from the audience, and he turns to the other reason that men dislike nude sunbathing:

> The terror, the absolute mind-numbing, ball-crunching, spine-tingling terror of the *unwanted erection*! ... Topless beach – fuck me, I'm surrounded by tits – boing! I'm a lefty, I'm trying to hang on to my politics, I'm thinking, 'I will not ogle, I will not look, I'm not going to stare, it's oppressive, it's invading her environment' ... *but the dick is not a hypocrite*!

After a while, Alexei Sayle left the Comedy Store and took his act on the road, performing to big audiences in rock venues; as Roger Wilmut has noted, alternative comedy does not really belong in the theatre, but in the world of rock concerts. Sayle's place as Comedy Store compère was taken by Ben Elton, until the original venue closed at the end of 1982. By that time another of the regular performers, Peter Richardson, had established the Comic Strip, a five-nights-a-week show in Paul Raymond's Boulevard Theatre just around the corner in Soho.

Meanwhile television was hastily reorganizing its views about comedy. Producer John Lloyd, who had worked on *Week Ending* before moving to TV, recalls this period of upheaval: 'I was astonished to go along to the Comic Strip and see people like Alexei Sayle and Ben Elton, all making jokes from the "wrong" angle' – that is, from an explicitly left-wing viewpoint, quite different from that of most broadcast comedy, which now seemed to Lloyd 'full of the most flaccid, out-dated, old-fashioned right-wing propaganda'. Lloyd realized that 'the world has changed, and we're still whanging on with the clichés, so we've got to look at everything anew and say, what do we really think about this, not, what's the easy gag'.

The first result was the BBC television series *Not! the Nine O'Clock News*, co-produced by Lloyd, which began in 1979 and ran until 1982. This featured three young Oxbridge graduates, Rowan Atkinson, Griff Rhys Jones and Mel Smith, in a show that aimed to blend *Monty Python*-style surrealism with a degree of topical satire. Many of its writers came from

Week Ending, but *Not! the Nine O'Clock News* lacked the radio show's political bite. Meanwhile the arrival in late 1982 of Channel Four, itself more 'alternative' than the other networks, gave the new wave of comedians their chance. Curiously, as Harry Thompson points out, this was because of one of Mrs Thatcher's key policies:

> Ironically, alternative comedy might well have stayed where it was – as nothing more than an unusual night out in central London – if it wasn't for the capitalist ideology of its principal target, Mrs Thatcher herself. In her hunger for the free market, the lady ruled that 25 per cent of BBC TV programmes (not to mention 100 per cent of Channel Four shows) should come from the independent sector. A rash of hurriedly created independent companies suddenly needed to find wholesale new talent, new ideas and a whole new outlook.

For a while, the contributions of Comedy Store and Comic Strip comedians to television were largely as writers, essentially within the old sitcom format. Ben Elton, for example, co-wrote for *The Young Ones* and *Blackadder*. Then in 1986 he began to host Channel Four's *Saturday Live* and to make solo tours of the big venues, earning a reputation for his 'right-on' (fashionably left-wing) attacks on Thatcher. This is a typical snatch of one of his stand-up performances in 1989, the time of the Thatcher government's programme of privatizing almost all the country's public services:

> They're beginning to advertise things that personally I thought I owned...It's a surreal experience when you're watching the telly and suddenly there's an advert for something you thought was already yours. There's Telecom and then there's the gas, and then there's water, and I'm saying to my girlfriend, 'I could have sworn that was ours.'...But no, apparently we've got to buy it back, and if we don't, some Japanese investors will buy it, and then won't we feel silly? I confidently expect to see my sofa advertised on the telly! 'The Ben's Sofa Share Opportunity.' Mrs Thatch would say, 'Well, what are you doing with your sofa?' I'd say, 'I'm sitting on it, Mrs Thatch.' She says, 'Well, that's no fucking good, it should be making a profit.'

There was more subtle satire of Thatcherism in some of the characters invented by Harry Enfield. On Channel Four early in 1988 he appeared as a loud-mouthed workman waving a bundle of banknotes: 'Look at that! Look at my wad! I've got loadsamoney.' Enfield explains: 'We were at the height of the mid-1980s housing boom, and plasterers saw themselves as the aristocracy of builders.' This character, Loadsamoney, quickly became a symbol of Thatcherite new wealth and the vulgarity that often went with it. Enfield was soon able to make him into a more specific political weapon:

One night, I did a benefit gig at Ealing Town Hall for the nurses, who were on strike in an attempt to get their pay increased. Before I went on, various 'right-on' stand-up comics did their acts, getting huge rounds of applause for all their anti-Tory and anti-Thatcher jokes. Then it was my turn. Loadsamoney walked on stage, surveyed the audience with contempt and shouted, 'GET BACK TO WORK, YOU SCUM!' I pranced around the stage telling them what wankers they were, how great BUPA was, how they should close the NHS down and develop the hospitals into flats for me to plaster … The nurses were asking for a £7-a-week rise – so I took out a tenner and burnt it on stage.

Enfield adds that 'the nurses loved it', but the comics' attacks on Thatcher and Thatcherism seemed to have no effect on the vote. Ian Hislop remarks of this:

Sometimes it's very difficult to make satire work. A classic case is Mrs Thatcher. And it would be difficult to find any evidence of satire having dented Mrs Thatcher's popularity or strength – largely because the perceived vision of her, as an extremely strong, arrogant, aggressive woman, was exactly the image she wanted to project. So there was no gap between the reality and the caricature. She didn't mind the caricature: it was part of what she was.

Just as his predecessor Christopher Booker had taken time off from *Private Eye* to help write *TW3*, Hislop was enlisted as one of the regular writers on *Spitting Image*, the TV satirical puppet show which ran from 1984 to 1996 – that is, for most of the life of the Thatcher government. *Spitting Image* was masterminded, and its puppets were created, by Roger Law, who had provided The Establishment with giant satirical drawings in the early 1960s, in collaboration with another artist whom he had known since Cambridge art-school days, Peter Fluck.

Since the days of The Establishment, Law had been working as an illustrator for newspapers and colour supplements:

I did strange things like covering the Moors murder trials when they couldn't use a camera. And I went to America on a Rockefeller grant, and made a satirical puppet film. Back home, I started to make three-dimensional caricatures and photograph them. Eventually, Peter Fluck and I set up a partnership doing this, and we worked for *The Sunday Times* and *The Economist*. Eventually we decided to make these three-dimensional figures move, thinking that perhaps we could do cartoons on TV after the news – commenting on the news with these personality puppets.

Law is quick to credit John Lloyd, who co-produced *Spitting Image*, with making the programme feasible: 'John shrewdly sugared the pill. We wanted half an hour of heavy satire – "I hate Thatcher, I hate Thatcher, I hate

Thatcher" – which you can't do on mainstream television. John knew what you could get away with.'

Spitting Image has been criticized for confusing satire with shallow slapstick, for mocking inconsequential showbiz celebrities as much as politicians, and for conferring glamour on the Thatcher government by portraying its members as highly distinctive puppets. Roger Law is the first person to admit the programme's limitations:

> I don't believe satire changes anything, though you think it will when you're young. But on *Spitting Image* in the Thatcher days, we sometimes had the feeling we were the only effective opposition. At least we were airing the issues; the Labour Party wasn't. They were fucking useless.
>
> For example, when Reagan bombed Libya from British air-bases, we had a sketch of him as one man and his dog, and Thatcher was the dog, and it wound up with him telling her to lick his bottom, and she did. And there was another one set in the men's toilet – typical *Spitting Image*, not very subtle! – and he just uses his cock to unload the bombs, pisses all over everybody uncontrollably. I was back in Cambridge the weekend that show went out, and the left were for it, of course, and the extreme right were for it too, because they were absolutely horrified that the Americans had just used us as an air-base – we still don't know if they even *asked* Thatcher. So people who'd been crossing the street to avoid me, as a well-known troublemaker and old lefty fart, came across and shook my hand.

*

Superficially, there seems to be even more satire around these days in Britain than there was in the 1960s. In recent years a wave of new comedy clubs and pubs, on the Comedy Store model, has washed across the country.[5] So-called satirists abound on television, and in the mid-1990s even John Bird and John Fortune reappeared on the screen, this time as 'The Long Johns', semi-improvising as they did in the days of The Establishment:

> BIRD: George Parr, you have just been appointed the co-ordinator of the Millennium celebrations … What sort of ideas have been coming from private sources? …
>
> FORTUNE: We've actually come up with the Queen Mother … I think she's the last thing we have left that can unify us.
>
> BIRD: Unify the nation, yes. The problem is, of course, I mean, the Queen Mother is ninety-six years old, and without wishing to be pessimistic in any way … do you have a fall-back position on the Queen Mother at all?

---

[5] According to Bryan Appleyard in *The Sunday Times* (18 July 1999), the comedian Eddie Izzard 'has counted eighty-five comedy clubs in London compared to five each in New York and Los Angeles. And now drama and media studies courses at a number of British universities are offering courses in stand-up.'

FORTUNE: Of course we do, yes...a giant hologram of Her Majesty, which
would be projected on to the night sky above London... We're already feeding
the Queen Mother's co-ordinates into a computer program ...

BIRD: They must be very complex, the co-ordinates... The hat alone is very –

FORTUNE: Yes, I'm glad you mentioned the hat, because that's all we've
managed to map so far. And I'm afraid the hat alone is beginning to soak up
our budget.

As to topical satire, BBC Radio's *The News Quiz* and its television
offspring *Have I Got News For You* have provided a weekly deflation of the
latest absurdities – the participants in the latter sometimes being the very
politicians who are being mocked. No sooner had the Tory MP Neil
Hamilton lost his seat in the 1997 General Election, following accusations
that he had accepted cash in brown envelopes for asking questions in the
House of Commons, than he appeared on *Have I Got News For You* with his
wife Christine.[6] Yet Gerald Kaufman compares the programme's regular
participants unfavourably with the creators of *TW3*:

> They're cheekier, but it's juvenile humour – they don't deal with issues. The
> thing that distinguished *TW3* was that it pursued issues. I doubt if the BBC
> would do most of the sketches I wrote nowadays – it's timid and conventional,
> though it pretends to be forward-looking and thrusting.

'Satire is now an industry,' declares Harry Thompson.

> TV satirists are now paid more than captains of industry, which begs the
> question of whether they still have the moral authority to attack the rich and
> powerful merely for their rich-and-powerfulness. I read a Sunday opinion piece
> by one outraged captain of a satirical panel game, protesting vigorously that
> Cedric Brown, over at British Gas, was getting £10,000 of public money for just
> three days' work a week. And I happened to know that the self-same satirist was
> getting £10,000 of public money for just three hours' work a week.

John Bird comments: 'Satire has become one among many entertainment
options for the consumer to buy, and its success or failure is determined by
the market.' He adds:

> What I find dispiriting is, there now seems to be a whole lot of smart-arse
> journalists practising the humour of the *Guardian* 'Pass Notes' column, which

6 John O'Farrell, who had moved on from *Spitting Image* to *Have I Got News For You*, recalls the
occasion: 'Neil Hamilton's wife Christine... was such a phenomenon that someone had the idea of inviting
her... This was arranged during the campaign, although she said she would not have time until after polling
day... Once Hamilton was turfed out, we thought we might as well ask him on as well. Their immediate
reaction was, "Will it mean another appearance fee?" It did and we gave them the money in brown
envelopes at the end of the show.'

I find very resistible. And all the parliamentary sketch-writers are dismissive, and even the sports writers, the restaurant criticisms, the television reviews. Everything is a branch of comedy now. Everybody is a comedian. Everything is subversive. And I find that very tiresome.

Gerald Kaufman agrees with this:

Journalism now is all gossip. All the people who write those ghastly parliamentary sketches only write gossip – they don't report what's happening. In fact the problem now with most newspapers is finding any sort of news as distinct from the opinions – the *Guardian* is now nothing but opinions, and very callow, stupid opinions too.

Christopher Booker is similarly irritated by the perpetual facetiousness of the media:

I can't stand the relentless punning in newspaper headlines. *Private Eye* was in on the beginning of that, but now everyone does it, and even for serious things. Peter Cook once said, back in the 1960s, 'Britain is in danger of sinking giggling into the sea,' and I think we really are doing that now.

Barry Humphries agrees: 'Everyone is being satirical; everything is a send-up. There's an infuriating frivolity, cynicism and finally a vacuousness. Everyone is a satirist.'

This sounds like the grumbling of the older generation. Yet a much younger, current practitioner of what now passes for satire, the television performer and newspaper columnist Jeremy Hardy, makes the same points:

There's frankly too much comedy. It's absolutely invasive. I've been asked to go on *Question Time*, but I don't know whether as a humorist or whether they think I'm a serious journalist. I think it's part of the dumbing-down process. They have comedians on *Newsnight* now to do funny little skits. And I think that's hateful, and it's very dangerous. What it's basically saying is, oh no, this isn't really that important – it's all just frippery, really, what goes on in politics.

Michael Frayn agrees – and takes a little of the blame himself: 'I think we who were involved with "satire" in the 1960s may all have been partially responsible for the fact that there is now a tone in a lot of the press of a permanent sneer at almost everything, which is very depressing.' Christopher Booker, however, feels that 1960s satire was not itself to blame for what has happened since:

If we're talking about the disintegration of shared culture and values, and the general drift towards the moral wasteland that we now live in, to what extent has *Private Eye* and the satire movement been instrumental in helping to bring that about, or did we just reflect it? When I wrote *The Neophiliacs* I saw the satire movement as very destructive. But looking back on it now, I think the destruction was going on anyway, and I would much rather be associated with the *Private Eye* strand in that.

On the day in 1998 that the *Private Eye* spoof of Tony Blair, *Sermon from St Albion's*, was first seen on television (with Booker among the writing team), Bryan Appleyard wrote in *The Sunday Times*:

> There is a problem … with all contemporary attempts at political satire … The idea of the old left is intrinsically incredible. Nobody can appeal to a collapsed socialist ideal any more than they can appeal to a collapsed right-wing nationalist ideal. We know they don't work. But equally, we don't know what does … This is a loss that damps the satirical fire … No cultural change appears to be at hand, and the charge against New Labour is not that it is wrong, but simply that it is inauthentic … Politics has shrunk from matters of life and death to matters of presentation. Satire is in danger of shrinking with it.

David Nobbs, who wrote for *TW3*, remarks, 'In those days, it was a revelation that our lords and masters were capable of folly on a grand scale. Now it would be a revelation if we found that any of them weren't.' And John Fortune believes that satire is powerless in the face of the cynicism which he thinks pervades the present government:

> We now have a kind of politics which is almost mockery-proof. You felt with the last Conservative government that politicians were saying, let's just get whatever we can out of this – it may not be legal or moral, but nothing's going to last long, so let's grab it. And now the New Labour agenda seems to be that the purpose of politics is merely to stay in power. Labour's whole philosophy is to get re-elected – there's absolutely nothing else. And that's a cynicism beyond anything that a satirist can offer.

Finally, it seems to be a symptom of this post-ideological, highly consumerist age that, if you look up *Beyond the Fringe* on the Internet, you will find it is now the name of a ladies' hairdresser in Alan Bennett's native city of Leeds.

Curtain call: where are they now?

After the end of *TW3*, John Bassett, 'the Father of English Satire', did a number of jobs in television, and a spell as a literary agent. Later, he converted and ran a canal hotel-boat on European waterways. These days he lives in Hampstead. He is planning to issue a record made (but never released) by his Bassett Hounds forty years ago, with Dudley Moore on piano.

Four years after *Forty Years On*, in 1972, came Alan Bennett's first television play, *A Day Out*. Today, many people would pick as the peak of his career his series of dramatic monologues for television, *Talking Heads* (1987, with a second series in 1999); though it was arguably the autobiographical book *Writing Home* (1994), chiefly a selection from his diaries, that finally established his status as a national institution, a symbol of a certain kind of Englishness, much like John Betjeman.

His house in Camden Town stands just a few doors from Jonathan Miller's, peaks of whose polymathic career have included an idiosyncratic television version of *Alice in Wonderland* (1966) with Peter Cook as the Mad Hatter, and the 1978 television series he presented on the history of medicine, *The Body in Question*. He moved into opera directing in the 1970s. When asked how he feels about giving up writing and performing comedy, he says, 'I never repudiated it. I've just not done it any more, professionally – I've not performed and I've not written. Though I would hope that any of the actors and singers with whom I've worked would say that my direction is largely the result of my amusing them. So I keep doing that sort of thing by virtue of being a director.'

Dudley Moore teamed up with Peter Cook for the legendary television series *Not Only... But Also* (1965–6), and for some comically obscene 'Derek and Clive' sound recordings (originally circulated as bootlegged copies); and they appeared together in several films, including *The Wrong Box* (1965) and *Bedazzled* (1967). Then, quite unpredictably, Moore went on to become a film star in his own right, leaving Cook behind him and eventually settling in Hollywood. His movies included *Thirty is a Dangerous Age, Cynthia* (1967), for which John Wells co-wrote the screenplay, *'10'* (1979), *Arthur* (1980), and *Santa Claus* (1985). He has had a turbulent private life, with four marriages, and at the time of writing is in very poor health.

Willie Donaldson, who brought *Beyond the Fringe* to London, lost all his money in a 1965 theatrical flop. He then had various picaresque adventures in the underworld of gangsters, prostitution and drugs, and wrote these up, suitably embroidered, in several idiosyncratic books, including *Both the Ladies and the Gentlemen* (1975), which Kenneth Tynan likened to Evelyn Waugh. Fame came to him in 1979 with *The Henry Root Letters*, in which under the persona of Root he coaxed the famous into writing him straight-faced replies to ludicrous requests. Taxed with the accusation that he is a satirist at heart, Donaldson typically disclaims any originality in the Root book: 'I pinched the idea from an American book by a comedian who wrote to right-wing people in an invented persona – I stole the idea lock, stock and barrel.'

Richard Ingrams still contributes to *Private Eye*, but since 1992 his main preoccupation has been editing the *Oldie*, a magazine written by and intended for the middle aged and elderly. Christopher Booker continues to resent the Ingrams coup which displaced him in 1963, but comes into the *Eye* once a fortnight to help Ingrams, Ian Hislop and Barry Fantoni to write the Tony Blair spoof, 'Sermon From St Albion's'. He has written books attacking bureaucracy and the European Community, and has seethed in a *Sunday Telegraph* column about how Britain should get out of Europe before it is too late.

The Foreign Office posted Andrew Osmond to Africa and Rome, where he met Douglas Hurd; together they wrote several bestselling political thrillers. Osmond returned to *Private Eye* as managing director in 1969, spent six years greatly improving its finances, then directed two companies specializing in writing for businesses. He died of cancer in 1999. Peter Usborne left *Private Eye* in 1965, and eventually became a publisher; these days he runs the highly successful Usborne Publishing, specializing in educational and non-fiction books for children.

Nicholas Luard has been a prolific travel-writer and novelist. His wife Elisabeth writes about food, and made a considerable impression with her 1991 book *Family Life*, which concludes with the death from AIDS of their daughter Francesca.

Having established himself as a performer in *TW3*, Willie Rushton remained much in demand for television and radio comedy and quiz shows, but he continued as a cartoonist, illustrating Auberon Waugh's Diary in

Private Eye from 1978 (following the death of its previous illustrator, Nicholas Bentley), and later decamping with Waugh to the *Literary Review*, which he illustrated prolifically, and the *Daily Telegraph*. His only remaining regular contribution to *Private Eye* in his latter years was the author caricature on the 'Literary Review' book page. He died in December 1996 while in hospital for a heart operation.

John Wells died of cancer in 1998, after a busy life which, besides his satirical and comic activities, included translating and directing operas, and writing histories of the London Library and the House of Lords and biographical plays about Swift and Wesley.

'After the satire shows of the 1960s,' writes John Bird, 'I did a few comedy series, either on my own or with John Fortune and/or John Wells, for the BBC and various ITV companies. I wrote a stage play, *Council of Love*, freely adapted from a turn-of-the-century German piece, which was put on at the Criterion, directed by Jack Gold. In 1973 I appeared in the original West End production of Alan Bennett's *Habeas Corpus*, and collaborated on the screenplay of Terence Donovan's film *Yellow Dog*. In 1981 and 1983 I directed a couple of off-Broadway productions. The rest of the 1970s and 1980s were mostly taken up with television acting, of which the highlights (for me, anyway) were Dennis Potter's *Blue Remembered Hills*, Andrew Davies's *A Very Peculiar Practice*, and my only, unlikely venture into starring in a cop series, Granada's *El Cid*. At the beginning of the 1990s, Rory Bremner asked me to work with him on his television series, initially as a writer, and at some point it was suggested that John Fortune and I try our hand at the semi-improvised conversations on topical subjects which we've been doing for Rory ever since, as "The Long Johns". So the wheel has come full circle and I'm back doing very much the sort of thing we did at The Establishment.'

Eleanor Bron, on the other hand, has tended to do straight theatre and screen work rather than comedy. She has also written *Life, and Other Punctures* (1978) and *The Pillow Book of Eleanor Bron* (1985), and a novel, *Double Take* (1996). Jeremy Geidt went back to America where he has had many successful years acting with Yale Repertory Theater and the American Repertory Theater, and teaching acting at Yale and Harvard Universities.

David Kernan says that life was difficult for some of the *TW3* cast when the show was abruptly axed – 'we were type-cast as "those satirists", and I was out of work for several months'. He himself teamed up again with Ned Sherrin in 1976, when they devised *Side by Side by Sondheim*, in which Kernan sometimes still performs. 'I wrote to Sondheim asking if he would let us do it,' Kernan recalls. 'Back came a telegram – there weren't any faxes in those days – saying: "By all means have a try, but apart from the Book of

Kells, I can't think of anything more boring." In fact it revolutionized the small-scale musical.'

As to the rest of the *TW3* cast, Roy Kinnear's later acting career included appearances with the Royal Shakespeare Company and the National Theatre, and he was in the Beatles film *Help!* He died in 1988. Kenneth Cope went on to star in *Randall and Hopkirk Deceased* before leaving showbiz to run a restaurant in Oxfordshire. He is now acting again, in *Brookside*. Lance Percival will still oblige with a topical calypso, but these days he mainly concentrates on after-dinner speaking, and writing scripts for corporate events.

Millicent Martin was given her own television show, *Mainly Millicent*, and appeared in a sitcom, *From a Bird's Eye View*. Then she returned to stage musicals, and was in the original *Side by Side by Sondheim*. Three times married (her first husband was singer Ronnie Carroll), she now lives in America, where she has been playing a wealthy European woman, Miss Faversham, in the hugely popular soap opera *Days of Our Lives*. 'People still remember me most for *TW3*,' she says. 'I loved the show … They were some of the happiest days of my life.' Bernard Levin, on the other hand, has always refused to talk about *TW3*: 'It was a long time ago and I have nothing to say.' He left the *Daily Mail* in 1971 to write a column for *The Times*, which continued (with breaks) for more than twenty-five years.

After his television satire shows Ned Sherrin became a film producer for a while, beginning with *The Virgin Soldiers* (1968), and also wrote television plays with Caryl Brahms. These days he works mainly in the theatre – he directed Keith Waterhouse's *Jeffrey Bernard is Unwell* in 1989 (and in a recent revival) – and is still within the BBC fold, having hosted the Radio 4 chat show *Loose Ends* for many years.

David Frost finally got his knighthood in 1993, long after Barry Humphries awarded Edna Everage the DBE.

As Dudley Moore rose to stardom, Peter Cook's career slowly fizzled out, though most of his friends still found him the funniest man in the world. Nick Luard says of him, 'Peter didn't go into a decline. He was simply bored. He found too much absurdity, too much pretension, too much vanity, and in the end he couldn't really be bothered.' After Cook had drunk himself to death in 1995, Alan Bennett gave the address at his memorial service at Hampstead Parish Church, describing him as 'a figure from the Parables, a publican, a sinner, but never a Pharisee'. So, in a way, the story of satire in the 1960s ends, as it began, with Bennett giving a sermon; this time a real one.

Bibliography

....

Interviews with HC

Bassett, John *19 January 1999*
Bennett, Alan *13 January 1999*
Berry, Adrian *6 June 1998*
Bird, John *16 February 1999*
Booker, Christopher *1 March 1999*
Bron, Eleanor *17 March 1999*
Callil, Carmen *3 March 1999*
Cleese, John *5 April 1999*
Cope, Kenneth *18 March 1999*
Donaldson, William *10 March 1999*
Duncan, John (Jack) *14 January 1999*
Fortune, John *4 February 1999*
Frayn, Michael *27 January 1999*
Garland, Nicholas *9 March 1999*
Geidt, Jeremy *1 April 1999* (written material)
Gillespie, Robert *9 March 1999*
Humphries, Barry *7 June 1999*
Ingrams, Richard *25 January 1999; and 10 October 1998 (interview by HC with Harry Thompson at Cheltenham Festival of Literature)*

Kaufman, Gerald *10 March 1999*
Kernan, David *8 April 1999*
Lang, Ian (Rt Hon Lord Lang of Monkton) *4 February 1999*
Law, Roger *17 March 1999*
Lewis, Peter *8 March 1999*
Luard, Nicholas *17 May 1999*
Lycett Green, Candida *28 March 1999*
MacLehose, Christopher *27 June 1998*
Martin, Millicent *24 April 1999*
Miller, Jonathan *8 February 1999*
Percival, Lance *23 February 1999*
Ponsonby, Robert *16 January 1999*
Roberts, Adam *25 May 1998*
Shallcross, Alan *19 May 1998*
Sherrin, Ned *27 January 1999*
Simpson, Carole *16 April 1999*
Steadman, Ralph *22 March 1999*
Usborne, Peter *28 April 1999*
Waugh, Auberon *17 March 1997*
Wells, John *5 May 1997*

Books and articles

Appignanesi, Lisa, *The Cabaret* (Studio Vista, 1975)
Bennett, Alan, *The Writer in Disguise* (Faber and Faber, 1985)
Bennett, Alan, *Writing Home* (Faber and Faber, rev. edn, 1997)
Bennett, Alan, Peter Cook, Jonathan Miller, and Dudley Moore, *The Complete Beyond the Fringe*, with an introduction by Michael Frayn, edited by Roger Wilmut (Mandarin, 1993)
Bergan, Ronald, *Beyond the Fringe... and Beyond: A Critical Biography of Alan Bennett, Peter Cook, Jonathan Miller and Dudley Moore* (Virgin Publishing, 1989)

Booker, Christopher, *The Neophiliacs: A Study of the Revolution in English Life in the Fifties and Sixties* (Collins, 1969)

Bron, Eleanor, *The Pillow Book of Eleanor Bron, or An Actress Despairs* (Jonathan Cape, 1985)

Bruce, Lenny, *How to Talk Dirty and Influence People*, with an introduction by Kenneth Tynan (Peter Owen, 1966)

Carpenter, Humphrey, *OUDS: A Centenary History of the Oxford University Dramatic Society, 1885–1985* (Oxford University Press, 1985)

Cook, Lin (ed.), *Something Like Fire: Peter Cook Remembered* (Methuen, 1996)

Enfield, Harry, *Harry Enfield and His Humorous Chums* (Penguin, 1997)

Frost, David, *An Autobiography: Part One: From Congregations to Audiences* (HarperCollins, 1993)

Frost, David, and Ned Sherrin (eds.), *That Was The Week That Was* (W.H. Allen, 1963)

Hewison, Robert, *Footlights! A Hundred Years of Cambridge Comedy* (Methuen, 1983)

Humphries, Barry, *More Please* (Penguin, 1993)

Ingrams, Richard (ed.), *The Life and Times of Private Eye* (Penguin, 1971)

Jelavich, Peter, *Berlin Cabaret* (Harvard University Press, 1993)

Johnston, John, *The Lord Chamberlain's Blue Pencil* (Hodder & Stoughton, 1990)

Lessing, Doris, *Walking in the Shade: Volume Two of My Autobiography, 1949–1962* (HarperCollins, 1997)

Levin, Bernard, *The Pendulum Years: Britain and the Sixties* (Jonathan Cape, 1970)

McKay, Peter, *Inside Private Eye* (Fourth Estate, 1986)

Marnham, Patrick, *The Private Eye Story: The First 21 Years* (Fontana/Collins, 1983)

Marwick, Arthur, *The Sixties: Cultural Revolution in Britain, France, Italy and the United States, c. 1958–c. 1974* (Oxford University Press, 1998)

Melly, George, *Revolt into Style: The Pop Arts* (Oxford University Press, 1970; rp 1989)

Rushton in the Eye, a *Private Eye* special number [n.d.; 1997]

Miller, Jonathan, 'Can English Satire Draw Blood?', *Observer*, 1 October 1961

Morley, Lewis, *Black and White Lies* (Angus & Robertson, 1992)

O'Farrell, John, *Things Can Only Get Better: Eighteen Miserable Years in the Life of a Labour Supporter 1979–1997* (Doubleday, 1998)

Paskin, Barbara, *The Authorised Biography of Dudley Moore* (Sidgwick & Jackson, 1997)

Raphael, Frederic, 'Son of Enoch', *Prospect*, June 1997 [a short story in which Jonathan Miller appears in thin disguise as 'Methuselah']

Romain, Michel, *A Profile of Jonathan Miller* (Cambridge University Press, 1992)

Schiff, Stephen, 'The Poet of Embarrassment' [profile of Alan Bennett], *New Yorker*, 6 September 1993

Segel, Harold, *Turn-of-the-Century Cabaret* (Columbia University Press, 1987)

Sherrin, Ned, *A Small Thing – Like an Earthquake* (Weidenfeld & Nicolson, 1983)

Tennant, Emma, *Girlitude: A Memoir of the 50s and 60s* (Jonathan Cape, 1999)

Thompson, Douglas, *Dudley Moore on the Couch* (Little, Brown, 1996)

Thompson, Harry, *Richard Ingrams: Lord of the Gnomes* (Heinemann, 1994)

Thompson, Harry, *Peter Cook: A Biography* (Hodder & Stoughton, 1997)

Wells, John, 'Satire: The End of the Party', *Scotsman*, 25 September 1965

Wilmut, Roger, *From Fringe to Flying Circus: Celebrating a Unique Generation of Comedy, 1960–1980* (Methuen, 1982)

Television and radio broadcasts and commercial recordings

Beyond the Fringe cast interviewed by Wilfred De'Ath, recorded 18 October 1961 (BBC Sound Archives LP 27094)

Cartoons, Lampoons and Buffoons, BBC Radio 4, 8, 15, 22 and 29 April and 6 May 1998: series on satire

The Establishment, recorded live in the UK and the USA (1992), with John Bird, Eleanor Bron, John Fortune and Jeremy Geidt (EMI Comedy Classics double cassette 077 7 99839 4 0)

That Was The Week That Was (TW3), video-cassettes (VHS), BBC Broadcast Archives

Third Ear, BBC Radio 3, 29 March 1988 (BBC Sound Archives T87406): Alan Bennett interviewed by Paul Bailey

Willie's Wake, BBC Radio 4, 31 May 1997: reminiscences of Willie Rushton

Unpublished scripts and other archival material

Beyond the Fringe (1960), script of the August 1960 production at the Lyceum Theatre, Edinburgh (Lord Chamberlain's Playscripts (LCP), held by the British Library Department of Manuscripts)

Beyond the Fringe (1961), script of the April 1961 production at the Arts Theatre, Cambridge (Lord Chamberlain's Playscripts (LCP), held by the British Library Department of Manuscripts)

Booker, Christopher, 'David Frost: The Man Who Rose Without Trace', and 'The Rise and Fall of the Super-Egotists' (texts supplied by Christopher Booker)

That Was The Week That Was, Films 47/48, TV Talks Scripts, BBC Written Archives Centre (WAC), Caversham Park, Reading

Source Notes

. . . .

Sources are identified by the first words quoted. When two or more quotations from the same source follow each other with little intervening narrative, I have used only the first quotation for identification. Sources clearly identified in the text are not cited in the notes. Texts in the Lord Chamberlain's Playscripts collection (LCP), held in the British Library Department of Manuscripts, are identified by year and file number, and material held at the BBC Written Archives Centre (WAC) are identified, where possible, by file number.

Preface
'It's an interesting story', Jonathan Miller interview

Prologue: Permission to speak
'Satire is what closes', Sherrin, *A Small Thing*, 88
'I hear that you', ibid.
'Continental conception of human society', L.C.B. Seaman, *Post-Victorian Britain, 1902–1951* (Routledge, 1966), 423
'He was triumphantly going', Jonathan Miller interview
'That London of the late 1940s', Lessing, *Walking in the Shade*, 4f.
'In cinemas and theatres', ibid.
'attempt to echo the decade', Tennant, *Girlitude*, 10f.
'We had queued', ibid., 30
'Prince Charles, six next month', *Daily Herald*, 5 October 1954
'Shortly afterwards, other verses', *Private Eye*, 7 August 1964
'The Society of Old Seafordians', *The Times*, 1 January 1955
'Mr Mailer is a writer', quoted in *The Sunday Times* books section, 6 September 1998
'Is it a book you would even wish', *The Times*, 21 October 1960
'English upper-class girls', Melly, *Revolt into Style*, 165
'You bought what your parents', Miller interview
'The Young – Who are the Young?', *Daily Herald*, 7 October 1954
'I felt increasingly distressed', Adrian Walker, *Six Campaigns: National Servicemen on Active Service 1948–1960* (Leo Cooper, 1993), 4
'Living with them', ibid., 18
'never really understood', ibid., 26
'I spent life in a complete cross-section', ibid., 47

'The Army changed me immensely', B.S. Johnson, *All Bull: The National Servicemen*
    (Alison & Busby, 1973), 24
'burlesque ... interlarded with scenes of horror', ibid., 257
'Most of all, best of all', ibid., 24
'Permission to speak', *Radio Times*, 20–26 February 1993
'Authority was everything', Nicholas Luard interview
'a firm stand', Hugh Thomas, *The Suez Affair* (Weidenfeld & Nicolson, rev. edn, 1986),
    41
'We can't have this malicious swine', ibid., 45
'This is Munich all over again', ibid., 66
'Egypt's challenge', ibid., 56
'THIS IS FOLLY', *Daily Herald*, 31 October 1956
'Eden must go' and 'deep anxiety', *Daily Telegraph*, 2 November 1956
'very great risks', *The Times*, 31 October 1956
'bollocks', Johnson, op. cit., 11
'A squalid episode', *Daily Herald*, 7 November 1956
'the folly of the government's crime', *Isis*, 7 November 1956
'of colossal ferocity', Michael Frayn interview
'Suez ... was a shock', *New Statesman*, 21 June 1958
'He's ... still casting well-fed glances', John Osborne, *Look Back in Anger* (Faber and
    Faber, 1957), 15f., 17, 34f.
'To Charles and me', John Braine, *Room at the Top* (Mandarin, 1990), 16
'That's what all these', Alan Sillitoe, *Saturday Night and Sunday Morning* (Flamingo,
    1994), 36
'a very angry young man', Harry Ritchie, *Success Stories: Literature and the Media in
    England, 1950–59* (Faber and Faber, 1988), 26f.
'a rambling survey', Booker, *The Neophiliacs*, 112
'Somehow, Osborne and I were supposed to prove', Colin Wilson, introduction to *The
    Outsider* (Indigo, 1997), 7
'a new animal', Melly, 26
'Before, when the men came back from work', Lessing, 16
'The literary world ha[d] welcomed', Tennant, 112
'The bearded boys in blue jeans', Herb Greer, *Mud Pie: The CND Story* (Max Parrish,
    1964), 36
'The marches united the whole spectrum', Lessing, 266
'The next war will destroy', *Isis*, 26 February 1958
'all along the frontier', ibid.
'I believe that there is a real chance', *Isis*, 5 March 1958
'Gaitskell and Macmillan came close', Dennis Potter, *The Glittering Coffin* (Gollancz,
    1960), 161
'the struggle of the 1950s', Tennant, 94
'Let's be frank about it', Alistair Horne, *Macmillan 1957–1986: Volume II of the Official
    Biography* (Macmillan, 1989), 64
'Maybe the big emotional orgies', *Isis*, 4 June 1958

PART ONE: I've got a viper in this box

1 Doing silly turns

'The lodge of my college', Bennett, *Writing Home*, 502
'I was born and brought up', ibid., 592

'the Utility version', *London Review of Books*, 3–16 December 1981

'People ... think I'm sad ...', Schiff, 'The Poet of Embarrassment'

'I already knew at the age of five', Bennett, *Writing Home*, 3

'a telling phrase', ibid., 10

'they took my scout', ibid.

'When we were at home', ibid., 58f.

'They imagined that books', ibid., 12

'that great hopes', ibid., 593

'It wasn't old', Bennett, ibid., 500

'The families I read about', ibid., 5

'I always feel guilty', *Third Ear*, 29 March 1988

'my favourite', Bennett, *Writing Home*, 8

'music showed you how to live', *London Review of Books*, 1 January 1998

'I saw myself modestly ascending', ibid., 2 January 1997

'I thought life was going to be like', Alan Bennett, *Plays One: Forty Years On, Getting On, Habeas Corpus and Enjoy* (Faber and Faber, 1996), 174

'a fervent Anglican', Bennett, *Writing Home*, 191

'Easter at St Michael's', ibid., 198

'devoutly religious, a regular communicant', Alan Bennett, *Objects of Affection and Other Plays for Television* (British Broadcasting Corporation, 1982), 12

'an awful Tory', Schiff

'the only work of literature', *Man of Action*, BBC Radio 3, 20 October 1973 (BBC Sound Archives T51299)

'I ... thought I would be', Schiff

'it was touch and go', Bennett, *Writing Home*, 354

'the happiest time of my life', *Yorkshire Post*, 7 May 1977

'I actually didn't even mind', ibid.

'a cushy number', Bergan, *Beyond the Fringe*, 77

'the Russian soul', Bennett, *Writing Home*, 238

'the discipline was lax', *Yorkshire Post*, 7 May 1977

'What most people get at university', ibid.

'a congenial group', ibid.

'He wrote a few items', Michael Frayn interview

'I did something with Frayn', Alan Bennett interview

'He did it as a minor canon', Frayn interview

'If it was based on anybody', Bennett interview

'I think that until I went into the army', ibid.

'It would be easy to say', Schiff

'I had a hopeless crush', Bennett, *Writing Home*, 354

'I'd always been in love with guys', Schiff

'I suppose you could describe me', *Daily Mail*, 15 September 1993

'inward-looking', Bennett, *Writing Home*, 22f.

'I'm sure if there had been', Wilmut, *From Fringe to Flying Circus*, 8f.

'As a repository of actual suggestions', Bennett, *Writing Home*, 23f.

'Thir, Pleathe can we have', Exeter College JCR Suggestions Book, Michelmas Term 1955

'Sir, A *serious*', ibid.

'Marcel Proust had a very poor figure', ibid., Hilary Term 1957

'There were some other verses', Bennett interview

'what in a later age', Hewison, *Footlights!*, 11

'a living person', John Johnston, *The Lord Chamberlain's Blue Pencil* (Hodder & Stoughton, 1990), 110

....

'Oh it's going just a bit too far', Hewison, 35
'trenchant enough to rouse', ibid., 36
'An Act of 1737', Hewison, 2f.
'The admission of smoking', ibid., 14
'imitations of various musical instruments', ibid., 23
'Sketches of the crudest ribaldry', Carpenter, *OUDS*, 87
'just a dramatized version', Bennett, *Writing Home*, 24
'If one had to point', ibid., 64, 68
'It's not based on him at all', Bennett interview
'Once I had hit on the form', *Vanity Fair*, December 1995
'regular feature', Bennett, *Writing Home*, 24
'They were so obscene', Bennett interview
'They were incredibly, magically funny', Frayn interview
'my slightly sickening obsession', *London Review of Books*, 1 January 1998
'Art ... begins with imitation', Bennett, *Writing Home*, xiii
'It *is* contradictory', Schiff
'My room-mate was from Eton', Harry Thompson, *Richard Ingrams*, 82
'When I was an undergraduate', Alan Shallcross interview
'fluke result', *London Review of Books*, 1 January 1998
'doing his shy best', Bergan, 79
'breathing space', *London Review of Books*, 1 January 1998
'Nobody knew anything about him', Andrew Hichens to HC, 27 April 1998
'And there was a very very funny one', John Wells interview
'I had a sort of molecular diagram', Bennett interview
'I thought it was infinitely better', Wells interview

2 This suet and this sangfroid will get you nowhere
'From Southampton', John Wells interview
'silent ... sober ... still a child', Harry Thompson, *Richard Ingrams*, 32
'Willie knew quite a lot of it', Richard Ingrams interview
'The other person beside Beachcomber', ibid.
'From the earliest days', *Willie's Wake* (BBC Radio 4); *Rushton in the Eye*, 1997
'He'd dash his drawings off', Christopher MacLehose interview
'Herbert "Bertie" Rushton', *Rushton in the Eye*, 1997
'Good heavens, no', Harry Thompson, *Ingrams*, 35
'I never thought Willie changed', *Rushton in the Eye*; *Willie's Wake*
'I understand now', *Salopian*, December 1952
'They called the Bishops naughty names', ibid., 31 May 1953
'He was the reason I pursued comedy', Harry Thompson, *Ingrams*, 42
'He kept the rules', ibid., 46
'The more I saw of Ingrams', ibid., 2f.
'an ultra-traditionalist', ibid., 22
'the stocks were the answer to everything', *Salopian*, 1 March 1953
'The secretary said', ibid., 13 December 1953
'R.R. Ingrams was very effective', ibid., 30 May 1954
'Rushton ... specializes in the impersonation', ibid., 24 July 1955
'It has now been working', ibid., 1 March 1953
'Shrewsbury was isolated', Harry Thompson, *Ingrams*, 35
'They say that these are', *Salopian*, 19 December 1954
'There is a tribe', ibid., 23 July 1954
'*total* hero-worship', Harry Thompson, *Ingrams*, 44

'taking things too seriously', ibid.
'He delivered the most ferocious attack', ibid.
'a light interlude', *Salopian*, 6 November 1955
'He had spectacles and golden curls', Harry Thompson, *Ingrams*, 44
'It's true that I was keen on geology', Christopher Booker interview
'Booker is the only man I know', Harry Thompson, *Ingrams*, 44
'Richard's invention of the concept of the Pseud', Christopher Booker interview
'It was then the turn of Mr Rushton and Mr Ingrams', *Salopian*, 25 February 1956
'I wrote an editorial', Booker interview
'All you had to do', Harry Thompson, *Ingrams*, 55
'We neither of us made it', *Willie's Wake*
'with that satirical and contemptuous attitude', Harry Thompson, *Ingrams*, 55
'deep shock', ibid.
'I saw him playing the harmonium', Wells interview
'the officers weren't really fit', Harry Thompson, *Ingrams*, 59
'It was the first time I had met my fellow man', *Oldie*, July 1997
'original, humorous and satirical articles', *Punch*, week ending 17 July 1841
'Its position can best be defined', John Sutherland's introduction to his edition of W.M.
    Thackeray, *The Book of Snobs* (University of Queensland Press, 1978), 9
'An original factor was Mark Lemon's system', ibid., 10
'O! men with sisters dear', *Oxford Dictionary of Quotations* (Oxford University Press,
    3rd edn, 1980), 255
'Why is a loud laugh', *Punch*, week ending 9 October 1841
'We have washed, combed, clothed', Robert C. Elliott, *The Power of Satire: Magic,
    Ritual, Art* (Princeton University Press, 1960), 270, quoting Thackeray's 1854 essay
    'John Leech's Pictures of Life and Character'
'the development of the nineteenth-century English public school', Miller, 'Can English
    Satire Draw Blood?'
'Our deliberations on the week's cartoon', *Private Eye*, 7 August 1964

3 Joined at the hip
'I heard this voice saying "Foot"', Harry Thompson, *Richard Ingrams*, 78
'eccentrics and aesthetes', ibid., 80
'But they were too nervous', Adrian Berry interview
'The aim and purpose of this magazine', *Parson's Pleasure*, 28 May 1958
'Kenneth Baker', ibid., 2 June 1958
'His frequent displays of histrionics', ibid., 10 June 1958
'the opening meet', ibid., 5 November 1958
'A Day with the Drag Hounds', ibid., 12 November 1958
'I remember Adrian Berry', Richard Ingrams interview
'It brought home to me', Harry Thompson, *Ingrams*, 84
'There are too many foreigners', *Parson's Pleasure*, 9 May 1959
'Who is the Provok'd Wife', ibid.
'Razor, played by Richard Ingrams', ibid., n.d. [spring 1960]
'unhappily neither of these', ibid., 9 May 1959
'We would like to welcome', ibid., n.d. [summer 1959]
'I've always been a rotten editor', Harry Thompson, *Ingrams*, 74f.
'In conversation', ibid., 35
'No, no, I insist', *Parson's Pleasure*, n.d. [October 1959]
'When we tried to enclose the gnomes', ibid.
'The story so far', ibid., n.d. [November 1959]

'someone who lives in Africa', Berry interview

'I made a sort of takeover bid', Auberon Waugh interview

'Eventually I realized that *Parson's Pleasure*', Berry interview

'At school, I'd always thought', Peter Usborne interview

'a progressive, meaningful, distinctive', *Mesopotamia*, May 1959

'He was nearly run over', *Willie's Wake* (BBC Radio 4)

'Briefly I served under Michael Foot', introduction to *Willie Rushton's Great Moments of History* (Victoria & Albert Museum, 1984)

'I remember him always wearing', *Rushton in the Eye*, 1997

'arrogant', Harry Thompson, *Ingrams*, 63

'Outrageously handsome ex-Gurkha', quoted in ibid., 88

'I was what was called', ibid., 79

'Political satire, cartoons and captions', *Mesopotamia*, n.d. [1959]

'All generations of Corrodians', ibid.

'I am tall and dark', ibid.

'DO YOUR FRIENDS SMELL?', ibid.

'Coming from Eastbourne College', Wells interview

'an instinctive feel for the bogus', Wells, 'Satire: The End of the Party'

'Well, I'd been brought up', Wells interview

'You there – that guard over there!', Roger Wilmut and Jimmy Grafton, *The Goon Show Companion* (Robson Books, 1976), 27

'The English Channel, 1941', Spike Milligan, *The Goon Show Scripts* (Woburn Press, 1972), 23

'SEAGOON: Major Bloodnok', ibid., 27

'MORIARTY: My socks keep coming down', Spike Milligan, *The Book of the Goons* (Robson Books, 1974), 92

'The Goons did an enormous amount', Jonathan Miller interview

'Colonel Sir Ethelred Cabbage', *Mesopotamia*, n.d. [summer 1960]

'sold like the clappers', Harry Thompson, *Ingrams*, 91

'What's your name?', ibid., 92

'my new glasses!', *Mesopotamia*, n.d. [summer 1960]

'They were all brilliant and funny', Caroline Seebohm to HC, 29 May and 20 September 1998

'There was a little boy called Gnittie', *Mesopotamia*, n.d. [autumn 1960]

'Willie was marking time', *Rushton in the Eye*

'We were lying there in the sunshine', Harry Thompson, *Ingrams*, 111

'Professor Kneale's treatment', *Isis*, 25 January 1961

'had a nervous breakdown', Wells interview

'Censored by the Proctors', *Isis*, 1 February 1961

'a sense of outrage among graver minds', quoted ibid., 8 February 1961

'agitation', ibid., 15 February 1961

4 A little bit of something for everyone

'I paid a disastrous visit', *London Review of Books*, 4 September 1997

'Thereafter I used to go down and see him', ibid., and Bennett, *Writing Home*, 356

'I could never find sufficient comments', ibid., 25

'I knew Alan already', Adam Roberts interview

'long practice of imitating sermons', Exeter College JCR Suggestions Book, Michelmas Term 1957

'I was never sure', Alan Bennett interview

'This side of the book', Exeter College JCR Suggestions Book, Michelmas Term 1958

'daunting', Bennett, *Writing Home*, 27
'I found that, in sitting down', *Observer*, 28 May 1967
'total silence', Bergan, *Beyond the Fringe*, 80
'The only thing that fitted me', *The Times*, 27 November 1978
'The professor kicked off the interview', Bennett, *Writing Home*, 562
'making people laugh', ibid., 25
'What was Intimate Revue?', Sandy Wilson, *I Could Be Happy* (Michael Joseph, 1975), 129f.
'Directors literally insisted', Wells, 'Satire: The End of the Party'
'Half-past ten and curtain time', *After the Show* (LCP 1950/57)
'Oh you've all read in the Old Testament', *Cakes and Ale* (LCP 1953/47)
'immensely old', Bennett, *Writing Home*, 26
'In our cottage by the sea', *Better Never* (LCP 1959/33)
'Good evening. I'm a scientist', ibid.
'It was an unforgivable thing', Bergan, 80
'done on a shoestring', *Observer*, 13 September 1959
'the sharp, acid wit', *Daily Herald*, 23 February 1962
'a great success', Bennett, *Writing Home*, 26
'a testing ground for subsequent London productions', *Observer*, 30 August 1959
'put on a revue', Bennett, *Writing Home*, 26

5 Danny Kaye of Cambridge

'a bit pompous', Bergan, *Beyond the Fringe*, 5
'And it was all going fine', Robert Ponsonby interview
'My grandmother was a Gaiety Girl', John Bassett interview
'We didn't seem poor', Douglas Thompson, *Dudley Moore on the Couch*, 49
'My mother didn't want me to feel', ibid., 48
'I was a very pompous little boy', ibid., 50
'I had to stand on a pile of bricks', Paskin, *The Authorised Biography of Dudley Moore*, 25
'I was quite attuned to the possibility', Douglas Thompson, 47
'I went right from the midwife', ibid., 10f., 45
'There was I', Paskin, 37
'The toughest part that first year', Douglas Thompson, 59
'He had an unforced, unpretentious wit', Paskin, 36
'Then in my third year', Douglas Thompson, 60
'Dudley was a soloist', Paskin, 55
'hilarious', John Bassett to HC, 3 February 1999
'and I recommended another person', Douglas Thompson, 57
'saw Alan doing cabaret', Bassett interview
'had a very early established feeling', Bergan, 57
'Bergson claimed that we laugh', John Durant and Jonathan Miller (eds.), *Laughing Matters: A Serious Look at Humour* (Longman Scientific & Technical, 1988), 10
'I am Jewish', Bergan, 58
'There were strange, long-delayed train journeys', ibid., 58
'a giant, Darwinian struggle', *Listener*, 10 February 1977
'a world of such wonderful', Romain, *A Profile of Jonathan Miller*, 21, 24f.
'When I was thirteen', *Observer*, undated cutting [1967], in BBC News Information Archive
'words jostled, and sometimes jammed', Raphael, 'Son of Enoch'
'built like an Anglepoise', Bergan, 56, 58

'eloquent hands', Raphael
'It was a very important part of my life', Bergan, 58f.
'It's gloom, gloom, gloom', *Out of the Blue* (LCP 1954/33)
'Pandemonium reigns supreme', Hewison, *Footlights!*, 115
'The South of England will move', *Out of the Blue*
'In the third of our series', *Beyond the Fringe* (1961), 119f.
'asked to request a tune', *Out of the Blue*
'a mimic the like of whom', *The Sunday Times*, 11 July 1954
'DANNY KAYE OF CAMBRIDGE', *Daily Telegraph*, 7 June 1955
'Enter: Talk in a homely voice', *Between the Lines* (LCP 1955/32)
'His portrayal of the sword Excalibur', *Daily Telegraph*, 29 June 1955
'imitations of Isaiah Berlin', *Between the Lines*
'But what *were* his dying words?', *Beyond the Fringe* (1961), 135
'even funnier', *Daily Telegraph*, 29 June 1955
'I was interested in higher disorders', Bergan, 62
'Jonathan has a very good double act', ibid.
'A hilarious turn', ibid., 63
'This man Bassett came and asked', Miller interview
'I did it because it was going to be', Romain, 26
'I said Peter Cook', Miller interview

6 At right-angles to all the comedy we'd heard
'Are you *virgo intacta*?', *Pieces of Eight* (LCP 1959/36)
'I've got a viper in this box', ibid.
'There was this astonishing, strange, glazed', Harry Thompson, *Peter Cook*, 77
'My father used to receive news', ibid., 2
'He was a total stranger', ibid., 10
'I disliked being away from home', ibid., 18
'a bit of a loner', ibid., 29
'He told me quite seriously', to HC, 20 September 1998
'It was the first time it had been done complete', John Bird interview
'Peter exemplified the idea', ibid.
'I said I'd only do it', ibid.
'has always been very political', John Fortune interview
'At Cambridge I was much more interested', Bird interview
'the funniest man I'd ever seen', Harry Thompson, *Cook*, 63
'probably the worst producer ever', William Donaldson interview
'It was something like half a million', ibid.
'This is a member', *Here is the News* (LCP 1960/24)
'We opened in midsummer in Coventry', Lance Percival interview
'the jolly opening', Sheila Hancock, *Ramblings of an Actress* (Hutchinson, 1987), 57f.
'terrible gloomy stuff', Donaldson interview
'a revue that Moira Lister and David Kernan were in', Ned Sherrin interview

PART TWO: Boom

1 Funnier than anything we had ever seen
'famously difficult', Geoffrey Grigson (ed.), *The Oxford Book of Satirical Verse* (Oxford University Press, 1980), v
'Satire is a sort of glass', Jonathan Swift, Preface to *The Battle of the Books* (1704)

'satura quidem tota nostra est', Quintilian, *Institutiones Oratiorae*, x.1.93

'the greatest monster in the land', Aristophanes, *The Wasps, The Poet and the Women,
    The Frogs* (Penguin Classics, 1964), 76

'Whenever a person deserved', Horace, *Satires and Epistles*, translated by Niall Rudd
    (Penguin, 1979), 55

'Don't you want to cram', Juvenal, *The Sixteen Satires*, translated by Peter Green
    (Penguin Books, 1974), 67f.

'very keen on Juvenal', *Cartoons, Lampoons and Buffoons* (BBC Radio 4)

'The hungry Judges soon the Sentence sign', Alexander Pope, *The Rape of the Lock*, III:
    21–2

'horrible, shameful, unmanly', Victoria Glendinning, *Jonathan Swift* (Hutchinson,
    1998), 253

'We had intended you to be', *Oxford Dictionary of Quotations* (Oxford University Press,
    3rd edn, 1980), 39

'I should very much like to join you', Peter Cook to John Bassett, 12 January 1960,
    courtesy of John Bassett

'on Goodge Street', Bennett, *Writing Home*, 77

'an Italian restaurant in Swiss Cottage', *The Times*, 27 November 1978

'near to University College Hospital', John Bassett interview

'We met…in a "cayf"', *Daily Express*, 16 May 1961

'We were all jealously guarding', Harry Thompson, *Peter Cook*, 90

'He dressed out of Sportique', Bennett, *Writing Home*, 77

'As soon as Peter sat down', Harry Thompson, *Cook*, 91

'I was there under false pretences', ibid.

'completely mute in front of these intellectual giants', ibid.

'doing a Groucho Marx walk', Bassett interview

'played the fool', Wilmut, *From Fringe to Flying Circus*, 8

'You have *carte blanche*', Robert Ponsonby interview

'because it came from Ponsonby', Alan Bennett interview

'Four very funny men', *Queen*, 15 February 1960

'We wrote a lot of our own monologues', Jonathan Miller interview

'We had various meetings', Bennett interview

'Peter wrote most of it', Douglas Thompson, *Dudley Moore on the Couch*, 57f.

'there was no unified approach', Harry Thompson, *Cook*, 92

'We do not gather our material', *Daily Herald*, 13 May 1961

'At the moments in writing the script', *Beyond the Fringe* cast interview (BBC)

'We don't intend to be specifically didactic', *Daily Express*, 16 May 1961; *Daily Herald*,
    13 May 1961

'but I never had the Latin', Bennett et al., *The Complete Beyond the Fringe*, 97

'surreptitious right-wing sketch', Wells, 'Satire: The End of the Party'

'They were fooling about on the stage', ibid.; John Wells interview

'It has always seemed to be', Bergan, *Beyond the Fringe*, 10

'We didn't come from the straightforward theatrical tradition', Romain, *A Profile of
    Jonathan Miller*, 25; *Beyond the Fringe* cast interview (BBC)

'Beckett's ragamuffin metaphysics', Jonathan Miller, 'Can English Satire Draw Blood?'

'softened and blurred', ibid.

'delighted…a hundred chorus girls', Wilmut, 12

'they wanted to have Julie Christie', Ned Sherrin interview

'It was just a schoolboy dream', Bassett interview

'American cabaret presents a different aspect', Miller, 'Can English Satire Draw Blood?'

'Mort Sahl is thirty-four', *New Statesman*, 21 July 1961

'Mel Brooks takes a swipe', Miller, 'Can English Satire Draw Blood?'

'A lot of people, like myself', Mort Sahl, *The Future Lies Ahead* (HMV CLP 1252)

'It's a good question', Miller interview

'The idea of somebody just *talking*', John Bird interview

'We were creatures of the post-war generation', Romain, 25

'*man*'s cigarette', ibid., 30

'love' and 'darling', *Beyond the Fringe* (1960)

'fair game in sketches', Johnston, *The Lord Chamberlain's Blue Pencil*, 110

'PETER: Who is that fellow', *Beyond the Fringe* (1960)

'THE DAILY MIRACLE', ibid.

'Don't let's take any notice', Bennett et al., *The Complete Beyond the Fringe*, 27

'I've a dreadful feeling', ibid., 154

'but Jonathan added things', Bennett interview

'BLEANEY: Well, I think we might make a start', *Beyond the Fringe* (1960)

'I still hadn't got one', Bennett et al., *The Complete Beyond the Fringe*, 157f.

'That's what they call the Royal Box', ibid., 20

'Good God, J.G.!', *Pieces of Eight* (LCP 1959/36)

'it had never occurred to any of us', John Fortune interview

'Good evening. I have recently been travelling', Bennett et al., *The Complete Beyond the Fringe*, 54

'PESKER: Now, you may realize, Johann', *Beyond the Fringe* (1960)

'I had to take my clothes off', Bennett interview

'Let us, in the silence together', *Beyond the Fringe* (1960)

'on a kind of automatic pilot', Bennett interview

'A: Come in', *Beyond the Fringe* (1960)

'ALL: (*Chanting*) Now is the end', Bennett et al., *The Complete Beyond the Fringe*, 113

'I think we did', Romain, 25

'In any case, they really directed', Bassett interview

'saw an early rehearsal', Ponsonby interview

'the person who really impressed me', Richard Ingrams interview

'It had opened with no fanfares', *Cartoons* (BBC Radio 4); Billington to HC, 16 October 1998

'The first night at Edinburgh', Bassett interview

'long queues for returns', Bennett et al., *The Complete Beyond the Fringe*, 155

'The pleasingness of this revue', quoted in Wilmut, 12

'economy and ensemble sympathy', *Observer*, 28 August 1960

'touches of irrational genius', *The Sunday Times*, 28 August 1960

'I was sent up there', Peter Lewis interview

'So I went to see the four boys', ibid.

'I asked them', *Cartoons* (BBC Radio 4)

'Jonathan seemed to take the point', Billington to HC, 16 October 1998

'ever so relieved', Bennett interview

'earnest and rather evangelical', Wells, 'Satire: The End of the Party'

'the hit of the festival', Harry Thompson, *Cook*, 97

'rolling about and roaring', Wells, 'Satire: The End of the Party'

'Langdon had advised Peter Cook', William Donaldson interview

'My lasting regret', Ponsonby interview

'Only Dudley and I seemed to want', Bennett et al., *The Complete Beyond the Fringe*, 159

'Codron tried to persuade me', Donaldson interview

'The fair-haired one will have to go', Bennett et al., *The Complete Beyond The Fringe*, 154

'It's ten times what I'd be receiving', ibid., 155
'pretty mean, considering', Donaldson interview
'They threw everything in', Bassett interview
'We sat round a table', Miller interview
'*Two men sitting on couch*', *Beyond the Fringe* (1961)
'Jonathan Miller and myself', Bennett et al., *The Complete Beyond the Fringe*, 84
'because when I went up to Cambridge', Fortune interview
'PETER: Now, we shall receive', Bennett et al., *The Complete Beyond the Fringe*, 79
'a joke which brilliantly clamped', Harry Thompson, *Cook*, 93
'quite simply the funniest show', Romain, 138f.
'Only when confronted with the excellent', *Broadsheet*, 26 April 1961 (copy kindly lent
    by John Bassett)
'the seats were going up like pistol shots', Bennett, *Writing Home*, 321, 472
'ALAN: I had a pretty quiet war', Bennett et al., *The Complete Beyond the Fringe*, 74
'coming downstairs with a pipe', Bennett, *Writing Home*, 170
'nearly sent me to sleep', quoted in Bergan, 18
'We loved it, darlings', Bennett, *Writing Home*, 413
'The Fortune was a funny little theatre', Barry Humphries interview
'appropriately stark and gritty', Bennett, *Writing Home*, 593

2 It really is a Rolls

'If you have ever been tickled', *Daily Mail*, 11 May 1961
'the perfect revue', quoted in *The Sunday Times*, 14 May 1961 (advertisement on p. 41)
'We sent round a referendum', Bennett et al., *The Complete Beyond the Fringe*, 93
'unashamed, adult, provocative', *Evening Standard*, 11 May 1961
'cascades of delighted laughter', *Daily Telegraph*, 11 May 1961
'the kind of thing people will go to', quoted in *The Sunday Times*, 14 May 1961
    (advertisement on p. 41)
'the clichés of Shaftesbury Avenue', *The Times*, 11 May 1961
'the official opening of the Satirical Sixties', Bennett et al., *The Complete Beyond the
    Fringe*, 7
'Moral Re-Gurgitation', *Guardian*, 12 May 1961
'To readers of this newspaper', ibid.
'I suppose there were satirical elements', Michael Frayn interview
'Bernard's father was a Camden Town tailor', Peter Lewis interview
'Several of the items', Bennett et al., *The Complete Beyond the Fringe*, 8f.
'four young men, till recently undergraduates', *The Sunday Times*, 14 May 1961
'as one Scottish old-age pensioner', Bennett et al., *The Complete Beyond the Fringe*, 55
'That's the rule', ibid., 82
'What if one of our American friends', ibid., 81
'God is as old as he feels', ibid., 23
'They're not worth the fifteen shillings', ibid., 20
'Are you using "yes"', ibid., 50
'When I went up to Cambridge', *Vanity Fair*, December 1995
'the actor Sebastian Shaw', Nicholas Garland interview
'the best young play of its decade', Bergan, *Beyond the Fringe*, 22
'the theatre as a whole', Kathleen Tynan, *The Life of Kenneth Tynan* (Methuen, 1988),
    179
'The curtain rises on what might be', *Observer*, 14 May 1961
'shoved this banner', Wilmut, *From Fringe to Flying Circus*, 17
'Whether *Beyond the Fringe* was satire', Bennett, *Writing Home*, xii

'London's show-busiest restaurant', *Daily Herald*, 13 May 1961
'performs at the Fortune Theatre', *Daily Mail*, 16 May 1961
'It was just a hired car', Alan Bennett interview
'wasn't getting any better', Bennett, *Writing Home*, 28
'Every night after the curtain falls', *Daily Mail*, 11 July 1961
'and he hadn't really cared for it', Barry Humphries interview
'when *Beyond the Fringe* took off', Douglas Thompson, *Dudley Moore on the Couch*, 61
'At parties, we would recap', Billington to HC, 16 October 1998
'At my boarding school', *Vanity Fair*, December 1995
'Peter could tap a flow', Bennett, *Writing Home*, 78
'I did have a hand', Bennett et al., *The Complete Beyond the Fringe*, 154
'He gets bored very easily', Wilmut, 20
'He had a sort of pin-sharp accuracy', ibid.
'I felt that I was regarded', Schiff, 'The Poet of Embarrassment'
'were always getting on one another's nerves', *Observer*, 28 May 1967
'There was one sketch', Schiff
'I laughed more than I can ever remember', *Observer*, 28 May 1967
'Alan was delightfully shockable', Bennett et al., *The Complete Beyond the Fringe*, 159
'Peter therefore went several steps further', Wilmut, 20
'When I've a spare evening', Harry Thompson, *Peter Cook*, 114
'Macmillan buried his face', Wilmut, 20
'I priggishly refused', ibid.
'Albery and myself were pocketing', William Donaldson, *From Winchester to This*
    (Peter Owen, 1998), 11
'If we go to New York', *Daily Express*, 16 May 1961
'Peter Cook has sunk his savings', *Daily Mail*, 11 July 1961

3 Satire was in

'the great myth of the satire boom', Wells, 'Satire: The End of the Party'
'The show was terribly bad', Wilmut, *From Fringe to Flying Circus*, 6
'in a brittle voice, slightly monotonous', Harold B. Segel, *Turn-of-the-Century Cabaret*,
    159
'European satire thrived best', Miller, 'Can English Satire Draw Blood?'
'*That's* how deep we're in', Alex de Jonge, *The Weimar Chronicle: Prelude to Hitler*
    (Paddington Press, 1978), 16of.
'but they deal with the abuses', Miller, 'Can English Satire Draw Blood?'
'I lived in Germany for a year', John Wells interview
'I did a very odd National Service', Nicholas Luard interview
'We'd both seen political–satirical cabaret', Lin Cook, *Something Like Fire*, 39, 41
'Until one could escape', Miller, 'Can English Satire Draw Blood?'
'where we could be more outrageous', Harry Thompson, *Peter Cook*, 120
'the prize', *Evening Standard*, 7 August 1961
'The Establishment aims to be', *Daily Mail*, 11 July 1961
'Mort Sahlon', *Evening Standard*, 4 October 1961
'No plush, nothing Caribbean', *Observer*, 23 June 1961
'members who simply want', *The Sunday Times*, 1 October 1961
'from Macmillan to Macmillan', *Evening Standard*, 4 October 1961
'I directed two shows there', John Bird interview
'John was a brilliant director', Nicholas Garland interview
'When John Barton directed', John Fortune interview
'As far as I know', Jeremy Geidt interview

'I was an awestruck colonial', Barry Humphries interview
'The only suitable person', Fortune interview
'a boisterous, wonderful straight man', Bird interview
'great at falling over', Harry Thompson, *Cook*, 123
'There is no one to touch Jeremy', Bron, *The Pillow Book*, 14
'The people we liked', Bird interview
'the boys will come in', *Observer*, 23 June 1961
'The *Beyond the Fringe* team will do', *Evening Standard*, 4 October 1961
'Alan Bennett is really behind', *Daily Express*, 5 October 1961
'To help him concentrate', tape supplied by Jeremy Geidt
'two doctored wartime films', Geidt interview
'rather humiliating', Jonathan Miller interview
'Jonathan appeared more than once', Geidt interview
'Peter asked me to do the first night', John Wells interview
'He was incredibly well mannered', Harry Thompson, *Cook*, 122
'These are the people he aims to attack', *Evening Standard*, 4 October 1961
'People went there just to hear something', *Cartoons, Lampoons and Buffoons* (BBC
    Radio 4)
'I'm sure poor Jonathan thought', Fortune interview
'felt that this was not the stuff', *Observer*, 8 October 1961
'small enough to be stacked', *Daily Express*, 5 October 1961
'Television arc lights blazed', Wells, 'Satire: The End of the Party'
'angry members … who had arrived', *The Times*, 6 October 1961
'The thing I remember is John Sparrow', Alan Bennett interview
'To add to the confusion', Wells, 'Satire: The End of the Party'
'a good actress', Fortune interview
'roly-poly', *San Francisco Chronicle*, 14 August 1963
'sweaty brutes and insensitive rogues', *Observer*, 14 January 1962
'because of everybody trying to get in', Fortune interview
'objecting that Jesus was (a) higher up', Wilmut, 54
'FORTUNE: (*upper-class*) Eli, Eli, lama sabachthani', Geidt interview
'The punchline was me explaining', Fortune interview
'extremely bad taste', Wilmut, 54
'How do you do. My name is God', David Nobbs to HC, 5 February 1999
'Who is the only true, revealed, living God', *The Establishment* (EMI, 1992)
'another religious one, called "Strangler Martin"', Geidt interview
'Of course "Eli, Eli"', ibid.
'First of all, of course', *The Establishment* (EMI, 1992)
'The fact that we were going to open a club', Fortune interview
'The idea of the club', Bird interview
'which you'd recognize now', Wells interview
'I was rather disgusted by it', Peter Lewis interview
'Not at all, because none of us', Fortune interview
'My favourite poet was Pope', Bird interview
'He would start on some typical train of fantasy', Fortune interview
'subjects for satire', *The Times*, 6 October 1961
'MACMILLAN: I believe he was with Neville', *The Establishment* (EMI, 1992)
'Elections as such', ibid.
'I wasn't a mimic', Bird interview
'LINKMAN: Sports Report', *The Establishment* (EMI, 1992)
'seems very, very un-politically correct', Bird interview

'Jonathan saying that, as a doctor', Fortune interview
'Of course they'd love to be able', *The Establishment* (EMI, 1992)
'I did a bit of John Betjeman', Wells interview
'Now you must admit', *Late Night Final* (LCP 1961/40)
'I'd missed the last train', Wells interview
'sardine spirit', *The Sunday Times*, 8 October 1961
'the most brilliant number', *Observer*, 8 October 1961
'Oh! Oh!', *Beyond the Fringe* cast interview (BBC)
'There was an atmosphere', Cook, 69
'it was so fashionable', Bird interview
'We were introduced to him', Fortune interview
'most of the fashionable lunatics', Wells, 'Satire: The End of the Party'
'That's not what you're here for', Wilmut, 54f.
'grasshopper whimsy', *Observer*, 14 January 1962
'studying them as he talked', Cook, 47
'sub-Weillian', *Observer*, 14 January 1962
'they were just as good', Carole Simpson interview
'But then John lured me', Eleanor Bron interview
'She just was fantastic fun', Wells interview
'No, but I was less interested', Bron interview
'the boy seeing a girl home', Bron, *Pillow Book*, 12
'type-casting', Lewis interview
'BRON: It was awfully sweet of you', *The Establishment* (EMI, 1992)
'Not very much', Fortune interview
'I can remember Eleanor saying', Bennett interview
'the failure of one person', Bron interview
'TOBY: You need an image', 'Labour's New Image', attached to Cambridge script of
    Beyond the Fringe (LCP 1961/24)
'I remember they opened', Ned Sherrin interview
'always felt a little apart', Humphries interview
'a none-too-hilarious monologue', Humphries, *More Please*, 216f.
'He was terrified', Geidt interview
'It wasn't really directing', Garland interview
'surrounded by the best-looking birds', Harry Thompson, *Cook*, 127
'I come from the East Anglia', Roger Law interview
'this series of bloody great drawings', Garland interview
'a reasonably good and cheap lunch', Wells, 'Satire: The End of the Party'
'I was actually very annoyed', Harry Thompson, *Cook*, 133

4 Fortnightly lampoon
'I didn't think *Fringe* was anything', Richard Ingrams (Cheltenham) interview
'that it was possible to sell', Ingrams, *The Life and Times of Private Eye*, 7
'I thought Wells was much funnier', Richard Ingrams interview
'Staging is good and deceptively simple', *Scotsman*, 23 August 1961
'All the focus was on her', Ingrams interview
'a miserable job in a press bureau', Peter Usborne interview
'wasted my three years at Cambridge', Christopher Booker interview
'POLITICIAN WITH DRAWLING UPPER-CLASS VOICE', *The Best of Sellers* (Parlophone PMD
    1069)
'CHAIRMAN: Good afternoon', *Songs for Swinging Sellers* (Parlophone PMC 1111)
'I felt that I would like to do', Booker interview
'had a lot of jokes in common', Nicholas Garland interview

'spent most of my lunchtimes', Harry Thompson, *Richard Ingrams*, 120f.
'Booker, Rushton and a bit of John Wells', Marnham, *The Private Eye Story*, 26
'MESPOT RIDES AGAIN', ibid.
'by the time I got back', ibid.
'I had been looking at the Lord Kitchener', ibid.
'by that time everyone was so bored', Ingrams, *Life and Times*, 8
'I pounded out words', *Rushton in the Eye* (1997)
'When we produced the first *Private Eye*', Booker interview
'terrible stuff like Sellotape', Marnham, 30
'a fuck-up by the Light Entertainment department', Sherrin interview
'The decrepitude of *Punch*', Marnham, 29
'almost entirely the work', Ingrams, *Life and Times*, 8
'I've probably written more words', Booker interview
'sold in fashionable restaurants', Ingrams, *Life and Times*, 8
'set out for the part of London', Marnham, 29
'I would put a stack out', ibid.
'I expect he was just being kind', Candida Lycett Green interview
'The first copies of a magazine', Ingrams, *Life and Times*, 8
'You can imprison some of the people', *Private Eye*, 30 November 1961
'Yes, in diplomatic circles', ibid.
'We … survive by getting the hot potatoes', Marnham, 32
'Editor, typist: Christopher Booker', *Private Eye*, 7 February 1962
'Pressdram was simply the name', Marnham, 37
'This is a great day for PRIVATE EYE', *Private Eye*, 7 February 1962
'An engaging eight-page fortnightly', *Observer*, 18 February 1962
'PRIVATE EYE COMPETITION', *Private Eye*, 23 February 1962
'Within six issues, we were being approached', Booker interview
'*Private Eye* was very short of money', Michael Heseltine to HC, 12 March 1999
'cavernous', Ingrams, *Life and Times*, 9
'We never paid a penny's rent', Marnham, 35
'and subscribers ranged from', Ingrams, *Life and Times*, 9
'I was very worried about money', Marnham, 35
'Hew Wellbread', *Private Eye*, 23 March 1962
'Ambrose Weskit', ibid., 4 May 1962
'Bernard Unleaven', ibid., 13 July 1962
'I don't know whether Peter', Nicholas Luard interview
'I left them feeling that they wouldn't survive', Marnham, 37
'I had passed my Foreign Office exam', ibid., 35

5 Balls to the lot of them
'So Booker, Rushton and I', Ingrams, *The Life and Times of Private Eye*, 9
'I was working downstairs', Carmen Callil interview
'the very minor role', Richard Ingrams interview
'Unfortunately we only got 1 per cent', Jack Duncan interview
'I put what I'd inherited', Ingrams interview
'constant quarrelling', Marnham, *The Private Eye Story*, 38
'tense, desperately short-sighted', *Observer*, 8 July 1962 and 3 February 1963
'I was saying "This has got to be"', Christopher Booker interview
'everyone was suffering greatly', Marnham, 37
'smashed telephones', ibid., 41
'This story about my tearing things up', Booker interview

'Old mac, he's hed of Skool', *Private Eye*, 15 June 1962
'We've got to put the Tories in', *Observer*, 3 February 1963
'Sir, I was delighted to read', *Private Eye*, 27 July 1962
'Surrounded by a two-fold 12-foot-high electric fence', ibid., 18 May 1962
'One morning the editor of *Debrett*', ibid., 15 June 1962
'It was just fantastic being there', John Wells interview
'That's even true of the cartoons', Booker interview
'My idea was to take the job', Wells interview
'The silly man who owned the place', William Donaldson interview
'But we had a lot to drink', Wells interview
'We really got the bird', Ingrams interview
'Once I'd gritted my teeth', Wells interview
'We just did our old sketches', Ingrams interview
'Ingrams did his John Gielgud', Wilmut, *From Fringe to Flying Circus*, 59
'Stephen came over here', Ned Sherrin interview
'Stephen was a brilliant lyricist', Carl Davis to HC, 25 February 1999
'a very odd evening', Sherrin interview
'Despite the publicity', Wells interview
'103-year-old Mr Justice Dribble', *Private Eye*, 29 June 1962
'The satire industry is booming', *Observer*, 8 July 1962
'merely one of Peter's teases', Nicholas Luard interview
'SCONE – the new all-hip weekly paper', *Private Eye*, 24 August 1962
'Smooth and twenty-five', *Observer*, 8 July 1962
'the Brian Epstein of the satire boom', Ingrams, *Life and Times*, 9
'It was usually full of the very people', Harry Thompson, *Peter Cook*, 135
'"Naïvely, I brought the Establishment cast', Lin Cook (ed.), *Something Like Fire*, 50
'The two factions sat on opposite sides', Wells, 'Satire: The End of the Party'
'The Establishment group', Cook, 50
'Actually we (me anyway)', Jeremy Geidt interview
'We didn't really get on', Ingrams interview
'Willie Rushton always said', John Bird interview
'I've read a memoir saying', John Fortune interview
'The two Johns don't come', Booker interview
'a reject from *Punch*', Ralph Steadman interview
'I have been granted Welsh Citizenship', *Private Eye*, 18 May 1962
'You stupid bloody irresponsible cunts', Marnham, 42
'We've always got those leather-elbowed thugs', *The Sunday Times*, 6 September 1998
'Jonathan Miller thought that *Private Eye*', Ingrams interview
'I was simply annoyed that they called me', Jonathan Miller interview
'niggers, beatniks, Angry Young Men', *Private Eye*, 4 May 1962
'tendency ... to go to yet greater lengths', Ingrams, *Life and Times*, 9
'A FLABBY-FACED OLD COWARD', *Private Eye*, 15 June 1962
'hailed by some as, at last', Ingrams, *Life and Times*, 9
'When are you going to', ibid.
'Underneath all this business enterprise', *Observer*, 8 July 1962
'Mr Butler today announced', *Private Eye*, 9 March 1962
'I am one of the new, young', ibid., 27 July 1962
'TORIES SNATCH BIG LEAD POLL SHOWS', ibid., 9 March 1962
'Pablo Picasso is 100 today', *Private Eye*, 2 November 1962
'Nigel, I think we're going', ibid., 9 March 1962
'I'm sorry, but the ethical position', ibid., 10 August 1962

'any human life is a gift', *Private Eye*, 10 August 1962
'*Private Eye* says, "Balls"', ibid., 6 April 1962
'To me, if you live in New York', Bruce, *How to Talk Dirty and Influence People*, 17f.
'an absolute, shambling wreck', Harry Thompson, *Cook*, 131
'fragile, sick, white-faced', Cook, 44f.
'Clad in a black tunic sans lapels', Bruce, 10
'He was completely wonderful', Callil interview
'The smoking of marijuana should be encouraged', Bruce, 10
'agreed with me', ibid., 11
'I spent about four nights a week', Miller interview
'Lenny Bruce stayed with me', Fortune interview
'Scarcely a night passed', Bruce, 11
'I've been thinking about what the ad companies', 'The Almost Unpublished Lenny Bruce' website: www/members.aol.com/dcspohr/lenny/unshow.htm
'John Fortune and I had become quite hostile', Bird interview
'Get this vile creature', Cook, 44f.
'the conservative press baying', Bruce, 12
'had a lot of fun', ibid., 179

6 A highly successful year for British satire
'The revue is primarily concerned', *Time & Tide*, 17 May 1962
'crude allegory', ibid., 21 June 1962
'SHOULD THE QUEEN MOVE?', *Private Eye*, 19 October 1962
'A PESSIMIST thinks every woman', *Relax*, November 1962
'an inept new "satirical" magazine', *Observer*, 30 December 1962
'"Do stop calling me "Brother"', ibid., 27 May 1962
'You have continued to progress', *The Establishment* (EMI, 1992)
'It was a period when America thought', John Bird interview
'so polite', Carole Simpson interview
'the devastating brilliance of their satire', *San Francisco Chronicle*, 14 August 1963
'Even though many thought the evening', *The Sunday Times*, 9 September 1962
'DUDLEY: Isn't there a very seriour colour problem', Bennett et al., *The Complete Beyond the Fringe*, 12f.
'Fagots ... or Pooves', *Private Eye*, 2 November 1962
'In a time of peril', *Daily Mirror*, 10 November 1962
'repeated the *coup de théâtre*', *Guardian*, 30 October 1962
'put ... an end to my dwindling hopes', Bennett, *Writing Home*, 28
'slightly gone off Oxford', *The Sunday Times*, 8 April 1962
'tending to turn away from straight medicine', ibid.
'I don't want to do ordinary reviewing', *Observer*, 9 June 1963
'He'd found a really nice place', Cook (ed.), *Something Like Fire*, 69
'a very corny-looking version', *Evening News*, 16 April 1964
'a satiric view of English life', *Observer*, 8 July 1962
'We in the British government', *The Establishment* (EMI, 1992)
'When we were opening in New York', John Fortune interview
'which is in some places', *The Establishment* (EMI, 1992)
'Good evening. I am blind', Harry Thompson, *Peter Cook*, 144
'On the opening night in New York', Fortune interview
'There may have been big men', Jeremy Geidt interview
'I remember how efficient', Bird interview
'invisible mastermind', Robert Brustein, *Seasons of Discontent* (Cape, 1966), 194ff.

'a series of nuclear explosions', Robert Brustein, *The Third Theatre* (Cape, 1970), 234

'This refers to Carole Simpson's last song', Jeremy Geidt interview

'Though they calculatedly defame', *The Sunday Times*, 21 October 1962

'Lord Gnome stated that the closing year', *Private Eye*, 19 October 1962

'The latest figures … show', ibid., 10 August 1962

'Hard hearts and coronets', *New Statesman*, 24 August 1962

'which would be genuinely satirical', Richard Ingrams, *Muggeridge: The Biography* (HarperCollins, 1995), xi

'We haven't heard it', *Private Eye*, 14 December 1963

'K is for KEN', *Spectator*, 23 November 1962

'The BBC has rashly handed over', *Private Eye*, 24 August 1962

'We're right on the trail', ibid., 7 September 1962

PART THREE: 'The BBC moved in on the act'

1 A mixture of News, Interviews, Satire and Controversy

'Peter and I were developing the idea', John Bird interview

'wild, voluble Welshman', Alasdair Milne, *DG: The Memoirs of a British Broadcaster* (Coronet, 1989), 23

'The next thing I knew', Bird interview

'We had a long lunch', Sherrin, *A Small Thing – Like an Earthquake*, 62

'But Ned is so convinced', Bird interview

'Douglas engaged in wild attempts', Sherrin, *A Small Thing*, 27

'it is much better for your programme', ibid. 24f.

'scanned the obituary columns', ibid., 40f.

'as harmless as a punch', *Daily Herald*, 20 October 1962

'There is an absolute ban', *BBC Variety Programmes Policy Guide for Writers and Producers* (WAC, R34/259)

'dark, tiny, with a very prominent nose', *Dictionary of National Biography, 1981–1985*

'an unstoppable authority', Sherrin, *A Small Thing*, 56f.

'The joker stood up', ibid., 60

'a new sort of revolutionary programme', Sherrin to Mike Williams-Thompson, 6 July 1962 (WAC, T32/1, 650/1)

'an experimental two-hour mixture', Sherrin to Peter Maloney, 6 July 1962 (WAC, T32/1, 650/1)

'Ned said, would I be', Bird interview

'It is hard to convey', Booker, 'David Frost'

'Compared with Cookie', Christopher Booker interview

'There was a lot of snobbery', Barry Humphries interview

'that wonderfully silly voice', *The Sunday Times*, 17 August 1997

'The first night I spent', Frost, *An Autobiography*, 19

'David's most obvious quality', Booker, 'David Frost'

'made a real impression', Frost, 9

'Although he never produced anything', Booker, 'David Frost'

'the new wave of satirical comedy', Frost, 37

'David did some nights of cabaret', Bird interview

'Ask me about any subject', Frost, 39

'When Cook introduced', Booker, 'David Frost'

'He was adept at provoking questions', Sherrin, *A Small Thing*, 63

'small and select audience', Sherrin to Mike Williams-Thompson, 6 July 1962 (WAC, T32/1, 650/1)

'He was tirelessly inventive', Sherrin, *A Small Thing*, 63
'no attempt to disguise the studio walls', ibid., 65
'the casual let-it-all-hang-out style', Frost, 43
'The opening credits of ITV's *Armchair Theatre*', Ned Sherrin interview
'a great deal of pop's televisual language', Melly, *Revolt into Style*, 182f.
'JEREMY GEIDT: Utyligenesis, you may remember', *The Establishment* (EMI, 1992)
'My memory may be playing me false', Sherrin, *A Small Thing*, 64
'Insert four pennies', Michael Frayn, *The Book of Fub* (Collins, 1963), 86
'It's my only impersonation', Wilmut, *From Fringe to Flying Circus*, 64
'their traditional hats', Sherrin, *A Small Thing*, 65
'by the end the audience', Frost, 44
'The object was not to produce', Sherrin to Kenneth Adam, Director of Television, 17
    July 1962 (WAC, T32/1, 650/1)
'Frost is a winner', Donald Baverstock to Grace Wyndham Goldie, 23 July 1962
'not without humour', Sherrin, *A Small Thing*, 33
'amateurish in its endeavours', quoted in ibid., 66
'The competitor is going to attempt', Stuart Hood to Grace Wyndham Goldie, 3 August
    1962 (WAC, T32/1, 650/1
'From then on I was full-time', Frost, 47
'We were summoned to Lime Grove', Waterhouse, 140
'Frost was never', Booker, 'David Frost'
'This programme does not spring', Baverstock to Stuart Hood, 15 November 1962 (WAC,
    T16/589)
'We did not come to *TW3*', Frost, 47f.
'It was late-night, ghetto television', Sherrin, *A Small Thing*, 67
'If I'd known I was part of an era', ibid.
'ITV are ... mounting a late-night satirical spot', *Daily Herald*, 20 October 1962

2 'Live' as hell
'That Was The Week That Was', *TW3* (WAC, 24 November 1962)
'It was produced under Talks', Wilmut, *From Fringe to Flying Circus*, 61
'Scarcely the stuff of which revolutions', Frost, *An Autobiography*, 51
'DAVID: By-elections in Central Dorset', *TW3* (WAC, 24 December 1962)
'What is our policy?', ibid.; Frost and Sherrin (eds), *That Was The Week That Was*, 55f.
'a mock tribute to Norrie Paramor', Frost, 49
'We had the same timing', *Vanity Fair*, December 1995; Jonathan Miller interview
'Our humour is based', quoted in Booker, *The Neophiliacs*, 187
'Bernard Levin, in unarmed combat', *Sunday Telegraph*, 25 November 1962
'I don't know why', *The Times*, undated cutting [1976]
'CHRISTIAN: Look, sir', *TW3* (WAC, 24 December 1962)
'Sex before Marriage', ibid.
'he had appeared in our office', Frost, 53
'Birdsall ... almost by accident', Sherrin, *A Small Thing*, 67
'NIGEL: Where did you come by', *TW3* (WAC, 24 December 1962)
'Time, gentlemen, please', *TW3* (VHS, 24 December 1962)
'and we shared a feeling', Sherrin, *A Small Thing*, 69
'moment of pure joy', Frost, 54
'LATE-NIGHT TV SATIRE', *Sunday Telegraph*, 25 November 1962
'David Frost, the anchor man', quoted in Frost, 56
'Satire – or how to laugh', *Daily Herald*, 26 November 1962
'Only five viewers phoned', quoted in Frost, 56

'D.G. says that he wants', *Daily Herald*, 8 December 1962
'I was delighted', Wilmut, 60
'Whenever he was asked about satire', ibid., 59
'His curious classless accent', Sherrin, *A Small Thing*, 68
'I was unemployed', Jack Duncan interview
'The music for my songs', Millicent Martin interview
'brilliant', Lance Percival interview
'Up to that point', Christopher Booker interview
'In the first programme', Duncan interview
'He seems to me to have', *Sunday Telegraph*, 24 February 1963
'Sherrin's "invention" of David Frost', Melly, *Revolt into Style*, 183
'Perhaps David Frost grasped', Levin, *The Pendulum Years*, 321
'The programme will be a weekly dose', *TV Times*, 19 October 1962
'any offensive representation', *Daily Mirror*, 20 December 1962
'they appointed our very own censor', Philip Oakes to HC, 31 March 1999
'terrible trouble with the legal department', Aubrey Woods to HC, 8 April 1999
'turned it in', *Sunday Telegraph*, 30 December 1962
'I had the idea', Wilmut, 58
'Never forget Mr Henry Brooke', *TW3* (WAC, 1 December 1962)
'The American, who had been convicted', Booker, *The Neophiliacs*, 176
'David was then the only person', John Cleese interview
'Three hundred and seventeen light years', *TW3* (WAC, 1 December 1962)
'*Dixon of Dock Green* was no longer', Frost, 56
'LANCE *enters in policeman uniform*', *TW3* (WAC, 1 December 1962)
'37 complaints', *Daily Telegraph*, 3 December 1962
'Any ignorant git that says', *TW3* (WAC, 1 December 1962)
'Before it was taken over', *Daily Herald*, 8 December 1962
'I must have seen the show', John Bassett interview
'He was edged out', Alan Bennett interview
'Then Ned very kindly took me on', Bassett interview
'He knew lots of jazz musicians', Ned Sherrin interview
'Both men shy at the word "satire"', *Daily Herald*, 8 December 1962
'Again, as in *Beyond the Fringe*', Wells, 'Satire: The End of the Party'
'Ned asked me up to the gallery', John Wells interview
'The only way to cope', Sherrin interview
'Sherrin was talking to Willis Hall', *Daily Herald*, 8 December 1962
'Willis and I tended to write', Waterhouse, 141
'Peter and I once wrote', David Nobbs to HC, 5 January 1999
'I would have some idea', Wilmut, 62
'Suddenly, at the age of just twenty-three', Booker, 'David Frost'
'H-bombed its way', *Daily Sketch*, 10 December 1962
'Britain is not quite as important', *TW3* (WAC, 8 December 1962; Booker, *The Neophiliacs*, 181
'Dean Acheson says we're played out', *TW3* (WAC, 8 December 1962)
'The truth was too obvious', Booker, *The Neophiliacs*, 181
'About this Acheson thing', *TW3* (VHS, 8 December 1962)
'For forty-three years now', *TW3* (WAC, 8 December 1962)
'I'd been friends with Dobereiner', Peter Lewis interview
'the folly of youth', David Kernan interview
'Lionel was in America', Sherrin interview
'authorized vernacular translation', *TW3* (WAC, 8 December 1962)

'Dear me! In Africa, you see', ibid.
'Why is the catering at London Airport', Paisner & Co. to BBC Solicitor, 20 December
    1962 (WAC, T32/1, 652/1)
'vicious and unwarranted attack', ibid.
'Mr Forte … was originally invited', Alasdair Milne to Assistant Solicitor, 12 December
    1962 (WAC, T32/1, 652/1)
'I've got work to do', *Daily Telegraph*, 10 December 1962
'we can all sleep more safely', *Sunday Telegraph*, 9 December 1962
'RELIGION was ridiculed', *Daily Mail*, 10 December 1962
'You want to stamp out', *TW3* (WAC, 8 December 1962)
'It is difficult to believe today', Sherrin, *A Small Thing*, 83
'Old-style revue-writers', *Observer*, 9 December 1962
'When the programme began', David Nobbs to HC, 5 February 1999
'less inbred', *Observer*, 9 December 1962
'Satire is an intimate thing', *Daily Telegraph*, 10 December 1962
'I'm all for the BBC's new satire show', *Private Eye*, 21 December 1962
'Let us be thankful', *Daily Telegraph*, 11 December 1962
'If I find that there was anything said', ibid.
'I hope you will not, repeat not', quoted in Frost, 61

3 The death of deference

'*TW3* was definitely', Frost, *An Autobiography*, 61
'David Frost, eh?', *TW3* (WAC, 15 December 1962)
'irresistible to add the words', Frost, 62
'We in America have always had', *TW3* (WAC, 15 December 1962)
'the colonies we've still got', ibid., 22 December 1962
'I am sure it would be a great mistake', *Daily Telegraph*, 11 December 1962
'We're in favour of nationalization', *TW3* (WAC, 22 December 1962)
'We had no campaigning motives', Jack Duncan interview
'was a Tory then', Gerald Kaufman interview
'It helped me to be impartial', Ned Sherrin interview
'irreligious and cynical undertones', *Daily Telegraph*, 24 December 1962
'cease making references to the Royal Family', *The Times*, 18 December 1962
'have a bit of fun', Sherrin interview
'diminished interest', *Daily Telegraph*, 24 December 1962
'A script arrived from him', Sherrin, *A Small Thing*, 71
'I was visiting Leeds', *Observer*, 8 September 1985
'WILLIE RUSHTON: "1 July"', Frost, 63
'Clement, who had been running cabaret', Sherrin interview
'What predictions had he made', Frost, 63
'There are dangers in indiscriminate knocking', *Sunday Telegraph*, 30 December 1962
'there used to be letters in the *Telegraph* saying', *Willie's Wake* (BBC Radio 4)
'very funny indeed', *The Times*, 31 December 1962
'D.G. says he has not laughed as much', Kenneth Adam to Stuart Hood, 7 January 1963
    (WAC, T16/589)
'I wanted to examine the career', Sherrin, *A Small Thing*, 72
'who had many individual complaints', R.D. Pendlebury to 'HS', 11 January 1963 (WAC,
    T16/589)
'Personally, I am against', Frank Gillard to Director of Television, 14 January 1963
'an excitable middle-aged woman', *TW3* (WAC, 12 January 1963)
'Ah God, to see the branches stir', *TW3* (WAC, 15 December 1962), by kind permission of
    Malcolm Bradbury

'enormous euphoria', Malcolm Bradbury to HC, 10 January 1999
'the death of deference', Keith Waterhouse to HC, 14 February 1999
'My own religious background', Robert Gillespie interview
'What do you put into it?', Frost and Sherrin (eds.), *That Was The Week That Was*, 78ff.
'It is a good example', Sherrin, *A Small Thing*, 83
'having a pack of Fleet Street tigers', Frost, 66
'Do you believe a man's religion', *Daily Express*, 14 January 1963
'As I understood it', *Daily Telegraph*, 15 January 1963
'If we were 100 per cent Christian', Frost, 65
'deplorably bad taste', Bishop of Swansea and Brecon to Director-General, 13 January 1963
'It was very good', Sherrin, *A Small Thing*, 83
'giving a sermon in favour', Frost, 66
'a kindly Old Man', John A.T. Robinson, *Honest to God* (SCM Press, 1963), 41
'In a satirical programme', Hugh Greene to Bishop of Swansea and Brecon, 15 January 1963 (WAC, T16/726)
'This note is not concerned with the argument', Donald Baverstock to Alasdair Milne, 14 January 1963 (WAC, T16/589)
'We were surprised to find', *TW3* (WAC), 16 February 1963
'incredibly daring new outlook', *Willie's Wake* (BBC Radio 4)

4 Sick jokes and lavatory humour

'It is sad, but not surprising', *Sunday Telegraph*, 24 February 1963
'around 500 scripts', *Daily Mail*, 28 January 1963
'Salute Sir Norman Hulbert', *TW3* (WAC, T16/589)
'It entailed an enormous amount of research', Gerald Kaufman interview
'Go to sleep, my little baby', *TW3* (WAC), 19 January 1963
'*That Was The Week That Was* ... is already beginning', *Evening Standard*, 28 January 1963
'In really advanced circles', *Daily Telegraph*, 5 February 1963
'I'd done quite a few things', Richard Ingrams interview
'appearing occasionally as an extra', Ned Sherrin interview
'the climax of the Satire Boom', Ingrams, *The Life and Times of Private Eye*, 11
'For a short time I went to Frostie's flat', Marnham, *The Private Eye Story*, 48
'the lure of the telly', Ingrams, *Life and Times*, 11
'But seriously, viewers', *Private Eye*, 22 February 1963
'curtailed in length', minutes of Controllers' Meeting (WAC, T16/589)
'I think it needs shortening', *Time & Tide*, 21 February 1963
'The Royal Barge is, as it were, sinking', *TW3* (WAC), 16 March 1963
'It started when I saw *Beyond the Fringe*', Ian Lang interview
'None of our items dealing with the Royal Family', Sherrin, *A Small Thing*, 84
'It was wonderful going into the pub', Jack Duncan interview
'West End restaurants had to install TV sets', Kenneth Cope interview
'Thou shalt have no other gods', *TW3* (WAC), 9 March 1963
'an Italo-American zany', *Tatler*, 20 February 1963
'In the beginning there was darkness', Frost and Sherrin, *That Was The Week That Was*, 119
'Can we concentrate on non-violence?', Frost, *An Autobiography*, 84
'met in Dublin on a rainy day', *The Times*, undated cutting [1976]
'And so, Henry, to this week', *TW3* (WAC), 23 March 1963
'When people ask what practical effect', Sherrin, *A Small Thing*, 79

'SENIOR OFFICIAL: (*Reading a letter*) "To Mr Jenkins"', *TW3* (VHS), 29 December 1962

'What do you give these homosexual johnnies?', Frost, 82

'One was a little worried', *Oldie*, July 1997

'fashionable', Sherrin, *A Small Thing*, 88

'George Brown came, and was seen laughing', Sherrin interview

'thought it was only right', Kenneth Adam to Alasdair Milne, 8 April 1963

'I wanna go back to Mississippi', Frost and Sherrin, *That Was The Week That Was*, 13

'May 23rd. Christine Keeler appointed', *TW3* (WAC), 27 April 1963

'See him in the 'Ouse of Commons', ibid., 23 March 1963

'I had a lot of work to persuade', Sherrin interview

'I was on first-name terms', *TW3* (WAC), 30 March 1963

'I see you know everything', Marnham, 63

'It was satire, wasn't it?', *TW3* (WAC), 27 April 1963

'It looked delightfully easy', Frost, 82f.

'mildly dirty jokes', Bennett et al., *The Complete Beyond the Fringe*, 8f.

'Goodbye to a Gang of Low Schoolboys', Frost, 85

'an apparent victory of evil', ibid.

'thrilling', ibid.

'I had a sixth sense', Sherrin, *A Small Thing*, 87

'of all places', ibid., 85

'finally unravelled', Frost, 89

'The film company representatives', Morley, *Black and White Lies*, 58

'hardly an operator', *Oldie*, January 1999

'bumped off by the police', *Private Eye*, 9 August 1963

'the Kennedys came backstage', Bennett, *Writing Home*, 445

'Jackie Kennedy asked us to have supper', Schiff, 'The Poet of Embarrassment'

'Mrs Kennedy absently stroking', Cook (ed.), *Something Like Fire*, 35

'And then it all got taken up', *Vanity Fair*, December 1995

'We were undergraduate comedians', Jonathan Miller interview

'Ah, ho ho, David is making', Frost, 91

'The only regret he regularly voiced', Bennett, *Writing Home*, 79

'I hadn't seen David', John Bird interview

'simpering and whimpering', Cook, *Something Like Fire*, 43

'slightly pathetic', Sherrin, *A Small Thing*, 60

'the amazing fee of £100', Cook, *Something Like Fire*, 63

'a huge success', Nicholas Garland interview

'I was absolutely petrified', Frankie Howerd, *On the Way I Lost It* (W.H. Allen, 1976), 187

'winsome, roguish, naughty', Cook, *Something Like Fire*, 44

'About *time*. I've been waiting', *TW3* (VHS), compilation programme, 1 October 1993

'There was nothing coming on', Sherrin interview

'a cult figure', Howerd, op. cit., 194

'sick jokes and lavatory humour', *Private Eye*, 19 April 1963

'I actually flew to London', Bruce, *How to Talk Dirty*, 181

'Thickset gentlemen began to pay', Harry Thompson, *Peter Cook*, 130

'most of the waiters', ibid., 135

'proved incapable of keeping out', Wells, 'Satire: The End of the Party'

'because I had had a fantastic year', John Wells interview

'We would have stayed on', John Fortune interview

'On November 4th, the return', Bron, *The Pillow Book*, 31

'the new show I wrote', Peter Cook to David Nathan, 21 November 1963, by kind permission of David Nathan

'a sentimental occasion for old satire hands', *Sunday Telegraph*, 17 November 1963
'The fact is that The Establishment', David Nathan to Peter Cook, 29 November 1963, by kind permission of David Nathan
'underworld aura', Morley, 84
'It quickly became obvious', Fortune interview
'I felt particularly responsible', John Bird interview
'Side-effects from extra-mural activities', Morley, 85
'It's now a gambling club', Wells, 'Satire: The End of the Party'
'I handed over my *Private Eye* shares', Cook, *Something Like Fire*, 50f.
'*Private Eye* is safe now', *The Sunday Times*, 16 September 1963
'I have met a satirist', Tennant, *Girlitude*, 157
'absurd', Wells interview
'almost nothing in common', Tennant, *Girlitude*, 161
'Booker got terribly taken up', Ingrams interview
'Booker had a kind of preachy quality', Garland interview
'horrified', Marnham, 87
'Richard's ambition to be editor', Christopher Booker interview
'a blow', Tennant, *Girlitude*, 159, 166
'The programme will be 50 minutes long', Roland Fox to Donald Baverstock, 18 September 1963 (WAC, T32/1, 649/2)
'The programme was criticized', Frost, 93; Sherrin, *A Small Thing*, 88
'It was such a gift', Frost, 93
'We had never really worried', Sherrin, *A Small Thing*, 89
'On the island', quoted in Booker, *The Neophiliacs*, 191
'I don't think we have had smut', Frost, 93f.
'First Mr Stuart Hood', ibid.
'Why the BBC has so evidently decided', ibid.
'Ned loved the idea', ibid.
'That Was The Week That Was', *TW3* (WAC), 22 September 1963 (pilot)
'ROY: What's on next, love?', *TW3* (WAC), 28 September 1963
'incipient Grundyism', Frost, 95
'Abolish matrimony', *TW3* (WAC), 28 September 1963
'very important', John Mortimer to HC, 6 January 1999
'Take sex out of this show', Frost, 96
'Does it matter if some German Jews', *TW3* (WAC), 28 September 1963
'The plane, which Harry Lime', *TW3* (VHS), 28 September 1963
'The audience greatly enjoyed', Frost, 97
'I am very anxious', Sherrin to Legal Department, 1 October 1963 (WAC, T16/589)
'does not think it right', Legal Department to Sherrin (WAC, T16/589)
'D.G. and I feel', Kenneth Adam to Alasdair Milne, 2 October 1963 (WAC, T16/589)
'Please note that Board of Management', Kenneth Adam to Stuart Hood, 7 October 1963 (WAC, T16/589)
'Dear Sir, I hope I am not a prude', *TW3* (WAC), 5 October 1963
'dull … stilted and self-conscious', Sherrin, *A Small Thing*, 89
'a general feeling in the air', Frost, 97f.
'too hot not to cool down', Sherrin, *A Small Thing*, 88
'NOW THE SHOCK HAS GONE', *Daily Herald*, 30 September 1963
'audience and performers now form', Kenneth Adam to Hugh Greene, 9 October 1963
'Once [satire] had annihilated', Bennett et al., *The Complete Beyond the Fringe*, 9

5 The party's over

'O Squire, who once had England', *TW3* (WAC), 12 October 1963

'very sweetly', *Willie's Wake* (BBC Radio 4)

'because he lost a very good part', ibid.

'Drab Butler', *TW3* (WAC), 12 October 1963

'[He] joined the Cabinet', *TW3* (VHS), 9 March 1963

'the Conservative Party appeared to have learned', Frost, *An Autobiography*, 99

'retrograde', Sherrin *A Small Thing*, 78

'Benjamin Disraeli writing a letter', Frost, 99

'My Lord: When I say', *TW3* (WAC), 19 October 1963

'The Director-General had summoned me', Grace Wyndham Goldie, *Facing the Nation: Television and Politics 1936–1976* (Bodley Head, 1977), 231–3

'I remember standing in the hospitality room', Wilmut, *From Fringe to Flying Circus*, 71

'no such savage attack', Sherrin, *A Small Thing*, 78f.

'And so, there is the choice', ibid.

'New Instant Wilson', *TW3* (WAC), 16 February 1963

'more than six hundred phone calls', Frost, 100

'The only time I think I really', BBC Sound Archives (LP 37341)

'not discernibly positive', Frost, 100

'tell us that it would be an infringement', Stuart Hood to Ned Sherrin, 24 October 1963 (WAC, T16/589)

'Of course we will not mention', Ned Sherrin to Stuart Hood, 25 October 1963, ibid.

'I'm going to start taking', *TW3* (WAC), 26 October 1963

'[Milne] had said to me', Grace Wyndham Goldie to Hugh Carleton Greene, 28 October 1963 (WAC, T16/589)

'offensive, undergraduate, potentially venomous', Michael Tracey, *A Variety of Lives: A Biography of Sir Hugh Greene* (Bodley Head, 1963), 216

'I think this is one of', ibid., 219

'had recurred as a subject', Board of Governors Minutes, 7 December 1963 (WAC)

'an absolutely personal conclusion', *Observer*, 22 March 1964

'What happened was that the Board', *Private Eye*, 29 November 1963

'Sir Arthur fforde, the Chairman', Wilmut, 71

'The BBC announces that the present run' (WAC, T16/589)

'a stunner', Frost, 100

'Election year?', ibid.

'as usual, perfectly calm', Grace Wyndham Goldie to Chief Assistant to Greene, 15 November 1963 (WAC, T16/589)

'I think we would have been needed', *Daily Sketch*, 14 November 1963

'It's a compliment', ibid.

'damned pleased', Frost, 101

'I deplore this decision', *Daily Express*, 14 November 1963

'Dick Crossman … was going round', Wilmut, 64f.

'Have you ever in your born days', *Daily Herald*, 14 November 1963

'satire came in as a craze', *Guardian*, 14 November 1963

'We had to do six more', Sherrin, *A Small Thing*, 90

'Happy days are here, my dears', *TW3* (WAC), 16 November 1963

'As we arrived, the news', Frost, 104

'disappeared in a blaze', Sherrin, *A Small Thing*, 90

'That was the week that was', *TW3* (WAC), 28 December 1963

'deceitfully', Sherrin, *A Small Thing*, 72

'I hope that you and your wife', Hugh Carleton Greene to Lord Chancellor, 16 December 1963 (WAC, T16/589)

PART FOUR: Everyone is a satirist

1 Swimming is out of fashion
'After I'd done *Beyond the Fringe*', Jonathan Miller interview
'COOK: I'd like to make one thing quite clear', Bennett et al., *The Complete Beyond the Fringe*, 133
'in a voice that was my own', Bennett, *Writing Home*, xii
'After a few days', Bennett et al., *The Complete Beyond the Fringe*, 123f.
'and when the revue ended', Bennett, *Writing Home*, xii–xiii
'I couldn't see myself', Schiff, 'The Poet of Embarrassment'
'and I look forward', Cook to Nathan, 21.11.63, by kindness of David Nathan
'When people talk to my return', Harry Thompson, *Peter Cook*, 159
'I do have to say', Christopher Booker interview
'Richard [had] made himself effectively editor', Harry Thompson, *Richard Ingrams*, 143
'The thing to remember', John Wells interview
'Eventually Norman … said', Harry Thompson, *Ingrams*, 148
'He finds himself disconcertingly unable', ibid., 152
'the last thing to be seen carrying', Marnham, *The Private Eye Story*, 90
'the last and dying echo', Harry Thompson, *Ingrams*, 161
'this rather shy man', Harry Thompson, *Cook*, 165
'If it wasn't for Peter Cook', Harry Thompson, *Ingrams*, 162
'He invented catchphrases', Harry Thompson, *Cook*, 161
'seize hold of young women', *Private Eye*, 24 July 1964
'I had made a gramophone record', Humphries, *More Please*, 228f.
'I had trained in Fine Art', Nicholas Garland interview
'made up', Humphries, *More Please*, 231
'Barry used to sit in the Coach', Wells interview
'In those days I was rushing round', Barry Humphries interview
'It was beautifully American', Ned Sherrin interview
'The Conservatives – under Alec Douglas-Home', Gerald Kaufman interview
'Consciously or not, the satire movement', Harry Thompson, *Ingrams*, 178
'As with Tony Blair in 1997', Richard Ingrams (Cheltenham) interview
'I don't remember Peter ever sitting down', ibid.
'We on the magazine pinch', Wells, 'Satire: The End of the Party'
'You make something up', Harry Thompson, *Ingrams*, 177
'"Mrs Wilson's Diary" turned out to be', Humphries interview
'Salopian snobbery', Wells interview
'very snobbish and name-dropping', Humphries interview

2 I still think there is room for satire
'had more pilots than the average', Sherrin, *A Small Thing*, 97
'Frost was determined in his heart of hearts', Wilmut, *From Fringe to Flying Circus*, 76
'Ned's plot was that I should replace', P.J. Kavanagh to HC, 6 January 1999
'worked himself (again not as originally intended)', Booker, 'David Frost'
'Why does TV stick to this superstition', Frost, *An Autobiography*, 139
'This was one of the first appearances', Wilmut, 75
'a fair disaster', Sherrin, *A Small Thing*, 102
'lumbering', Booker, *The Neophiliacs*, 239
'There is certainly very little', Wells, 'Satire: The End of the Party'
'The reason television came in for me', John Wells interview
'Good evenin'. Well, I always say', Frost, 139

'I'm not a mimic', John Bird interview
'I'd come down on the train', John Fortune interview
'I think people have been jolly unkind', Wilmut, 77
'The best thing I did with Eleanor', Fortune interview
'I really felt that the thing was', Bird interview
'NOT SO MUCH A FROST', *Private Eye*, 27 November 1963
'Yes, I've been Father Christmas now', *The Best of Private Eye: Volume One: The
    Famous Flexies*, Comedy Club audio cassettes (GAGDMC 085)
'Hello, good evening, welcome', ibid.
'in a place called Magnagraph', Barry Humphries interview
'Have you sinned, Mrs O'Hara?', Frost, 145f.
'cretin', ibid., 150f.
'I still think there is room for satire', ibid., 152
'David had become an international traveller', *Willie's Wake* (BBC Radio 4)
'It was clear that our careers', Sherrin, *A Small Thing*, 105
'visited by lovely ladies', Harry Thompson, *Peter Cook*, 177
'the most popular show on television', ibid., 182
'I remember watching', *Observer*, 28 May 1967
'I used to work with John Bird and John Fortune', *Third Ear* (BBC Radio 3)
'Ned had fitted us all up', Wells interview
'Of all the honours that fell upon', Wilmut, 83
'a thing I did with John Fortune', Alan Bennett interview
'Now I imagine you'll think', Wilmut, 82
'Last weekend we had a big party', *Private Eye*, 27 November 1964
'*BBC3* was certainly the wrong title', Sherrin, *A Small Thing*, 111
'watery relic', Booker, *The Neophiliacs*, 271
'I doubt if there are any rational people', Wilmut, 82
'did everything for our viewing figures', Sherrin, *A Small Thing*, 113
'CLEESE: I look down on him', Wilmut, 141
'from then on he was', Booker, 'David Frost'
'very uneven in quality', Humphries, *More Please*, 255
'not successful', Bird interview
'in which the painter Millais', Humphries, *More Please*, 258
'Across the darkening room', *Daily Mail*, 26 January 1966
'(NIGEL KNOCKER-THREW *is talking to* SAM)', *On the Margin* (WAC), 9 November 1966
'In *On the Margin* we were still trying', Bennett interview
'as much a revue', Bennett, *Writing Home*, 317
'I had been producing', Anthony Smith to HC, 25 January 1999
'It became clear very quickly', David Nathan, 'Between the Winds', an unpublished
    autobiography, by kind permission of David Nathan
'I had to leave the BBC staff', Alan Shallcross interview
'hated the programme', Anthony Smith to HC, 25 January 1999
'*Lingerie shop set*', Graham Chapman et al., *Monty Python's Flying Circus: Just the
    Words*, vol. 1 (Mandarin, 1990), 121f.
'Nothing makes me laugh more', *Daily Mail*, 9 December 1978
'We experienced a sort of after-life', Wells interview

3 Giggling into the sea
'key features of the 1950s', Marwick, *The Sixties*, 3
'presented in witty and potent form', ibid., 143
'The British New Wave', ibid., 118

'I am a heterosexual', Frost and Sherrin (eds.), *That Was The Week That Was*, 93

'A Northerner is a scrap of humanity', ibid., 11

'I don't think we were', Jonathan Miller interview

'wasn't a crusade', Bennett interview

'Satire spanned the period', Melly, *Revolt into Style*, 183

'symptoms rather than causes', Levin, *The Pendulum Years*, 320

'all male', Tennant, *Girlitude*, 158

'really *Daily Telegraph* readers', ibid., 166

'the last and dying echo', Harry Thompson, *Richard Ingrams*, 161

'It has run nearly as long', *The Times*, 5 October 1991

'a colossal sum', Ingrams, *The Life and Times of Private Eye*, 19

'In his new manifestation', ibid., 20

'A number of foreign observers', *Private Eye*, 25 June 1965

'an enormously exciting mini-skirted place', Jonathan Miller interview

'I started to do a few jokes', Christopher Booker interview

'If some of its material was witty', Booker, *The Neophiliacs*, 181

'Tim and I used to look', Booker interview

'We watched *TW3* to see how ghastly', Nicholas Garland interview

'He got very thick with Muggeridge', Richard Ingrams interview

'twentieth-century dream', Booker, *The Neophiliacs*, 299, 331

'With Foot's invaluable help', Ingrams, *Life and Times*, 21

'Y'know, Jack Kennedy's parties', ibid., 18

'Sad and terrible news', Marnham, *The Private Eye Story*, 80

'Dempster wore expensively made suits', McKay, *Inside Private Eye*, 68

'I think Goldsmith was a great blessing', Ingrams interview

'genius at living with, and avoiding', Auberon Waugh interview

'We're administering the last writs', *Private Eye*, 22 November 1991

'I suspect satire depends on verbal dexterity', *Guardian*, 13 July 1995

'To my mind, it was just a straightforward case', Richard Ingrams (Cheltenham) interview

'Denis Thatcher was furious', John Wells interview

'Neither Denis Thatcher nor I', *Cartoons, Lampoons and Buffoons* (BBC Radio 4)

'Denis ... became a keen reader', Carol Thatcher, *Below the Parapet* (HarperCollins, 1997), 141

'My mother *loathed* it', *Dear John: A Tribute to John Wells*, BBC2, 24 December 1998

'The "Dear Bill" letters made her more human', ibid.

'Welcome aboard!', Harry Thompson, *Cook*, 425

'Today every newspaper and news magazine', ibid., 332

'cleared with the Palace', *Private Eye*, 19 September 1997

'The biting satire mined rich veins', ibid.

'When we left the club', Wilmut and Rosengard, *Didn't You Kill My Mother-in-law?*, 2f.

'I got through a lot of raincoats', Mike Yarwood, *Impressions of My Life* (Willow Books, 1986), 109

'all those bigoted, illiberal chauvinists', Johnny Speight, *For Richer, for Poorer: A Kind of Autobiography* (BBC Books, 1991), 143

'ALF: Where d'you get this meat?', Johnny Speight, *Till Death Us Do Part Scripts* (Woburn Press, 1973), 26

'probed, with an admirable contempt', *Observer*, 25 February 1968

'One chap came up over to me', Johnny Speight, *Till Death Us Do Part Scripts*, 17

'After the great dinosaurs of the satire boom', *Cartoons, Lampoons and Buffoons* (BBC Radio 4)

'Writing left-wing satirical sketches', O'Farrell, *Things Can Only Get Better*, 172
'COMEDIANS WANTED for new comedy', *Private Eye*, 27 April 1979
'My first mistake had been to put an ad', Wilmut and Rosengard, 3–5
'Turn it up, knock it on the 'ead', ibid., 23
'Dudley Moore used to say he did comedy', ibid., 49
'I'd sent out over three hundred invitations', ibid., 5
'from all walks of life', ibid., 9
'Have you heard the story', *Guardian*, 21 May 1979
'it seemed to young people', Enfield, *Harry Enfield and His Humorous Chums*, 18f.
'All Rosengard has to do now', Wilmut and Rosengard, 8
'I kept trying to get well-known comedians', ibid., 8f.
'My dad's an academic', ibid., 90
'What I don't like is nudie sunbathing', ibid., 93f.
'I was astonished to go along', *Cartoons, Lampoons and Buffoons* (BBC Radio 4)
'Ironically, alternative comedy', ibid.
'They're beginning to advertise things', *Ben Elton Live 1989* CD (Laughing Stock,
    LAFFCD 16)
'Look at that! Look at my wad!', Enfield, 24–6
'Sometimes it's very difficult', *Cartoons, Lampoons and Buffoons* (BBC Radio 4)
'I did strange things', Roger Law interview
'BIRD: George Parr, you have just been appointed', John Bird and John Fortune, *The Long
    Johns* (Hutchinson, 1996), 225–31
'Neil Hamilton's wife Christine', O'Farrell, 265f.
'They're cheekier, but it's juvenile humour', Gerald Kaufman interview
'Satire is now an industry', *Cartoons, Lampoons and Buffoons* (BBC Radio 4)
'Satire has become one among many', John Bird interview
'Journalism now is all gossip', Kaufman interview
'I can't stand the relentless punning', Booker interview
'Everyone is being satirical', Barry Humphries interview
'There's frankly too much comedy', *Cartoons, Lampoons and Buffoons* (BBC Radio 4)
'I think we who were involved', Michael Frayn interview
'If we're talking about the disintegration', Booker interview
'There is a problem', *The Sunday Times*, 15 November 1998
'In those days, it was a revelation', David Nobbs to HC, 5 February 1999
'We now have a kind of politics', John Fortune interview

Curtain call: where are they now?
'I never repudiated it', Jonathan Miller interview
'I pinched the idea', William Donaldson interview
'After the satire shows of the 1960s', John Bird interview
'we were type-cast as "those satirists"', David Kernan interview
'People still remember me', *Daily Express*, 26 November 1992; *Sun*, 31 August 1982
'It was a long time ago', *Daily Express*, 26 November 1992
'Peter didn't go into a decline', Nicholas Luard interview
'a figure from the Parables', Bennett, *Writing Home*, 81

Acknowledgements

....

In the Introduction to the paperback edition of *Writing Home*, Alan Bennett describes his experiences signing in bookshops:

> Readers do ask one to write some very peculiar things in their books. One youth said, 'Could you put "To Christine. I'm sorry about last night and it won't happen again!" This I dutifully did and then had to sign it 'Alan Bennett'. If I'm ever deemed worthy of a biography I'd like to see what Andrew Motion or Humphrey Carpenter will make of that.

Possibly it was this that prompted a publisher – Roland Philipps of Hodder Headline – to suggest that I *should* write Bennett's biography. Of course Bennett didn't seriously want me to; but the idea led to this 'group biography' of the Sixties satirists, so I am very grateful to Roland for starting the whole thing off.

Alan Bennett himself must head the list of those I want to thank for help with the text, since he gave me tea and answered my questions patiently. Jonathan Miller gave me a characteristically breathless interview over the phone, and kindly read and approved the finished text; alas, Dudley Moore was too unwell to oblige (despite efforts on my behalf by his biographer Barbara Paskin); and Peter Cook was of course dead; but John Bassett and Robert Ponsonby, begetters of *Beyond the Fringe*, were generous with their time.

The other surviving satirists and their associates who patiently answered my questions were, in alphabetical order: John Bird, Christopher Booker, Eleanor Bron, Kenneth Cope, Willie Donaldson, Jack Duncan, John Fortune, Michael Frayn, Nicholas Garland, Jeremy Geidt, Barry Humphries, Richard Ingrams, David Kernan, Roger Law, Nicholas Luard, Millicent Martin, Lance Percival, Ned Sherrin, Ralph Steadman, Peter Usborne, Auberon Waugh and John Wells. *TW3* writers who helped abundantly were: Malcolm Bradbury, John Cleese, Robert Gillespie, Gerald Kaufman, Ian Lang (Lord

Lang of Monkton), Peter Lewis, Charles Lewsen, Sir John Mortimer, David Nathan, David Nobbs and Keith Waterhouse.

For reminiscences and other kinds of help I am very grateful to: Adrian Berry, Michael Billington, T.J. Binyon, Alan Brien, Carmen Callil, Michael Codron, Carl Davis, John Davis, Michael Heseltine, Bishop Eric Kemp, John Lloyd, Ken Loach, Christopher Logue, Candida Lycett Green, Christopher MacLehose, David Marquand, Philip Oakes, Mira Osmond, Brian Rees, Adam Roberts, Alan Shallcross, Anthony Smith, John Sutherland, Harry Thompson, Paul Thompson, David Vaisey, Peter and Elisabeth Way, Teresa Wells and Aubrey Woods.

Lewis Morley generously allowed me to use his photographs, and I am also grateful to his agent, Nicky Akehurst. Bobby Mitchell of the BBC Photo Library, and Jacquie Kavanagh and Jeff Walden of the BBC Written Archives, were as usual tirelessly helpful; Angela O'Leary of BBC TV kindly provided a photograph from her programme on John Wells; and Mark Crossan, Rob Ketteridge, Timothy Prosser and Neil Trevithick at Broadcasting House assisted me in getting hold of other archival material, including the videotapes of *That Was The Week That Was*. Vanessa Green at *The Sunday Times* found me a wealth of photographs; Dr John Maddicott of Exeter College, Oxford and his assistant Lorise Topliffe allowed me to inspect Alan Bennett's contributions to the college Suggestions Books; and Paul Rossiter, librarian of the *Daily Mail*, unearthed an obscure but vital cutting.

At Gollancz, Sara Holloway was that rare bird in today's publishing world, an editor who edits closely, demandingly, yet immensely helpfully (this sounds so ferocious that I have to add that we also became great friends). Jill Burrows copy-edited and indexed with a skill that I am in danger of taking for granted, since we have worked together before. Lastly, my agent Felicity Bryan made the whole project possible.

It seems a pity to end on a sad note, but I am particularly sorry that John Wells, the first person I interviewed for the book, did not survive to read it, since he had probably thought and written more about the subject of 1960s satire than anyone else alive. His is the name with which I would like to end these 'credits', as I belatedly dedicate my text to his memory.

List of illustrations and sources

....

Index